Introduction to Financial
Henry Dauderis & David Annand

Edited by Athabasca University

Version 2016 — Revision B

Copyright

This work is licensed under a Creative Commons Attribution-NonCommercial-ShareAlike 3.0 Unported License.

To view a copy of this license, visit https://creativecommons.org/licenses/by-nc-sa/3.0/

lyryx
advancing learning

LYRYX WITH OPEN TEXTS

The form of this book is completely new to the Canadian market. As authors we have many years of experience in hard copy book publishing with a major international publisher. This time we are publishing an **open text** in collaboration with Lyryx Learning, supporting open content as part of their Lyryx with Open Texts products & services.

While there is no requirement that users of the book do anything more than download the pdf files and use them for non-profit educational purposes, the texts are aligned with Lyryx with Open Texts products and services offering the following benefits.

OPEN TEXT

The text can be downloaded in electronic format, printed, and can be distributed to students at no cost. Instructors who adopt Lyryx with Open Texts may obtain the relevant original text files from the authors if the instructors decide they wish to amplify certain sections for their own students. In collaboration with the authors, Lyryx will also adapt the content and provide custom editions for specific courses.

ONLINE ASSESSMENT

Lyryx has developed corresponding formative online assessment for homework and quizzes. These are genuine questions for the subject and adapted to the content. Student answers are carefully analyzed by the system and personalized feedback is immediately provided to help students improve on their work. Lyryx provides all the tools required to manage your online assessment including student grade reports and student performance statistics.

INSTRUCTOR SUPPLEMENTS

A number of resources are available, including a full set of slides for instructors and students. These are available in their original format, and consequently can be further adapted by instructors. An Exam Builder tool is also available allowing instructors to easily create paper quizzes and exams.

SUPPORT

Lyryx provides all of the support you and your students need! Starting from the course preparation time to beyond the end of the course, the Lyryx staff is available 7 days/week to provide assistance. This may include adapting the text, managing multiple sections of the course, providing course supplements, as well as timely assistance to students with registration, navigation, and daily organization.

Contact Lyryx!
info@lyryx.com

Table of Contents

Table of Contents v

1   Introduction to Financial Accounting **1**

    Chapter 1 Learning Objectives 1

    Concept Self-Check 1

    1.1   Accounting Defined 3

    1.2   Business Organizations 3

    1.3   Generally Accepted Accounting Principles (GAAP) 5

    1.4   Financial Statements 8

    1.5   Transaction Analysis and Double-entry Accounting 15

    Summary of Chapter 1 Learning Objectives 23

    Discussion Questions 24

    Exercises 25

    Problems 34

2   The Accounting Process **37**

    Chapter 2 Learning Objectives 37

    Concept Self-Check 37

    2.1   Accounts 38

    2.2   Transaction Analysis Using Accounts 43

    2.3   The Trial Balance 50

    2.4   Using Formal Accounting Records 55

    2.5   The Accounting Cycle 59

Summary of Chapter 2 Learning Objectives		60
Discussion Questions		61
Exercises		62
Problems		68

3 Financial Accounting and Adjusting Entries — 73

Chapter 3 Learning Objectives . . . 73

Concept Self-Check . . . 73

3.1 The Operating Cycle . . . 74

3.2 Adjusting Entries . . . 80

3.3 The Adjusted Trial Balance . . . 93

3.4 Using the Adjusted Trial Balance to Prepare Financial Statements . . . 94

3.5 The Accounting Cycle . . . 98

3.6 The Closing Process . . . 99

Summary of Chapter 3 Learning Objectives . . . 103

Discussion Questions . . . 105

Exercises . . . 107

Problems . . . 114

4 The Classified Balance Sheet and Related Disclosures — 123

Chapter 4 Learning Objectives . . . 123

Concept Self-Check . . . 123

4.1 Financial Statement Disclosure Decisions . . . 124

4.2 Classified Balance Sheet . . . 126

4.3 Notes to Financial Statements . . . 130

4.4 Auditor's Report . . . 133

4.5 Management's Responsibility for Financial Statements . . . 135

Summary of Chapter 4 Learning Objectives . . . 136

Discussion Questions 138

Exercises 139

Problems 141

5 Accounting for the Sale of Goods — 143

Chapter 5 Learning Objectives 143

Concept Self-Check 143

5.1 The Basics of Merchandising 145

5.2 The Purchase and Payment of Merchandise Inventory (Perpetual) 147

5.3 Merchandise Inventory: Sales and Collection (Perpetual) 150

5.4 Adjustments to Merchandise Inventory (Perpetual) 153

5.5 Merchandising Income Statement 157

5.6 Closing Entries for a Merchandiser 159

5.7 Appendix A: The Periodic Inventory System 159

Summary of Chapter 5 Learning Objectives 163

Discussion Questions 164

Exercises 165

Problems 168

6 Assigning Costs to Merchandise — 173

Chapter 6 Learning Objectives 173

Concept Self-Check 173

6.1 Inventory Cost Flow Assumptions 174

6.2 Financial Statement Impact of Different Inventory Cost Flows 187

6.3 Lower of Cost and Net Realizable Value (LCNRV) 189

6.4 Estimating the Balance in Merchandise Inventory 191

6.5 Appendix A: Ratio Analysis—Merchandise Inventory Turnover 195

6.6 Appendix B: Inventory Cost Flow Assumptions Under the Periodic System 196

Summary of Chapter 6 Learning Objectives 198

Discussion Questions 200

Exercises 201

Problems 205

7 Cash and Receivables — 207

Chapter 7 Learning Objectives 207

Concept Self-Check 207

7.1 Internal Control 208

7.2 Petty Cash 210

7.3 Cash Collections and Payments 212

7.4 Accounts Receivable 221

7.5 Short-Term Notes Receivable 229

7.6 Appendix A: Ratio Analysis—Acid Test 231

7.7 Appendix B: Ratio Analysis—Accounts Receivable Turnover 232

Summary of Chapter 7 Learning Objectives 233

Discussion Questions 235

Exercises 235

Problems 240

8 Long-lived Assets — 243

Chapter 8 Learning Objectives 243

Concept Self-Check 243

8.1 Establishing the Cost of Property, Plant, and Equipment (PPE) 244

8.2 Depreciation 248

8.3 Partial Year Depreciation 254

8.4 Revising Depreciation 255

8.5 Impairment of Long-lived Assets 259

	8.6	Derecognition of Property, Plant, and Equipment	260
	8.7	Intangible Assets	264
	8.8	Goodwill	266
	8.9	Disclosure	267
	Summary of Chapter 8 Learning Objectives		267
	Discussion Questions		271
	Exercises		273
	Problems		278
9	**Debt Financing: Current and Long-term Liabilities**		**281**
	Chapter 9 Learning Objectives		281
	Concept Self-Check		281
	9.1	Current versus Long-term Liabilities	282
	9.2	Known Current Liabilities	284
	9.3	Estimated Current Liabilities	288
	9.4	Long-Term Liabilities—Bonds Payable	291
	9.5	Long-term Liabilities—Loans Payable	298
	9.6	Appendix A: Present Value Calculations	301
	9.7	Appendix B: Additional Payroll Transactions	304
	Summary of Chapter 9 Learning Objectives		307
	Discussion Questions		308
	Exercises		309
	Problems		312
10	**Equity Financing**		**315**
	Chapter 10 Learning Objectives		315
	Concept Self-Check		315
	10.1	The Corporate Structure	316

10.2 Recording Share Transactions 322

10.3 Cash Dividends 326

10.4 Share Dividends 330

10.5 Book Value 332

Summary of Chapter 10 Learning Objectives 333

Discussion Questions 335

Exercises 336

Problems 340

11 The Statement of Cash Flows 345

Chapter 11 Learning Objectives 345

Concept Self-Check 345

11.1 Financial Statement Reporting 346

11.2 Preparing the Statement of Cash Flows 347

11.3 Interpreting the Statement of Cash Flows 360

Summary of Chapter 11 Learning Objectives 361

Discussion Questions 362

Exercises 363

Problems 365

12 Financial Statement Analysis 369

Chapter 12 Learning Objectives 369

Concept Self-Check 369

12.1 Introduction to Ratio Analysis 370

12.2 Liquidity Ratios: Analyzing Short-term Cash Needs 373

12.3 Profitability Ratios: Analyzing Operating Activities 381

12.4 Leverage Ratios: Analyzing Financial Structure 385

12.5 Market Ratios: Analysis of Financial Returns to Investors 389

12.6 Overall Analysis of Big Dog's Financial Statements 392

12.7 Horizontal and Vertical Trend Analysis 392

Summary of Chapter 12 Learning Objectives 398

Discussion Questions 399

Exercises 400

Problems 404

13 Proprietorships and Partnerships 407

Chapter 13 Learning Objectives 407

Concept Self-Check 407

13.1 Proprietorships 408

13.2 Partnerships 413

Summary of Chapter 13 Learning Objectives 419

Discussion Questions 419

Exercises 420

Problems 422

Chapter 1

Introduction to Financial Accounting

Accounting involves a process of collecting, recording, and reporting a business's economic activities to users. It is often called the language of business because it uses a unique vocabulary to communicate information to decision makers. To understand accounting, we first look at the basic forms of business organizations. The concepts and principles that provide the foundation for financial accounting are then discussed. With an emphasis on the corporate form of business organization, we will examine how we communicate to users of financial information using financial statements. Finally, we will review how financial transactions are analyzed and then reported on financial statements.

Chapter 1 Learning Objectives

LO1 – Define accounting.

LO2 – Identify and describe the forms of business organization.

LO3 – Identify and explain the Generally Accepted Accounting Principles (GAAP).

LO4 – Identify, explain, and prepare the financial statements.

LO5 – Analyze transactions by using the accounting equation.

Concept Self-Check

Use the following as a self-check while working through Chapter 1.

1. What is accounting?
2. What is the difference between internal and external users of accounting information?
3. What is the difference between managerial and financial accounting?
4. What is the difference between a business organization and a non-business organization?
5. What are the three types of business organizations?
6. What is a PAE? A PE?
7. What does the term *limited liability* mean?

8. Explain how ethics are involved in the practice of accounting.
9. Describe what GAAP refers to.
10. Identify and explain the six qualitative characteristics of GAAP.
11. Identify and explain at least five of the nine principles that support the GAAP qualitative characteristics.
12. How is financial information communicated to external users?
13. What are the four financial statements?
14. Which financial statement measures financial performance? Financial position?
15. What information is provided in the statement of cash flows?
16. Explain how retained earnings and dividends are related.
17. What are the three primary components of the balance sheet?
18. Equity consists of what two components?
19. How are assets financed?
20. Identify and explain the three types of activities a business engages in.
21. What are *notes to the financial statements*?
22. What is the accounting equation?
23. What are the distinctions among calendar, interim, and fiscal year ends?

NOTE: The purpose of these questions is to prepare you for the concepts introduced in the chapter. Your goal should be to answer each of these questions as you read through the chapter. If, when you complete the chapter, you are unable to answer one or more the Concept Self-Check questions, go back through the content to find the answer(s). Solutions are not provided to these questions.

1.1 Accounting Defined

LO1 – Define accounting.

Accounting is the process of identifying, measuring, recording, and communicating an organization's economic activities to users. Users need information for decision making. **Internal users** of accounting information work for the organization and are responsible for planning, organizing, and operating the entity. The area of accounting known as **managerial accounting** serves the decision-making needs of internal users. External users do not work for the organization and include investors, creditors, labour unions, and customers. **Financial accounting** is the area of accounting that focuses on external reporting and meeting the needs of external users. This book addresses financial accounting. Managerial accounting is covered in other books.

1.2 Business Organizations

LO2 – Identify and describe the forms of business organization.

An **organization** is a group of individuals who come together to pursue a common set of goals and objectives. There are two types of business organizations: *business* and *non-business*. A **business organization** sells products and/or services for profit. A **non-business organization**, such as a charity or hospital, exists to meet various societal needs and does not have profit as a goal. All businesses, regardless of type, record, report, and, most importantly, *use* accounting information for making decisions.

This book focuses on business organizations. There are three common forms of business organizations — a *proprietorship*, a *partnership*, and a *corporation*.

Proprietorship

A **proprietorship** is a business owned by one person. It is not a separate legal entity, which means that the business and the owner are considered to be the same entity. This means, for example, that from an income tax perspective, the profits of a proprietorship are taxed as part of the owner's personal income tax return. **Unlimited liability** is another characteristic of a sole proprietorship meaning that if the business could not pay its debts, the owner would be responsible even if the business's debts were greater than the owner's personal resources.

Partnership

A **partnership** is a business owned by two or more individuals. Like the proprietorship, it is not a separate legal entity and its owners are typically subject to unlimited liability.

Corporation

A **corporation** is a business owned by one or more owners. The owners are known as *shareholders*. A **shareholder** owns shares of the corporation. **Shares**[1] are units of ownership in a corporation. For example, if a corporation has 1,000 shares, there may be three shareholders where one has 700 shares, another has 200 shares, and the third has 100 shares. The number of shares held by a shareholder represents how much of the corporation they own. A corporation can have different types of shares; this topic is discussed in a later chapter. When there is only one type of share, it is usually called **common shares**.

A corporation's shares can be privately held or available for public sale. A corporation that holds its shares privately and does not sell them publicly is known as a **private enterprise (PE)**. A corporation that sells its shares publicly, typically on a stock exchange, is called a **publicly accountable enterprise (PAE)**.

Unlike the proprietorship and partnership, a corporation is a separate legal entity. This means, for example, that from an income tax perspective, a corporation files its own tax return. The owners or shareholders of a corporation are not responsible for the corporation's debts so have **limited liability** meaning that the most they can lose is what they invested in the corporation.

In larger corporations, there can be many shareholders. In these cases, shareholders do not manage a corporation but participate indirectly through the election of a **Board of Directors**. The Board of Directors does not participate in the day-to-day management of the corporation but delegates this responsibility to the officers of the corporation. An example of this delegation of responsibility is illustrated in Figure 1.1.

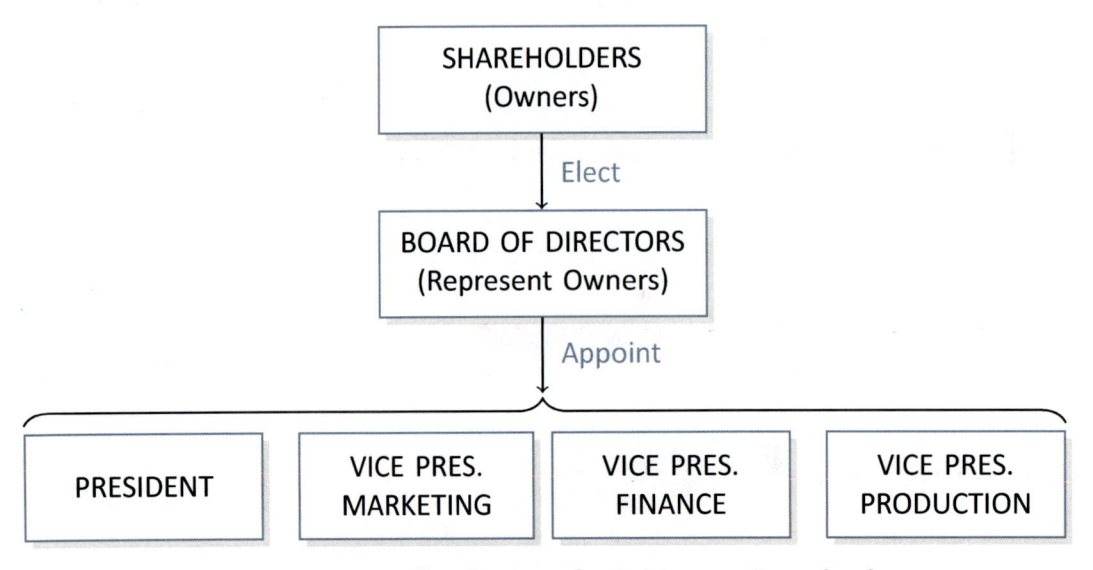

Figure 1.1: Generalized Form of a Corporate Organization

Shareholders usually meet annually to elect a Board of Directors. The Board of Directors meets

---

[1]Shares are also called **stock**.

regularly to review the corporation's operations and to set policies for future operations. Unlike shareholders, directors can be held personally liable if a company fails.

The focus of these chapters will be on the corporate form of business organization. The proprietorship and partnership organizations will be discussed in more detail in Chapter 13.

An exploration is available on the Lyryx site. Log into your Lyryx course to run Forms of Organization.

1.3 Generally Accepted Accounting Principles (GAAP)

LO3 – Identify and explain the Generally Accepted Accounting Principles (GAAP).

The goal of accounting is to ensure information provided to decision makers is useful. To be useful, information must be relevant and faithfully represent a business's economic activities. This requires **ethics**, beliefs that help us differentiate right from wrong, in the application of underlying accounting concepts or principles. These underlying accounting concepts or principles are known as **Generally Accepted Accounting Principles (GAAP)**.

GAAP in Canada, as well as in many other countries, is based on International Financial Reporting Standards (IFRS) for publicly accountable enterprises (PAE). IFRS are issued by the **International Accounting Standards Board (IASB)**. The IASB's mandate is to promote the adoption of a single set of global accounting standards through a process of open and transparent discussions among corporations, financial institutions, and accounting firms around the world. Private enterprises (PE) in Canada are permitted to follow either IFRS or **Accounting Standards for Private Enterprises (ASPE)**, a set of less onerous GAAP-based standards developed by the Canadian Accounting Standards Board (AcSB). The **AcSB** is the body that governs accounting standards in Canada. *The focus in this book will be on IFRS for PAEs*[2].

Accounting practices are guided by GAAP which are comprised of qualitative characteristics and principles. As already stated, relevance and faithful representation are the primary qualitative characteristics. Comparability, verifiability, timeliness, and understandability are additional qualitative characteristics.

Information that possesses the quality of:

- **relevance** has the ability to make a difference in the decision-making process.

- **faithful representation** is complete, neutral, and free from error.

---

[2]It should be noted, however, that at the introductory level, there are no significant differences in how IFRS and ASPE are applied.

- **comparability** tells users of the information that businesses utilize similar accounting practices.
- **verifiability** means that others are able to confirm that the information faithfully represents the economic activities of the business.
- **timeliness** is available to decision makers in time to be useful.
- **understandability** is clear and concise.

Table 1.1 lists the nine principles that support these qualitative characteristics.

Accounting Principle	Explanation/Example
Business entity	Requires that each economic entity maintain separate records. Example: A business owner keeps separate accounting records for business transactions and for personal transactions.
Consistency	Requires that a business use the same accounting policies and procedures from period to period. Example: A business uses a particular inventory costing method. It cannot change to a different inventory costing method in the next accounting period.
Cost	Requires that each economic transaction be based on the actual original cost (also known as historical cost principle). Example: The business purchases a delivery truck advertised for $75,000 and pays $70,000. The truck must be recorded at the cost of $70,000, the amount actually paid.
Full disclosure	Requires that accounting information communicate sufficient information to allow users to make knowledgeable decisions. Example: A business is applying to the bank for a $1,000,000 loan. The business is being sued for $20,000,000 and it is certain that it will lose. The business must tell the bank about the lawsuit even though the lawsuit has not yet been finalized.
Going concern	Assumes that a business will continue for the foreseeable future. Example: All indications are that Business X will continue so it is reported to be a 'going concern'. Business Z is being sued for $20,000,000 and it is certain that it will lose. The $20,000,000 loss will force the business to close. Business Z must not only disclose the lawsuit but it must also indicate that there is a 'going concern' issue.
Matching	Requires that financial transactions be reported in the period in which they occurred/were realized. Example: Supplies were purchased March 15 for $700. They will be recorded as an asset on March 15 and then expensed as they are used.
Materiality	Requires a business to apply proper accounting only for items that would affect decisions made by users. Example: The business purchases a stapler for $5 today. Technically, the stapler will last several years so should be recorded as an asset. However, the business will record the $5 as an expense instead because depreciating a $5 item will not impact the decisions of financial information.

Accounting Principle	Explanation/Example
Monetary unit	Requires that financial information be communicated in stable units of money. Example: Land was purchased in 1940 for $5,000 Canadian. It is maintained in the accounting records at $5,000 Canadian and is not adjusted.
Recognition	Requires that revenues be recorded when earned and expenses be recorded when incurred, which is not necessarily when cash is received (in the case of revenues) or paid (in the case of expenses). Example: A sale occurred on March 5. The customer received the product on March 5 but will pay for it on April 5. The business records the sale on March 5 when the sale occurred even though the cash is not received until April 5.

Table 1.1: Accounting Principles

Note: Some of the principles discussed above may be challenging to understand because related concepts have not yet been introduced. Therefore, most of these principles will be discussed again in more detail in a later chapter.

1.4 Financial Statements

LO4 – Identify, explain, and prepare the financial statements.

Recall that financial accounting focuses on communicating information to external users. That information is communicated using **financial statements**. There are four financial statements: the income statement, statement of changes in equity, balance sheet, and statement of cash flows. Each of these is introduced in the following sections using an example based on a fictitious corporate organization called Big Dog Carworks Corp.

The Income Statement

An **income statement** communicates information about a business's financial performance by summarizing **revenues** less **expenses** over a period of time. Revenues are created when a business provides products or services to a customer in exchange for assets. Assets are resources resulting from past events and from which future economic benefits are expected to result. Examples of assets include cash, equipment, and supplies. Assets will be discussed in more detail later in this chapter. Expenses are the assets that have been used up or the obligations incurred in the course of earning revenues. When revenues are greater than expenses, the difference is called **net income** or **profit**. When expenses are greater than revenue, a **net loss** results.

Consider the following income statement of Big Dog Carworks Corp. (BDCC). This business was started on January 1, 2015 by Bob "Big Dog" Baldwin in order to repair automobiles. All the shares of the corporation are owned by Bob.

At January 31, the income statement shows total revenues of $10,000 and various expenses totaling $7,800. Net income, the difference between $10,000 of revenues and $7,800 of expenses, equals $2,200.

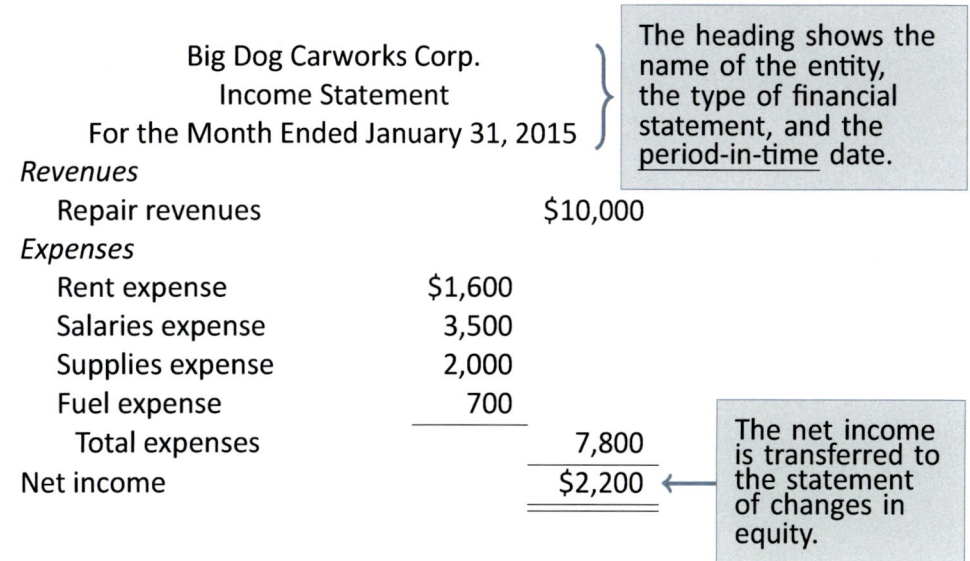

Big Dog Carworks Corp.
Income Statement
For the Month Ended January 31, 2015

Revenues		
Repair revenues		$10,000
Expenses		
Rent expense	$1,600	
Salaries expense	3,500	
Supplies expense	2,000	
Fuel expense	700	
Total expenses		7,800
Net income		$2,200

The heading shows the name of the entity, the type of financial statement, and the period-in-time date.

The net income is transferred to the statement of changes in equity.

An exploration is available on the Lyryx site. Log into your Lyryx course to run Income Statement.

The Statement of Changes in Equity

The **statement of changes in equity** provides information about how the balances in Share capital and Retained earnings changed during the period. **Share capital** is a heading in the shareholders' equity section of the balance sheet and represents how much shareholders have invested. When shareholders buy shares, they are investing in the business. The number of shares they purchase will determine how much of the corporation they own. The type of ownership unit purchased by Big Dog's shareholders is known as common shares. Other types of shares will be discussed in a later chapter. When a corporation sells its shares to shareholders, the corporation is said to be **issuing shares** to shareholders.

In the statement of changes in equity shown below, Share capital and Retained earnings balances at January 1 are zero because the corporation started the business on that date. During January, Share capital of $10,000 was issued to shareholders so the January 31 balance is $10,000.

Retained earnings is the sum of all net incomes earned by a corporation over its life, less any distributions of these net incomes to shareholders. Distributions of net income to shareholders are called **dividends**. Shareholders generally have the right to share in dividends according to the percentage of their ownership interest. To demonstrate the concept of retained earnings, recall that Big Dog has been in business for one month in which $2,200 of net income was reported. Additionally, $200 of dividends were distributed, so these are subtracted from retained earnings. Big Dog's retained earnings were therefore $2,000 at January 31, 2015 as shown in the statement of changes in equity below.

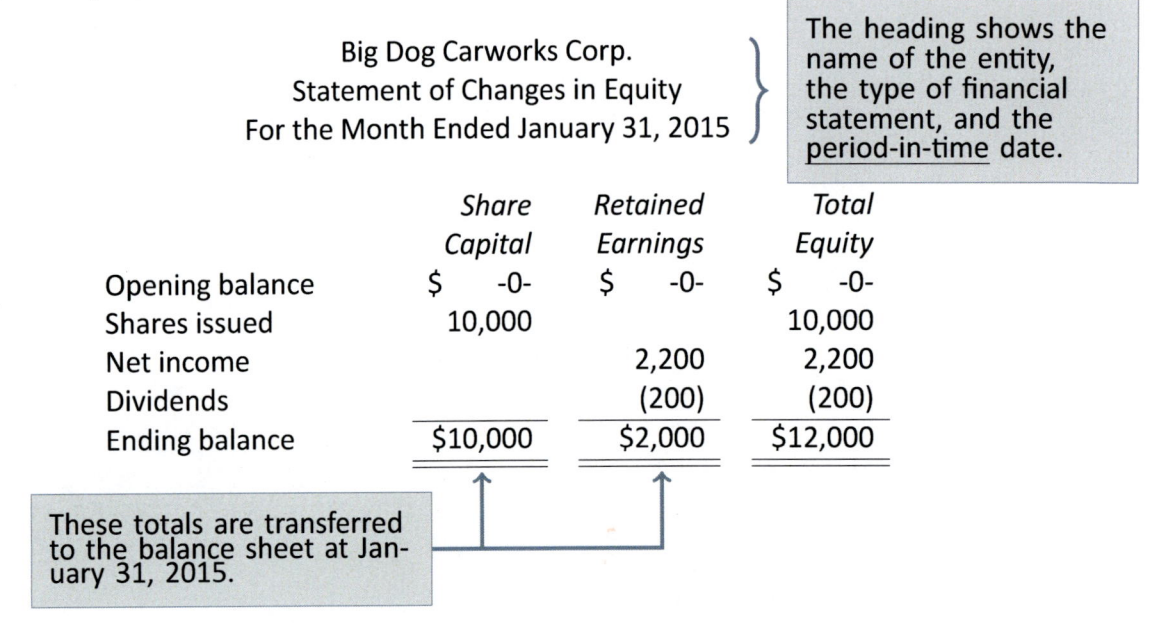

Big Dog Carworks Corp.
Statement of Changes in Equity
For the Month Ended January 31, 2015

The heading shows the name of the entity, the type of financial statement, and the period-in-time date.

	Share Capital	Retained Earnings	Total Equity
Opening balance	$ -0-	$ -0-	$ -0-
Shares issued	10,000		10,000
Net income		2,200	2,200
Dividends		(200)	(200)
Ending balance	$10,000	$2,000	$12,000

These totals are transferred to the balance sheet at January 31, 2015.

To demonstrate how retained earnings would appear in the next accounting period, let's assume that Big Dog reported a net income of $5,000 for February, 2015 and dividends of $1,000 were given to the shareholder. Based on this information, retained earnings at the end of February would be $6,000, calculated as the $2,000 January 31 balance plus the $5,000 February net income less the $1,000 February dividend. The balance in retained earnings continues to change over time because of additional net incomes/losses and dividends.

An exploration is available on the Lyryx site. Log into your Lyryx course to run Statement of Changes in Equity.

The Balance Sheet

The **balance sheet**, or **statement of financial position**, shows a business's assets, liabilities, and equity at a point in time. The balance sheet of Big Dog Carworks Corp. at January 31, 2015 is shown below.

Big Dog Carworks Corp.
Balance Sheet
At January 31, 2015

> The heading shows the name of the entity, the type of financial statement, and the point-in-time date.

Assets		Liabilities		
Cash	$ 3,700	Bank Loan	$ 6,000	
Accounts receivable	2,000	Accounts payable	700	
Prepaid insurance	2,400	Unearned revenue	400	
Equipment	3,000	Total liabilities		$ 7,100
Truck	8,000			
		Equity		
		Share capital	$10,000	
		Retained earnings	2,000	
		Total equity		12,000
Total assets	$19,100	Total liabilities and equity		$19,100

> Total assets ($19,100 here) always equal Total liabilities ($7,100) plus Equity ($12,000).

What Is an Asset?

Assets are economic resources that provide future benefits to the business. Examples include cash, accounts receivable, prepaid expenses, equipment, and trucks. **Cash** is coins and currency, usually held in a bank account, and is a financial resource with future benefit because of its purchasing power. **Accounts receivable** represent amounts to be collected in cash in the future for goods sold or services provided to customers on credit. **Prepaid expenses** are assets that are paid in cash in advance and have benefits that apply over future periods. For example, a one-year insurance policy purchased for cash on January 1, 2015 will provide a benefit until December 31, 2015 so is a prepaid asset. The equipment and truck were purchased on January 1, 2015 and will provide benefits for 2015 and beyond so are assets.

What Is a Liability?

A **liability** is an obligation to pay an asset in the future. For example, Big Dog's bank loan represents an obligation to repay cash in the future to the bank. **Accounts payable** are obligations to pay a creditor for goods purchased or services rendered. A **creditor** owns the right to receive payment from an individual or business. **Unearned revenue** represents an advance payment of cash from a customer for Big Dog's services or products to be provided in the future. For example, Big Dog collected cash from a customer in advance for a repair to be done in the future.

What Is Equity?

Equity represents the net assets owned by the owners (the shareholders). **Net assets** are assets minus liabilities. For example, in Big Dog's January 31 balance sheet, net assets are $12,000, calculated as total assets of $19,100 minus total liabilities of $7,100. This means that although there are $19,100 of assets, only $12,000 are owned by the shareholders and the balance, $7,100, are financed by debt. Notice that net assets and total equity are the same value; both are $12,000. Equity consists of share capital and retained earnings. Share capital represents how much the shareholders have invested in the business. Retained earnings is the sum of all net incomes earned by a corporation over its life, less any dividends distributed to shareholders.

In summary, the balance sheet is represented by the equation: Assets = Liabilities + Equity. Assets are the investments held by a business. The liabilities and equity explain how the assets have been financed, or funded. Assets can be financed through liabilities, also known as **debt**, or equity. Equity represents amounts that are owned by the owners, the shareholders, and consists of share capital and retained earnings. Investments made by shareholders, namely share capital, are used to finance assets and/or pay down liabilities. Additionally, retained earnings, comprised of net income less any dividends, also represent a source of financing.

An exploration is available on the Lyryx site. Log into your Lyryx course to run Account Types.

The Statement of Cash Flows (SCF)

Cash is an asset reported on the balance sheet. Ensuring there is sufficient cash to pay expenses and liabilities as they come due is a critical business activity. The **statement of cash flows (SCF)** explains how the balance in cash changed over a period of time by detailing the sources (inflows) and uses (outflows) of cash by type of activity: operating, investing, and financing, as these are the three types of activities a business engages in. **Operating activities** are the day-to-day processes involved in selling products and/or services to generate net income. Examples of operating activities include the purchase and use of supplies, paying employees, fuelling equipment, and renting space for the business. **Investing activities** are the buying of assets needed to generate revenues. For example, when an airline purchases airplanes, it is investing in assets required to help it generate revenue. **Financing activities** are the raising of money needed to invest in assets. Financing can involve issuing share capital (getting money from the owners known as shareholders) or borrowing. Figure 1.2 summarizes the interrelationships among the three types of business activities.

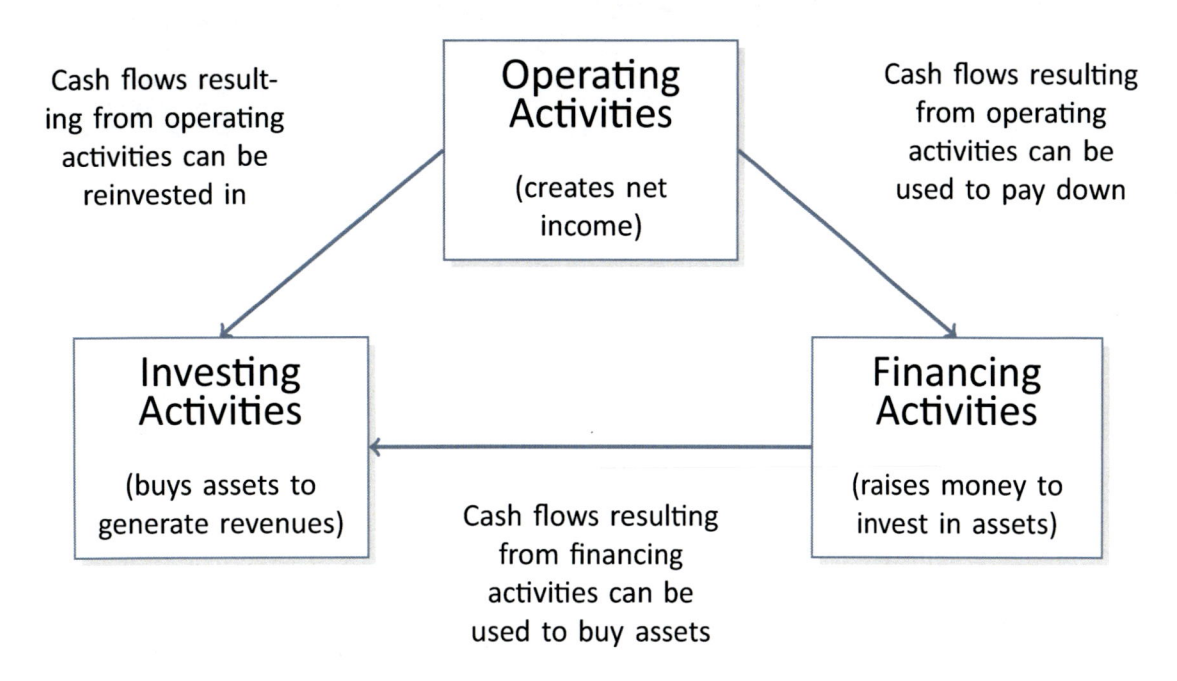

```
                    Operating
                    Activities
Cash flows result-                          Cash flows resulting
ing from operating                          from operating
activities can be   (creates net            activities can be
reinvested in       income)                 used to pay down


   Investing                                   Financing
   Activities                                  Activities

   (buys assets to   Cash flows resulting      (raises money to
   generate revenues) from financing           invest in assets)
                     activities can be
                     used to buy assets
```

Figure 1.2: Relationships Among the Three Types of Business Activities

The statement of cash flows for Big Dog is shown below.

Big Dog Carworks Corp.
Statement of Cash Flows
For the Month Ended January 31, 2015

> The heading shows the name of the entity, the type of financial statement, and the period-in-time date.

Operating activities:		
Net income		$ 2,200
Adjustments:		
Increase in unearned revenues	400	
Increase in accounts payable	700	
Increase in prepaid insurance	(2,400)	
Increase in accounts receivable	(2,000)	
Net cash used by operating activities		$(1,100)
Investing activities:		
Purchase of equipment	$(3,000)	
Purchase of truck	(3,000)	
Net cash used by investing activities		(6,000)
Financing activities:		
Issued shares	$10,000	
Borrowed from bank	3,000	
Payment on bank loan	(2,000)	
Paid dividends	(200)	
Net cash provided by financing activities		10,800
Net increase in cash		3,700
Cash balance, January 1		-0-
Cash balance, January 31		$3,700

This agrees with the Cash amount shown on the Balance Sheet at January 31, 2015.

The statement of cash flows is useful because cash is one of the most important assets of a corporation. Information about expected future cash flows are therefore important for decision makers. For instance, Big Dog's bank manager needs to determine whether the remaining $6,000 loan can be repaid, and also whether or not to grant a new loan to the corporation if requested. The statement of cash flows helps inform those who make these decisions.

Notes to the Financial Statements

An essential part of financial statements are the notes that accompany them. These notes are generally located at the end of a set of financial statements. The notes provide greater detail about various amounts shown in the financial statements, or provide non-quantitative information that is useful to users. For example, a note may indicate the estimated useful lives of long-lived assets, or loan repayment terms. Examples of note disclosures will be provided later.

An exploration is available on the Lyrx site. Log into your Lyrx course to run Communicating Through Financial Statements.

1.5 Transaction Analysis and Double-entry Accounting

LO5 – Analyze transactions by using the accounting equation.

The **accounting equation** is foundational to accounting. It shows that the total assets of a business must always equal the total claims against those assets by creditors and owners. The equation is expressed as:

$$\text{ASSETS} = \text{LIABILITIES} + \text{EQUITY}$$

(economic resources owned by an entity) (creditors' claims on assets) (owners' claims on assets)

When financial transactions are recorded, combined effects on assets, liabilities, and equity are always exactly offsetting. This is the reason that the balance sheet always balances.

Each economic exchange is referred to as a **financial transaction** — for example, when an organization exchanges cash for land and buildings. Incurring a liability in return for an asset is also a financial transaction. Instead of paying cash for land and buildings, an organization may borrow money from a financial institution. The company must repay this with cash payments in the future. The accounting equation provides a system for processing and summarizing these sorts of transactions.

Accountants view financial transactions as economic events that change components within the accounting equation. These changes are usually triggered by information contained in **source documents** (such as sales invoices and bills from creditors) that can be verified for accuracy.

The accounting equation can be expanded to include all the items listed on the Balance Sheet of Big Dog at January 31, 2015, as follows:

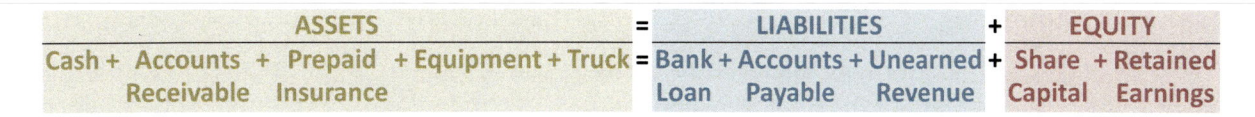

ASSETS	=	LIABILITIES	+	EQUITY
Cash + Accounts + Prepaid + Equipment + Truck	=	Bank + Accounts + Unearned	+	Share + Retained
Receivable Insurance		Loan Payable Revenue		Capital Earnings

If one item within the accounting equation is changed, then another item must also be changed to balance it. In this way, the equality of the equation is maintained. For example, if there is an increase in an asset account, then there must be a decrease in another asset or a corresponding increase in a liability or equity account. This equality is the essence of *double-entry accounting*. The equation itself always remains in balance after each transaction. The operation of double-entry accounting is illustrated in the following section, which shows 10 transactions of Big Dog Carworks Corp. for January 2015.

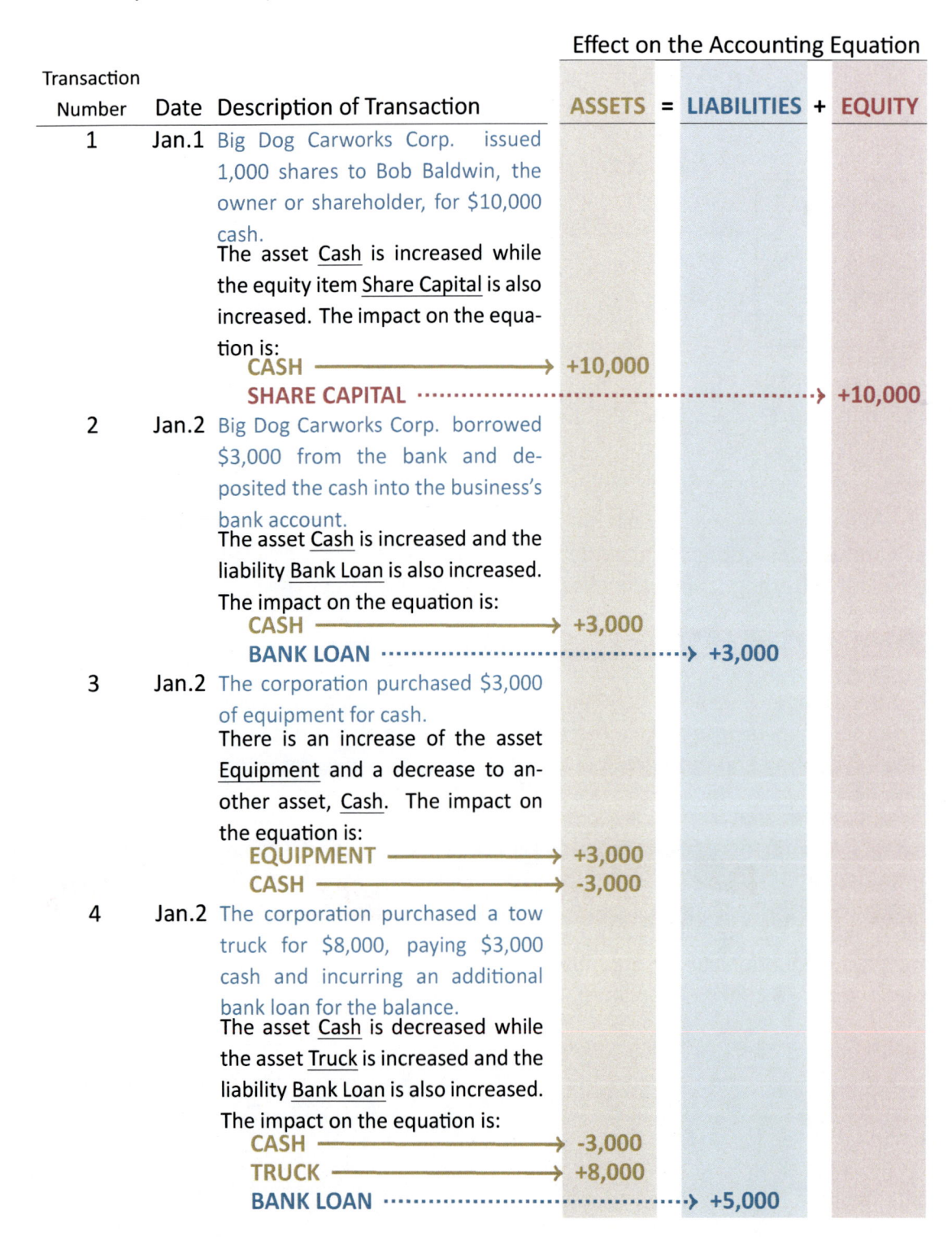

Effect on the Accounting Equation

Transaction Number	Date	Description of Transaction	ASSETS	=	LIABILITIES	+	EQUITY
1	Jan.1	Big Dog Carworks Corp. issued 1,000 shares to Bob Baldwin, the owner or shareholder, for $10,000 cash. The asset Cash is increased while the equity item Share Capital is also increased. The impact on the equation is: CASH → +10,000 SHARE CAPITAL ⋯⋯⋯⋯⋯⋯⋯⋯⋯⋯⋯⋯⋯⋯⋯→ +10,000					
2	Jan.2	Big Dog Carworks Corp. borrowed $3,000 from the bank and deposited the cash into the business's bank account. The asset Cash is increased and the liability Bank Loan is also increased. The impact on the equation is: CASH → +3,000 BANK LOAN ⋯⋯⋯⋯⋯⋯⋯⋯⋯→ +3,000					
3	Jan.2	The corporation purchased $3,000 of equipment for cash. There is an increase of the asset Equipment and a decrease to another asset, Cash. The impact on the equation is: EQUIPMENT → +3,000 CASH → -3,000					
4	Jan.2	The corporation purchased a tow truck for $8,000, paying $3,000 cash and incurring an additional bank loan for the balance. The asset Cash is decreased while the asset Truck is increased and the liability Bank Loan is also increased. The impact on the equation is: CASH → -3,000 TRUCK → +8,000 BANK LOAN ⋯⋯⋯⋯⋯⋯⋯⋯⋯→ +5,000					

1.5. Transaction Analysis and Double-entry Accounting

Effect on the Accounting Equation

Transaction Number	Date	Description of Transaction	ASSETS	= LIABILITIES	+ EQUITY
5	Jan. 5	Big Dog Carworks Corp. paid $2,400 for a one-year insurance policy, effective January 1.			

Here the asset <u>Prepaid Insurance</u> is increased and the asset <u>Cash</u> is decreased. The impact on the equation is:

    PREPAID INSURANCE ⟶ +2,400
    CASH ⟶ -2,400

Since the one-year period will not be fully used at January 31 when financial statements are prepared, the insurance cost is considered to be an asset at the payment date. The transaction does not affect liabilities or equity.

| 6 | Jan. 10 | The corporation paid $2,000 cash to the bank to reduce the loan outstanding. | | | |

The asset <u>Cash</u> is decreased and there is a decrease in the liability <u>Bank Loan</u>. The impact on the equation is:

    BANK LOAN ·········⟶ -2,000
    CASH ⟶ -2,000

| 7 | Jan. 15 | The corporation received $400 as an advance payment from a customer for services to be performed over the next two months as follows: $300 for February, $100 for March. | | | |

The asset <u>Cash</u> is increased by $400 and a liability, <u>Unearned Revenue</u>, is also increased since the revenue will not be earned by the end of January. It will be earned when the work is performed in later months. At January 31, these amounts are repayable to customers if the work is not done (and thus a liability). The impact on the equation is:

    CASH ⟶ +400
    UNEARNED REVENUE ·········⟶ +400

18 ■ Introduction to Financial Accounting

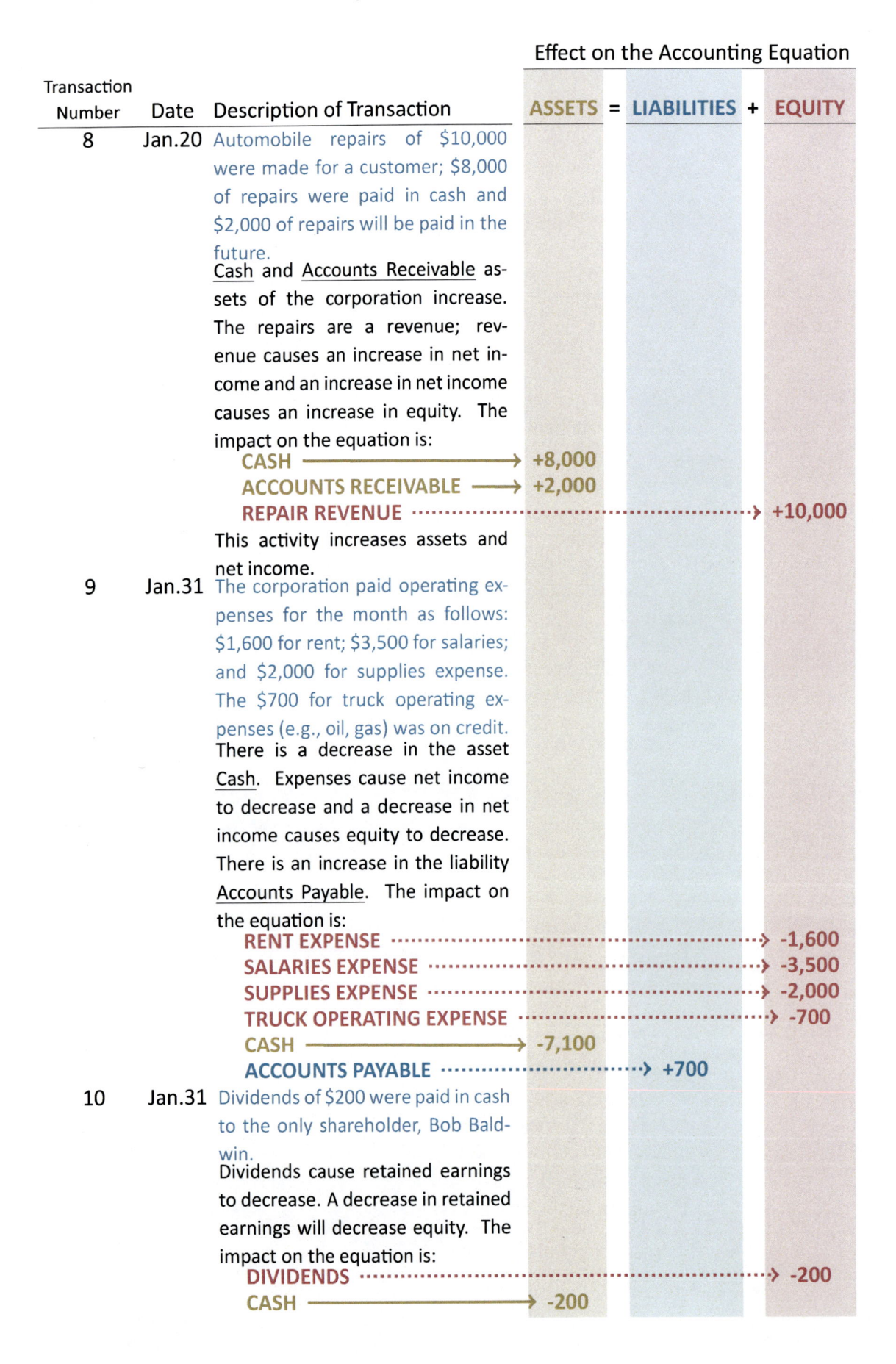

Effect on the Accounting Equation

Transaction Number	Date	Description of Transaction	ASSETS =	LIABILITIES +	EQUITY
8	Jan. 20	Automobile repairs of $10,000 were made for a customer; $8,000 of repairs were paid in cash and $2,000 of repairs will be paid in the future.			
		Cash and Accounts Receivable assets of the corporation increase. The repairs are a revenue; revenue causes an increase in net income and an increase in net income causes an increase in equity. The impact on the equation is:			
		CASH	+8,000		
		ACCOUNTS RECEIVABLE	+2,000		
		REPAIR REVENUE			+10,000
		This activity increases assets and net income.			
9	Jan. 31	The corporation paid operating expenses for the month as follows: $1,600 for rent; $3,500 for salaries; and $2,000 for supplies expense. The $700 for truck operating expenses (e.g., oil, gas) was on credit.			
		There is a decrease in the asset Cash. Expenses cause net income to decrease and a decrease in net income causes equity to decrease. There is an increase in the liability Accounts Payable. The impact on the equation is:			
		RENT EXPENSE			−1,600
		SALARIES EXPENSE			−3,500
		SUPPLIES EXPENSE			−2,000
		TRUCK OPERATING EXPENSE			−700
		CASH	−7,100		
		ACCOUNTS PAYABLE		+700	
10	Jan. 31	Dividends of $200 were paid in cash to the only shareholder, Bob Baldwin.			
		Dividends cause retained earnings to decrease. A decrease in retained earnings will decrease equity. The impact on the equation is:			
		DIVIDENDS			−200
		CASH	−200		

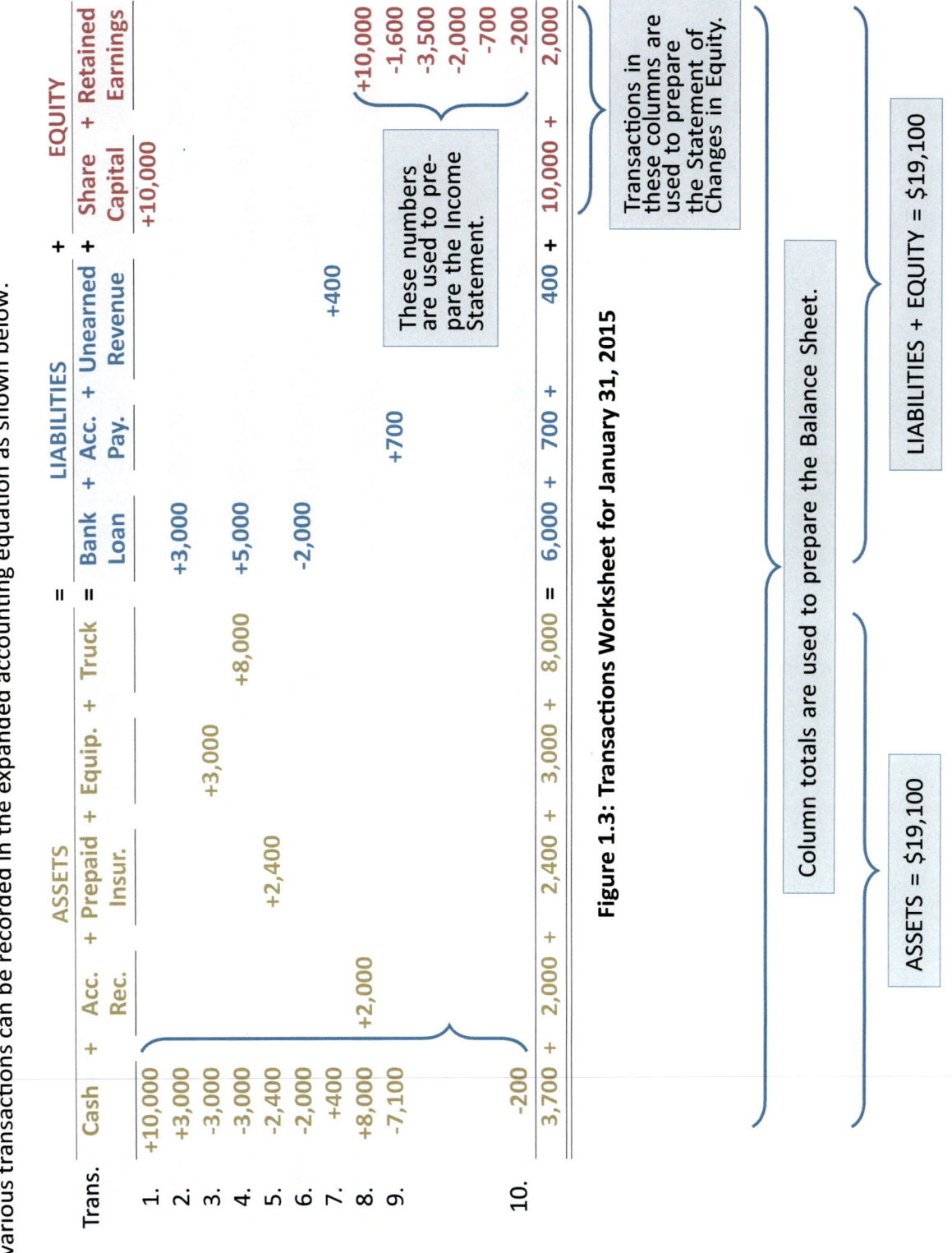

These various transactions can be recorded in the expanded accounting equation as shown below:

Trans.	Cash	+ Acc. Rec.	+ Prepaid Insur.	+ Equip.	+ Truck	=	Bank Loan	+ Acc. Pay.	+ Unearned Revenue	+	Share Capital	+ Retained Earnings
1.	+10,000										+10,000	
2.	+3,000						+3,000					
3.	−3,000			+3,000								
4.	−3,000				+8,000		+5,000					
5.	−2,400		+2,400									
6.	−2,000						−2,000					
7.	+400								+400			
8.	+8,000	+2,000						+700				+10,000
9.	−7,100											−1,600
												−3,500
												−2,000
												−700
10.	−200											−200
	3,700 +	2,000 +	2,400 +	3,000 +	8,000 =		6,000 +	700 +	400 +		10,000 +	2,000

These numbers are used to prepare the Income Statement.

Transactions in these columns are used to prepare the Statement of Changes in Equity.

Figure 1.3: Transactions Worksheet for January 31, 2015

Column totals are used to prepare the Balance Sheet.

ASSETS = $19,100

LIABILITIES + EQUITY = $19,100

Transactions summary:

1. Issued share capital for $10,000 cash.
2. Received a bank loan for $3,000.
3. Purchased equipment for $3,000 cash.
4. Purchased a truck for $8,000; paid $3,000 cash and incurred a bank loan for the balance.
5. Paid $2,400 for a comprehensive one-year insurance policy effective January 1.
6. Paid $2,000 cash to reduce the bank loan.
7. Received $400 as an advance payment for repair services to be provided over the next two months as follows: $300 for February, $100 for March.
8. Performed repairs for $8,000 cash and $2,000 on credit.
9. Paid a total of $7,100 for operating expenses incurred during the month; also incurred an expense on account for $700.
10. Dividends of $200 were paid in cash to the only shareholder, Bob Baldwin.

The transactions summarized in Figure 1.3 were used to prepare the financial statements described earlier, and reproduced in Figure 1.4 below.

Big Dog Carworks Corp.
Balance Sheet
At January 31, 2015

Assets
Cash $3,700
Accounts receivable 2,000
Prepaid insurance 2,400
Equipment 3,000
Truck 8,000
$19,100

Liabilities
Bank loan $6,000
Accounts payable 700
Unearned revenue 400   7,100

Equity
Share capital $10,000
Retained earnings 2,000
12,000
$19,100

Big Dog Carworks Corp.
Income Statement
For the Month Ended January 31, 2015

Revenue
Repairs $10,000

Expenses
Rent $1,600
Salaries 3,500
Supplies 2,000
Truck operation 700
Total expenses 7,800

Net income $2,200

The components of equity are shown on the Balance Sheet.

Net Income becomes part of Retained Earnings.

Big Dog Carworks Corp.
Statement of Changes in Equity
For the Month Ended January 31, 2015

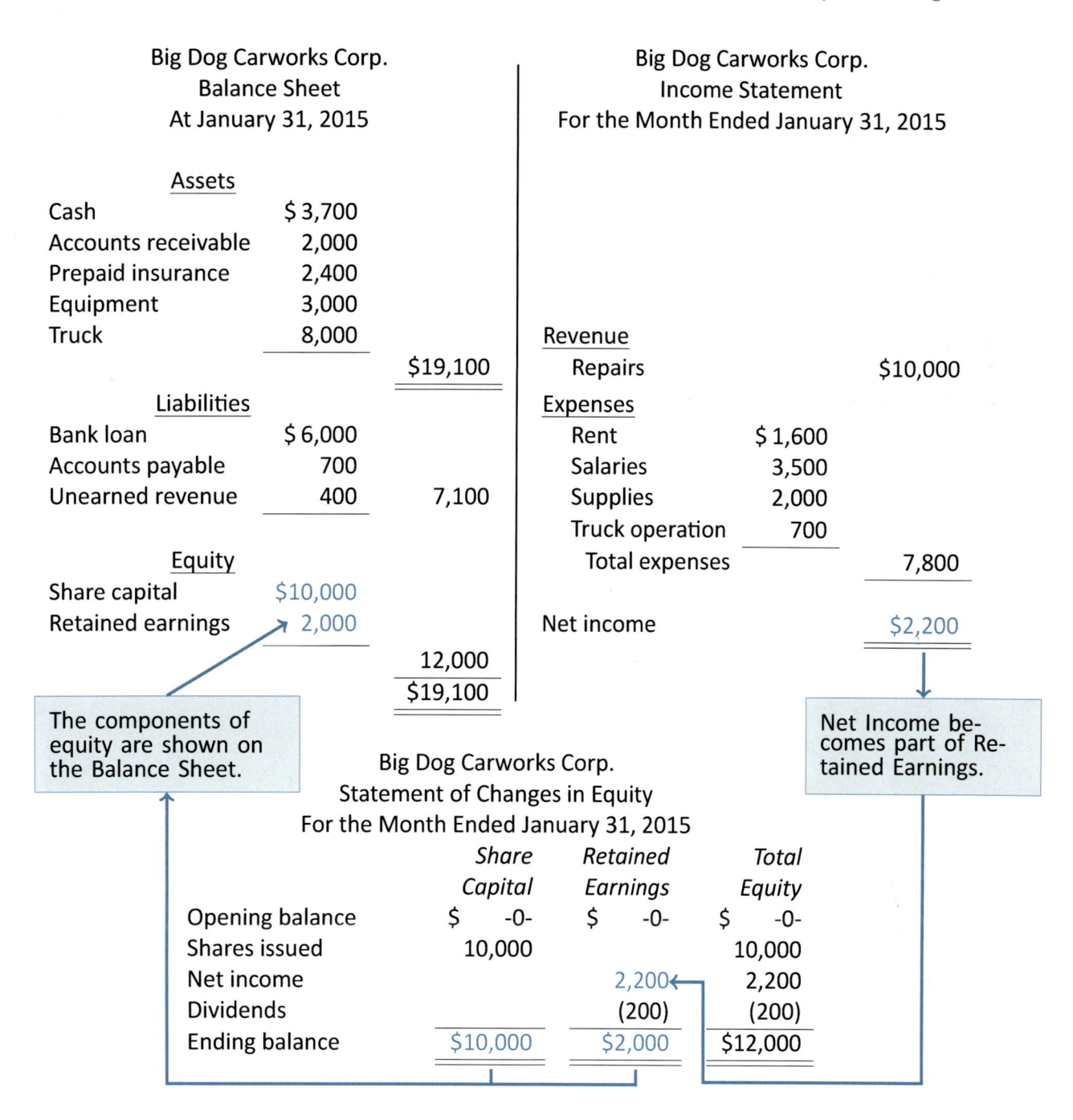

	Share Capital	Retained Earnings	Total Equity
Opening balance	$ -0-	$ -0-	$ -0-
Shares issued	10,000		10,000
Net income		2,200	2,200
Dividends		(200)	(200)
Ending balance	$10,000	$2,000	$12,000

Figure 1.4: Financial Statements of Big Dog Carworks Corp.

Accounting Time Periods

Financial statements are prepared at regular intervals — usually monthly or quarterly — and at the end of each 12-month period. This 12-month period is called the **fiscal year**. The timing of the financial statements is determined by the needs of management and other users of the financial statements. For instance, financial statements may also be required by outside parties, such as bankers and shareholders. However, accounting information must possess the qualitative characteristic of timeliness — it must be available to decision makers in time to be useful — which is typically a minimum of once every 12 months.

Accounting reports, called the *annual financial statements*, are prepared at the end of each 12-month period, which is known as the **year-end** of the entity. Some companies' year-ends do not follow the calendar year (year ending December 31). This may be done so that the fiscal year coincides with their *natural year*. A **natural year** ends when business operations are at a low point. For example, a ski resort may have a fiscal year ending in late spring or early summer when business operations have ceased for the season.

Corporations listed on **stock exchanges** are generally required to prepare **interim financial statements**, usually every three months, primarily for the use of shareholders or creditors. Because these types of corporations are large and usually have many owners, users require more up-to-date financial information.

The relationship of the interim and year-end financial statements is illustrated in Figure 1.5.

Jan. 1, 2015 (commencement of operations) — Jan. 31, 2015 (interim) — Dec. 31, 2015 (fiscal year end)

INTERIM INCOME STATEMENT
INTERIM STATEMENT OF CHANGES IN EQUITY
INTERIM STATEMENT OF CASH FLOWS
(for the month of January)

INTERIM BALANCE SHEET (prepared on this date)

YEAR END BALANCE SHEET (prepared on this date)

These *may* be prepared.

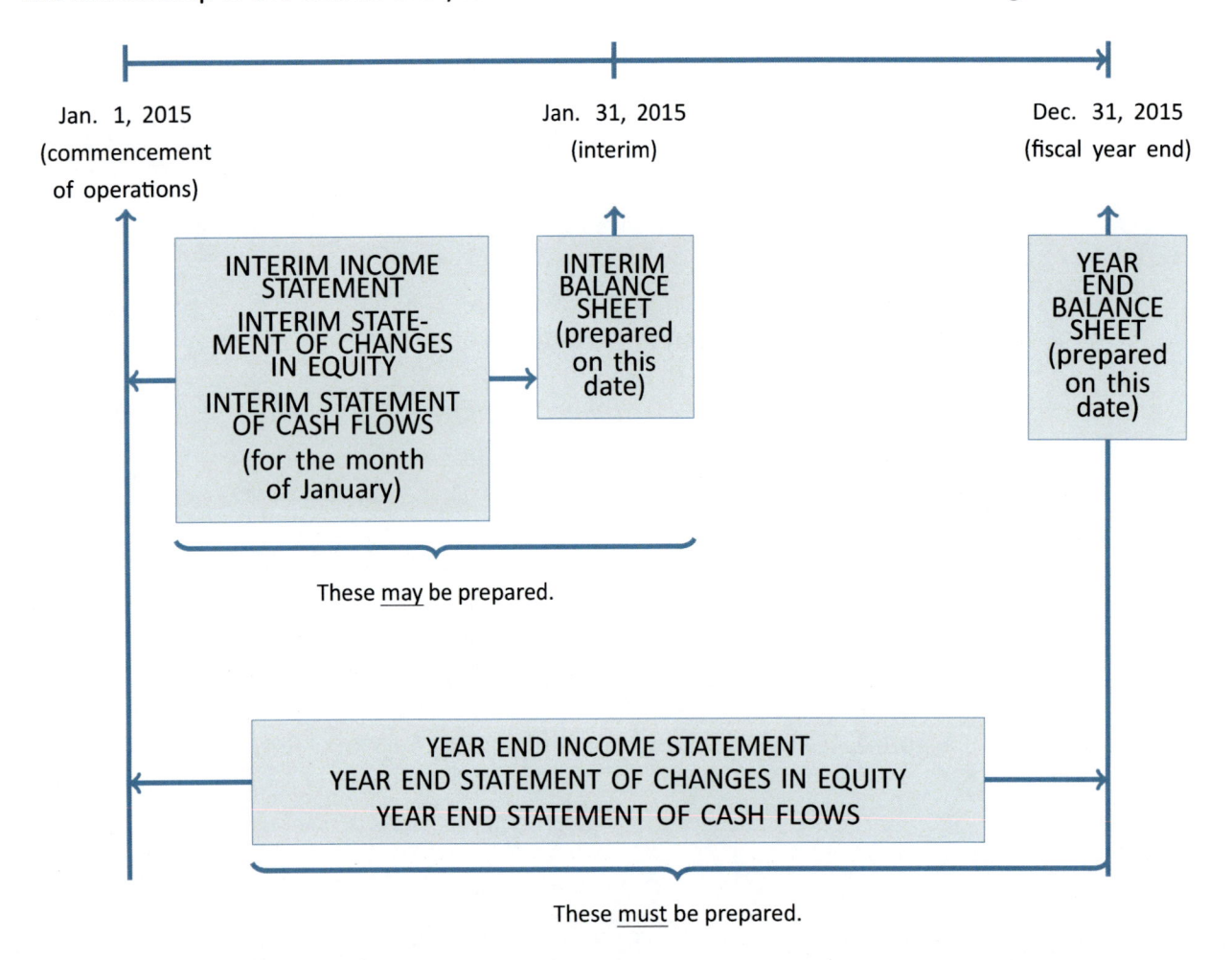

YEAR END INCOME STATEMENT
YEAR END STATEMENT OF CHANGES IN EQUITY
YEAR END STATEMENT OF CASH FLOWS

These *must* be prepared.

Figure 1.5: Relationship of Interim and Year-end Financial Statements

An exploration is available on the Lyryx site. Log into your Lyryx course to run Accounting Equation.

Summary of Chapter 1 Learning Objectives

LO1 – Define accounting.

Accounting is the process of identifying, measuring, recording, and communicating an organization's economic activities to users for decision making. Internal users work for the organization while external users do not. Managerial accounting serves the decision-making needs of internal users. Financial accounting focuses on external reporting to meet the needs of external users.

LO2 – Identify and describe the forms of business organization.

The three forms of business organizations are a proprietorship, partnership, and corporation.

The following chart summarizes the key characteristics of each form of business organization.

Characteristic	Proprietorship	Partnership	Corporation
Separate legal entity	No	No	Yes
Business income is taxed as part of the business	No[3]	No[4]	Yes
Unlimited liability	Yes	Yes	No
One owner permitted	Yes	No	Yes[5]
Board of Directors	No	No	Yes

LO3 – Identify and explain the Generally Accepted Accounting Principles (GAAP).

GAAP followed in Canada by PAEs (Publicly Accountable Enterprises) are based on IFRS (International Financial Reporting Standards). PEs (Private Enterprises) follow GAAP based on ASPE (Accounting Standards for Private Enterprises), a less onerous set of GAAP maintained by the AcSB (Accounting Standards Board). GAAP have qualitative characteristics (relevance, faithful representation, comparability, verifiability, timeliness, and understandability) and principles (business entity, consistency, cost, full disclosure, going concern, matching, materiality, monetary unit, and recognition).

---

[3] Business income is added to the owner's personal income and the owner pays tax on the sum of the two.
[4] Business income is added to the owner's personal income and the owner pays tax on the sum of the two.
[5] A corporation can have one or more owners.

LO4 – Identify, explain, and prepare the financial statements.

The four financial statements are: income statement, statement of changes in equity, balance sheet, and statement of cash flows. The income statement reports financial performance by detailing revenues less expenses to arrive at net income/loss for the period. The statement of changes in equity shows the changes during the period to each of the components of equity: share capital and retained earnings. The balance sheet identifies financial position at a point in time by listing assets, liabilities, and equity. Finally, the statement of cash flows details the sources and uses of cash during the period based on the three business activities: operating, investing, and financing.

LO5 – Analyze transactions by using the accounting equation.

The accounting equation, A = L + E, describes the asset investments (the left side of the equation) and the liabilities and equity that financed the assets (the right side of the equation). The accounting equation provides a system for processing and summarizing financial transactions resulting from a business's activities. A financial transaction is an economic exchange between two parties that impacts the accounting equation. The equation must always balance.

Discussion Questions

1. What are generally accepted accounting principles (GAAP)?
2. When is revenue recognised?
3. How does the matching concept more accurately determine the Net Income of a business?
4. What are the qualities that accounting information is expected to have? What are the limitations on the disclosure of useful accounting information?
5. What are assets?
6. To what do the terms *liability* and *equity* refer?
7. Explain the term *financial transaction*. Include an example of a financial transaction as part of your explanation.
8. Identify the three forms of business organization.
9. What is the business entity concept of accounting? Why is it important?
10. What is the general purpose of financial statements? Name the four financial statements?

11. Each financial statement has a title that consists of the name of the financial statement, the name of the business, and a date line. How is the date line on each of the four financial statements the same or different?

12. What is the purpose of an income statement? a balance sheet? How do they interrelate?

13. Define the terms *revenue* and *expense*.

14. What is net income? What information does it convey?

15. What is the purpose of a statement of changes in equity? a statement of cash flows?

16. Why are financial statements prepared at regular intervals? Who are the users of these statements?

17. What is the accounting equation?

18. Explain double-entry accounting.

19. What is a year-end? How does the timing of year-end financial statements differ from that of interim financial statements?

20. How does a fiscal year differ from a calendar year?

Exercises

EXERCISE 1–1   (LO1,2,3)   Matching

Ethics
Financial accounting
International Financial Reporting Standards
Limited liability
Managerial accounting
Partnership
Separate legal entity
Unlimited liability

Required: Match each term in the above alphabetized list to the corresponding description below.

a. _____   The owners pay tax on the business' net income.
b. _____   Accounting standards followed by PAEs in Canada.
c. _____   Rules that guide us in interpreting right from wrong.
d. _____   Accounting aimed at communicating information to external users.
e. _____   Accounting aimed at communicating information to internal users.
f. _____   The business is distinct from its owners.
g. _____   The owner(s) are not responsible for the debts of the business.
h. _____   If the business is unable to pay its debts, the owner(s) is responsible.

EXERCISE 1–2   (LO4)   Calculating Missing Amounts

	Assets	=	Liabilities	+	Equity
a.	50,000	=	20,000	+	?
b.	10,000	=	?	+	1,000
c.	?	=	15,000	+	80,000

Required: Calculate the missing amounts in **a**, **b**, and **c** above. Additionally, answer each of the questions in **d** and **e** below.

d. Assets are financed by debt and equity. The greatest percentage of debt financing is reflected in **a**, **b**, or **c**?

e. The greatest percentage of equity financing is reflected in **a**, **b**, or **c**?

EXERCISE 1–3 (LO4) Calculating Missing Amounts

Required: Calculate the missing amounts for companies A to E.

	A	B	C	D	E
Cash	$3,000	$1,000	$?	$6,000	$2,500
Equipment	8,000	6,000	4,000	7,000	?
Accounts Payable	4,000	?	1,500	3,000	4,500
Share Capital	2,000	3,000	3,000	4,000	500
Retained Earnings	?	1,000	500	?	1,000

EXERCISE 1–4 (LO4) Calculating Missing Amounts

	Assets	=	Liabilities	+	Equity
Balance, Jan. 1, 2015	$50,000		$40,000		?
Balance, Dec. 31, 2015	40,000		20,000		?

Required: Using the information above, calculate net income under each of the following assumptions.

a. During 2015, no share capital was issued and no dividends were declared.

b. During 2015, no share capital was issued and dividends of $5,000 were declared.

c. During 2015, share capital of $12,000 was issued and no dividends were declared.

d. During 2015, share capital of $8,000 was issued and $12,000 of dividends were declared.

EXERCISE 1–5 (LO4) Identifying Assets, Liabilities, Equity Items

Required: Indicate whether each of the following is an asset (A), liability (L), or an equity (E) item.

a. Accounts Payable
b. Accounts Receivable
c. Bank Loan Payable
d. Building
e. Cash
f. Share Capital
g. Loan Payable
h. Office Supplies
i. Prepaid Insurance
j. Utilities Expense
k. Dividends
l. Interest Receivable
m. Retained Earnings
n. Interest Revenue
o. Interest Payable
p. Interest Expense
q. Prepaid Insurance
r. Insurance Expense
s. Insurance Revenue
t. Machinery

EXERCISE 1–6 (LO4) Calculating Financial Statement Components

The following information is taken from the records of Jasper Inc. at January 31, 2015, after its first month of operations. Assume no dividends were declared in January.

Cash	$33,000	Equipment	$30,000
Accounts Receivable	82,000	Bank Loan	15,000
Unused Supplies	2,000	Accounts Payable	27,000
Land	25,000	Share Capital	?
Building	70,000	Net Income	40,000

Required:

a. Calculate total assets.

b. Calculate total liabilities.

c. Calculate share capital.

d. Calculate retained earnings.

e. Calculate total equity.

EXERCISE 1–7 (LO4) Net Income, Shares Issued

Accounts Receivable	$4,000	Miscellaneous Expense	$ 2,500
Accounts Payable	5,000	Office Supplies Expense	1,000
Cash	1,000	Service Revenue	20,000
Equipment	8,000	Share Capital	?
Insurance Expense	1,500	Wages Expense	9,000

Required: Using the alphabetized information above for EDW Inc. after its first month of operations, complete the income statement, statement of changes in equity, and balance sheet using the templates provided below.

EDW Inc.
Income Statement
Month Ended March 31, 2015

Revenues
  Service Revenue $
Expenses
  Wages Expense $
  Miscellaneous Expense
  Insurance Expense
  Office Supplies Expense
Net Income $

EDW Inc.
Statement of Changes in Equity
Month Ended March 31, 2015

	Share Capital	Retained Earnings	Total Equity
Opening Balance	$	$	$
Shares Issued			
Net Income			
Ending Balance	$	$	$

EDW Inc.
Balance Sheet
March 31, 2015

Assets
  Cash $
  Accounts Receivable
  Equipment

Total Assets $

Liabilities
  Accounts Payable $

Equity
  Share Capital $
  Retained Earnings
  Total Equity
Total Liabilities and Equity $

EXERCISE 1–8 (LO4) Net Income, Dividends

Accounts Receivable	$17,000	Machinery	$14,000
Accounts Payable	3,000	Note Payable	18,000
Advertising Expense	5,000	Retained Earnings	6,000
Cash	9,000	Salaries Expense	64,000
Dividends	2,000	Service Revenue	81,000
Insurance Expense	7,000	Share Capital	10,000

Required: Algonquin Inc. began operations on August 1, 2013. After its second year, Algonquin Inc.'s accounting system showed the information above. During the second year, no additional shares were issued. Complete the income statement, statement of changes in equity, and balance sheet using the templates provided below.

Algonquin Inc.
Income Statement
Year Ended July 31, 2015

Revenues
  Service Revenue $
Expenses
  Advertising Expense $
  Insurance Expense
  Salaries Expense
Net Income $

Algonquin Inc.
Statement of Changes in Equity
Year Ended July 31, 2015

	Share Capital	Retained Earnings	Total Equity
Opening Balance	$ 10,000	$ 6,000	$ 16,000
Net Income			
Dividends			
Ending Balance	$	$	$

Algonquin Inc.
Balance Sheet
July 31, 2015

Assets
  Cash $
  Accounts Receivable
  Machinery

Total Assets $

Liabilities
  Accounts Payable $
  Note Payable
  Total Liabilities $

Equity
  Share Capital $
  Retained Earnings
  Total Equity
Total Liabilities and Equity $

EXERCISE 1–9 (LO4) Net Income, Dividends, Shares Issued

Required: Refer to EXERCISE 1–8. Use the same information EXCEPT assume that during the second year, additional shares were issued for cash of $3,000. Complete the income statement, statement of changes in equity, and balance sheet using the templates provided below.

Algonquin Inc.
Income Statement
Year Ended July 31, 2015

Revenues
  Service Revenue $
Expenses
  Advertising Expense $
  Insurance Expense
  Salaries Expense
Net Income $

Algonquin Inc.
Statement of Changes in Equity
Year Ended July 31, 2015

	Share Capital	Retained Earnings	Total Equity
Opening Balance	$	$	$
Shares Issued			
Net Income			
Dividends			
Ending Balance	$	$	$

Algonquin Inc.
Balance Sheet
July 31, 2015

Assets
  Cash $
  Accounts Receivable
  Machinery

Total Assets $

Liabilities
  Accounts Payable $
  Note Payable
  Total Liabilities $

Equity
  Share Capital $
  Retained Earnings
  Total Equity
Total Liabilities and Equity $

EXERCISE 1–10 (LO4) Net Loss

Accounts Receivable	$1,600	Rent Payable	$2,500
Cash	6,000	Retained Earnings	4,000
Equipment Rental Expense	9,400	Share Capital	6,400
Fees Earned	12,000	Truck	22,000
Fuel Expense	500	Wages Expense	3,400
Note Payable	18,000		

Required: Wallaby Inc. began operations on February 1, 2014. After its second month, Wallaby Inc.'s accounting system showed the information above. During the second month, no dividends were declared and no additional shares were issued. Complete the income statement, statement of changes in equity, and balance sheet using the templates provided below.

Wallaby Inc.
Income Statement
Month Ended March 31, 2015

Revenues
  Fees Earned $
Expenses
  Equipment Rental Expense $
  Wages Expense
  Fuel Expense
Net Loss $

Wallaby Inc.
Statement of Changes in Equity
Month Ended March 31, 2015

	Share Capital	Retained Earnings	Total Equity
Opening Balance	$ 6,400	$ 4,000	$ 10,400
Net Loss			
Ending Balance	$	$	$

Wallaby Inc.
Balance Sheet
March 31, 2015

Assets
  Cash $
  Accounts Receivable
  Truck

Liabilities
  Rent Payable $
  Note Payable
  Total Liabilities $

Equity
  Share Capital $
  Retained Earnings
  Total Equity

Total Assets $ Total Liabilities and Equity $

EXERCISE 1–11   (LO4)   Correcting Financial Statements

A junior bookkeeper of Adams Ltd. prepared the following incorrect financial statements at the end of its first month of operations.

Adams Ltd.
Income Statement
For the Month Ended January 31, 2015

Service Revenue		$3,335
Expenses		
Accounts Payable	$300	
Land	1,000	
Miscellaneous Expenses	335	1,635
Net Income		$1,700

Balance Sheet

Assets		Liabilities and Equity	
Cash	$1,000	Rent Expense	$300
Repairs Expense	500	Share Capital	3,000
Salaries Expense	1,000	Retained Earnings	1,700
Building	2,500		
	$5,000		$5,000

Required: Prepare a corrected income statement, statement of changes in equity, and balance sheet.

EXERCISE 1–12 (LO4,5) Equity – What Causes it to Change

	Assets	=	Liabilities	+	Equity
Balances at April 1, 2015	$100,000		$60,000		$40,000
					? Shares issued in April
					? April net income(loss)
					? Dividends paid in April
Balances at April 30, 2015	$180,000	=	$130,000	+	?

Required: Using the information provided above, calculate the net income or net loss realized during April under each of the following independent assumptions.

a. No shares were issued in April and no dividends were paid.

b. $50,000 of shares were issued in April and no dividends were paid.

c. No shares were issued in April and $4,000 of dividends were paid in April.

EXERCISE 1–13 (LO4,5) Equity – What Causes it to Change

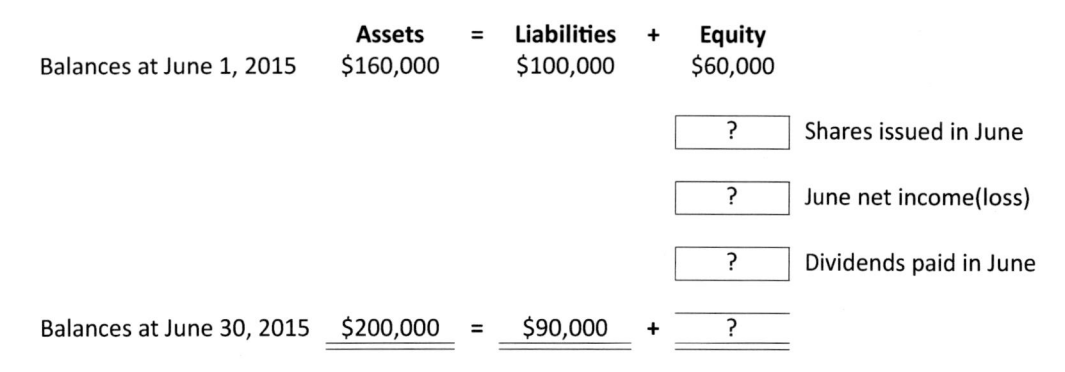

	Assets	=	Liabilities	+	Equity
Balances at June 1, 2015	$160,000		$100,000		$60,000

?	Shares issued in June
?	June net income(loss)
?	Dividends paid in June

Balances at June 30, 2015 $200,000 = $90,000 + ?

Required: Using the information provided above, calculate the dividends paid in June under each of the following independent assumptions.

a. In June no shares were issued and a $70,000 net income was earned.

b. $40,000 of shares were issued in June and a $90,000 net income was earned.

c. In June $130,000 of shares were issued and an $80,000 net loss was realized.

EXERCISE 1–14 (LO5) Impact of Transactions on the Accounting Equation

The following list shows the various ways in which the accounting equation might be affected by financial transactions.

	Assets	=	Liabilities	+	Equity
1.	(+)				(+)
2.	(+)		(+)		
3.	(+)(−)				
4.	(−)				(−)
5.	(−)		(−)		
6.			(+)		(−)
7.			(−)		(+)
8.			(+)(−)		
9.					(+)(−)

Required: Match one of the above to each of the following financial transactions. If the description below does not represent a financial transaction, indicate 'NT' for 'No Transaction'. The first one is done as an example.

a. _____3_____ Purchased a truck for cash.
b. _____ Issued share capital for cash.
c. _____ Incurred a bank loan as payment for equipment.
d. _____ Made a deposit for electricity service to be provided to the company in the future.
e. _____ Paid rent expense.
f. _____ Signed a new union contract that provides for increased wages in the future.
g. _____ Wrote a letter of complaint to the prime minister about a mail strike and hired a messenger service to deliver letters
h. _____ Received a collect telegram from the prime minister; paid the messenger.
i. _____ Billed customers for services performed.
j. _____ Made a cash payment to satisfy an outstanding obligation.
k. _____ Received a payment of cash in satisfaction of an amount owed by a customer.
l. _____ Collected cash from a customer for services rendered.
m. _____ Paid cash for truck operation expenses.
n. _____ Made a monthly payment on the bank loan; this payment included a payment on part of the loan and also an amount of interest expense. (*Hint*: This transaction affects more than two parts of the accounting equation.)
o. _____ Issued shares in the company to pay off a loan.

Problems

PROBLEM 1–1 (LO4,5) **Preparing Financial Statements**

Following are the asset, liability, and equity items of Dumont Inc. at January 31, 2015, after its first month of operations.

ASSETS		=	LIABILITIES		+	EQUITY	
Cash	$1,300		Bank Loan	$8,000		Share Capital	$2,000
Accounts Receivable	2,400		Accounts Payable	1,000		Service Revenue	7,500
Prepaid Expenses	550					Advertising Expense	500
Unused Supplies	750					Commissions Expense	720
Truck	9,000					Insurance Expense	50
						Interest Expense	80
						Rent Expense	400
						Supplies Expense	100
						Telephone Expense	150
						Wages Expense	2,500

Required:

1. Prepare an income statement and statement of changes in equity for Dumont's first month

ended January 31, 2015.

2. Prepare a balance sheet at January 31, 2015.

PROBLEM 1–2 (LO4) Preparing Financial Statements

Laberge Sheathing Inc. began operations on January 1, 2015. The office manager, inexperienced in accounting, prepared the following statement for the business's most recent month ended August 31, 2015.

Laberge Sheathing Inc.
Financial Statement
Month Ended August 31, 2015

Cash	$400	Accounts Payable	$7,800
Accounts Receivable	3,800	Share Capital	3,200
Unused Supplies	100	Service Revenue	2,000
Equipment	8,700	Retained Earnings	4,000
Advertising Expense	300		
Interest Expense	500		
Maintenance Expense	475		
Supplies Used	125		
Wages Expense	2,600		
	$17,000		$17,000

Required:

1. Prepare an income statement and statement of changes in equity for the month ended August 31, 2015, and a balance sheet at August 31, 2015. No shares were issued in August.

2. Using the information from the balance sheet completed in Part 1, calculate the percentage of assets financed by equity.

PROBLEM 1–3 (LO5) Transaction Analysis

The following transactions of Larson Services Inc. occurred during August 2015, its first month of operations.

Aug. 1 Issued share capital for $3,000 cash
1 Borrowed $10,000 cash from the bank
1 Paid $8,000 cash for a used truck
3 Signed a contract with a customer to do a $15,000 job beginning in November
4 Paid $600 for a one-year truck insurance policy effective August 1
5 Collected fees of $2,000 for work to be performed in September
7 Billed a client $5,000 for services performed today
9 Paid $250 for supplies purchased and used today
12 Purchased $500 of supplies on credit
15 Collected $1,000 of the amount billed August 7
16 Paid $200 for advertising in The News that ran the first two weeks of August
20 Paid $250 of the amount owing regarding the credit purchase of August 12
25 Paid the following expenses: rent for August, $350; salaries, $2,150; telephone, $50; truck operation, $250
28 Called clients for payment of the balances owing from August 7
31 Billed a client $6,000 for services performed today
31 $500 of the amount collected on August 5 has been earned as of today

Required:

1. Create a table like the one below by copying the headings shown.

ASSETS	=	LIABILITIES	+	EQUITY
Cash + Acct. Rec. + Ppd. Exp. + Unused Supplies + Truck	=	Bank Loan + Acct. Pay. + Unearned Revenue	+	Share Capital + Retained Earnings

2. Use additions and subtractions in the table created in Part 1 to show the effects of the August transactions. For non-transactions that do not impact the accounting equation items (such as August 3), indicate 'NE' for 'No Effect'.

3. Total each column and prove the accounting equation balances.

PROBLEM 1–4 **(LO4)** **Preparing Financial Statements**

Required: Refer to your answer for Problem 1–3. Prepare an income statement and a statement of changes in equity for the month ended August 31, 2015. Label the revenue earned as Fees Earned. Prepare a balance sheet at August 31, 2015.

Chapter 2

The Accounting Process

Chapter 2 looks more closely at asset, liability, and equity accounts and how they are affected by double-entry accounting, namely, debits and credits. The transactions introduced in Chapter 1 for Big Dog Carworks Corp. are used to explain debit and credit analysis. The preparation of a trial balance will be introduced. Additionally, this chapter will demonstrate how transactions are recorded in a general journal and posted to a general ledger. Finally, the concept of the accounting cycle is presented.

Chapter 2 Learning Objectives

LO1 – Describe asset, liability, and equity accounts, identifying the effect of debits and credits on each.

LO2 – Analyze transactions using double-entry accounting.

LO3 – Prepare a trial balance and explain its use.

LO4 – Record transactions in a general journal and post in a general ledger.

LO5 – Define the accounting cycle.

Concept Self-Check

Use the following as a self-check while working through Chapter 2.

1. What is an asset?
2. What is a liability?
3. What are the different types of equity accounts?
4. What is retained earnings?
5. How are retained earnings and revenues related?
6. Why are T-accounts used in accounting?
7. How do debits and credits impact the T-account?
8. What is a chart of accounts?

9. Are increases in equity recorded as a debit or credit?

10. Are decreases in equity recorded as a debit or credit?

11. Does issuing shares and revenues cause equity to increase or decrease?

12. Are increases in the share capital account recorded as a debit or credit?

13. Are increases in revenue accounts recorded as debits or credits?

14. Do dividends and expenses cause equity to increase or decrease?

15. Are increases in the dividend account recorded as a debit or credit?

16. Are increases in expense accounts recorded as debits or credits?

17. How is a trial balance useful?

18. What is the difference between a general journal and a general ledger?

19. Explain the posting process.

20. What is the accounting cycle?

NOTE: The purpose of these questions is to prepare you for the concepts introduced in the chapter. Your goal should be to answer each of these questions as you read through the chapter. If, when you complete the chapter, you are unable to answer one or more the Concept Self-Check questions, go back through the content to find the answer(s). Solutions are not provided to these questions.

2.1 Accounts

LO1 – Describe asset, liability, and equity accounts, identifying the effect of debits and credits on each.

Chapter 1 reviewed the analysis of financial transactions and the resulting impact on the accounting equation. We now expand that discussion by introducing the way transaction is recorded in an *account*. An **account** accumulates detailed information regarding the increases and decreases in a specific asset, liability, or equity item. Accounts are maintained in a **ledger** also referred to as the **books**. We now review and expand our understanding of asset, liability, and equity accounts.

Asset Accounts

Recall that assets are resources that have future economic benefits for the business. The primary purpose of assets is that they be used in day-to-day operating activities in order to generate revenue either directly or indirectly. A separate account is established for each asset. Examples of asset accounts are reviewed below.

- **Cash** has future purchasing power. Coins, currency, cheques, and bank account balances are examples of cash.

- **Accounts receivable** occur when products or services are sold on account or on credit. When a sale occurs on account or on credit, the customer has not paid cash but promises to pay in the future.

- **Notes receivable** are a promise to pay an amount on a specific future date plus a predetermined amount of interest.

- **Office supplies** are supplies to be used in the future. If the supplies are used before the end of the accounting period, they are an expense instead of an asset.

- **Merchandise inventory** are items to be sold in the future.

- **Prepaid insurance** represents an amount paid in advance for insurance. The prepaid insurance will be used in the future.

- **Prepaid rent** represents an amount paid in advance for rent. The prepaid rent will be used in the future.

- **Land** cost must be in a separate account from any building that might be on the land. Land is used over future periods.

- **Buildings** indirectly help a business generate revenue over future accounting periods since they provide space for day-to-day operating activities.

Liability Accounts

As explained in Chapter 1, a liability is an obligation to pay for an asset in the future. The primary purpose of liabilities is to finance investing activities that include the purchase of assets like land, buildings, and equipment. Liabilities are also used to finance operating activities involving, for example, accounts payable, unearned revenues, and wages payable. A separate account is created for each liability. Examples of liability accounts are reviewed below.

- **Accounts payable** are debts owed to creditors for goods purchased or services received as a result of day-to-day operating activities. An example of a service received on credit might be a plumber billing the business for a repair.

- **Wages payable** are wages owed to employees for work performed.

- **Short-term notes payable** are a debt owed to a bank or other creditor that is normally paid within one year. Notes payable are different than accounts payable in that notes involve interest.

- **Long-term notes payable** are a debt owed to a bank or other creditor that is normally paid beyond one year. Like short-term notes, long-term notes involve interest.

- **Unearned revenues** are payments received in advance of the product or service being provided. In other words, the business owes a customer the product/service.

Equity Accounts

Chapter 1 explained that equity represents the net assets owned by the owners of a business. In a corporation, the owners are called shareholders. Equity is traditionally one of the more challenging concepts to understand in introductory financial accounting. The difficulty stems from there being different types of equity accounts: share capital, retained earnings, dividends, revenues, and expenses. Share capital represents the investments made by owners into the business and causes equity to increase. Retained earnings is the sum of all net incomes earned over the life of the corporation to date, less any dividends distributed to shareholders over the same time period. Therefore, the Retained Earnings account includes revenues, which cause equity to increase, along with expenses and dividends, which cause equity to decrease. Figure 2.1 summarizes equity accounts.

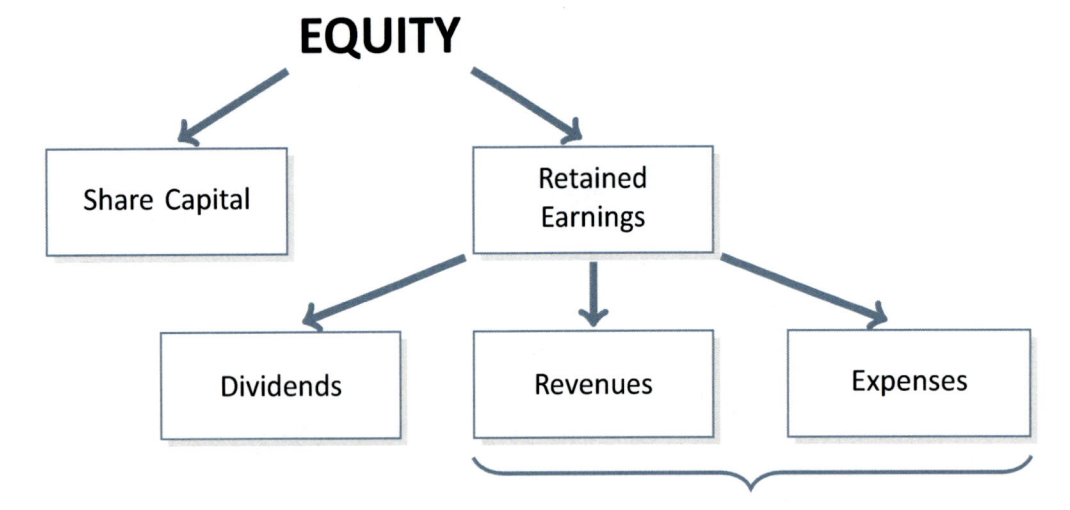

```
                        EQUITY
                       /      \
                      /        \
              Share Capital   Retained
                              Earnings
                             /    |    \
                            /     |     \
                       Dividends Revenues Expenses
```

Recall that revenues less expenses equals net income/net loss. Net income/net loss is not an account but is the result of subtracting expenses from revenues.

Figure 2.1: Composition of Equity Accounts

T-accounts

A simplified account, called a **T-account**, is often used as a teaching/learning tool to show increases and decreases in an account. It is called a T-account because it resembles the letter *T*. As shown in the T-account below, the left side records **debit** entries and the right side records **credit** entries.

Account Name
Debit	Credit
(always on left)	(always on right)

The *type* of account determines whether an increase or a decrease in a particular transaction is represented by a debit or credit. For financial transactions that affect *assets*, *dividends*, and *expenses*, increases are recorded by debits and decreases by credits. This guideline is shown in the following T-account.

Assets, Dividends, Expenses	
Debits are always increases ⬆	Credits are always decreases ⬇

For financial transactions that affect *liabilities, share capital*, and *revenues*, increases are recorded by credits and decreases by debits, as follows:

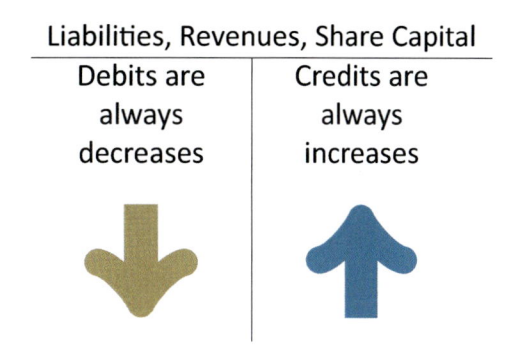

Liabilities, Revenues, Share Capital	
Debits are always decreases ⬇	Credits are always increases ⬆

Another way to illustrate the debit and credit rules is based on the accounting equation. Remember that dividends, expenses, revenues, and share capital are equity accounts.

	Assets	=	Liabilities	+	Equity
Increases are recorded as:	Debits		Credits		Credits[1]
Decreases are recorded as:	Credits		Debits		Debits[2]

---

[1] Revenues and the issuance of Share Capital are equity accounts. They cause equity to increase so increases in these account types are recorded as credits.

[2] Expenses, and Dividends are equity accounts. They cause equity to decrease. Decreases in equity are always recorded as debits so as expenses and dividends are realized, they are debited.

The following summary shows how debits and credits are used to record increases and decreases in various types of accounts.

ASSETS *(Normal Balance ✓)*	LIABILITIES *(Normal Balance X)*
DIVIDENDS	
EXPENSES	SHARE CAPITAL
Increases are DEBITED.	REVENUE increases are CREDITED.
Decreases are CREDITED.	Decreases are DEBITED.

This summary will be used in a later section to illustrate the recording of debits and credits regarding the transactions of Big Dog Carworks Corp. introduced in Chapter 1.

An exploration is available on the Lyryx site. Log into your Lyryx course to run Account Types.

The **account balance** is determined by adding and subtracting the increases and decreases in an account. Two assumed examples are presented below.

Cash			Accounts Payable	
10,000	3,000		700	5,000
3,000	3,000			
400	2,400			4,300 Balance
8,000	2,000			
	7,100			
	200			
Balance 3,700				

The $3,700 debit balance in the Cash account was calculated by adding all the debits and subtracting the sum of the credits. The $3,700 is recorded on the debit side of the T-account because the debits are greater than the credits. In Accounts Payable, the balance is a $4,300 credit calculated by subtracting the debits from the credits.

Notice that Cash shows a debit balance while Accounts Payable shows a credit balance. The Cash account is an asset so its *normal balance* is a debit. A **normal balance** is the side on which increases occur. Accounts Payable is a liability and because liabilities increase with credits, the normal balance in Accounts Payable is a credit as shown in the T-account above.

An exploration is available on the Lyryx site. Log into your Lyryx course to run Account Balances.

An exploration is available on the Lyryx site. Log into your Lyryx course to run Normal

Balance.

Chart of Accounts

A business will create a list of accounts called a **chart of accounts** where each account is assigned both a name and a number. A common practice is to have the accounts arranged in a manner that is compatible with the order of their use in financial statements. For instance, Asset accounts begin with the digit '1', Liability accounts with the digit '2'. Each business will have a unique chart of accounts that corresponds to its specific needs. Big Dog Carworks Corp. uses the following numbering system for its accounts:

100-199	Asset accounts
200-299	Liability accounts
300-399	Share capital, retained earnings, and dividend accounts
500-599	Revenue accounts
600-699	Expense accounts

An exploration is available on the Lyryx site. Log into your Lyryx course to run Account Numbers.

2.2 Transaction Analysis Using Accounts

LO2 – Analyze transactions using double-entry accounting.

In Chapter 1, transactions for Big Dog Carworks Corp. were analyzed to determine the change in each item of the accounting equation. In this next section, these same transactions will be used to demonstrate double-entry accounting. **Double-entry accounting** means each transaction is recorded in at least two accounts where the total debits ALWAYS equal the total credits. As a result of double-entry accounting, the sum of all the debit balance accounts in the ledger must equal the sum of all the credit balance accounts. The rule that debits = credits is rooted in the accounting equation:

	ASSETS	=	LIABILITIES	+	EQUITY[3]
Increases are:	Debits		Credits		Credits
Decreases are:	Credits		Debits		Debits

---

[3]The issuance of share capital and revenues cause equity to increase; as indicated above, increases in equity are recorded as credits. Dividends and expenses cause equity to decrease; decreases in equity are recorded as debits.

Illustrative Problem—Double-Entry Accounting and the Use of Accounts

In this section, the following debit and credit summary will be used to record the transactions of Big Dog Carworks Corp. into T-accounts.

ASSETS	LIABILITIES
DIVIDENDS	SHARE CAPITAL
EXPENSES	REVENUE
Increases are DEBITED.	Increases are CREDITED.
Decreases are CREDITED.	Decreases are DEBITED.

Transaction 1

Jan. 1 – Big Dog Carworks Corp. issued 1,000 shares to Bob Baldwin, a shareholder, for a total of $10,000 cash.

Analysis:

Debit: An asset account, Cash, is increased resulting in a debit. ─────→ Cash 10,000

Credit: Share Capital, an equity account, is increased resulting in a credit.* ─────→ Share Capital 10,000

*Note: An alternate analysis would be that the issuance of shares causes equity to increase and increases in equity are always recorded as a credit.

Transaction 2

Jan. 2 – Borrowed $3,000 from the bank.

Analysis:

Debit: An asset account, Cash, is increased resulting in a debit. ─────→ Cash 3,000

Credit: A liability account, Bank Loan, is increased resulting in a credit. ─────→ Bank Loan 3,000

Transaction 3

Jan. 3 – Equipment is purchased for $3,000 cash.

Analysis:

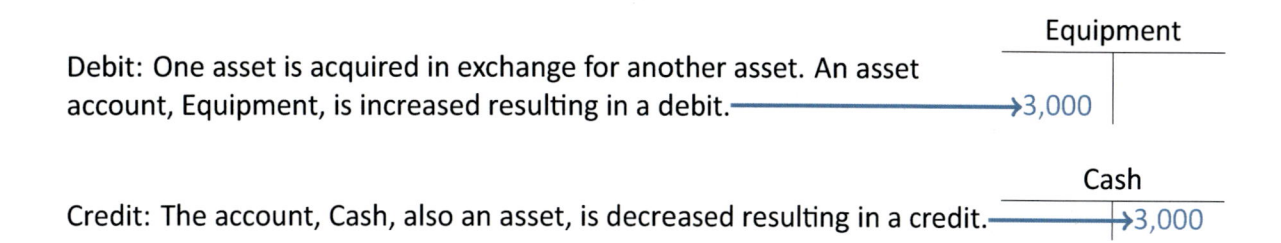

Debit: One asset is acquired in exchange for another asset. An asset account, Equipment, is increased resulting in a debit.———→

Equipment

→3,000

Credit: The account, Cash, also an asset, is decreased resulting in a credit.———→

Cash

→3,000

Transaction 4

Jan. 3 – A truck was purchased for $8,000; Big Dog paid $3,000 cash and incurred a $5,000 bank loan for the balance.

Analysis:

Debit: An asset account, Truck, is increased resulting in a debit.———→

Truck

→8,000

Credit: An asset account, Cash, is decreased resulting in a credit.———→

Cash

→3,000

Credit: A liability account, Bank Loan, is increased resulting in a credit.———→

Bank Loan

→5,000

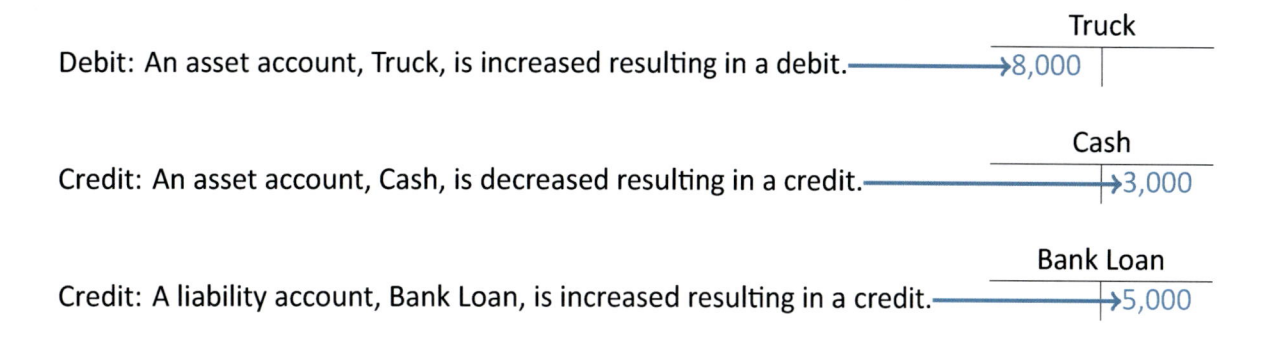

Note: Transaction 4 involves one debit and two credits. Notice that the total debit of $8,000 equals the total credits of $8,000 which satisfies the double-entry accounting rule requiring that debits ALWAYS equal credits.

Transaction 5

Jan. 5 – Big Dog Carworks Corp. paid $2,400 cash for a one-year insurance policy, effective January 1.

Analysis:

Debit: An asset account, Prepaid Insurance, is increased resulting in a debit. Because the insurance provides future benefit, it is recorded as an asset until it is used.———→

Prepaid Insurance

→2,400

Credit: Payment of the insurance results in a decrease in the asset account, Cash, resulting in a credit.———→

Cash

→2,400

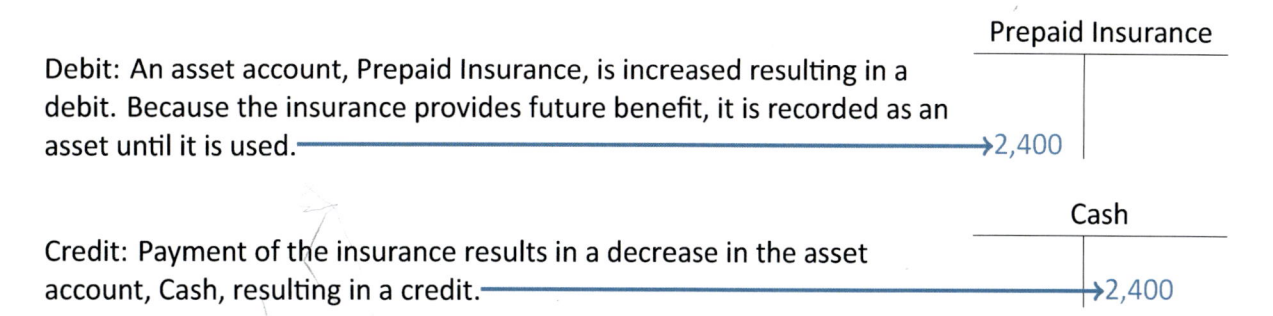

Transaction 6

Jan. 10 – The corporation paid $2,000 cash to reduce the bank loan.

Analysis:

Debit: This payment decreases the liability, Bank Loan, resulting in a debit. → Bank Loan 2,000

Credit: The payment also decreases the asset, Cash, resulting in a credit. → Cash 2,000

Transaction 7

Jan. 15 – The corporation received an advance payment of $400 for repair services to be performed as follows: $300 in February and $100 in March.

Analysis:

Debit: An asset, Cash, is increased at the time the cash is received resulting in a debit. → Cash 400

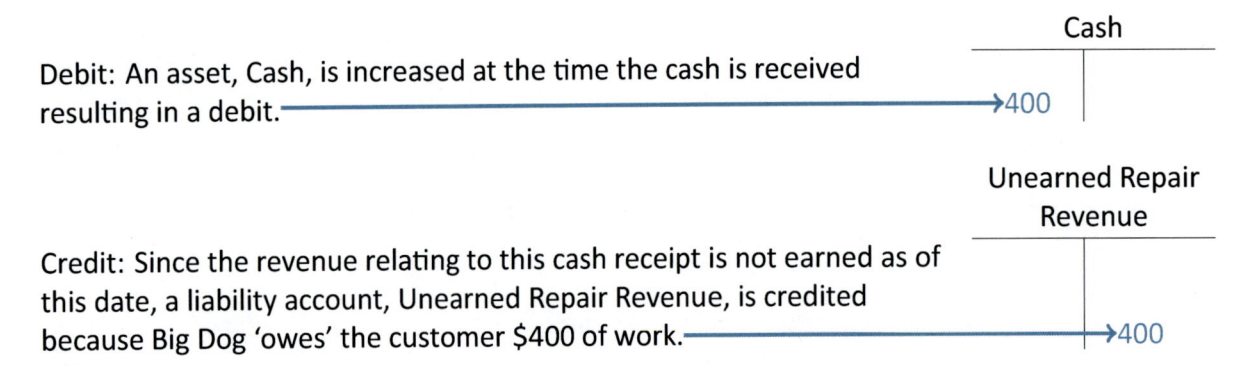

Credit: Since the revenue relating to this cash receipt is not earned as of this date, a liability account, Unearned Repair Revenue, is credited because Big Dog 'owes' the customer $400 of work. → Unearned Repair Revenue 400

Transaction 8

Jan. 31 – A total of $10,000 of automotive repair services is performed for a customer who paid $8,000 cash. The remaining $2,000 will be paid in 30 days.

Analysis:

Debit: An asset, Cash, is increased resulting in a debit. → Cash 8,000

Debit: An asset, Accounts Receivable, is increased resulting in a debit. → Accounts Receivable 2,000

Credit: An equity, Repair Revenue, is increased resulting in a credit. → Repair Revenue 10,000

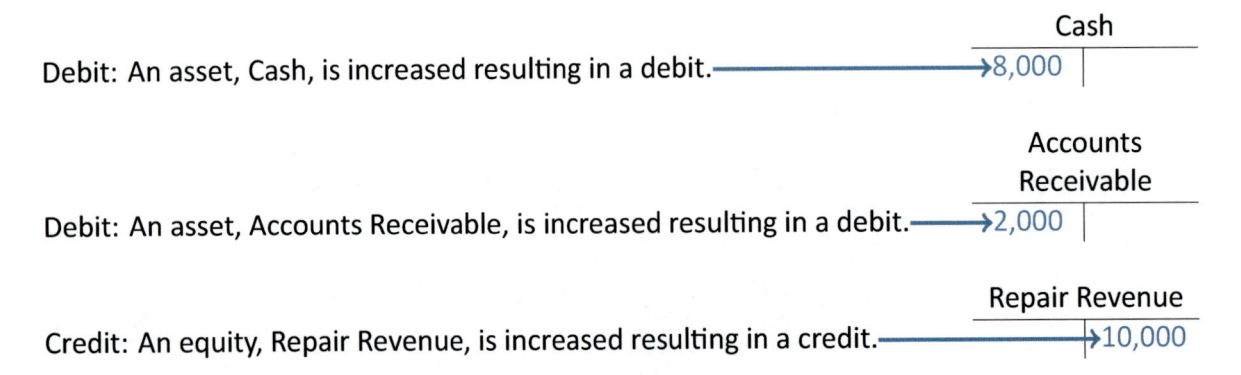

Transaction 9

Jan. 31 – Operating expenses of $7,100 were paid in cash: Rent expense, $1,600; salaries expense, $3,500; and supplies expense of $2,000. $700 for truck operating expenses (e.g., oil, gas) were incurred on credit.

Analysis:

Debit: This transaction increases four expense accounts resulting in a debit to each.

Rent Expense
1,600

Salaries Expense
3,500

Supplies Expense
2,000

Truck Operating Expense
700

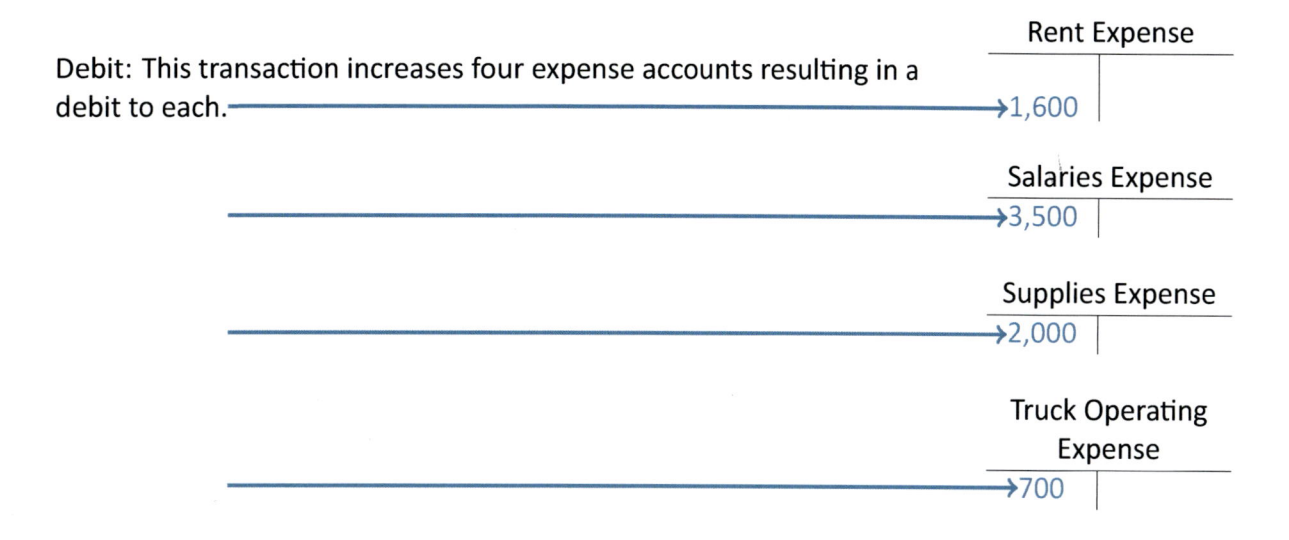

Note: Each expense is recorded in an individual account.

Credit: An asset, Cash, is decreased resulting in a credit.

Cash
7,100

Credit: A liability, Accounts Payable, is increased resulting in a credit.

Accounts Payable
700

Transaction 10

Jan. 31 – Dividends of $200 were paid in cash to the only shareholder, Bob Baldwin.

Analysis:

Debit: Dividends, an equity account, is increased resulting in a debit.

Dividends
200

Note: An alternate analysis would be that dividends cause equity to decrease and that decreases in equity are always recorded as a debit.

Credit: An asset, Cash is decreased resulting in a credit.

Cash
200

After the January transactions of Big Dog Carworks Corp. have been recorded in the T-accounts, each account is totalled and the difference between the debit balance and the credit balance is calculated, as shown in the following diagram. The numbers in parentheses refer to the transaction numbers used in the preceding section. To prove that the accounting equation is in balance, the account balances for each of assets, liabilities, and equity are added. Notice that total assets of $19,100 equal the sum of total liabilities of $7,100 plus equity of $12,000.

2.2. Transaction Analysis Using Accounts

ASSETS

Cash

(1) 10,000	(3) 3,000
(2) 3,000	(4) 3,000
(7) 400	(5) 2,400
(8) 8,000	(6) 2,000
	(9) 7,100
	(10) 200

Bal. 3,700

Accounts Receivable

(8) 2,000

Prepaid Insurance

(5) 2,400

Equipment

(3) 3,000

Truck

(4) 8,000

$19,100^1$

LIABILITIES

Bank Loan

(6) 2,000	(2) 3,000
	(4) 5,000
	Bal. 6,000

Accounts Payable

| | (9) 700 |

Unearned Repair Revenue

| | (7) 400 |

$7,100^2$

EQUITY

Share Capital

| | (1) 10,000 |

Dividends

(10) 200

Repair Revenue

| | (8) 10,000 |

Rent Expense

(9) 1,600

Salaries Expense

(9) 3,500

Supplies Expense

(9) 2,000

Truck Operation Expense

(9) 700

$12,000^3$

= +

1. 3,700 + 2,000 + 2,400 + 3,000 + 8,000 = 19,100
2. 6,000 + 700 + 400 = 7,100
3. 10,000 − 200 + 10,000 − 1,600 − 3,500 − 2,000 − 700 = 12,000

2.3 The Trial Balance

LO3 – Prepare a trial balance and explain its use.

To help prove that the accounting equation is in balance, a trial balance is normally prepared instead of the T-account listing shown in the previous section. A **trial balance** is an internal document that lists all the account balances at a point in time. The total debits must equal total credits on the trial balance. The form and content of a trial balance is illustrated below, using the account numbers, account names, and account balances of Big Dog Carworks Corp. at January 31, 2015. Assume that the account numbers are those assigned by the business.

Big Dog Carworks Corp.
Trial Balance
At January 31, 2015

Acct. No.	Account	Debit	Credit
101	Cash	$3,700	
110	Accounts receivable	2,000	
161	Prepaid insurance	2,400	
183	Equipment	3,000	
184	Truck	8,000	
201	Bank loan		$6,000
210	Accounts payable		700
247	Unearned revenue		400
320	Share capital		10,000
330	Dividends	200	
450	Repair revenue		10,000
654	Rent expense	1,600	
656	Salaries expense	3,500	
668	Supplies expense	2,000	
670	Truck operation expense	700	
		$27,100	$27,100

Double-entry accounting requires that debits equal credits. The trial balance establishes that this equality exists for Big Dog but it does not ensure that each item has been recorded in the proper account. Neither does the trial balance ensure that all items that should have been entered have been entered. In addition, a transaction may be recorded twice. Any or all of these errors could occur and the trial balance would still balance. Nevertheless, a trial balance provides a useful mathematical check before preparing financial statements.

An exploration is available on the Lyryx site. Log into your Lyryx course to run Trial Balance.

Preparation of Financial Statements

Financial statements for the one-month period ended January 31, 2015 can now be prepared from the trial balance figures. First, an income statement is prepared.

52 ■ The Accounting Process

Big Dog Carworks Corp.
Trial Balance
At January 31, 2015

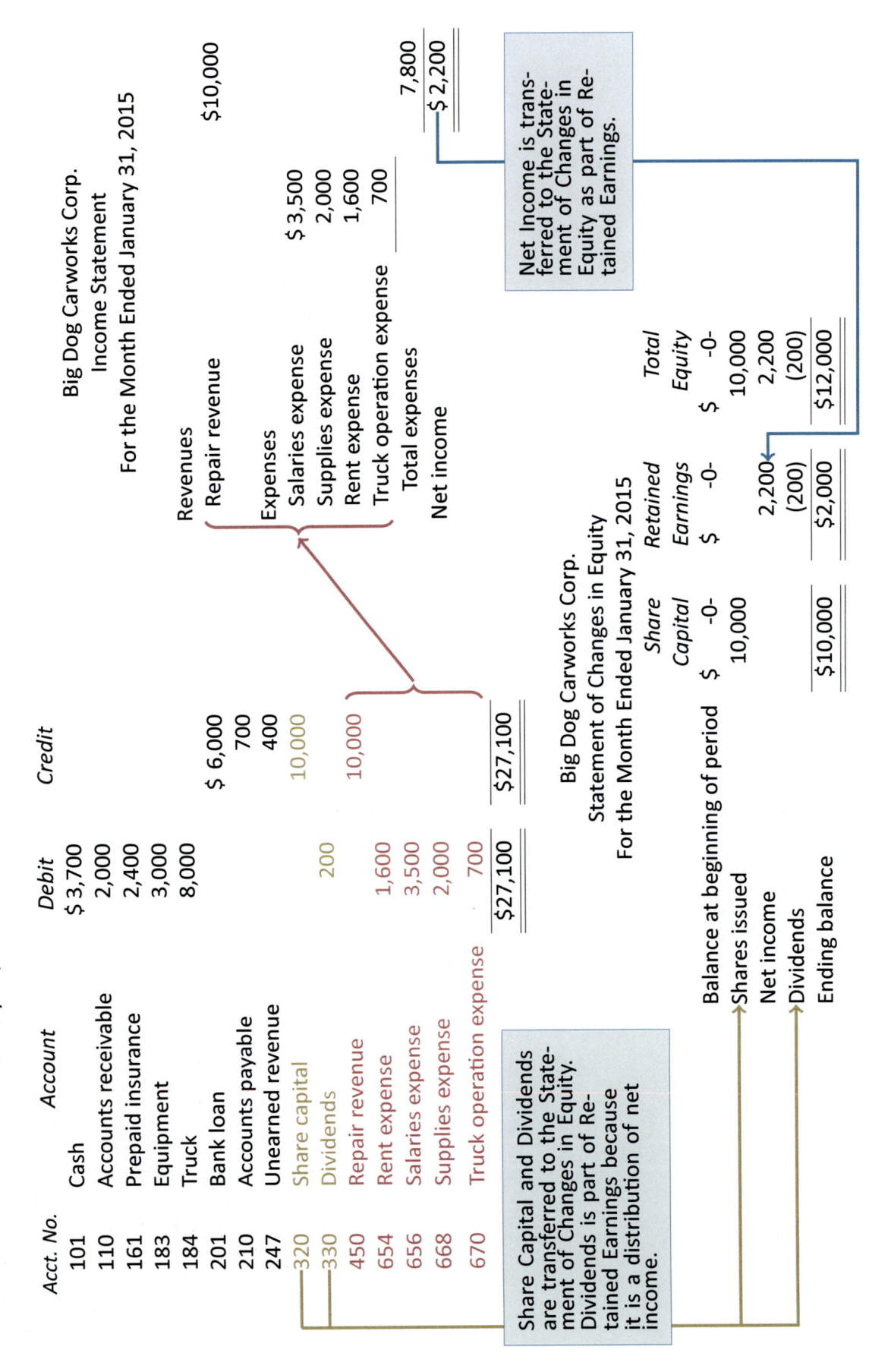

Acct. No.	Account	Debit	Credit
101	Cash	$ 3,700	
110	Accounts receivable	2,000	
161	Prepaid insurance	2,400	
183	Equipment	3,000	
184	Truck	8,000	
201	Bank loan		$ 6,000
210	Accounts payable		700
247	Unearned revenue		400
320	Share capital		10,000
330	Dividends	200	
450	Repair revenue		10,000
654	Rent expense	1,600	
656	Salaries expense	3,500	
668	Supplies expense	2,000	
670	Truck operation expense	700	
		$27,100	$27,100

Share Capital and Dividends are transferred to the Statement of Changes in Equity. Dividends is part of Retained Earnings because it is a distribution of net income.

Big Dog Carworks Corp.
Income Statement
For the Month Ended January 31, 2015

Revenues
Repair revenue $10,000

Expenses
Salaries expense .... $ 3,500
Supplies expense 2,000
Rent expense 1,600
Truck operation expense 700
Total expenses 7,800
Net income .... $ 2,200

Net Income is transferred to the Statement of Changes in Equity as part of Retained Earnings.

Big Dog Carworks Corp.
Statement of Changes in Equity
For the Month Ended January 31, 2015

	Share Capital	Retained Earnings	Total Equity
Balance at beginning of period	$ -0-	$ -0-	$ -0-
Shares issued	10,000		10,000
Net income		2,200	2,200
Dividends		(200)	(200)
Ending balance	$10,000	$2,000	$12,000

2.3. The Trial Balance 53

The asset and liability accounts from the trial balance and the ending balances for share capital and retained earnings on the statement of changes in equity are used to prepare the balance sheet.

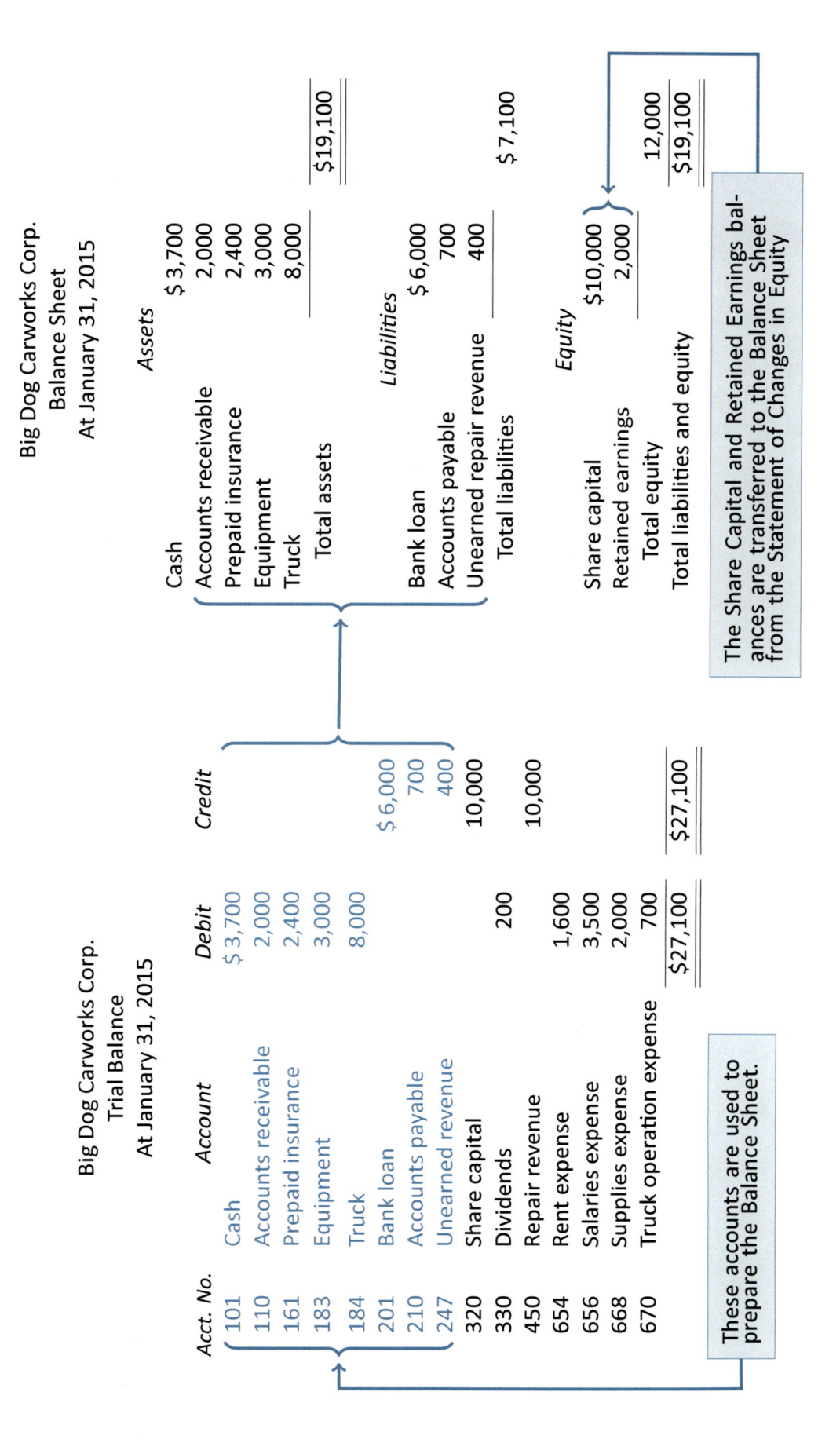

Big Dog Carworks Corp.
Trial Balance
At January 31, 2015

Acct. No.	Account	Debit	Credit
101	Cash	$ 3,700	
110	Accounts receivable	2,000	
161	Prepaid insurance	2,400	
183	Equipment	3,000	
184	Truck	8,000	
201	Bank loan		$ 6,000
210	Accounts payable		700
247	Unearned revenue		400
320	Share capital		10,000
330	Dividends	200	
450	Repair revenue		10,000
654	Rent expense	1,600	
656	Salaries expense	3,500	
668	Supplies expense	2,000	
670	Truck operation expense	700	
		$27,100	$27,100

These accounts are used to prepare the Balance Sheet.

Big Dog Carworks Corp.
Balance Sheet
At January 31, 2015

Assets

Cash	$ 3,700
Accounts receivable	2,000
Prepaid insurance	2,400
Equipment	3,000
Truck	8,000
Total assets	$19,100

Liabilities

Bank loan	$ 6,000
Accounts payable	700
Unearned repair revenue	400
Total liabilities	$ 7,100

Equity

Share capital	$10,000
Retained earnings	2,000
Total equity	12,000
Total liabilities and equity	$19,100

The Share Capital and Retained Earnings balances are transferred to the Balance Sheet from the Statement of Changes in Equity

NOTE: Pay attention to the links between financial statements.

The income statement is linked to the statement of changes in equity: Revenues and expenses are reported on the income statement to show the details of net income. Because net income causes equity to change, it is then reported on the statement of changes in equity.

The statement of changes in equity is linked to the balance sheet: The statement of changes in equity shows the details of how equity changed during the accounting period. The balances for share capital and retained earnings that appear on the statement of changes in equity are transferred to the equity section of the balance sheet.

The balance sheet SUMMARIZES equity by showing only account balances for share capital and retained earnings. To obtain the details regarding these equity accounts, we must look at the income statement and the statement of changes in equity.

2.4 Using Formal Accounting Records

LO4 – Record transactions in a general journal and post in a general ledger.

The preceding analysis of financial transactions used T-accounts to record debits and credits. T-accounts will continue to be used for illustrative purposes throughout this book. In actual practice, financial transactions are recorded in a general journal.

A **general journal**, or just **journal**, is a document that is used to chronologically record a business's debit and credit transactions (see Figure 2.2). It is often referred to as the *book of original entry*. **Journalizing** is the process of recording a financial transaction in the journal. The resulting debit and credit entry recorded in the journal is called a **journal entry**.

A **general ledger**, or just **ledger**, is a record that contains all of a business's accounts. **Posting** is the process of transferring amounts from the journal to the matching ledger accounts. Because amounts recorded in the journal eventually end up in a ledger account, the ledger is sometimes referred to as a *book of final entry*.

Recording Transactions in the General Journal

Each transaction is first recorded in the journal. The January transactions of Big Dog Carworks Corp. are recorded in its journal as shown in Figure 2.2. The journalizing procedure follows these steps (refer to Figure 2.2 for corresponding numbers):

1. The year is recorded at the top and the month is entered on the first line of page 1. This information is repeated only on each new journal page used to record transactions.

2. The date of the first transaction is entered in the second column, on the first line. The day of each transaction is always recorded in this second column.

3. The name of the account to be debited is entered in the description column on the first line. By convention, accounts to be debited are usually recorded before accounts to be credited. The column titled 'F' (for Folio) indicates the number given to the account in the General Ledger. For example, the account number for Cash is 101. The amount of the debit is recorded in the debit column. A dash is often used by accountants in place of .00.

4. The name of the account to be credited is on the second line of the description column and is indented about one centimetre into the column. Accounts to be credited are always indented in this way in the journal. The amount of the credit is recorded in the credit column. Again, a dash may be used in place of .00.

5. An explanation of the transaction is entered in the description column on the next line. It is not indented.

6. A line is usually skipped after each journal entry to separate individual journal entries and the date of the next entry recorded. It is unnecessary to repeat the month if it is unchanged from that recorded at the top of the page.

2.4. Using Formal Accounting Records ■ 57

GENERAL JOURNAL Page 1

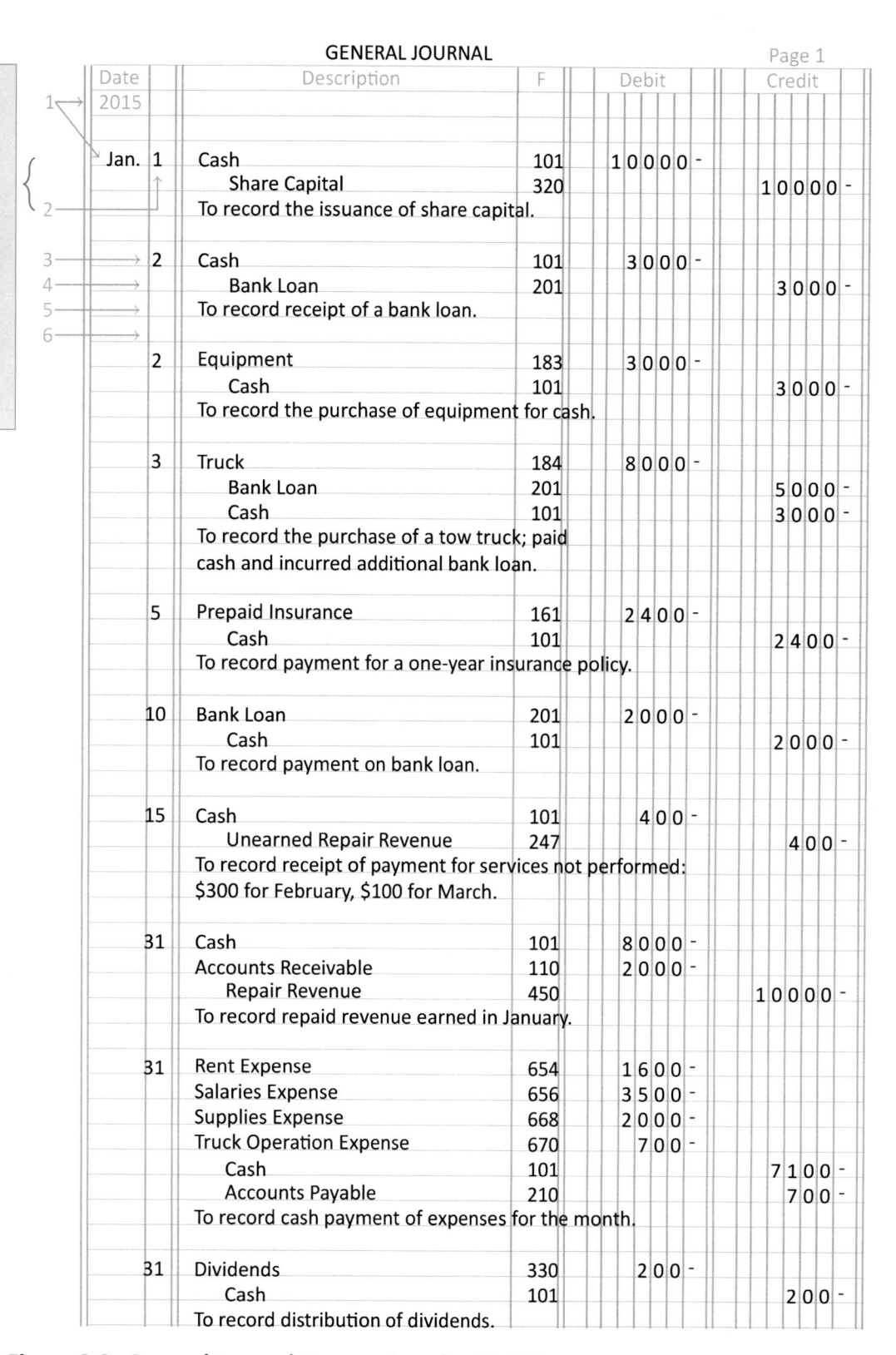

Date 2015		Description	F	Debit	Credit
Jan.	1	Cash	101	10000 -	
		Share Capital	320		10000 -
		To record the issuance of share capital.			
	2	Cash	101	3000 -	
		Bank Loan	201		3000 -
		To record receipt of a bank loan.			
	2	Equipment	183	3000 -	
		Cash	101		3000 -
		To record the purchase of equipment for cash.			
	3	Truck	184	8000 -	
		Bank Loan	201		5000 -
		Cash	101		3000 -
		To record the purchase of a tow truck; paid cash and incurred additional bank loan.			
	5	Prepaid Insurance	161	2400 -	
		Cash	101		2400 -
		To record payment for a one-year insurance policy.			
	10	Bank Loan	201	2000 -	
		Cash	101		2000 -
		To record payment on bank loan.			
	15	Cash	101	400 -	
		Unearned Repair Revenue	247		400 -
		To record receipt of payment for services not performed: $300 for February, $100 for March.			
	31	Cash	101	8000 -	
		Accounts Receivable	110	2000 -	
		Repair Revenue	450		10000 -
		To record repaid revenue earned in January.			
	31	Rent Expense	654	1600 -	
		Salaries Expense	656	3500 -	
		Supplies Expense	668	2000 -	
		Truck Operation Expense	670	700 -	
		Cash	101		7100 -
		Accounts Payable	210		700 -
		To record cash payment of expenses for the month.			
	31	Dividends	330	200 -	
		Cash	101		200 -
		To record distribution of dividends.			

> This entry tells us to:
>
> - Post $10,000 to the debit side of the Cash account (increasing Cash by $10,000), and
>
> - Post $10,000 to the credit side of the Share Capital account (increasing this account by $10,000).

Figure 2.2: General Journal Transactions for BDCC in January

Most of Big Dog's entries have one debit and credit. An entry can also have more than one debit

58 ■ The Accounting Process

or credit, in which case it is referred to as a **compound entry**. The entry dated January 3 is an example of a compound entry.

Posting Transactions to the General Ledger

The **ledger account** is a formal variation of the T-account. The ledger accounts shown in Figure 2.3 are similar to what is used in electronic/digital accounting programs. Ledger accounts are kept in the general ledger. Debits and credits recorded in the journal are posted to appropriate ledger accounts so that the details and balance for each account can be found easily. Figure 2.3 uses the first transaction of Big Dog Carworks Corp. to illustrate how to post amounts and record other information.

The journal records each financial transaction in double-entry form. Each side of the entry is transferred to a separate ledger account.

The ledger stores transactions according to account and keeps a running total of each account balance.

GENERAL JOURNAL — Page 1

Date 2015	Description	F	Debit	Credit
Jan. 1	Cash	**3** 101	10000 -	
	Share Capital	320		10000 -
	To record the issuance of share capital.			

GENERAL LEDGER

Cash — Acct. No. 101

Date 2015	Description	F	Debit	Credit	DR/CR	Balance
Jan. 1 **1**		**2** GJ1	10000 -		DR	10000 - **4**

Share Capital — Acct. No. 320

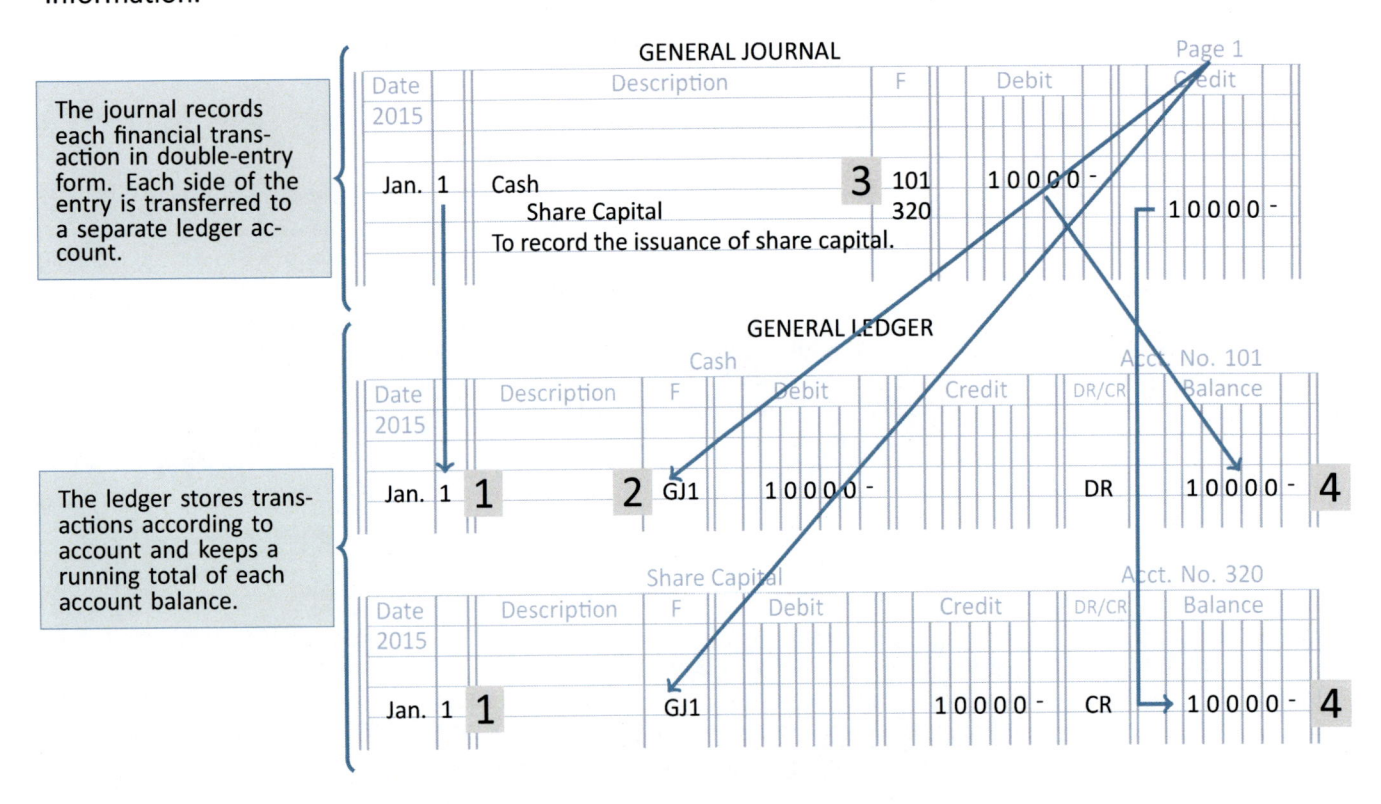

Date 2015	Description	F	Debit	Credit	DR/CR	Balance
Jan. 1 **1**		GJ1		10000 -	CR	10000 - **4**

Figure 2.3: Illustration of a Transaction Posted to Two Accounts in the General Ledger

1. The date and amount are posted to the appropriate ledger account. Here the entry debiting Cash is posted from the journal to the Cash ledger account. The entry crediting Share Capital is then posted from the journal to the Share Capital ledger account.

2. The journal page number is recorded in the folio (F) column of each ledger account as a cross reference. In this case, the posting has been made from general journal page 1; the reference is recorded as GJ1.

3. The appropriate ledger account number is recorded in the folio (F) column of the journal to indicate the posting has been made to that particular account. Here the entry debiting Cash

has been posted to Account No. 101. The entry crediting Share Capital has been posted to Account No. 320.

4. After posting the entry, a balance is calculated in the Balance column. A notation is recorded in the column to the left of the Balance column indicating whether the balance is a debit or credit. A brief description can be entered in the Description column but this is generally not necessary since the journal includes a detailed description for each journal entry.

This manual process of recording, posting, summarizing, and preparing financial statements is cumbersome and time-consuming. In virtually all businesses, the use of accounting software automates much of the process. In this and subsequent chapters, either the T-account or the ledger account can be used in working through exercises and problems. Both formats are used to explain and illustrate concepts in subsequent chapters.

An exploration is available on the Lyryx site. Log into your Lyryx course to run Journalizing Transactions.

2.5 The Accounting Cycle

LO5 – Define the accounting cycle.

In the preceding sections, the January transactions of Big Dog Carworks Corp. were used to demonstrate the steps performed to convert economic data into financial information. This conversion was carried out in accordance with the basic double-entry accounting model. These steps are summarized in Figure 2.4.

Step 1: Transactions are analyzed and journalized.
Journalizing consists of analyzing transactions as they occur to see how they affect the accounting equation. Then, the transactions are recorded chronologically in the general journal.

Step 2: Transactions are summarized by account.
Posting consists of transferring debits and credits from the general journal to the appropriate general ledger accounts.

Step 3: The equality of debits and credits is proved.
A trial balance is prepared, listing account numbers and names along with account balances to prove the equality of the debits and credits.

Step 4: The summarized transactions are communicated.
Preparing the financial statements consists of using the balances listed in the columns of the trial balance to prepare the income statement, statement of changes in equity, and balance sheet.

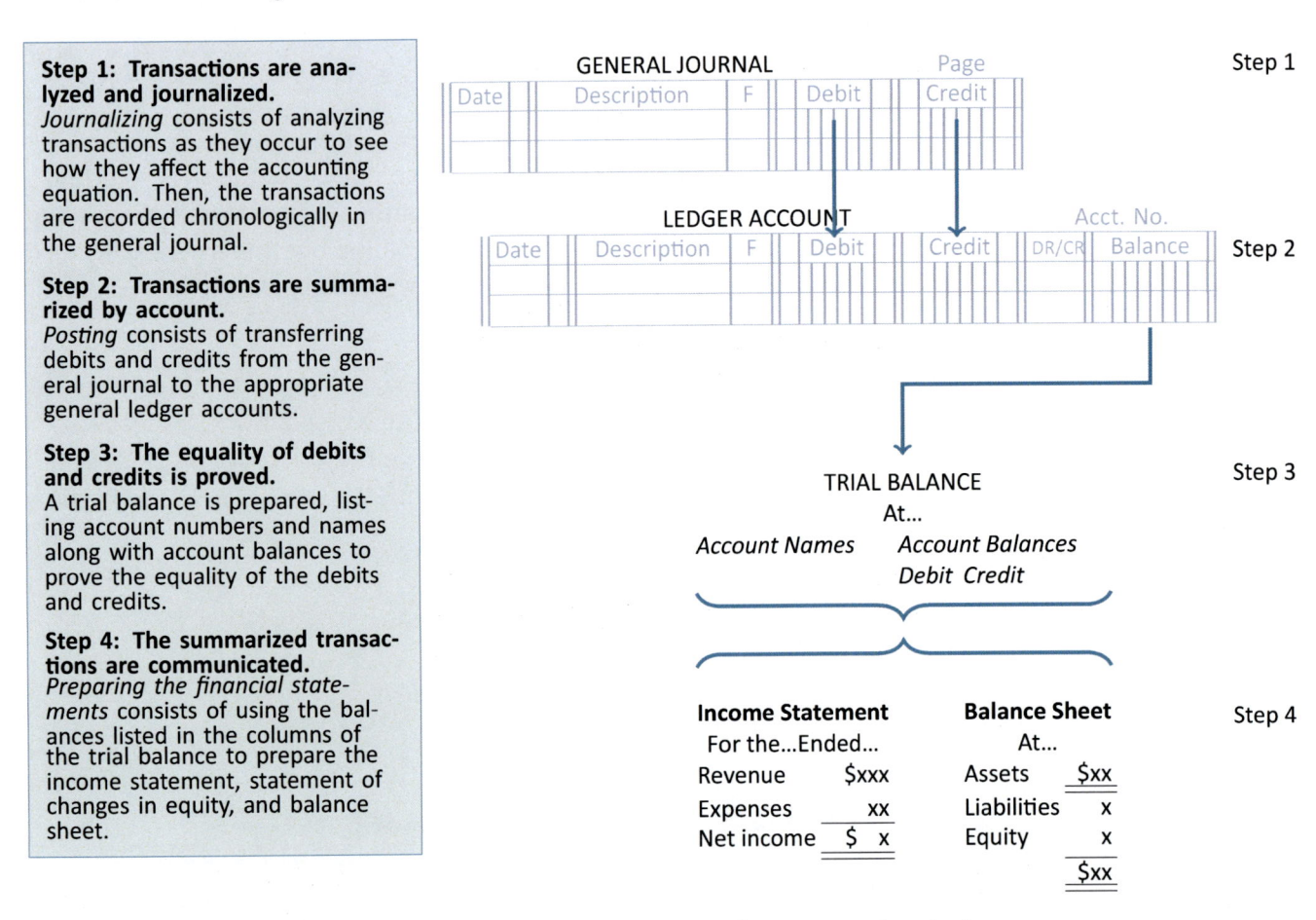

Figure 2.4: Illustrating the Steps in the Accounting Cycle

The sequence just described, beginning with the journalising of the transactions and ending with the communication of financial information in financial statements, is commonly referred to as the **accounting cycle**. There are additional steps involved in the accounting cycle and these will be introduced in Chapter 3.

Summary of Chapter 2 Learning Objectives

LO1 – Describe asset, liability, and equity accounts, identifying the effect of debits and credits on each.

Assets are resources that have future economic benefits such as cash, receivables, prepaids, and machinery. Increases in assets are recorded as debits and decreases as credits. Liabilities represent an obligation to pay an asset in the future and include payables and unearned revenues. Inceases in liabilities are recorded as credits and decreases as debits. Equity represents the net assets owned by the owners and includes share capital, dividends, revenues, and expenses. Increases in equity, caused by the issuance of shares and revenues, are recorded as credits, and decreases in equity, caused by dividends and expenses, are recorded as debits. The following summary can be used to show how debits and credits impact the types of accounts.

LO2 – Analyze transactions using double-entry accounting.

Double-entry accounting requires that each transaction be recorded in at least two accounts where the total debits always equal the total credits. The double-entry accounting rule is rooted in the accounting equation: Assets = Liabilities + Equity.

LO3 – Prepare a trial balance and explain its use.

To help prove the accounting equation is in balance, a trial balance is prepared. The trial balance is an internal document that lists all the account balances at a point in time. The total debits must equal total credits on the trial balance. The trial balance is used in the preparation of financial statements.

LO4 – Record transactions in a general journal and post in a general ledger.

The recording of financial transactions was introduced in this chapter using T-accounts, an illustrative tool. A business actually records transactions in a general journal, a document which chronologically lists each debit and credit journal entry. To summarize the debit and credit entries by account, the entries in the general journal are posted (or transferred) to the general ledger. The account balances in the general ledger are used to prepare the trial balance.

LO5 – Define the accounting cycle.

Analyzing transactions, journalizing them in the general journal, posting from the general journal into the general ledger, preparing the trial balance, and generating financial statements are steps followed each accounting period. These steps form the core of the accounting cycle. Additional steps involved in the accounting cycle will be introduced in Chapter 3.

Discussion Questions

1. Why is the use of a transactions worksheet impractical in actual practice?

2. What is an 'account'? How are debits and credits used to record transactions?

3. Some tend to associate "good" and "bad" or "increase" and "decrease" with credits and debits. Is this a valid association? Explain.

4. The pattern of recording increases as debits and decreases as credits is common to asset and expense accounts. Provide an example.

5. The pattern of recording increases and credits and decreases as debits is common to liabilities, equity, and revenue accounts. Provide an example.

6. Summarise the rules for using debits and credits to record assets, expenses, liabilities, equity, and revenues.

7. What is a Trial Balance? Why is it prepared?

8. How is a Trial Balance used to prepare financial statements?

9. A General Journal is often called a book of original entry. Why?

10. The positioning of a debit-credit entry in the General Journal is similar in some respects to instructions written in a computer program. Explain, using an example.

11. What is a General Ledger? Why is it prepared?

12. What is a Chart of Accounts? How are the accounts generally arranged and why?

13. List the steps in the accounting cycle.

Exercises

EXERCISE 2–1   (LO2)

Required: Record the debit and credit for each of the following transactions (transaction 1 is done for you):

	Assets		Liabilities		Equity	
	Debit (increase)	Credit (decrease)	Debit (decrease)	Credit (increase)	Debit (decrease)	Credit (increase)
1. Purchased a $10,000 truck on credit.	10,000			10,000		
2. Borrowed $5,000 cash from the bank.						
3. Paid $2,000 of the bank loan in cash.						
4. Paid $600 in advance for a one-year insurance policy.						
5. Received $500 in advance from a renter for next month's rental of office space.						

EXERCISE 2–2   (LO2)

Required: Record the debit and credit in the appropriate account for each of the following transactions (transaction 1 is done for you):

	Debit	Credit
1. Issued share capital for cash.	Cash	Share Capital
2. Purchased equipment on credit.		
3. Paid for a one-year insurance policy.		
4. Billed a customer for repairs completed today.		
5. Paid this month's rent.		
6. Collected the amount billed in transaction 4 above.		
7. Collected cash for repairs completed today.		
8. Paid for the equipment purchased in transaction 2 above.		
9. Signed a union contract.		
10. Collected cash for repairs to be made for customers next month.		
11. Transferred this month's portion of prepaid insurance that was used to Insurance Expense.		

EXERCISE 2–3 (LO2)

Required: Post the following transactions to the appropriate accounts:

(1) Issued share capital for $5,000 cash (posted as an example).

(2) Paid $900 in advance for three months' rent, $300 for each month.

(3) Billed $1,500 to customers for repairs completed today.

(4) Purchased on credit $2,000 of supplies to be used next month.

(5) Borrowed $7,500 from the bank.

(6) Collected $500 for the amount billed in transaction (3).

(7) Received a $200 bill for electricity used to date (the bill will be paid next month).

(8) Repaid $2,500 of the bank loan.

(9) Used $800 of the supplies purchased in transaction (4).

(10) Paid $2,000 for the supplies purchased in transaction (4).

(11) Recorded the use of one month of the rent paid for in transaction (2).

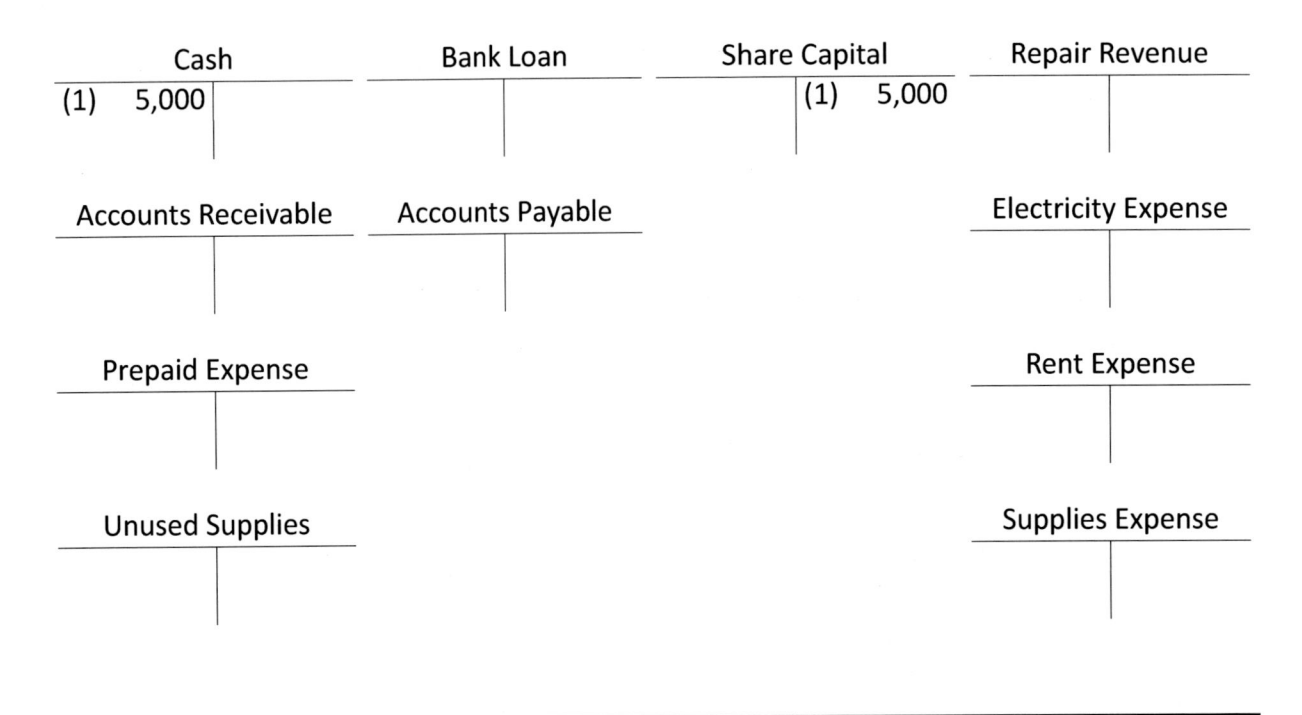

| Cash | Bank Loan | Share Capital | Repair Revenue |
| (1) 5,000 | | (1) 5,000 | |

| Accounts Receivable | Accounts Payable | | Electricity Expense |

| Prepaid Expense | | | Rent Expense |

| Unused Supplies | | | Supplies Expense |

EXERCISE 2–4   (LO3)

The following Trial Balance was prepared from the books of Cross Corporation at its year-end, December 31, 2015. After the company's bookkeeper left, the office staff was unable to balance the accounts or place them in their proper order. Individual account balances are correct, but debits may be incorrectly recorded as credits and vice-versa.

Account Title	Debits	Credits
Cash	$120,400	
Commissions Earned	5,000	
Share Capital		$170,000
Accounts Payable	30,000	
Insurance Expense	100	
Land		8,000
Building		120,000
Rent Expense		1,000
Accounts Receivable		26,000
Unused Supplies	6,000	
Supplies Expense		300
Loan Payable		80,000
Salaries Expense		3,000
Telephone Expense	200	
Totals	$161,700	$408,300

Required: Prepare a corrected Trial Balance showing the accounts in proper order and balances in the correct column. List expenses in alphabetical order. Total the columns and ensure total debits equal total credits.

EXERCISE 2–5   (LO4)

Required: Prepare journal entries for each of the following transactions:

(a) Issued share capital for $3,000 cash.

(b) Purchased $2,000 of equipment on credit.

(c) Paid $400 cash for this month's rent.

(d) Purchased on credit $4,000 of supplies to be used next month.

(e) Billed $2,500 to customers for repairs made to date.

(f) Paid cash for one-half of the amount owing in transaction (d).

(g) Collected $500 of the amount billed in transaction (e).

(h) Sold one-half of the equipment purchased in transaction 2 above for $1,000 in cash.

EXERCISE 2–6   (LO2,4)

Required: Prepare the journal entries and likely descriptions of the eleven transactions that were posted to the following General Ledger accounts for the month ended January 31, 2015. Do not include amounts. For instance, the first entry would be:

Date	Account/Explanation	PR	Debit	Credit
	Cash...............................		XX	
	Share Capital.......................			XX
	(1) To record issuance of share capital			

General Journal

Cash
1	2
3	5
8	10
11	

Bank Loan
	11

Share Capital
	1

Repair Revenue
	3
	4

Accounts Receivable
4	

Accounts Payable
10	2
	6
	7

Electricity Expense
9	

Prepaid Expense
5	9

Rent Expense
7	

Unused Supplies
2	8

Supplies Expense
6	

EXERCISE 2–7 (LO2,3,4)

The following journal entries were prepared for Elgert Corporation for its first month of operation, January 2015.

	General Journal			
Date	Account/Explanation	PR	Debit	Credit
Jan. 1	Cash		10,000	
	Share Capital			10,000
	To record the issuance of shares.			
5	Rent Expense		200	
	Cash			200
	To record the payment of rent for the month.			
9	Unused Supplies		4,000	
	Cash			4,000
	To record the purchase of supplies.			
11	Cash		1,300	
	Service Revenue			1,300
	To record service revenue earned.			
28	Truck Operation Expense		450	
	Accounts Payable			450
	To record truck repairs.			
30	Salaries Expense		1,800	
	Cash			1,800
	To record payment of salaries for the month.			
31	Accounts Receivable		1,600	
	Service Revenue			1,600
	To record service revenue earned during the month.			
31.	Supplies Expense		200	
	Unused Supplies			200
	To record supplies used during the month.			

Required:

a. Prepare necessary General Ledger T-accounts and post the transactions.

b. Prepare a Trial Balance at January 31, 2015.

c. Prepare an Income Statement and Statement of Changes in Equity for the month ended January 31, 2015 and a Balance Sheet at January 31, 2015.

Problems

PROBLEM 2–1   (LO3)

The following account balances are taken from the records of Fox Creek Service Limited at October 31, 2015 after its first year of operation:

Accounts Payable	$9,000	Insurance Expense	$ 500
Accounts Receivable	6,000	Repair Revenue	19,000
Advertising Expense	2,200	Supplies Expense	800
Bank Loan	5,000	Telephone Expense	250
Cash	1,000	Truck	9,000
Share Capital	2,000	Truck Operation	
Commissions Expense	4,500	Expense	1,250
Equipment	7,000	Wages Expense	4,000
		Wages Payable	1,500

Required:

1. Prepare a Trial Balance at October 31, 2015.

2. Prepare an Income Statement and Statement of Changes in Equity for the year ended October 31, 2015.

3. Prepare a Balance Sheet at October 31, 2015.

PROBLEM 2–2   (LO1,2,3,4)

The following ledger accounts were prepared for Davidson Tool Rentals Corporation during the first month of operation ending May 31, 2015. No journal entries were prepared in support of the amounts recorded in the ledger accounts.

Cash			101		Accounts Payable			210		Share Capital			320		Service Revenue			470
May 1	5,000	May 11	1,000		May 22	600	May 11	1,000				May 1	5,000				May 5	3,000
6	2,000	16	500				23	150									6	2,000
10	1,500	20	300				24	1,100									18	2,500
15	1,200	22	600															
21	800	28	400															
		29	3,500															

Accounts Receivable			110												Advertising Expense			610
May 5	3,000	May 10	1,500												May 31	250		
18	2,500	15	1,200															

Prepaid Advertising			160												Commissions Expense			615
May 16	500	May 31	250												May 24	1,100		

Unused Supplies			173												Rent Expense			654
May 20	300	May 30	100												May 28	400		

Equipment			183												Salaries Expense			656
May 11	2,000	May 21	800												May 29	3,500		

															Supplies Expense			668
															May 30	100		

															Telephone Expense			669
															May 23	150		

Required:

1. Reconstruct the transactions that occurred during the month and prepare journal entries to record these transactions, including appropriate descriptions. Include accounts numbers (Folio) using the Chart of Accounts provided. Calculate the balance in each account.

2. Total the transactions in each T-account above. Prepare a Trial Balance in proper order (list assets, liabilities, equity, revenue, then expenses) at May 31, 2015.

PROBLEM 2–3 (LO1,2,4)

The following balances appeared in the General Ledger of Fenton Table Rentals Corporation at April 1, 2015.

Cash	$1,400	Accounts Payable	$2,000
Accounts Receivable	3,600	Share Capital	4,350
Prepaid Rent	1,000		
Unused Supplies	350		

The following transactions occurred during April:

(a) Collected $2,000 cash owed by a customer.

(b) Billed $3,000 to customers for tables rented to date.

(c) Paid the following expenses: advertising, $300; salaries, $2,000; telephone, $100.

(d) Paid half of the accounts payable owing at April 1.

(e) Received a $500 bill for April truck repair expenses.

(f) Collected $2,500 owed by a customer.

(g) Billed $1,500 to customers for tables rented to date.

(h) Transferred $500 of prepaid rent to rent expense.

(i) Counted $200 of supplies on hand at April 30; recorded the amount used as an expense.

Required: Prepare journal entries to record the April transactions.

PROBLEM 2–4 (LO1,2,4)

The following transactions occurred in Thorn Accounting Services Inc. during August 2015, its first month of operation.

Aug. 1 Issued share capital for $3,000 cash.
1 Borrowed $10,000 cash from the bank.
1 Paid $8,000 cash for a used truck.
4 Paid $600 for a one-year truck insurance policy effective August 1.
5 Collected $2,000 fees in cash from a client for work performed today (recorded as Fees Earned).
7 Billed $5,000 fees to clients for services performed to date (recorded as Fees Earned).
9 Paid $250 for supplies used to date.
12 Purchased $500 of supplies on credit (recorded as Unused Supplies).
15 Collected $1,000 of the amount billed on August 7.
16 Paid $200 for advertising in The News during the first two weeks of August.
20 Paid half of the amount owing for the supplies purchased on August 12.
25 Paid cash for the following expenses: rent for August, $350; salaries, $2,150; telephone, $50; truck repairs, $250.
28 Called clients for payment of the balance owing from August 7.
29 Billed $6,000 of fees to clients for services performed to date (recorded as Fees Earned).
31 Transferred the amount of August's truck insurance ($50) to Insurance Expense.
31 Counted $100 of supplies still on hand (recorded the amount used as Supplies Expense).

Required: Prepare journal entries to record the August transactions.

Chapter 3

Financial Accounting and Adjusting Entries

Chapters 1 and 2 described the recording and reporting of economic transactions in detail. However, the account balances used to prepare the financial statements in these previous chapters did not necessarily reflect correct amounts. Chapter 3 introduces the concept of adjusting entries and how these satisfy the matching principle, ensuring revenues and expenses are reported in the correct accounting period. The preparation of an adjusted trial balance is discussed, as well as its use in completing financial statements. At the end of the accounting period, after financial statements have been prepared, it is necessary to close temporary accounts to retained earnings. This process is introduced in this chapter, as is the preparation of a post-closing trial balance. The accounting cycle, the steps performed each accounting period that result in financial statements, is also reviewed.

Chapter 3 Learning Objectives

LO1 – Explain how the timeliness, matching, and recognition GAAP require the recording of adjusting entries.

LO2 – Explain the use of and prepare the adjusting entries required for prepaid expenses, depreciation, unearned revenues, accrued revenues, and accrued expenses.

LO3 – Prepare an adjusted trial balance and explain its use.

LO4 – Use an adjusted trial balance to prepare financial statements.

LO5 – Identify and explain the steps in the accounting cycle.

LO6 – Explain the use of and prepare closing entries and a post-closing trial balance.

Concept Self-Check

Use the following as a self-check while working through Chapter 3.

1. What is the GAAP principle of timeliness?

2. What is the GAAP principle of matching?

3. What is the GAAP principle of revenue recognition?

4. What are adjusting entries and when are they journalized?

74 ■ Financial Accounting and Adjusting Entries

5. What are the five types of adjustments?
6. Why is an adjusted trial balance prepared?
7. How is the unadjusted trial balance different from the adjusted trial balance?
8. What are the four closing entries and why are they journalized?
9. Why is the Dividends account not closed to the income summary?
10. When is a post-closing trial balance prepared?
11. How is a post-closing trial balance different from an adjusted trial balance?

NOTE: The purpose of these questions is to prepare you for the concepts introduced in the chapter. Your goal should be to answer each of these questions as you read through the chapter. If, when you complete the chapter, you are unable to answer one or more the Concept Self-Check questions, go back through the content to find the answer(s). Solutions are not provided to these questions.

3.1 The Operating Cycle

> **LO1** – Explain how the timeliness, matching, and recognition GAAP require the recording of adjusting entries.

Financial transactions occur continuously during an accounting period as part of a sequence of operating activities. For Big Dog Carworks Corp., this sequence of operating activities takes the following form:

1. Operations begin with some cash on hand.
2. Cash is used to purchase supplies and to pay expenses.
3. Revenue is earned as repair services are completed for customers.
4. Cash is collected from customers.

This cash-to-cash sequence of transactions is commonly referred to as an **operating cycle** and is illustrated in Figure 3.1.

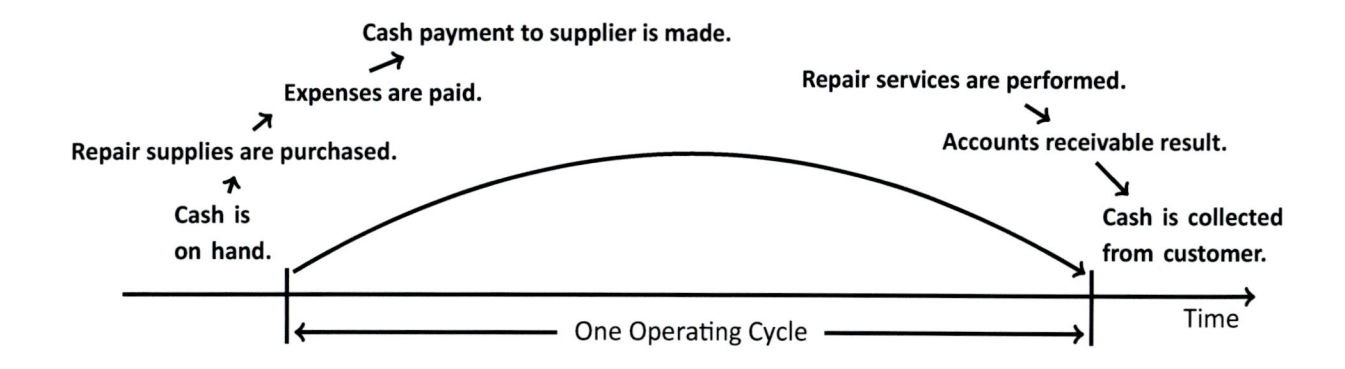

Figure 3.1: One Operating Cycle

Depending on the type of business, an operating cycle can vary in duration from short, such as one week (e.g., a grocery store) to much longer, such as one year (e.g., a car dealership). Therefore, an annual accounting period could involve multiple operating cycles as shown in Figure 3.2.

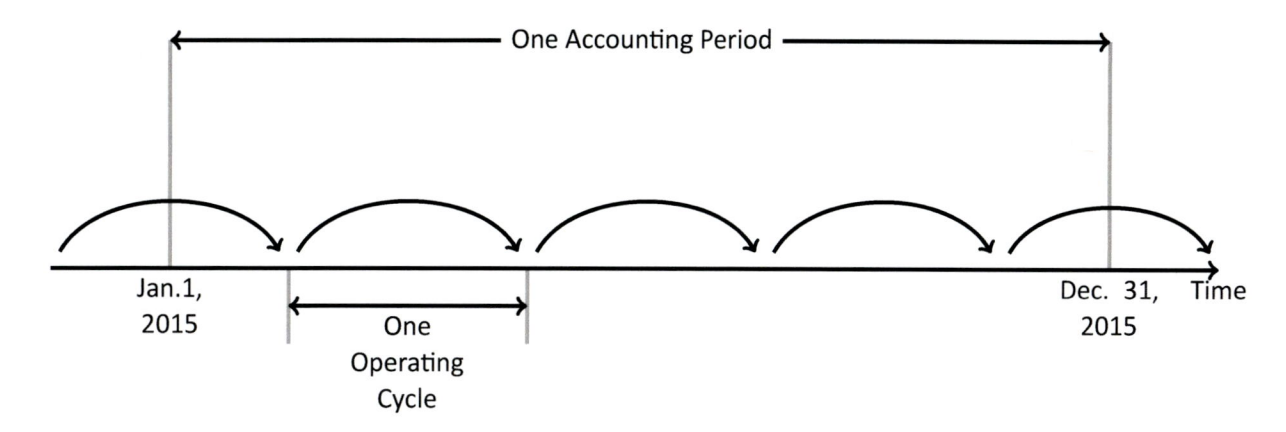

Figure 3.2: Operating Cycles Within an Annual Accounting Period

Notice that not all of the operating cycles in Figure 3.2 are completed within the accounting period. Since financial statements are prepared at specific time intervals to meet the GAAP requirement of timeliness, it is necessary to consider how to record and report transactions related to the accounting period's incomplete operating cycles. Two GAAP requirements — recognition and matching — provide guidance in this area, and are the topic of the next sections.

Recognition Principle in More Detail

GAAP provide guidance about when an economic activity should be recognized in financial statements. An economic activity is recognized when it meets two criteria:

1. it is probable that any future economic benefit associated with the item will flow to the business; and

2. it has a value that can be measured with reliability.

Revenue Recognition Illustrated

Revenue recognition is the process of recording revenue in the accounting period in which it was earned; this is not necessarily when cash is received. Most corporations assume that revenue has been earned at an objectively-determined point in the accounting cycle. For instance, it is often convenient to recognize revenue at the point when a sales invoice has been sent to a customer and the related goods have been received or services performed. This point can occur before receipt of cash from a customer, creating an asset called *Accounts Receivable* and resulting in the following entry:

\multicolumn{5}{c	}{General Journal}
Date	Account/Explanation	PR	Debit	Credit
	Accounts Receivable		XX	
	Revenue			XX
	To record revenue earned on account.			

When cash payment is later received, the asset *Accounts Receivable* is exchanged for the asset *Cash* and the following entry is made:

\multicolumn{5}{c	}{General Journal}
Date	Account/Explanation	PR	Debit	Credit
	Cash....................................		XX	
	Accounts Receivable			XX
	To record cash received from credit customer.			

Revenue is recognized in the first entry (the credit to revenue), prior to the receipt of cash. The second entry has no effect on revenue.

When cash is received at the same time that revenue is recognized, the following entry is made:

\multicolumn{5}{c	}{General Journal}
Date	Account/Explanation	PR	Debit	Credit
	Cash....................................		XX	
	Revenue			XX
	To record cash received from customer.			

When a cash deposit or advance payment is obtained **before** revenue is earned, a liability called Unearned Revenue is recorded as follows:

3.1. The Operating Cycle • 77

General Journal				
Date	Account/Explanation	PR	Debit	Credit
	Cash....................................		XX	
	Unearned Revenue			XX
	To record cash received from customer for work to be done in the future.			

Revenue is *not* recognized until the services have been performed. At that time, the following entry is made:

General Journal				
Date	Account/Explanation	PR	Debit	Credit
	Unearned Revenue......................		XX	
	Revenue............................			XX
	To record the earned portion of Unearned Revenue.			

The preceding entry reduces the unearned revenue account by the amount of revenue earned.

The matching of revenue to a particular time period, regardless of when cash is received, is an example of *accrual accounting*. **Accrual accounting** is the process of recognizing revenues when earned and expenses when incurred regardless of when cash is exchanged; it forms the basis of GAAP. Recognition of expenses is discussed in the next section.

Expense Recognition Illustrated

In a business, costs are incurred continuously. To review, a cost is recorded as an *asset* if it will be incurred in producing revenue in future accounting periods. A cost is recorded as an *expense* if it will be used or consumed during the current period to earn revenue. This distinction between types of cost outlays is illustrated in Figure 3.3.

```
                    COST OUTLAYS
                    /          \
   Recorded as ASSETS           Recorded as EXPENSES
   When costs are incurred to   When costs are incurred to
   produce revenue in future    earn revenue in the present
   accounting periods, for ex-  accounting period, for example:
   ample: prepaid rent, prepaid rent expense, insurance expense,
   insurance, and unused supplies. and office supplies expense.
```

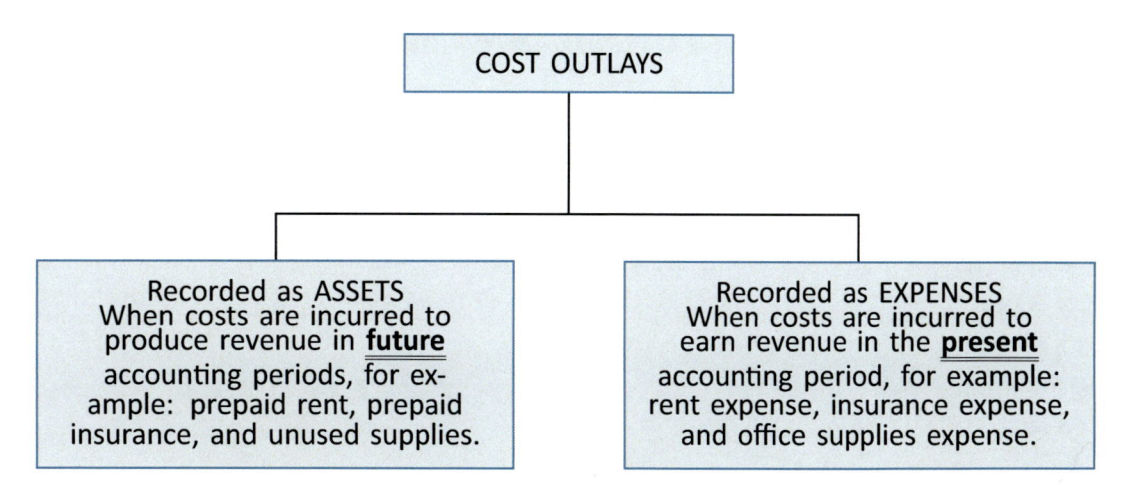

Figure 3.3: The Interrelationship Between Assets and Expense

In the previous section regarding revenue recognition, journal entries illustrated three scenarios where *revenue* was recognized before, at the same time as, and after cash was received. Similarly, expenses can be incurred before, at the same time as, or after cash is paid out. An example of when expenses are incurred before cash is paid occurs when the utilities expense for January is not paid until February. In this case, an *account payable* is created in January as follows:

	General Journal			
Date	Account/Explanation	PR	Debit	Credit
	Utilities Expense		XX	
	Accounts Payable (or Utilities Payable)			XX
	To record January utilities expense to be paid in February.			

The utilities expense is reported in the January income statement.

When the January utilities are paid in February, the following is recorded:

	General Journal			
Date	Account/Explanation	PR	Debit	Credit
	Accounts Payable (or Utilities Payable) ...		XX	
	Cash...............................			XX
	To record payment in February of utilities used in January.			

The preceding entry has no effect on expenses reported on the February income statement.

Expenses can also be recorded at the same time that cash is paid. For example, if salaries for January are paid on January 31, the entry on January 31 is:

	General Journal			
Date	Account/Explanation	PR	Debit	Credit
	Salaries Expense		XX	
	Cash...............................			XX
	To record payment of January salaries.			

As a result of this entry, salaries expense is reported on the January income statement when cash is paid.

Finally, a cash payment can be made **before** the expense is incurred, such as insurance paid in advance. A prepayment of insurance creates an asset *Prepaid Insurance* and is recorded as:

	General Journal			
Date	Account/Explanation	PR	Debit	Credit
	Prepaid Insurance.......................		XX	
	Cash...............................			XX
	To record payment of insurance in advance.			

As the prepaid insurance is used, it is appropriate to report an expense on the income statement by recording the following entry:

| General Journal |||||
Date	Account/Explanation	PR	Debit	Credit
	Insurance Expense.......................		XX	
	Prepaid Insurance....................			XX
	To record the use of Prepaid Insurance.			

The preceding examples illustrate how to *match* expenses to the appropriate accounting period. The **matching principle** requires that expenses be reported in the same period as the revenues they helped generate. That is, expenses are reported on the income statement: a) when related revenue is recognized, or b) during the appropriate time period, regardless of when cash is paid.

To ensure the recognition and matching of revenues and expenses to the correct accounting period, account balances must be reviewed and adjusted prior to the preparation of financial statements. This is the topic of the next section.

3.2 Adjusting Entries

LO2 – Explain the use of and prepare the adjusting entries required for prepaid expenses, depreciation, unearned revenues, accrued revenues, and accrued expenses.

At the end of an accounting period, before financial statements can be prepared, the accounts must be reviewed for potential adjustments. This review is done by using the *unadjusted trial balance*. The **unadjusted trial balance** is a trial balance where the accounts have not yet been adjusted. The trial balance of Big Dog Carworks Corp. at January 31 was prepared in Chapter 2 and appears in Figure 3.4 below. It is an unadjusted trial balance because the accounts have not yet been updated for adjustments. We will use this trial balance to illustrate how adjustments are identified and recorded.

Big Dog Carworks Corp.
Unadjusted Trial Balance
At January 31, 2015

Acct.	Account	Debit	Credit
101	Cash	$3,700	
110	Accounts receivable	2,000	
161	Prepaid insurance	2,400	
183	Equipment	3,000	
184	Truck	8,000	
201	Bank loan		$6,000
210	Accounts payable		700
247	Unearned revenue		400
320	Share capital		10,000
330	Dividends	200	
450	Repair revenue		10,000
654	Rent expense	1,600	
656	Salaries expense	3,500	
668	Supplies expense	2,000	
670	Truck operation expense	700	
		$27,100	$27,100

Figure 3.4: Unadjusted Trial Balance of Big Dog Carworks Corp. at January 31, 2015

Adjustments are recorded with *adjusting entries*. The purpose of **adjusting entries** is to ensure both the balance sheet and the income statement faithfully represent the account balances for the accounting period. Adjusting entries help satisfy the matching principle. There are five types of adjusting entries as shown in Figure 3.5, each of which will be discussed in the following sections.

Adjust prepaid assets | Adjust unearned liabilities | Adjust plant and equipment assets | Adjust for accrued revenues[1] | Adjust for accrued expenses[2]

1. An **accrued revenue** is a revenue that has been earned but has not been collected or recorded.
2. An **accrued expense** is an expense that has been incurred but has not yet been paid or recorded.

Figure 3.5: Five Types of Adjusting Entries

Adjusting Prepaid Asset Accounts

An asset or liability account requiring adjustment at the end of an accounting period is referred to as a **mixed account** because it includes both a balance sheet portion and an income statement portion. The income statement portion must be removed from the account by an adjusting entry.

Refer to Figure 3.4 which shows an unadjusted balance in prepaid insurance of $2,400. Recall from Chapter 2 that Big Dog paid for a 12-month insurance policy that went into effect on January 1 (transaction 5).

The unadjusted trial balance shows the following balance in the Prepaid Insurance account:

Prepaid Insurance
2,400

The balance resulted when the journal entry below was recorded:

Prepaid Insurance   2,400
   Cash   2,400

At January 31, one month or $200 of the policy has expired (been used up) calculated as $2,400/12 months = $200.

The adjusting entry on January 31 to transfer $200 out of prepaid insurance and into insurance expense is:

	General Journal			
Date	Account/Explanation	PR	Debit	Credit
Jan 31	Insurance Expense		200	
	Prepaid Insurance...................			200
	To adjust for the use of one month of Prepaid Insurance.			

As shown below, the balance remaining in the Prepaid Insurance account is $2,200 after the adjusting entry is posted. The $2,200 balance represents the unexpired asset that will benefit future periods, namely, the 11 months from February to December, 2015. The $200 transferred out of prepaid insurance is posted as a debit to the Insurance Expense account to show how much insurance has been used during January.

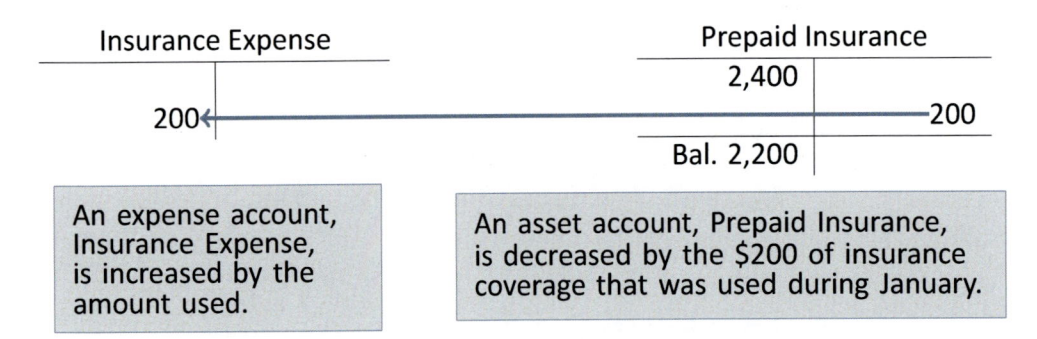

```
      Insurance Expense                           Prepaid Insurance
                                                  2,400
              200◄─────────────────────────────────────────── 200
                                                  Bal. 2,200
```

An expense account, Insurance Expense, is increased by the amount used.

An asset account, Prepaid Insurance, is decreased by the $200 of insurance coverage that was used during January.

If the adjustment was not recorded, assets on the balance sheet would be overstated by $200 and expenses would be understated by the same amount on the income statement.

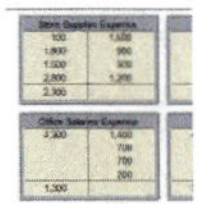

An exploration is available on the Lyryx site. Log into your Lyryx course to run Prepaid Expenses.

Adjusting Unearned Liability Accounts

On January 15, Big Dog received a $400 cash payment in advance of services being performed: $300 for January and $100 for February.

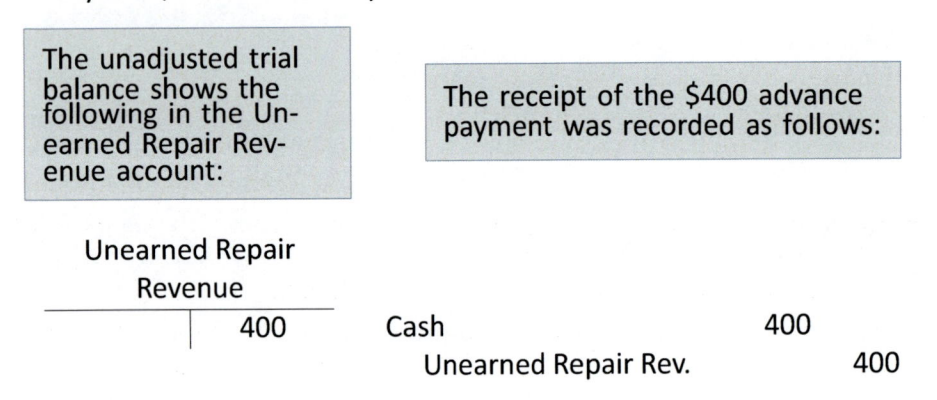

The unadjusted trial balance shows the following in the Unearned Repair Revenue account:

The receipt of the $400 advance payment was recorded as follows:

```
   Unearned Repair
       Revenue
             | 400            Cash                    400
                                 Unearned Repair Rev.        400
```

This advance payment was originally recorded as unearned, since the cash was received **before** repair services were performed. At January 31, $300 of the $400 unearned amount has been earned. Therefore, $300 must be transferred from unearned repair revenue into repair revenue. The adjusting entry at January 31 is:

General Journal				
Date	Account/Explanation	PR	Debit	Credit
Jan 31	Unearned Repair Revenue.............		300	
	Repair Revenuee....................			300
	To adjust for repair revenue earned.			

After posting the adjustment, the $100 remaining balance in unearned repair revenue ($400 − $300) represents the amount at the end of January that will be earned in February.

```
    Unearned Repair
        Revenue                                    Repair Revenue
                        400                                        10,000
           300                                                →300
                      Bal. 100                                   Bal. 10,300
```

A liability account, Unearned Repair Revenue, is decreased by the $300 adjustment.

A revenue account, Repair Revenue, is increased by the $300 adjustment.

If the adjustment was not recorded, unearned repair revenue would be overstated (too high) by $300 causing liabilities on the balance sheet to be overstated. Additionally, revenue would be understated (too low) by $300 on the income statement if the adjustment was not recorded.

An exploration is available on the Lyryx site. Log into your Lyryx course to run Unearned Revenues.

Adjusting Plant and Equipment Accounts

Plant and equipment assets, also known as long-lived assets, are expected to help generate revenues over the current and future accounting periods because they are used to produce goods, supply services, or used for administrative purposes. The truck and equipment purchased by Big Dog Carworks Corp. in January are examples of plant and equipment assets that provide economic benefits for more than one accounting period. Because plant and equipment assets are useful for more than one accounting period, their cost must be spread over the time they are used. This is done to satisfy the matching principle. For example, the $100,000 cost of a machine expected to be used over five years is not expensed entirely in the year of purchase because this would cause expenses to be overstated in Year 1 and understated in Years 2, 3, 4, and 5. Therefore, the $100,000 cost must be spread over the asset's five-year life.

The process of allocating the cost of a plant and equipment asset over the period of time it is expected to be used is called **depreciation**. The amount of depreciation is calculated using the actual cost and an estimate of the asset's *useful life* and *residual value*. The **useful life** of a plant and equipment asset is an estimate of how long it will actually be used by the business regardless of how long the asset is expected to last. For example, a car might have a manufacturer's suggested life of 10 years but a business may have a policy of keeping cars for only 2 years. The useful life for depreciation purposes would therefore be 2 years and not 10 years. The **residual value** is an estimate of what the plant and equipment asset will be sold for when it is no longer used by a business. Residual value can be zero. There are different formulas for calculating depreciation. We will use the **straight-line method of depreciation**:

$$\frac{\text{Cost} - \text{Estimated Residual Value}}{\text{Estimated Useful Life}}$$

The cost less estimated residual value is the total **depreciable cost** of the asset. The straight-line method allocates the depreciable cost equally over the asset's estimated useful life. When recording depreciation expense, our initial instinct is to debit depreciation expense and credit the Plant and Equipment asset account in the same way prepaids were adjusted with a debit to an expense and a credit to the Prepaid asset account. However, crediting the Plant and Equipment asset account is incorrect. Instead, a *contra account* called *accumulated depreciation* must be credited. A **contra account** is an account that is related to another account and typically has an opposite normal balance that is subtracted from the balance of its related account on the financial statements. **Accumulated depreciation** records the amount of the asset's cost that has been expensed since it was put into use. Accumulated depreciation has a normal credit balance that is subtracted from a Plant and Equipment asset account on the balance sheet.

Initially, the concept of crediting Accumulated Depreciation may be confusing because of how we learned to adjust prepaids (debit an expense and credit the prepaid). Remember that prepaids actually get used up and disappear over time. The Plant and Equipment asset account is not credited because, unlike a prepaid, a truck or building does not get used up and disappear. The goal in recording depreciation is to match the cost of the asset to the revenues it helped generate. For example, a $50,000 truck that is expected to be used by a business for 4 years will have its cost spread over 4 years. After 4 years, the asset will likely be sold (journal entries related to the sale of plant and equipment assets are discussed in Chapter 8).

The adjusting journal entry to record depreciation is:

	General Journal			
Date	Account/Explanation	PR	Debit	Credit
	Depreciation Expense		XX	
	Accumulated Depreciation............			XX
	To adjust for depreciation.			

Subtracting the accumulated depreciation account balance from the Plant and Equipment asset account balance equals the **carrying amount** or **net book value** of the plant and equipment asset that is reported on the balance sheet.

Let's work through two examples to demonstrate depreciation adjustments. Big Dog Carworks Corp.'s January 31, 2015 unadjusted trial balance showed the following two plant and equipment assets:

Big Dog Carworks Corp.
Unadjusted Trial Balance
At January 31, 2015

Acct.	Account	Debit	Credit
183	Equipment	3,000	
184	Truck	8,000	

The equipment was purchased for $3,000.

The Equipment general ledger account appears as follows:

Equipment
3,000

The balance resulted when this journal entry was recorded:

Equipment   3,000
    Cash   3,000

The equipment was recorded as a plant and equipment asset because it has an estimated useful life greater than 1 year. Assume its actual useful life is 10 years (120 months) and the equipment is estimated to be worth $0 at the end of its useful life (residual value of $0).

$$\frac{\text{Cost} - \text{Estimated Residual Value}}{\text{Estimated Useful Life}} = \frac{\$3,000 - \$0}{120 \text{ months}} = \$25/\text{month}$$

Note that depreciation is always rounded to the nearest whole dollar. This is because depreciation is based on estimates — an estimated residual value and an estimated useful life; it is not exact. The following adjusting journal entry is made on January 31:

	General Journal			
Date	Account/Explanation	PR	Debit	Credit
Jan 31	Depreciation Expense, Equipment		25	
	Accumulated Depreciation, Equipment			25
	To adjust for one month of depreciation on the equipment.			

When the adjusting entry is posted, the accounts appear as follows:

86 ■ Financial Accounting and Adjusting Entries

```
       Equipment              Accumulated                  Depreciation
                          Depreciation – Equipment      Expense – Equipment
        3,000                      25 ←——————————————————→ 25
```

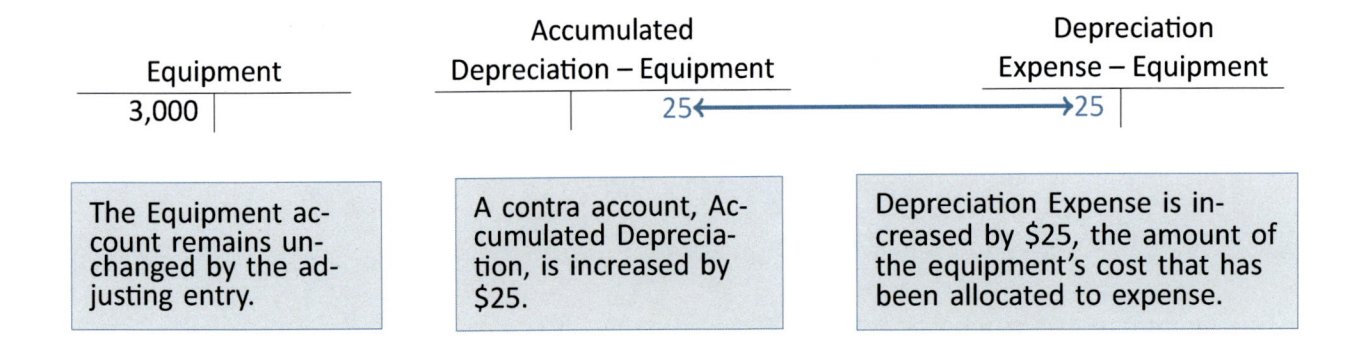

| The Equipment account remains unchanged by the adjusting entry. | A contra account, Accumulated Depreciation, is increased by $25. | Depreciation Expense is increased by $25, the amount of the equipment's cost that has been allocated to expense. |

For financial statement reporting, the asset and contra asset accounts are combined. The net book value of the equipment on the balance sheet is shown as $2,975 ($3,000 – $25).

BDCC also shows a truck for $8,000 on the January 31, 2015 unadjusted trial balance.

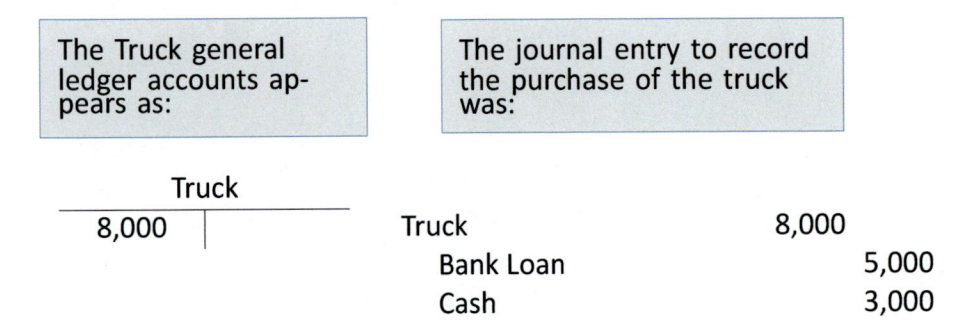

| The Truck general ledger accounts appears as: | The journal entry to record the purchase of the truck was: |

```
        Truck
        8,000                Truck              8,000
                             Bank Loan                    5,000
                             Cash                         3,000
```

Assume the truck has an estimated useful life of 80 months and a zero estimated residual value. At January 31, one month of the truck cost has expired since it was put into operation in January. Using the straight-line method, depreciation is calculated as:

$$\frac{\text{Cost} - \text{Estimated Residual Value}}{\text{Estimated Useful Life}} = \frac{\$8,000 - \$0}{80 \text{ months}} = \$100/\text{month}$$

The adjusting entry recorded on January 31 is:

| \multicolumn{5}{c}{General Journal} |
Date	Account/Explanation	PR	Debit	Credit
Jan 31	Depreciation Expense, Truck		100	
	Accumulated Depreciation, Truck			100
	To adjust for one month of depreciation on the truck.			

When the adjusting entry is posted, the accounts appear as follows:

Truck	Accumulated Depreciation – Truck	Depreciation Expense – Truck
8,000	100 ←	→ 100

| The Truck account remains unchanged by the adjusting entry. | A contra account, Accumulated Depreciation, is increased by $100. | Depreciation Expense is increased by $100, the amount of the truck's cost that has been allocated to expense. |

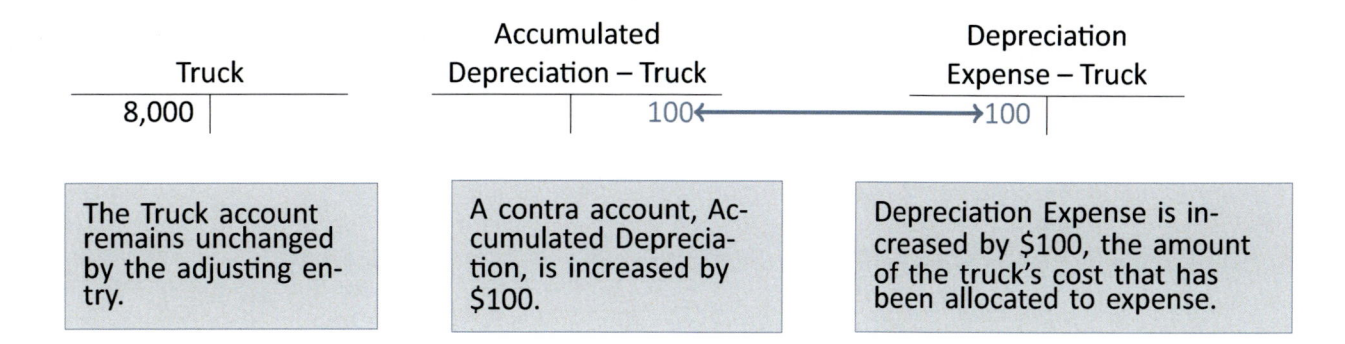

For financial statement reporting, the asset and contra asset accounts are combined. The net book value of the truck on the balance sheet is shown as $7,900 ($8,000 – $100).

If depreciation adjustments are not recorded, assets on the balance sheet would be overstated. Additionally, expenses would be understated on the income statement causing net income to be overstated. If net income is overstated, retained earnings on the balance sheet would also be overstated.

It is important to note that land is a long-lived asset. However, it is **not depreciated** because it does not get used up over time. Therefore, land is often referred to as a non-depreciable asset.

An exploration is available on the Lyryx site. Log into your Lyryx course to run Depreciation.

Adjusting for Accrued Revenues

Accrued revenues are revenues that have been earned but not yet collected or recorded. For example, a bank has numerous notes receivable. Interest is earned on the notes receivable as time passes. At the end of an accounting period, there would be notes receivable where the interest has been earned but not collected or recorded. The adjusting entry for accrued revenues is:

General Journal				
Date	Account/Explanation	PR	Debit	Credit
	Receivable		XXX	
	Revenue			XXX
	To adjust for accrued revenue.			

For Big Dog Carworks Corp., assume that on January 31, $400 of repair work was completed for a client but it had not yet been collected or recorded. BDCC must record the following adjusting entry:

88 ■ Financial Accounting and Adjusting Entries

General Journal				
Date	Account/Explanation	PR	Debit	Credit
Jan 31	Accounts Receivable		400	
	Repair Revenue......................			400
	To adjust for accrued revenue.			

```
      Accounts Receivable                              Repair Revenue
            2,000                                                     10,300
             400◄─────────────────────────────────────────►400
        Bal. 2,400                                              Bal. 10,700
```

An asset account, Accounts Receivable, is increased by the accrued amount.

An income statement account, Repair Revenue, is increased by the $400 of accrued revenue.

If the adjustment was not recorded, assets on the balance sheet would be understated by $400 and revenues would be understated by the same amount on the income statement.

An exploration is available on the Lyryx site. Log into your Lyryx course to run Accrued Revenues.

Adjusting for Accrued Expenses

Accrued expenses are expenses that have been incurred but not yet paid or recorded. For example, a utility bill received at the end of the accounting period is likely not payable for 2–3 weeks. Utilities for the period have been used but have not yet been paid or recorded. The adjusting entry for accrued expenses is:

General Journal				
Date	Account/Explanation	PR	Debit	Credit
	Expense..................................		XXX	
	Payable.................................			XXX
	To adjust for accrued expense.			

Accruing Interest Expense

For Big Dog Carworks Corp., the January 31, 2015 unadjusted trial balance shows a $6,000 bank loan balance. Assume it is a 4%, 60-day bank loan[1]. It was dated January 3 which means that on January 31, 28 days of interest have accrued (January 31 less January 3 = 28 days) as shown in Figure 3.6.

---

[1] The maturity date is March 4, 2015 calculated as: January 31 less January 3 = 28 days + 28 days in February = 56 days + 4 days = March 4.

```
                        60-day Note
    ←——————————————————————————————————————→
    |              |                              |
January 3      January 31                     March 4
                                              (Maturity
                                                date)

    ←——————————————→
     28 days of
     interest has
     been incurred
     at January 31
```

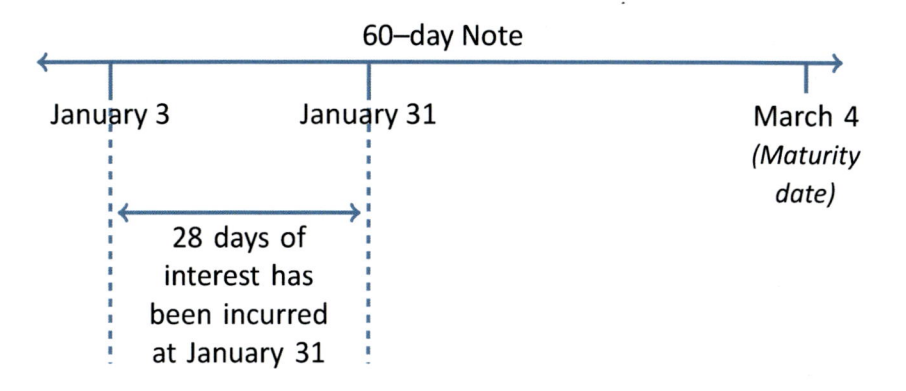

Figure 3.6: Interest Incurred During an Accounting Period

The formula for calculating interest when the term is expressed in days is:

$$\text{Interest} = \text{Principal} \times \text{Interest rate} \times \frac{\text{Elapsed time in days}}{365}$$

The interest expense accrued at January 31 is calculated as:

$$\text{Interest} = \$6{,}000 \times 0.04 \times \frac{28}{365} = \$18 \text{ (rounded to nearest whole dollar)}$$

Interest is normally expressed as an annual rate. Therefore, the 28 days must be divided by the 365 days in a year.[2] Normally all interest calculations in this textbook are rounded to two decimal places. However, for simplicity of demonstrations in this chapter, we will round to the nearest whole dollar.

BDCC's adjusting entry on January 31 is:

Date	Account/Explanation	PR	Debit	Credit
Jan 31	Interest Expense		18	
	Interest Payable			18
	To adjust for accrued interest; $6,000 X 4% X 28/365 = $18.41 (rounded to $18 for illustrative purposes in this chapter).			

This adjusting entry enables BDCC to include the interest expense on the January income statement even though the payment has not yet been made. The entry creates a payable that will be reported as a liability on the balance sheet at January 31.

When the adjusting entry is posted, the accounts appear as:

---

[2] To review interest calculations, refer to the Chapter 3 - Interest Tutorial.

90 ■ Financial Accounting and Adjusting Entries

```
Interest Expense                    Interest Payable
     18                                        18
```

An expense account is established to record the debit.

Interest payable is established to record the credit.

On February 28, interest will again be accrued and recorded as:

	General Journal			
Date	Account/Explanation	PR	Debit	Credit
Feb 28	Interest Expense		18	
	Interest Payable			18
	To adjust for accrued interest; $6,000 X 4% X 28/365 = $18.41 (rounded to $18 for illustrative purposes in this chapter).			

On March 4 when the bank loan matures, Big Dog will pay the interest and principal and record the following entry:

	General Journal			
Date	Account/Explanation	PR	Debit	Credit
Mar 4	Interest Expense		3	
	Interest Payable........................		36	
	Bank Loan..............................		6,000	
	Cash.....................................			6039
	To record payment of the bank loan and interest; interest expense for March is $6,000 X 4% X 4/365 = $2.63 (rounded to $3 for illustrative purposes in this chapter).			

The $36 debit to interest payable will cause the Interest Payable account to go to zero since the liability no longer exists once the cash is paid. Notice that the total interest expense recorded on the bank loan was $39 – $18 expensed in January, $18 expensed in February, and $3 expensed in March. The interest expense was matched to the life of the bank loan.

Accruing Income Tax Expense

Another adjustment that is required for Big Dog Carworks Corp. involves the recording of corporate income taxes. In most jurisdictions, a corporation is taxed as an entity separate from its shareholders. For simplicity, assume BDCC's income tax due for January 2015 is $500. The adjusting entry is at January 31:

	General Journal			
Date	Account/Explanation	PR	Debit	Credit
Jan 31	Income Tax Expense....................		500	
	Income Tax Payable			500
	To adjust for January accrued income tax.			

When the adjusting entry is posted, the accounts appear as follows:

Income Tax Expense
500◄

Income Tax Payable
►500

Income Tax Expense, an income statement account, is created at January 31.

A liability, Income Tax Payable, is created at January 31.

The above adjusting entry enables the company to match the income tax expense accrued in January to the income earned during the same month.

An exploration is available on the Lyryx site. Log into your Lyryx course to run Accrued Expenses.

An exploration is available on the Lyryx site. Log into your Lyryx course to run Collection/Payment of Accrual Adjustments in the Next Accounting Period.

The five types of adjustments discussed in the previous paragraphs are summarized in Figure 3.7.

Each of the five steps of adjusting entries either
debits an expense or **credits a revenue**.

Adjust Prepaid assets by recording:
Expense......................... XX
    Prepaid................... XX
To adjust a Prepaid for the amount used.

Adjust Unearned liabilities by recording:
Unearned Liability.............. XX
    Revenue................... XX
To adjust an Unearned Liability for the amount earned.

Adjust Plant and Equipment assets by recording:
Depreciation Expense........... XX
    Accumulated Depreciation.. XX
To adjust Plant and Equipment assets for depreciation.

Adjust for Accrued Revenues by recording:
Receivable..................... XX
    Revenue................... XX
To accrue a revenue.

Adjust for Accrued Expenses by recording:
Expense........................ XX
    Liability................. XX
To accrue an expense.

1. An **accrued revenue** is a revenue that has been earned but has not yet been collected or recorded.
2. An **accrued expense** is an expense that has been incurred but has not yet been paid or recorded.

Figure 3.7: Summary of the Five Types of Adjusting Entries

3.3 The Adjusted Trial Balance

LO3 – Prepare an adjusted trial balance and explain its use.

In the last section, adjusting entries were recorded and posted. As a result, some account balances reported on the January 31, 2015 unadjusted trial balance in Figure 2 have changed. Recall that an unadjusted trial balance reports account balances *before* adjusting entries have been recorded and posted. An **adjusted trial balance** reports account balances *after* adjusting entries have been recorded and posted. Figure 3.8 shows the adjusted trial balance for BDCC at January 31, 2015.

In Chapters 1 and 2, the preparation of financial statements was demonstrated using BDCC's *unadjusted* trial balance. We now know that an adjusted trial balance must be used to prepare financial statements.

Big Dog Carworks Corp.
Adjusted Trial Balance
At January 31, 2015

Account	Debit	Credit
Cash	$3,700	
Accounts receivable	2,400	
Prepaid insurance	2,200	
Equipment	3,000	
Accumulated depreciation – equipment		$ 25
Truck	8,000	
Accumulated depreciation – truck		100
Bank loan		6,000
Accounts payable		700
Interest payable		18
Unearned repair revenue		100
Income tax payable		500
Share capital		10,000
Dividends	200	
Repair revenue		10,700
Depreciation expense – equipment	25	
Depreciation expense – truck	100	
Rent expense	1,600	
Insurance expense	200	
Interest expense	18	
Salaries expense	3,500	
Supplies expense	2,000	
Truck operation expense	700	
Income tax expense	500	
Total debits and credits	$28,143	$28,143

Figure 3.8: BDCC's January 31, 2015 Adjusted Trial Balance

An exploration is available on the Lyryx site. Log into your Lyryx course to run *Adjusted*

Trial Balance.

3.4 Using the Adjusted Trial Balance to Prepare Financial Statements

LO4 – Use an adjusted trial balance to prepare financial statements.

In the last section, we saw that the adjusted trial balance is prepared after journalizing and posting the adjusting entries. This section shows how financial statements are prepared using the adjusted trial balance.

Big Dog Carworks Corp.
Adjusted Trial Balance
January 31, 2015

Account	Debit	Credit	
Cash	$ 3,700		Asset accounts, liability accounts, and the equity accounts from the statement of changes in equity are used to prepare the balance sheet.
Accounts receivable	2,400		
Prepaid insurance	2,200		
Equipment	3,000		
Accumulated depreciation – equipment		$ 25	
Truck	8,000		
Accumulated depreciation – truck		100	
Bank loan		6,000	
Accounts payable		700	
Interest payable		18	
Unearned repair revenue		100	Share capital, dividends, and the net income/loss from the income statement are used to prepare the statement of changes in equity.
Income tax payable		500	
Share capital		10,000	
Dividends	200		
Repair revenue		10,700	
Depreciation expense – equipment	25		
Depreciation expense – truck	100		Revenue and expense accounts are used to prepare the income statement.
Rent expense	1,600		
Insurance expense	200		
Interest expense	18		
Salaries expense	3,500		
Supplies expense	2,000		
Truck operation expense	700		
Income tax expense	500		
Total debits and credits	$28,143	$28,143	

Figure 3.9: BDCC's January 31, 2015 Adjusted Trial Balance and Links Among Financial Statements

The income statement is prepared first, followed by the statement of changes in equity as shown below.

96 ■ Financial Accounting and Adjusting Entries

Big Dog Carworks Corp.
Adjusted Trial Balance
At January 31, 2015

Account	Debit	Credit
Cash	$3,700	
Accounts receivable	2,400	
Prepaid insurance	2,200	
Equipment	3,000	
Accum. dep. – equipment		$ 25
Truck	8,000	
Accum. dep. – truck		100
Bank loan		6,000
Accounts payable		700
Interest payable		18
Unearned revenue		100
Income tax payable		500
Share capital		10,000
Dividends	200	
Repair revenue		10,700
Dep. expense – equipment	25	
Dep. expense – truck	100	
Rent expense	1,600	
Insurance expense	200	
Interest expense	18	
Salaries expense	3,500	
Supplies expense	2,000	
Truck operation expense	700	
Income tax expense	500	
	$28,143	$28,143

Share capital and dividends are transferred to the Statement of Changes in Equity. Dividends is part of retained earnings because it is a distribution of net income.

Big Dog Carworks Corp.
Income Statement
For the Month Ended January 31, 2015

Revenues		
Repair revenue		$10,700
Expenses		
Salaries expense	$3,500	
Supplies expense	2,000	
Rent expense	1,600	
Truck operating expense	700	
Income tax expense	500	
Insurance expense	200	
Dep. expense – truck	100	
Dep. expense – equipment	25	
Interest expense	18	
Total expenses		8,643
Net income		$2,057

Big Dog Carworks Corp.
Statement of Changes in Equity
For the Month Ended January 31, 2015

	Share capital	Retained earnings	Total equity
Balance at beginning of period	$ -0-	$ -0-	$ -0-
Shares issued	10,000		10,000
Dividends		(200)	(200)
Net income		2,057	2,057
Balance at end of period	$10,000	$1,857	$11,857

Net income is transferred to the Statement of Changes in Equity as part of retained earnings.

3.4. Using the Adjusted Trial Balance to Prepare Financial Statements

The balance sheet can be prepared once the statement of changes in equity is complete.

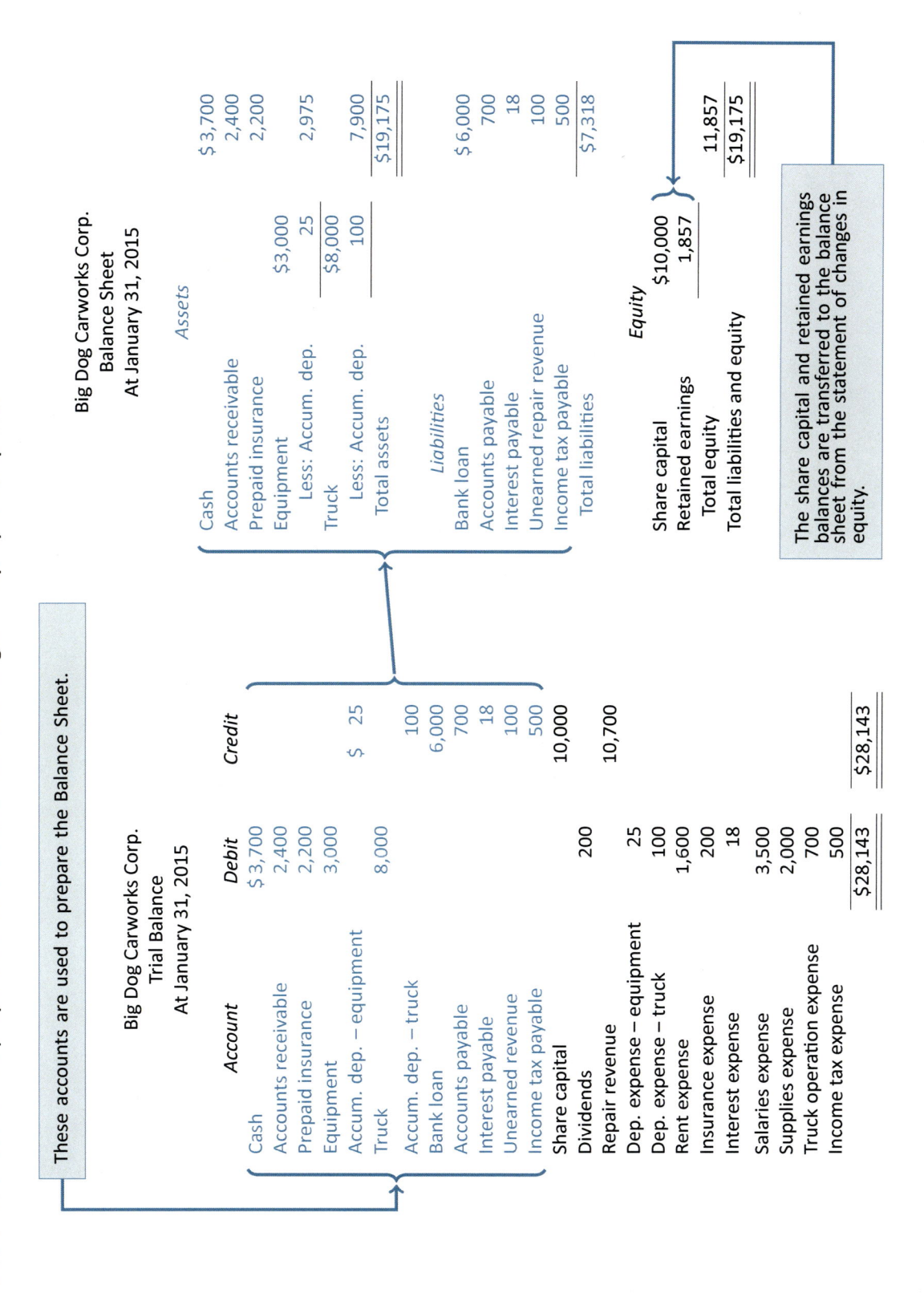

These accounts are used to prepare the Balance Sheet.

Big Dog Carworks Corp.
Trial Balance
At January 31, 2015

Account	Debit	Credit
Cash	$3,700	
Accounts receivable	2,400	
Prepaid insurance	2,200	
Equipment	3,000	
Accum. dep. – equipment		$ 25
Truck	8,000	
Accum. dep. – truck		100
Bank loan		6,000
Accounts payable		700
Interest payable		18
Unearned revenue		100
Income tax payable		500
Share capital		10,000
Dividends	200	
Repair revenue		10,700
Dep. expense – equipment	25	
Dep. expense – truck	100	
Rent expense	1,600	
Insurance expense	200	
Interest expense	18	
Salaries expense	3,500	
Supplies expense	2,000	
Truck operation expense	700	
Income tax expense	500	
	$28,143	$28,143

Big Dog Carworks Corp.
Balance Sheet
At January 31, 2015

Assets

Cash		$3,700
Accounts receivable		2,400
Prepaid insurance		2,200
Equipment	$3,000	
Less: Accum. dep.	25	2,975
Truck	$8,000	
Less: Accum. dep.	100	7,900
Total assets		$19,175

Liabilities

Bank loan	$6,000
Accounts payable	700
Interest payable	18
Unearned repair revenue	100
Income tax payable	500
Total liabilities	$7,318

Equity

Share capital	$10,000	
Retained earnings	1,857	
Total equity		11,857
Total liabilities and equity		$19,175

The share capital and retained earnings balances are transferred to the balance sheet from the statement of changes in equity.

Notice how accumulated depreciation is shown on the balance sheet.

An exploration is available on the Lyryx site. Log into your Lyryx course to run Adjustments and Financial Statements.

3.5 The Accounting Cycle

LO5 – Identify and explain the steps in the accounting cycle.

The concept of the accounting cycle was introduced in Chapter 2. The accounting cycle consists of the steps followed each accounting period to prepare financial statements. These eight steps are:

Step 1: Transactions are analyzed and recorded in the general journal

Step 2: The journal entries in the general journal are posted to accounts in the general ledger

Step 3: An unadjusted trial balance is prepared to ensure total debits equal total credits

Step 4: The unadjusted account balances are analyzed and adjusting entries are journalized in the general journal and posted to the general ledger

Step 5: An adjusted trial balance is prepared to prove the equality of debits and credits

Step 6: The adjusted trial balance is used to prepare financial statements

Step 7: Closing entries are journalized and posted

Step 8: Prepare a post-closing trial balance

Steps 1 through 6 were introduced in this and the preceding chapters. Steps 7 and 8 are discussed in the next section.

An exploration is available on the Lyryx site. Log into your Lyryx course to run Reviewing the Accounting Cycle.

3.6 The Closing Process

LO6 – Explain the use of and prepare closing entries and a post-closing trial balance.

At the end of a fiscal year, after financial statements have been prepared, the revenue, expense, and dividend account balances must be zeroed so that they can begin to accumulate amounts belonging to the new fiscal year. To accomplish this, *closing entries* are journalized and posted. **Closing entries** transfer each revenue and expense account balance, as well as any balance in the Dividend account, into retained earnings. Revenues, expenses, and dividends are therefore referred to as **temporary accounts** because their balances are zeroed at the end of each accounting period. Balance sheet accounts, such as retained earnings, are **permanent accounts** because they have a continuing balance from one fiscal year to the next. The closing process transfers temporary account balances into a permanent account, namely retained earnings. The four entries in the closing process are detailed below.

Entry 1: Close the revenue accounts to the income summary account

A single compound closing entry is used to transfer revenue account balances to the *income summary account*. The **income summary** is a checkpoint: once all revenue and expense account balances are transferred/closed to the income summary, the balance in the Income Summary account must be equal to the net income/loss reported on the income statement. If not, the revenues and expenses were not closed correctly.

Entry 2: Close the expense accounts to the Income Summary account

The expense accounts are closed in one compound closing journal entry to the Income Summary account. All expense accounts with a debit balance are credited to bring them to zero. Their balances are transferred to the Income Summary account as an offsetting debit.

After entries 1 and 2 above are posted to the Income Summary account, the balance in the income summary must be compared to the net income/loss reported on the income statement. If the income summary balance does not match the net income/loss reported on the income statement, the revenues and/or expenses were not closed correctly.

Entry 3: Close the income summary to retained earnings

The Income Summary account is closed to the Retained Earnings account. This procedure transfers the balance in the income summary to retained earnings. Again, the amount closed from the income summary to retained earnings must always equal the net income/loss as reported on the income statement.

Note that the Dividend account is **not** closed to the Income Summary account because dividends is not an income statement account. The dividend account is closed in Entry 4.

Entry 4: Close dividends to retained earnings

The Dividend account is closed to the Retained Earnings account. This results in transferring the balance in dividends, a temporary account, to retained earnings, a permanent account.

The balance in the Income Summary account is transferred to retained earnings because the net income (or net loss) belongs to the shareholders. The closing entries for Big Dog Carworks Corp. are shown in Figure 3.10.

Date	Description	F	Debit	Credit
2015	**Closing Entries**			
Jan. 31	Repair Revenue		10700	
	Income Summary			10700
	To close the revenue account balance.			
	Income Summary		8643	
	Depreciation expense – equipment			25
	Depreciation expense – truck			100
	Income tax expense			500
	Insurance expense			200
	Interest expense			18
	Rent expense			1600
	Salaries expense			3500
	Supplies expense			2000
	Truck operation expense			700
	To close expense account balances.			
	Income Summary		2057	
	Retained earnings			2057
	To close income summary to retained earnings.			
	Retained Earnings		200	
	Dividends			200
	To close dividends to retained earnings.			

Figure 3.10: Closing Entries

Posting the Closing Entries to the General Ledger

When entries 1 and 2 are posted to the general ledger, the balances in all revenue and expense accounts are transferred to the Income Summary account. The transfer of these balances is shown in Figure 3.11. Notice that a zero balance results for each revenue and expense account after the closing entries are posted, and there is a $2,057 credit balance in the income summary. The income summary balance agrees to the net income reported on the income statement.

1. Closing Expense Accounts

Dep. Expense – Equipment

Bal.	25	25
Bal.	-0-	

Dep. Expense – Truck

Bal.	100	100
Bal.	-0-	

Insurance Expense

Bal.	200	200
Bal.	-0-	

Interest Expense

Bal.	18	18
Bal.	-0-	

Rent Expense

Bal.	1,600	1,600
Bal.	-0-	

Salaries Expense

Bal.	3,500	3,500
Bal.	-0-	

Supplies Expense

Bal.	2,000	2,000
Bal.	-0-	

Truck Operation Expense

Bal.	700	700
Bal.	-0-	

Income Taxes Expense

Bal.	500	500
Bal.	-0-	

2. Closing Revenue Accounts

Repair Revenue

	10,700	10,700	
		-0-	Bal.

Income Summary

→ 8,643	10,700 ←
	2,057 Bal.

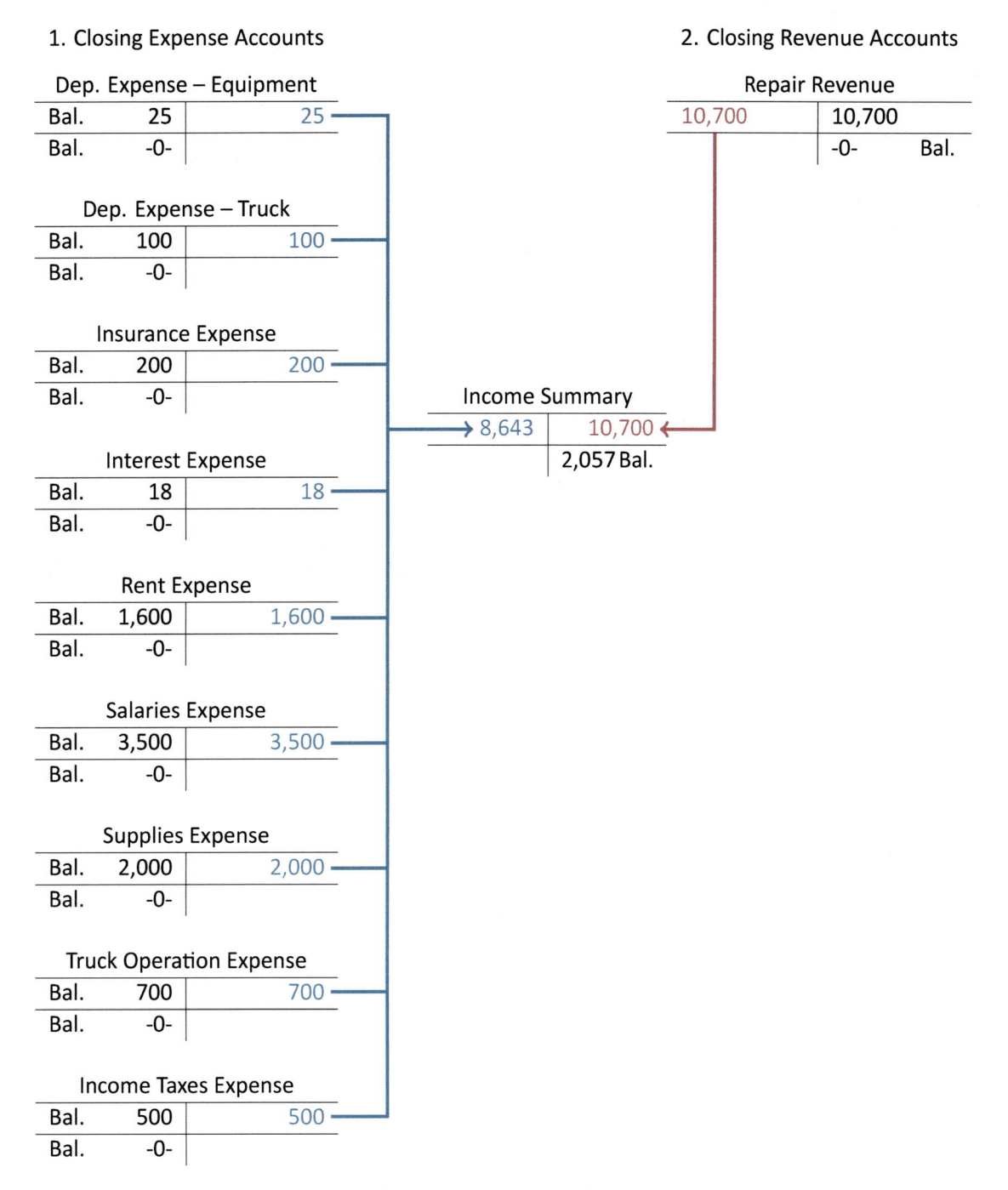

Figure 3.11: Closing Revenue and Expense Accounts

When the income summary is closed to retained earnings in the third closing entry, the $2,057 credit balance in the income summary account is transferred into retained earnings as shown in Figure 3.12. As a result, the income summary is left with a zero balance.

3. Closing the Income Summary Account

Income Summary			Retained Earnings
8,643	10,700		2,057
2,057	2,057 Bal.		
Bal. -0-			

Figure 3.12: Closing the Income Summary Account

This example demonstrated closing entries when there was a net income. When there is a net loss, the Income Summary account will have a debit balance after revenues and expenses have been closed. To close the Income Summary account when there is a net loss, the following closing entry is required:

	General Journal			
Date	Account/Explanation	PR	Debit	Credit
	Retained Earnings................		XX	
	Income Summary...............			XX
	To close the net loss, a debit balance in the income summary, to retained earnings.			

Finally, when dividends is closed to retained earnings in the fourth closing entry, the $200 debit balance in the Dividends account is transferred into retained earnings as shown in Figure 3.13. After the closing entry is posted, the Dividends account is left with a zero balance and retained earnings is left with a credit balance of $1,857. Notice that the $1,857 must agree to the retained earnings balance calculated on the statement of changes in equity.

4. Closing the Dividends Account

Dividends		Retained Earnings
200	200 →	200 2,057
Bal. -0-		1,857 Bal.

Figure 3.13: Closing the Dividends Account

An exploration is available on the Lyryx site. Log into your Lyryx course to run Closing Entries.

The Post–Closing Trial Balance

A **post-closing trial balance** is prepared immediately following the posting of closing entries. The purpose is to ensure that the debits and credits in the general ledger are equal and that all temporary accounts have been closed. The post-closing trial balance for Big Dog Carworks Corp. appears below.

Big Dog Carworks Corp.
Post-Closing Trial Balance
January 31, 2015

	Account Balance	
Account	Debit	Credit
Cash	$ 3,700	
Accounts receivable	2,400	
Prepaid insurance	2,200	
Equipment	3,000	
Accumulated depreciation – equipment		$ 25
Truck	8,000	
Accumulated depreciation – truck		100
Bank loan		6,000
Accounts payable		700
Interest payable		18
Unearned repair revenue		100
Income taxes payable		500
Share capital		10,000
Retained earnings		1,857
Total debits and credits	$19,300	$19,300

Only permanent accounts remain.

Note that only balance sheet accounts, the permanent accounts, have balances and are carried forward to the next accounting year. All temporary accounts begin the new fiscal year with a zero balance, so they can be used to accumulate amounts belonging to the new time period.

An exploration is available on the Lyryx site. Log into your Lyryx course to run Closing Errors.

Summary of Chapter 3 Learning Objectives

LO1 – Explain how the timeliness, matching, and recognition GAAP require the recording of adjusting entries.

Financial statements must be prepared in a timely manner, at minimum, once per fiscal year. For statements to reflect activities accurately, revenues and expenses must be recognized and reported in the appropriate accounting period. In order to achieve this type of matching, adjusting entries need to be prepared.

LO2 – Explain the use of and prepare the adjusting entries required for prepaid expenses, depreciation, unearned revenues, accrued revenues, and accrued expenses.

Adjusting entries are prepared at the end of an accounting period. They allocate revenues and expenses to the appropriate accounting period regardless of when cash was received/paid. The five types of adjustments are:

Expense	XX		Receivable	XX	
Prepaid		XX	Revenue		XX
To adjust prepaid for the amount used/expired.			*To adjust for accrued revenue.*		

Depreciation Expense	XX		Expense	XX	
Accumulated Depreciation		XX	Payable		XX
To allocate the cost of a plan or equipment asset over its useful life.			*To adjust for accrued expense.*		

Unearned Revenue	XX	
Revenue		XX
To adjust unearned amounts for amount earned.		

LO3 – Prepare an adjusted trial balance and explain its use.

The adjusted trial balance is prepared using the account balances in the general ledger after adjusting entries have been posted. Debits must equal credits. The adjusted trial balance is used to prepare the financial statements.

LO4 – Use an adjusted trial balance to prepare financial statements.

Financial statements are prepared based on adjusted account balances.

LO5 – Identify and explain the steps in the accounting cycle.

The steps in the accounting cycle are followed each accounting period in the recording and reporting of financial transactions. The steps are:

1. Transactions are analyzed and recorded in the general journal.
2. The journal entries in the general journal are posted to accounts in the general ledger.
3. An unadjusted trial balance is prepared to ensure total debits equal total credits.

4. The unadjusted account balances are analyzed, and adjusting entries are journalized in the general journal and posted to the general ledger.

5. An adjusted trial balance is prepared to prove the equality of debits and credits.

6. The adjusted trial balance is used to prepare financial statements.

7. Closing entries are journalized and posted.

8. Prepare a post-closing trial balance.

LO6 – Explain the use of and prepare closing entries and a post-closing trial balance.

After the financial statements have been prepared, the temporary account balances (revenues, expenses, and dividends) are transferred to retained earnings, a permanent account, via closing entries. The result is that the temporary accounts will have a zero balance and will be ready to accumulate transactions for the next accounting period. The four closing entries are:

```
Revenue.........................    XX
    Income Summary................           XX
To close each revenue to the income summary.

Income Summary...................    XX
    Expense ......................           XX
To close each expense to the income summary.
```

Income Summary.................... XX		OR	Retained Earnings................... XX
Retained Earnings XX			Income Summary................ XX
To close a net income in income summary to retained earnings.			To close a net loss in income summary to retained earnings.

```
Retained Earnings.................    XX
    Dividends.....................           XX
To close dividends to retained earnings.
```

The post-closing trial balance is prepared after the closing entries have been posted to the general ledger. The post-closing trial balance will contain only permanent accounts because all the temporary accounts have been closed.

Discussion Questions

1. Explain the sequence of financial transactions that occur continuously during an accounting time period. What is this sequence of activities called?

2. Do you have to wait until the operating cycle is complete before you can measure income using the accrual basis of accounting?

3. What is the relationship between the matching concept and accrual accounting? Are revenues matched to expenses, or are expenses matched to revenues? Does it matter one way or the other?

4. What is the impact of the going concern concept on accrual accounting?

5. Identify three different categories of expenses.

6. What are adjusting entries and why are they required?

7. Why are asset accounts like Prepaid Insurance adjusted? How are they adjusted?

8. How are plant and equipment asset accounts adjusted? Is the procedure similar to the adjustment of other asset and liability accounts at the end of an accounting period?

9. What is a *contra account* and why is it used?

10. How are liability accounts like Unearned Repair Revenue adjusted?

11. Explain the term *accruals*. Give examples of items that accrue.

12. Why is an adjusted trial balance prepared?

13. How is the adjusted trial balance used to prepare financial statements?

14. List the eight steps in the accounting cycle.

15. Which steps in the accounting cycle occur continuously throughout the accounting period?

16. Which steps in the accounting cycle occur only at the end of the accounting period? Explain how they differ from the other steps.

17. Give examples of revenue, expense, asset, and liability adjustments.

18. In general, income statement accounts accumulate amounts for a time period not exceeding one year. Why is this done?

19. Identify which types of general ledger accounts are temporary and which are permanent.

20. What is the income summary account and what is its purpose?

21. What is a post-closing trial balance and why is it prepared?

Exercises

EXERCISE 3–1   (LO1,2)   Adjusting Entries

The following are account balances of Graham Corporation:

Account Title	Amount in Unadjusted Trial Balance	Balance after Adjustment
Interest Receivable	$ -0-	$110
Prepaid Insurance	1,800	600
Interest Payable	-0-	90
Salaries Payable	-0-	450
Unearned Rent	700	200

Required:

a. Enter the unadjusted balance for each account in the following T-accounts: Interest Receivable, Prepaid Insurance, Interest Payable, Salaries Payable, Unearned Rent, Interest Earned, Rent Earned, Insurance Expense, Interest Expense, and Salaries Expense.

b. Reconstruct the adjusting entry that must have been recorded for each account.

c. Post these adjusting entries and agree ending balances in each T-account to the adjusted balances above.

d. List revenue and expense amounts for the period.

EXERCISE 3–2   (LO1,2)   Adjusting Entries

The trial balance of Lauer Corporation at December 31, 2015 follows, before and after the posting of adjusting entries.

	Trial Balance		Adjustments		Adjusted Trial Balance	
	Dr.	Cr.	Dr.	Cr.	Dr.	Cr.
Cash	$4,000				$4,000	
Accounts Receivable	5,000				5,000	
Prepaid Insurance	3,600				3,300	
Prepaid Rent	1,000				500	
Truck	6,000				6,000	
Accumulated Depreciation		$ -0-				$1,500
Accounts Payable		7,000				7,400
Salaries Payable						1,000
Unearned Rent		1,200				600
Share Capital		2,700				2,700
Revenue		25,000				25,000
Rent Earned						600
Advertising Expense	700				700	
Commissions Expense	2,000				2,000	
Depreciation Expense					1,500	
Insurance Expense					300	
Interest Expense	100				500	
Rent Expense	5,500				6,000	
Salaries Expense	8,000				9,000	
Totals	$35,900	$35,900			$38,800	$38,800

Required:

a. Indicate in the "Adjustments" column the debit or credit difference between the unadjusted trial balance and the adjusted trial balance.

b. Prepare in general journal format the adjusting entries that have been recorded. Include descriptions.

EXERCISE 3–3   (LO1,2)   Adjusting Entries

The following data are taken from an unadjusted trial balance at December 31, 2015:

Prepaid Rent	$ 600
Office Supplies	700
Income Taxes Payable	-0-
Unearned Commissions	1,500
Salaries Expense	5,000

Additional Information:

(a) The prepaid rent consisted of a payment for three months' rent at $200 per month for December 2015, January 2016, and February 2016.

(b) Office supplies on hand at December 31, 2015 amounted to $300.

(c) The estimated income taxes for 2015 are $5,000.

(d) All but $500 in the Unearned Commissions account has been earned in 2015.

(e) Salaries for the last three days of December amounting to $300 have not yet been recorded.

Required:

a. Prepare all necessary adjusting entries in general journal format.

b. Calculate the cumulative financial impact on assets, liabilities, equity, revenue and expense if these adjusting entries are not made.

EXERCISE 3–4   (LO1,2)   Adjusting Entries

The following are general ledger accounts extracted from the records of Bernard Inc. at December 31, 2015, its year-end ('Bal' = unadjusted balance):

110 ■ Financial Accounting and Adjusting Entries

```
    Prepaid Advertising              Accounts Payable              Share Capital
Bal.    1,000  |    500                       | Bal.  15,000              | Bal.  8,000
                                              |         200
                                              |         100          Supscription Revenue
     Unused Supplies                          |         400                |  5,000
Bal.     750   |    400                       |         800
                                                                     Advertising Expense
                                        Salaries Payable                  500  |
        Equipment                             |         700
Bal.   21,750  |                                                     Commissions Expense
                                      Unearned Subscriptions         Bal.  800  |
    Acc. Dep'n – Equipment              5,000  | Bal.  10,000
                |  Bal.  1,500                                       Dep'n Expense – Equipment
                |         250                                             250  |

                                                                     Maintenance Expense
                                                                          200  |

                                                                     Salaries Expense
                                                                     Bal.  9,500  |
                                                                           700  |

                                                                     Supplies Expense
                                                                     Bal.  2,500  |
                                                                           400  |

                                                                     Telephone Expense
                                                                          100  |

                                                                     Utilities Expense
                                                                          400  |
```

Required: Prepare in general journal format the adjusting entries that were posted. Include plausible descriptions/narratives for each adjustment.

EXERCISE 3–5 (LO1,2) Adjusting Entries

The following unadjusted accounts are extracted from the general ledger of A Corp. at December 31, 2015:

```
         Truck              Depreciation Expense – Truck        Acc. Dep'n – Truck
       10,000  |                    1,300  |                            |  1,300
```

Additional Information: The truck was purchased January 1, 2015. It has an estimated useful life of 4 years.

Required: Prepare the needed adjusting entry at December 31, 2015.

EXERCISE 3–6   (LO1,2)   Adjusting Entries

The following unadjusted accounts are taken from the records of B Corp. at December 31, 2015:

Bank Loan	Interest Expense	Interest Payable
12,000	1,100	100

Additional Information: The bank loan was received on January 1, 2015. It bears interest at 10 per cent.

Required: Prepare the adjusting entry at December 31, 2015.

EXERCISE 3–7   (LO1,2)   Adjusting Entries

The following general ledger accounts and additional information are taken from the records of Wolfe Corporation at the end of its fiscal year, December 31, 2015.

Cash	101	Unused Supplies	173	Advertising Exp.	610
Bal. 2,700		Bal. 700		Bal. 200	

Accounts Receivable	110	Share Capital	320	Salaries Expense	656
Bal. 2,000		Bal. 3,800		Bal. 4,500	

Prepaid Insurance	161	Repair Revenue	450	Telephone Expense	669
Bal. 1,200		Bal. 7,750		Bal. 250	

Additional Information:

(a) The prepaid insurance is for a one-year policy, effective July 1, 2015.

(b) A physical count indicated that $500 of supplies is still on hand.

(c) A $50 December telephone bill has been received but not yet recorded.

Required: Record all necessary adjusting entries in general journal format.

EXERCISE 3–8 (LO3) Prepare an Adjusted Trial Balance

After Bernard Inc. completed its first year of operations on December 31, 2015, the following adjusted account balances appeared in the general ledger.

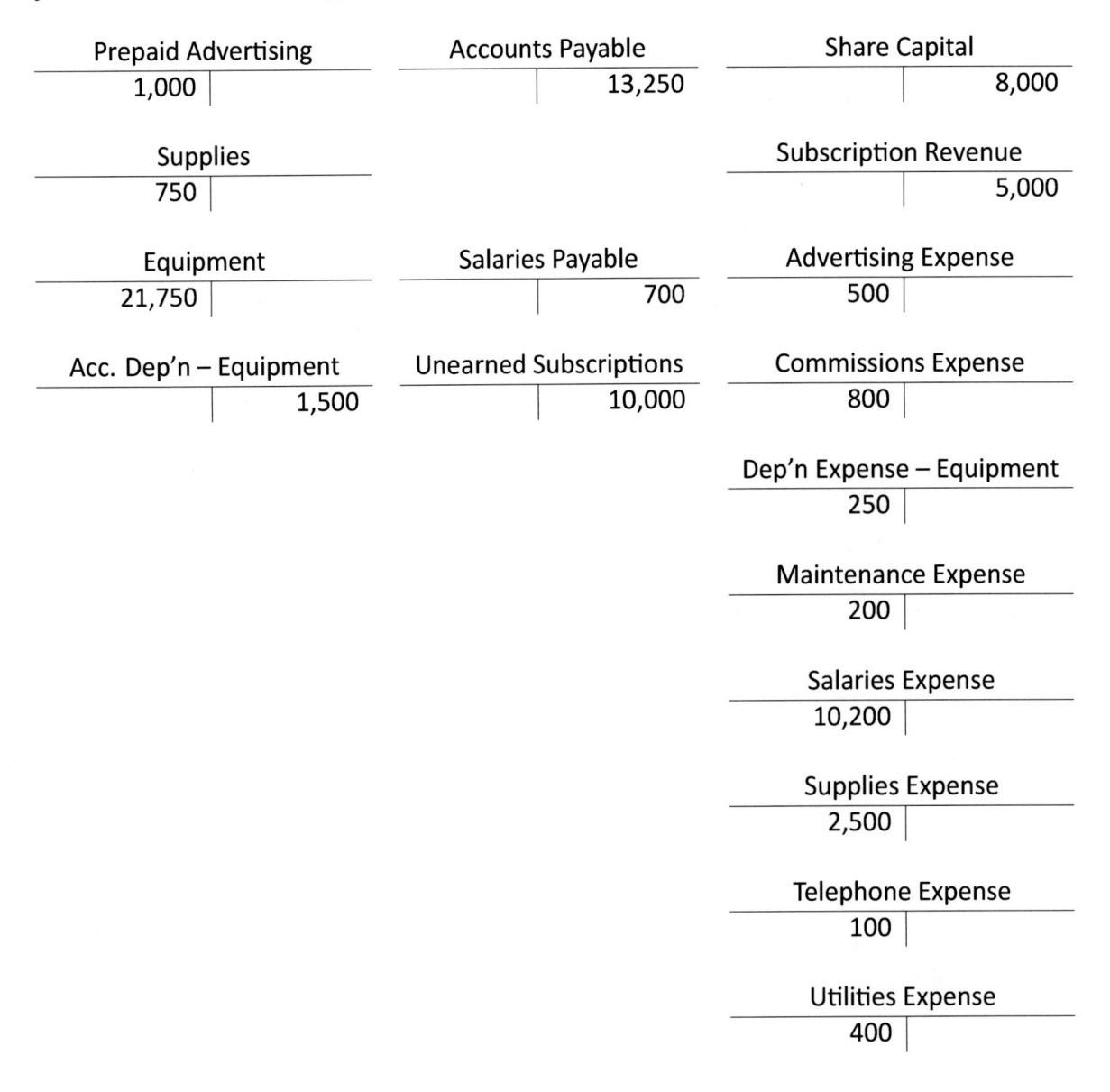

Account	Debit	Credit
Prepaid Advertising	1,000	
Supplies	750	
Equipment	21,750	
Acc. Dep'n – Equipment		1,500
Accounts Payable		13,250
Salaries Payable		700
Unearned Subscriptions		10,000
Share Capital		8,000
Subscription Revenue		5,000
Advertising Expense	500	
Commissions Expense	800	
Dep'n Expense – Equipment	250	
Maintenance Expense	200	
Salaries Expense	10,200	
Supplies Expense	2,500	
Telephone Expense	100	
Utilities Expense	400	

Required: Prepare an adjusted trial balance at December 31, 2015.

EXERCISE 3–9 (LO6) Prepare Closing Entries and a Post-Closing Trial Balance

The following alphabetized adjusted trial balance information is available for Willis Inc. at December 31, 2015. Assume all accounts have normal balances.

Accounts Payable	$ 4,400
Accounts Receivable	3,600
Accumulated Depreciation – Machinery	2,800
Accumulated Depreciation – Warehouse	8,000
Bank Loan	47,600
Cash	12,000
Commissions Earned	20,000
Depreciation Expense – Machinery	900
Depreciation Expense – Warehouse	1,200
Dividends	14,000
Insurance Expense	1,800
Interest Expense	2,365
Interest Payable	1,200
Land	15,000
Machinery	20,000
Retained Earnings	36,000
Salaries Expense	33,475
Salaries Payable	1,970
Share Capital	52,100
Subscriptions Revenue	17,630
Supplies	2,500
Supplies Expense	15,800
Unearned Fees	800
Utilities Expense	2,860
Warehouse	67,000

Required: Prepare closing entries and a post-closing trial balance.

Problems

PROBLEM 3–1 (LO1,2) **Adjusting Entries**

The following unrelated accounts are extracted from the records of Meekins Limited at December 31, its fiscal year-end:

		Balance Unadjusted	Balance Adjusted
(a)	Prepaid Rent	$ 900	$ 600
(b)	Wages Payable	500	700
(c)	Income Taxes Payable	-0-	1,000
(d)	Unearned Commissions Revenue	4,000	3,000
(e)	Other Unearned Revenue	25,000	20,000
(f)	Advertising Expense	5,000	3,500
(g)	Depreciation Expense – Equipment	-0-	500
(h)	Supplies Expense	850	625
(i)	Truck Operation Expense	4,000	4,500

Required: For each of the above unrelated accounts, prepare the most likely adjusting entry including plausible description/narrative.

PROBLEM 3–2 (LO1,2) **Adjusting Entries**

The unadjusted trial balance of Lukas Films Corporation includes the following account balances at December 31, 2015, its fiscal year-end. Assume all accounts have normal debit or credit balances as applicable.

Prepaid Rent	$ 1,500
Unused Supplies	-0-
Equipment	2,400
Unearned Advertising Revenue	1,000
Insurance Expense	900
Supplies Expense	600
Telephone Expense	825
Wages Expense	15,000

The following information applies at December 31:

a. A physical count of supplies indicates that $100 of supplies have not yet been used at December 31.

b. A $75 telephone bill for December has been received but not recorded.

c. One day of wages amounting to $125 remains unpaid and unrecorded at December 31; the amount will be included with the first Friday payment in January.

d. The equipment was purchased December 1; it is expected to last 2 years. No depreciation has yet been recorded.

e. The prepaid rent is for three months: December 2015, January 2016, and February 2016.

f. Half of the unearned advertising has been earned at December 31.

g. The $900 balance in Insurance Expense is for a one-year policy, effective August 1, 2015.

Required: Prepare all necessary adjusting entries at December 31, 2015. Descriptions are not needed.

PROBLEM 3–3   (LO1,2)   Adjusting Entries

The unadjusted trial balance of Mighty Fine Services Inc. includes the following account balances at December 31, 2015, its fiscal year-end. No adjustments have been recorded. Assume all accounts have normal debit or credit balances.

Notes Receivable	$10,000
Prepaid Rent	-0-
Prepaid Insurance	600
Unused Supplies	500
Bank Loan	5,000
Subscription Revenue	9,000
Rent Expense	3,900
Truck Operation Expense	4,000

The following information applies to the fiscal year-end:

(a) Accrued interest of $250 has not yet been recorded on the Notes Receivable.

(b) The $600 prepaid insurance is for a one-year policy, effective September 1, 2015.

(c) A physical count indicates that $300 of supplies is still on hand at December 31.

(d) Interest on the bank loan is paid on the fifteenth day of each month; the unrecorded interest for the last 15 days of December amounts to $25.

(e) The Subscription Revenue account consists of one $9,000 cash receipt for a 6-month subscription to the corporation's Computer Trends report; the subscription period began December 1, 2015.

(f) Three days of salary amounting to $300 remain unpaid and unrecorded at December 31.

(g) The rent expense account should reflect 12 months of rent. The monthly rent expense is $300.

(h) A bill for December truck operation expense has not yet been received; an amount of $400 is owed.

Required: Prepare all necessary adjusting entries at December 31, 2015. Descriptions are not needed.

PROBLEM 3–4 (LO1,2) Adjusting Entries

The following accounts are taken from the records of Bill Pitt Corp. at the end of its first 12 months of operations ended December 31, 2015, prior to any adjustments.

In addition to the balances in each set of accounts, additional data are provided for adjustment purposes if applicable. Treat each set of accounts independently of the others.

Truck	Depreciation Expense – Truck	Acc. Dep'n – Truck
6,000	600	600

(a) Additional information: The truck was purchased July 1; it has an estimated useful life of 4 years.

Cash	Unearned Rent	Rent Earned
600	-0-	600

(b) Additional information: A part of the office was sublet during the entire 12 months for $50 per month.

Unused Supplies	Supplies Expense
	1,250

(c) Additional information: A physical inventory indicated $300 of supplies still on hand at December 31.

Prepaid Rent	Rent Expense
1,200	4,400

(d) Additional information: The monthly rent is $400.

Wages Expense	Wages Payable
6,000	-0-

(e) Additional information: Unrecorded wages at December 31 amount to $250.

Bank Loan	Interest Expense	Interest Payable
8,000	600	100

(f) Additional information: The bank loan bears interest at 10 per cent. The money was borrowed on January 1, 2015.

Cash	Utilities Expense	Utilities Payable
1,000	1,200	200

(g) Additional information: The December bill has not yet been received or any accrual made; the amount owing at December 31 is estimated to be another $150.

Cash	Prepaid Insurance	Insurance Expense
1,200	600	600

(h) Additional information: A $1,200 one-year insurance policy had been purchased effective February 1, 2015; there is no other insurance policy in effect.

Unearned Rent Revenue	Rent Earned
900	-0-

(i) Additional information: The Unearned Rent Revenue balance applies to three months: November 2015, December 2015, and January 2016. $600 of the $900 has been earned as at December 31, 2015.

Cash	Other Unearned Revenue	Commissions Earned
25,200	-0-	25,200

(j) Additional information: $2,000 of the total $25,200 balance in commission revenue has not been earned at December 31, 2015.

Required: Prepare all necessary adjusting entries. Include descriptions/narratives.

PROBLEM 3–5   **(LO1,2,3)**   **Adjusting Accounts**

Roth Contractors Corporation was incorporated on December 1, 2015 and had the following transactions during December:

Part A

(a) Issued share capital for $5,000 cash.

(b) Paid $1,200 for three months' rent: December 2015; January and February 2016.

(c) Purchased a used truck for $10,000 on credit (recorded as an account payable).

(d) Purchased $1,000 of supplies on credit. These are expected to be used during the month (recorded as expense).

(e) Paid $1,800 for a one-year truck insurance policy, effective December 1.

(f) Billed a customer $4,500 for work completed to date.

(g) Collected $800 for work completed to date.

(h) Paid the following expenses: advertising, $350; interest, $100; telephone, $75; truck operation, $425; wages, $2,500.

(i) Collected $2,000 of the amount billed in (f) above.

(j) Billed customers $6,500 for work completed to date.

(k) Signed a $9,000 contract for work to be performed in January.

(l) Paid the following expenses: advertising, $200; interest, $150; truck operation, $375; wages, $2,500.

(m) Collected a $2,000 advance on work to be done in January (the policy of the corporation is to record such advances as revenue at the time they are received).

(n) Received a bill for $100 for electricity used during the month (recorded as utilities expense).

Required:

1. Open general ledger T-accounts for the following: Cash (101), Accounts Receivable (110), Prepaid Insurance (161), Prepaid Rent (162), Truck (184), Accounts Payable (210), Share Capital (320), Repair Revenue (450), Advertising Expense (610), Interest Expense (632), Supplies Expense (668), Telephone Expense (669), Truck Operation Expense (670), Utilities Expense (676), and Wages Expense (677).

2. Prepare journal entries to record the December transactions. Descriptions are not needed.

3. Post the entries to general ledger T-accounts.

Part B

At December 31, the following information is made available for the preparation of adjusting entries.

(o) One month of the Prepaid Insurance has expired.

(p) The December portion of the December 1 rent payment has expired.

(q) A physical count indicates that $350 of supplies is still on hand.

(r) The amount collected in transaction (m) is unearned at December 31.

(s) Three days of wages for December 29, 30, and 31 are unpaid; the unpaid amount of $1,500 will be included in the first Friday wages payment in January.

(t) The truck has an estimated useful life of 4 years.

Required:

4. Open additional general ledger T-accounts for the following: Supplies (173), Accumulated Depreciation – Truck (194), Wages Payable (237), Unearned Revenue (249), Depreciation Expense – Truck (624), Insurance Expense (631), and Rent Expense (654).

5. Prepare all necessary adjusting entries. Omit descriptions.

6. Post the entries to general ledger T-accounts and calculate balances.

7. Prepare an adjusted trial balance at December 31, 2015.

PROBLEM 3–6   (LO6)   Closing Accounts

Required:

1. Using the adjusted trial balance answer from Problem 3–5, journalize the appropriate closing entries (create additional accounts if required).

2. Prepare a post-closing trial balance.

PROBLEM 3–7   (LO1,2,3,4,5,6)   Comprehensive Accounting Cycle Review Problem

The unadjusted trial balance of Packer Corporation showed the following balances at the end of its first 12-month fiscal year ended August 31, 2015:

	Balance	
	Debits	Credits
Cash	$12,000	
Accounts Receivable	3,600	
Prepaid Insurance	-0-	
Supplies	2,500	
Land	15,000	
Building	60,000	
Furniture	3,000	
Equipment	20,000	
Accumulated Depreciation – Building		$ -0-
Accumulated Depreciation – Equipment		-0-
Accumulated Depreciation – Furniture		-0-
Accounts Payable		4,400
Salaries Payable		-0-
Interest Payable		-0-
Unearned Commissions Revenue		1,200
Unearned Subscriptions Revenue		800
Bank Loan		47,600
Share Capital		52,100
Retained Earnings		-0-
Income Summary		-0-
Commissions Earned		37,900
Subscriptions Revenue		32,700
Advertising Expense	4,300	
Depreciation Expense – Building	-0-	
Depreciation Expense – Equipment	-0-	
Depreciation Expense – Furniture	-0-	
Insurance Expense	1,800	
Interest Expense	2,365	
Salaries Expense	33,475	
Supplies Expense	15,800	
Utilities Expense	2,860	
Totals	$176,700	$176,700

At the end of August, the following additional information is available:

(a) The company's insurance coverage is provided by a single comprehensive 12-month policy that began on March 1, 2015.

(b) Supplies on hand total $2,850.

(c) The building has an estimated useful life of 50 years.

(d) The furniture has an estimated useful life of ten years.

(e) The equipment has an estimated useful life of 20 years.

(f) Interest of $208 on the bank loan for the month of August will be paid on September 1, when the regular $350 payment is made.

(g) A review of the unadjusted balance in the unearned commissions revenue account indicates the unearned balance should be $450.

(h) A review of the unadjusted balance in the subscription revenue account reveals that $2,000 has not been earned.

(i) Salaries that have been earned by employees in August but are not due to be paid to them until the next payday (in September) amount to $325.

Required:

1. Set up necessary general ledger T-accounts and record their unadjusted balances. Create and assign account numbers that you deem appropriate.

2. Prepare the adjusting entries. Descriptions are not needed.

3. Post the adjusting entries to the general ledger T-accounts and calculate balances.

4. Prepare an adjusted trial balance at August 31, 2015.

5. Prepare an income statement and balance sheet.

6. Prepare and post the closing entries.

7. Prepare a post-closing trial balance.

Chapter 4

The Classified Balance Sheet and Related Disclosures

Chapters 1 through 3 discussed and illustrated the steps in the accounting cycle. They also discussed the concepts, assumptions, and procedures that provide a framework for financial accounting as a whole. Chapter 4 expands upon the content and presentation of financial statements. It reinforces what has been learned in previous chapters and introduces the classification or grouping of accounts on the balance sheet. Chapter 4 expands on notes to the financial statements, the auditor's report, and the management's responsibility report which are all integral to meeting disclosure requirements.

Chapter 4 Learning Objectives

LO1 – Explain the importance of and challenges related to basic financial statement disclosure.

LO2 – Explain and prepare a classified balance sheet.

LO3 – Explain the purpose and content of notes to financial statements.

LO4 – Explain the purpose and content of the auditor's report.

LO5 – Explain the purpose and content of the report that describes management's responsibility for financial statements.

Concept Self-Check

Use the following as a self-check while working through Chapter 4.

1. What shapes and limits an accountant's measurement of wealth?
2. Are financial statements primarily intended for internal or external users?
3. What is a classified balance sheet?
4. What are the classifications within a classified balance sheet?
5. What are current assets?
6. What are non-current assets?
7. What are current liabilities?

8. What are long-term liabilities?

9. What is the current-portion of a long-term liability?

10. What is the purpose and content of the notes to the financial statements?

11. What is the purpose and content of the auditor's report?

12. What is the purpose and content of the report that describes management's responsibility for financial statements?

NOTE: The purpose of these questions is to prepare you for the concepts introduced in the chapter. Your goal should be to answer each of these questions as you read through the chapter. If, when you complete the chapter, you are unable to answer one or more the Concept Self-Check questions, go back through the content to find the answer(s). Solutions are not provided to these questions.

4.1 Financial Statement Disclosure Decisions

LO1 – Explain the importance of and challenges related to basic financial statement disclosure.

Financial statements communicate information, with a focus on the needs of financial statement users such as a company's investors and creditors. Accounting information should make it easier for management to allocate resources and for shareholders to evaluate management. A key objective of financial statements is to fairly present the entity's economic resources, obligations, equity, and financial performance.

Fulfilling these objectives is challenging. Accountants must make a number of subjective decisions about how to apply generally accepted accounting principles. For example, they must decide how to measure wealth and how to apply recognition criteria. They must also make practical cost-benefit decisions about how much information is useful to disclose. Some of these decisions are discussed in the following section.

Making Accounting Measurements

Economists often define wealth as an increase or decrease in the entity's ability to purchase goods and services. Accountants use a more specific measurement — they consider only increases and decreases resulting from actual transactions. If a transaction has not taken place, they do not record a change in wealth.

The accountant's measurement of wealth is shaped and limited by the generally accepted accounting principles introduced and discussed in Chapter 1, including cost, the monetary unit, the business entity, timeliness, recognition, and going concern. These principles mean that accountants record transactions in one currency (for example, dollars). They assume the monetary currency retains its purchasing power. Changes in market values of assets are generally not recorded. The entity is expected to continue operating into the foreseeable future.

Economists, on the other hand, do recognize changes in market value. For example, if an entity purchased land for $100,000 that subsequently increased in value to $125,000, economists would recognize a $25,000 increase in wealth. International Financial Reporting Standards generally do not recognize this increase until the entity actually disposes of the asset; accountants would continue to value the land at its $100,000 purchase cost. This practice is based on the application of the cost principle, which is a part of GAAP.

Economic wealth is also affected by changes in the purchasing power of the dollar. For example, if the entity has cash of $50,000 at the beginning of a time period and purchasing power drops by 10% because of inflation, the entity has lost wealth because the $50,000 can purchase only $45,000 of goods and services. Conversely, the entity gains wealth if purchasing power increases by 10%. In this case, the same $50,000 can purchase $55,000 worth of goods and services. However, accountants do not record any changes because the monetary unit principle assumes that the currency unit is a stable measure.

Qualities of Accounting Information

Financial statements are focused primarily on the needs of external users. To provide information to these users, accountants make cost-benefit judgments. They use materiality considerations to decide how particular items of information should be recorded and disclosed. For example, if the costs associated with financial information preparation are too high or if an amount is not sufficiently large or important, a business might implement a materiality policy for various types of asset purchases to guide how such costs are to be recorded. For example, a business might have a materiality policy for the purchase of office equipment whereby anything costing $100 or less is expensed immediately instead of recorded as an asset. In this type of situation, purchases of $100 or less are recorded as an expense instead of an asset to avoid having to record depreciation expense, a cost-benefit consideration that will not impact decisions made by external users of the business's financial statements.

Accountants must also make decisions based on whether information is useful. Is it comparable to prior periods? Is it verifiable? Is it presented with clarity and conciseness to make it understandable? Readers' perception of the usefulness of accounting information is determined by how well those who prepare financial statements address these qualitative considerations.

4.2 Classified Balance Sheet

LO2 – Explain and prepare a classified balance sheet.

The accounting cycle and double-entry accounting have been the focus of the preceding chapters. This chapter focuses on the presentation of financial statements, including how financial information is *classified* (the way accounts are grouped) and what is disclosed.

A common order for the presentation of financial statements is:

1. Income statement
2. Statement of changes in equity
3. Balance sheet
4. Statement of cash flows
5. Notes to the financial statements

In addition, the financial statements are often accompanied by an auditor's report and a statement entitled "Management's Responsibility for Financial Statements." Each of these items will be discussed below. Financial statement information must be disclosed for the most recent year with the prior year for comparison.

Because external users of financial statements have no access to the entity's accounting records, it is important that financial statements be organized in a manner that is easy to understand. Thus, financial data are grouped into useful, similar categories within *classified financial statements*, as discussed below.

The Classified Balance Sheet

A **classified balance sheet** organizes the asset and liability accounts into categories. The previous chapters used an **unclassified balance sheet** which included only three broad account groupings: assets, liabilities, and equity. The classification of asset and liability accounts into meaningful categories is designed to facilitate the analysis of balance sheet information by external users. Assets and liabilities are classified as either *current* or *non-current*. Another common term for *non-current* is *long-term*. Non-current assets, also referred to as long-term assets, can be classified further into *long-term investments*; *property, plant and equipment*; and *intangible assets*. The asset and liability classifications are summarized below:

Assets	Liabilities
Non-current or long-term assets:	Non-current or long-term liabilities
Long-term investments	
Property, plant and equipment (PPE)	
Intangible assets	

Current Assets

Current assets are those resources that the entity expects to convert to cash, or to consume during the next year or within the operating cycle of the entity, whichever is longer. Examples of current assets include:

- cash, comprising paper currency and coins, deposits at banks, cheques, and money orders.
- short-term investments, the investment of cash that will not be needed immediately, in short-term, interest-bearing notes that are easily convertible into cash.
- accounts receivable that are due to be collected within one year.
- notes receivable, usually formalized account receivables — written promises to pay specified amounts with interest, and due to be collected within one year.
- merchandise inventory that is expected to be sold within one year.

The current asset category also includes accounts whose future benefits are expected to expire in a short period of time. These are not expected to be converted into cash, and include:

- prepaid expenses that will expire within the next year, usually consisting of advance payments for insurance, rent, and other similar items.
- supplies on hand at the end of an accounting year that will be used during the next year.

On the balance sheet, current assets are normally reported before non-current assets. They are listed by decreasing levels of **liquidity** — their ability to be converted into cash. Therefore, cash appears first under the current asset heading since it is already liquid.

Non-current Assets

Non-current assets are assets that will be useful for more than one year; they are sometimes referred to as **long-lived assets**. Non-current assets include property, plant, and equipment (PPE) items used in the operations of the business. Some examples of PPE are: a) land, b) buildings, c) equipment, and d) motor vehicles such as trucks.

Other types of non-current assets include long-term investments and intangible assets. **Long-term investments** are held for more than one year or the operating cycle and include long-term notes receivable and investments in shares and bonds. **Intangible assets** are resources that do not have a physical form and whose value comes from the rights held by the owner. They are used over the long term to produce or sell products and services and include copyrights, patents, trademarks, and franchises.

Current Liabilities

Current liabilities are obligations that must be paid within the next 12 months or within the entity's next operating cycle, whichever is longer. They are shown first in the liabilities section of the balance sheet and listed in order of their due dates, with any bank loans shown first. Examples of current liabilities include:

- bank loans (or notes payable) that are payable on demand or due within the next 12 months
- accounts payable
- accrued liabilities such as interest payable and wages payable
- unearned revenue
- the current portion of long-term liabilities
- income taxes payable.

The **current portion of a long-term liability** is the principal amount of a long-term liability that is to be paid within the next 12 months. For example, assume a $24,000 note payable issued on January 1, 2015 where principal is repaid at the rate of $1,000 per month over two years. The current portion of this note on the January 31, 2015 balance sheet would be $12,000 (calculated as 12 months X $1,000/month). The remaining principal would be reported on the balance sheet as a long-term liability.

Non-Current or Long-Term Liabilities

Non-current liabilities, also referred to as long-term liabilities, are borrowings that do not require repayment for more than one year, such as the long-term portion of a bank loan or a mortgage. A **mortgage** is a liability that is secured by real estate.

Equity

The equity section of the classified balance sheet consists of two major accounts: share capital and retained earnings.

The following illustrates the presentation of Big Dog Carworks Corp.'s classified balance sheet after several years of operation.

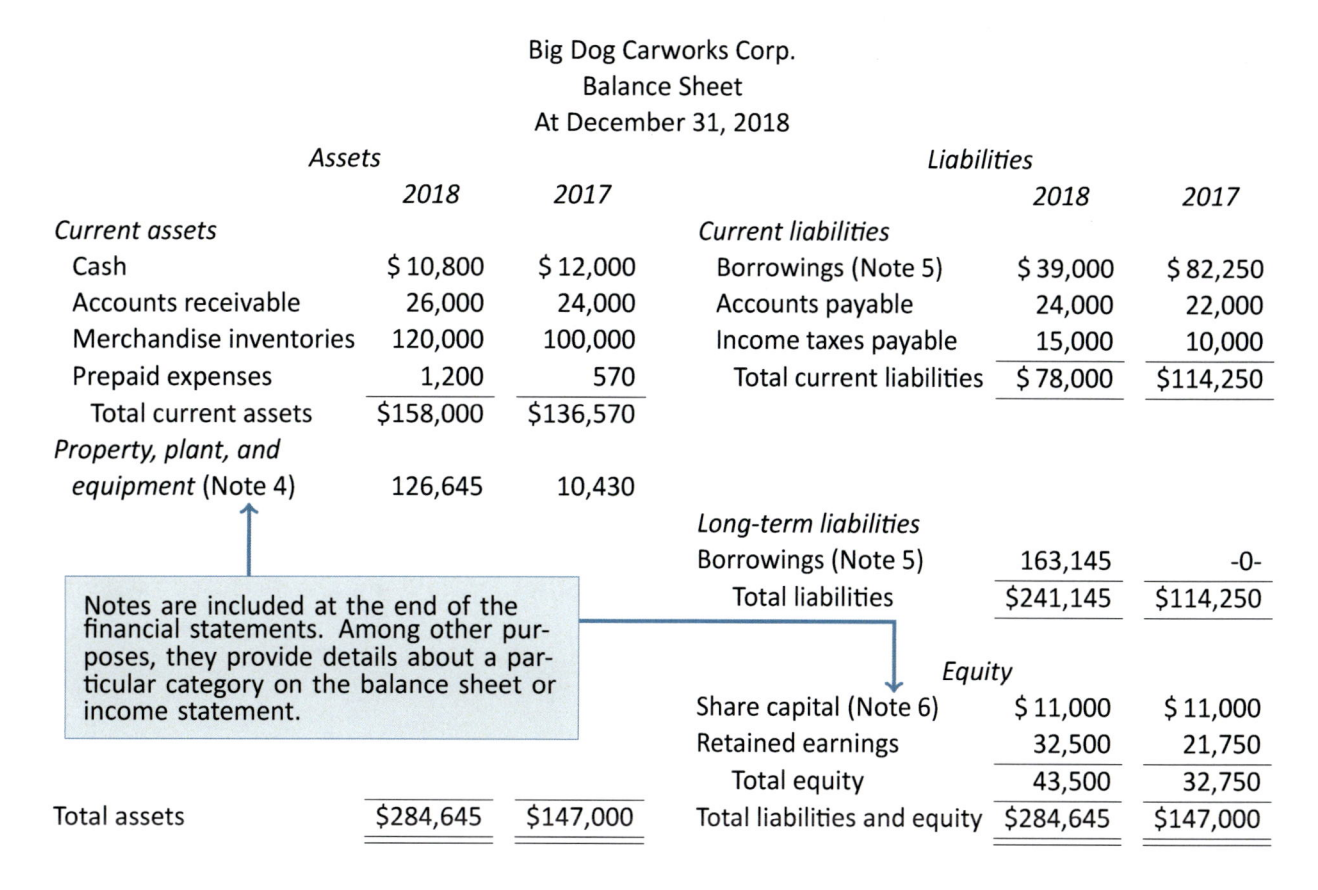

Big Dog Carworks Corp.
Balance Sheet
At December 31, 2018

Assets	2018	2017	Liabilities	2018	2017
Current assets			*Current liabilities*		
Cash	$ 10,800	$ 12,000	Borrowings (Note 5)	$ 39,000	$ 82,250
Accounts receivable	26,000	24,000	Accounts payable	24,000	22,000
Merchandise inventories	120,000	100,000	Income taxes payable	15,000	10,000
Prepaid expenses	1,200	570	Total current liabilities	$ 78,000	$114,250
Total current assets	$158,000	$136,570			
Property, plant, and equipment (Note 4)	126,645	10,430			
			Long-term liabilities		
			Borrowings (Note 5)	163,145	-0-
			Total liabilities	$241,145	$114,250
			Equity		
			Share capital (Note 6)	$ 11,000	$ 11,000
			Retained earnings	32,500	21,750
			Total equity	43,500	32,750
Total assets	$284,645	$147,000	Total liabilities and equity	$284,645	$147,000

> Notes are included at the end of the financial statements. Among other purposes, they provide details about a particular category on the balance sheet or income statement.

The balance sheet can be presented in the **account form** balance sheet, as shown above where liabilities and equities are presented to the right of the assets. An alternative is the **report form** balance sheet where liabilities and equity are presented below the assets.

The Classified Income Statement

Recall that the income statement summarizes a company's revenues less expenses over a period of time. An income statement for BDCC was presented in Chapter 1 as copied below.

Big Dog Carworks Corp.
Income Statement
For the Month Ended January 31, 2015

Revenues		
Repair revenues		$10,000
Expenses		
Rent expense	$1,600	
Salaries expense	3,500	
Supplies expense	2,000	
Fuel expense	700	
Total expenses		7,800
Net income		$2,200

The format used above was sufficient to disclose relevant financial information for Big Dog's simple start-up operations. Like the classified balance sheet, an income statement can be classified as well as prepared with comparative information. The classified income statement will be discussed in detail in Chapter 5.

Regardless of the type of financial statement, any items that are *material* must be disclosed separately so users will not otherwise be misled. Materiality is a matter for judgment. Office supplies of $2,000 per month used by BDCC in January 2015 might be a material amount and therefore disclosed as a separate item on the income statement for the month ended January 31, 2015. If annual revenues grew to $1 million, $2,000 per month for supplies might be considered immaterial. These expenditures would then be grouped with other similar items and disclosed as a single amount.

An exploration is available on the Lyryx site. Log into your Lyryx course to run Classified Balance Sheets.

4.3 Notes to Financial Statements

> **LO3** – Explain the purpose and content of notes to financial statements.

As an integral part of its financial statements, a company provides *notes to the financial statements*. In accordance with the disclosure principle, **notes to the financial statements** provide relevant details that are not included in the body of the financial statements. For instance, details about property, plant, and equipment are shown in Note 4 in the following sample notes to the financial statements. The notes help external users understand and analyze the financial statements.

Although a detailed discussion of disclosures that might be included as part of the notes is beyond the scope of an introductory financial accounting course, a simplified example of note disclosure is shown below for Big Dog Carworks Corp.

Big Dog Carworks Corp.
Notes to the Financial Statements
For the Year Ended December 31, 2018

1. Nature of operations

   The principal activity of Big Dog Carworks Corp. is the servicing and repair of vehicles.

2. General information and statement of compliance with IFRS

   Big Dog Carworks Corp. is a limited liability company incorporated and domiciled in Canada. Its registered office and principal place of business is 123 Fox Street, Owlseye, Alberta, T1K 0L1, Canada. Big Dog Carworks Corp.'s shares are listed on the Toronto Stock Exchange.

   The financial statements of Big Dog Carworks Inc. have been prepared in accordance with International Financial Reporting Standards (IFRS) as issued the International Accounting Standards Boards (IASB).

   The financial statements for the year ended December 31, 2018 were approved and authorised for issue by the board of directors on March 17, 2019.

3. Summary of accounting policies

   The financial statements have been prepared using the significant accounting policies and measurement bases summarized below.

   (a) Revenue

   Revenue arises from the rendering of service. It is measured by reference to the fair value of consideration received or receivable.

   (b) Operating expenses

   Operating expenses are recognized in the income statement upon utilization of the service or at the date of their origin.

   (c) Borrowing costs

   Borrowing costs directly attributable to the acquisition, construction, or production of property, plant, and equipment are capitalized during the period of time that is necessary to complete and prepare the asset for its intended use or sale. Other borrowing costs are expensed in the period in which they are incurred and reported as interest expense.

   (d) Property, plant, and equipment

   Land held for use in production or administration is stated at cost. Other property, plant, and equipment are initially recognized at acquisition cost plus any costs directly attributable to bringing the assets to the locations and conditions necessary to be employed in operations. They are subsequently measured using the cost model: cost less subsequent depreciation.

   Depreciation is recognized on a straight-line basis to write down the cost, net of estimated residual value. The following useful lives are applied:

   Buildings: 25 years

Equipment: 10 years

Truck: 5 years

Residual value estimates and estimates of useful life are updated at least annually.

(e) Income taxes

Current income tax liabilities comprise those obligations to fiscal authorities relating to the current or prior reporting periods that are unpaid at the reporting date. Calculation of current taxes is based on tax rates and tax laws that have been enacted or substantively enacted by the end of the reporting period.

(f) Share capital

Share capital represents the nominal value of shares that have been issued.

(g) Estimation uncertainty

When preparing the financial statements, management undertakes a number of judgments, estimates, and assumptions about the recognition and measurement of assets, liabilities, income, and expenses. Information about estimates and assumptions that have the most significant effect on recognition and measurement of assets, liabilities, income, and expenses is provided below. Actual results may be substantially different.

4. Property, plant, and equipment

Details of the company's property, plant, and equipment and their carrying amounts at December 31 are as follows:

	Land	Building	2018 Equip.	Truck	Total	2017 Total
Gross Carrying Amount						
Balance, January 1	$ -0-	$ -0-	$3,000	$8,000	$ 11,000	$11,000
Additions	30,000	90,000			120,000	
Balance, January 31	30,000	90,000	3,000	8,000	131,000	11,000
Depreciation						
Balance, January 1		-0-	90	480	570	285
Depreciation for year		3,500	45	240	3,785	285
Balance, December 31		3,500	135	720	4,355	570
Carrying Amount						
December 31	$30,000	$86,500	$2,865	$7,280	$126,645	$ 10,430

> These amounts agree to the amount of PPE shown in the assets section of BDCC's balance sheet.

5. Borrowings

Borrowings include the following financial liabilities measured at cost:

	Current		Non-Current	
	2018	2017	2018	2017
Demand blank loan	$ 20,000	$ 52,250	$ -0-	$ -0-
Subordinated shareholder loan	13,762	30,000	-0-	-0-
Mortgage	5,238	-0-	163,145	-0-
Total carrying amount	$39,000	$82,250	$163,145	$ -0-

The bank loan is due on demand and bears interest at 6% per year. It is secured by accounts receivable and inventories of the company.

The shareholder loan is due on demand, non-interest bearing, and unsecured.

The mortgage is payable to First Bank of Capitalville. It bears interest at 5% per year and is amortized over 25 years. Monthly payments including interest are $960. It is secured by land and buildings owned by the company. The terms of the mortgage will be re-negotiated in 2021.

6. Share capital

The share capital of Big Dog Carworks Corp. consists of fully-paid common shares with a stated value of $1 each. All shares are eligible to receive dividends, have their capital repaid, and represent one vote at the annual shareholders' meeting. There were no shares issued during 2017 or 2018.

4.4 Auditor's Report

> LO4 – Explain the purpose and content of the auditor's report.

Financial statements are often accompanied by an auditor's report. An **audit** is an external examination of a company's financial statement information and its system of *internal controls*.

Internal controls are the processes instituted by management of a company to direct, monitor, and measure the accomplishment of its objectives. This includes the prevention and detection of fraud and error. An audit seeks not certainty, but reasonable assurance that the financial statement information is not materially misstated.

The auditor's report is a structured statement issued by an independent examiner, usually a professional accountant, who is contracted by the company to report the audit's findings to the company's board of directors. An audit report provides some assurance to present and potential investors and creditors that the company's financial statements are trustworthy. Therefore, it is a useful means to reduce the risk of their financial decisions.

An example of an unqualified auditor's report for BDCC is shown below, along with a brief description of each component. Put in simple terms, an **unqualified auditor's report** indicates that the financial statements are truthful and a **qualified auditor's report** is one that indicates the financial statements are not or may not be truthful.

INDEPENDENT AUDITOR'S REPORT

The auditor's independence from the company is stated.

The Board of Directors of Big Dog Carworks Corp.
Owiseye, Alberta

The audit report is addressed to the board.

I have audited the accompanying financial statements of Big Dog Carworks Corp., which comprise the balance sheet as at December 31, 2018, the income statement, statement of changes in equity, and statement of cash flows for the year then ended, and a summary of significant accounting policies and other explanatory information.

The audited information is described.

Management Responsibility for the Financial Statements

Management is responsible for the preparation and fair presentation of these financial statements in accordance with Canadian generally accepted accounting principles, and for such internal control as management determines is necessary to enable the preparation of financial statements that are free from material misstatement, whether due to fraud or error.

Management's responsibilities are described.

Auditor's Responsibility

My responsibility is to express an opinion on the financial statements based on my audit. I conducted my audit in accordance with Canadian generally accepted auditing standards. Those standards require that I comply with ethical requirements, and plan and perform the audit to obtain reasonable assurance about whether the financial statements are free from material misstatement.

The auditor's responsibilities and the audit standards are described.

An audit involves performing procedures to obtain audit evidence about the amounts and disclosures in the financial statements. The procedures selected depend on the auditor's judgement, including assessment of the risks of material misstatement of the financial statements, whether due to fraud or error. In making those risk assessments, the auditor considers internal control relevant to the entity's preparation and fair presentation of the financial statements in order to design audit procedures that are appropriate in the circumstances, but not for the purpose of expressing an opinion on the effectiveness of the entity's internal control. An audit also includes evaluation of the appropriateness of accounting policies used and the reasonableness of accounting estimates made by management, as well as evaluating the overall presentation of the financial statement.

The audit procedures are described in general terms.

I believe that the audit evidence I have obtained is sufficient and appropriate to provide a basis for my audit opinion.

A conclusion about the adequacy of audit evidence is stated.

Opinion

In my opinion, the financial statements present fairly, in all material aspects, the financial position of Big Dog Carworks Corp. as at December 31, 2018, and its financial performance and its cash flows for the year then ended in accordance with Canadian generally accepted accounting principles.

An opinion is expressed about the financial statement information.

(signed)
H. K. Walker, CPA
March 15, 2019
Anywhereville, AB

The report is signed by the auditor and dated.

4.5 Management's Responsibility for Financial Statements

LO5 – Explain the purpose and content of the report that describes management's responsibility for financial statements.

The final piece of information often included with the annual financial statements is a statement describing management's responsibility for the accurate preparation and presentation of financial statements. This statement underscores the division of duties involved with the publication of financial statements. Management is responsible for preparing the financial statements, including estimates that underlie the accounting numbers. An example of an estimate is the useful life of long-lived assets in calculating depreciation.

The independent auditor is responsible for examining the financial statement information as prepared by management, including the reasonableness of estimates, and then expressing an opinion on their accuracy. In some cases, the auditor may assist management with aspects of financial statement preparation. For instance, the auditor may provide guidance on how a new accounting standard will affect financial statement presentation or other information disclosure. Ultimately, however, the preparation of financial statements is management's responsibility.

An example of a statement describing management's responsibility for the preparation and presentation of annual financial statements is shown below.

MANAGEMENT'S RESPONSIBILITY FOR FINANCIAL STATEMENTS

Management's responsibility for all aspects of financial statement presentation and disclosure is expressly stated.

The accompanying financial statements of the company are the responsibility of management. The financial statements were prepared by management in accordance with accounting principles generally accepted in Canada, applied on a consistent basis, and conform in all material respects with International Accounting Standards. The significant accounting policies, which management believes are appropriate for the company, are described in Note 3 to the financial statements.

Management's responsibility for estimates used and maintenance of internal controls is acknowledged.

Management is responsible for the integrity and objectivity of the financial statements. Estimates are necessary in the preparation of these statements and, based on careful judgements, have been properly reflected. Management has established systems of internal control that are designed to provide reasonable assurance that assets are safeguarded from loss or unauthorized use, and to produce reliable accounting records for the preparation of financial information.

The board of directors' and audit committee's respective roles are explained.	The board of directors is responsible for ensuring that management fulfils its responsibilities for financial reporting and internal control. The audit committee of the board, which is comprised solely of directors who are not employees of the company, is appointed by the board of directors annually. The audit committee of the board meets regularly with financial management of the company and with the shareholders' independent auditor to discuss internal controls, audit matters, including audit scope and auditor remuneration, and financial reporting issues. The independent shareholders' auditor has unrestricted access to the audit committee. The audit committee reviews the annual financial statements and reporting to the board, and makes recommendations with respect to their acceptance. The audit committee also makes recommendations to the board with respect to the appointment and remuneration of the company's auditor.
Management acknowledges its obligation to oversee all aspects of the company's operations in a legal and ethical manner.	Management recognizes its responsibility for conducting the company's affairs in compliance with established financial standards and applicable laws, and maintains proper standards of conduct for its activities.
The officer responsible for the financial affairs of the company signs and dates the statement.	(signed) Bill Brown II, Chief Financial Officer March 3, 2019

Summary of Chapter 4 Learning Objectives

LO1 – Explain the importance of and challenges related to basic financial statement disclosure.

The objective of financial statements is to communicate information to meet the needs of external users. In addition to recording and reporting verifiable financial information, accountants make decisions regarding how to measure transactions. Applying GAAP can present challenges when judgment must be applied as in the case of cost-benefit decisions and materiality.

LO2 – Explain and prepare a classified balance sheet.

A classified balance sheet groups assets and liabilities as follows:

Assets:	Liabilities:
Current assets	Current liabilities
Non-current assets: - Property, plant, and equipment - Long-term investments - Intangible assets	Non-current or long-term liabilities

Current assets are those that are used within one year or one operating cycle, whichever is longer, and include cash, accounts receivables, and supplies. Non-current assets are used beyond one year or one operating cycle. There are three types of non-current assets: property, plant, and equipment (PPE), long-term investments, and intangible assets. Long-term investments include investments in shares and bonds. Intangible assets are rights held by the owner and do not have a physical substance; they include copyrights, patents, franchises, and trademarks. Current liabilities must be paid within one year or one operating cycle, whichever is longer. Long-term liabilities are paid beyond one year or one operating cycle. Income statements are also classified (discussed in Chapter 5).

LO3 – Explain the purpose and content of notes to financial statements.

In accordance with the GAAP principle of full disclosure, relevant details not contained in the body of financial statements are included in the accompanying notes to financial statements. Notes would include a summary of accounting policies, details regarding property, plant, and equipment assets, and specifics about liabilities such as the interest rates and repayment terms.

LO4 – Explain the purpose and content of the auditor's report.

An audit as it relates to the auditor's report is an external examination of a company's financial statement information and its system of internal controls. Internal controls are the processes instituted by management of a company to direct, monitor, and measure the accomplishment of its objectives including the prevention and detection of fraud and error. The auditor's report provides some assurance that the financial statements are trustworthy. In simple terms, an unqualified auditor's report indicates that the financial statements are truthful and a qualified auditor's report is one that indicates the financial statements are not or may not be truthful.

LO5 – Explain the purpose and content of the report that describes management's responsibility for financial statements.

This report makes a statement describing management's responsibility for the accurate preparation and presentation of financial statements.

Discussion Questions

Refer to the Big Dog Carworks Corp. financial statements for the year ended December 31, 2018 and other information included in this chapter to answer the following questions.

1. Identify the economic resources of Big Dog Carworks Corp. in its financial statements.

2. What comprise the financial statements of BDCC?

3. Why does BDCC prepare financial statements?

4. From the balance sheet at December 31, 2018 extract the appropriate amounts to complete the following accounting equation:

    ASSETS = LIABILITIES + EQUITY

5. If ASSETS − LIABILITIES = NET ASSETS, how much is net assets at December 31, 2018? Is net assets synonymous with equity?

6. What types of assets are reported by Big Dog Carworks Corp.? What types of liabilities?

7. What kind of assumptions is made by Big Dog Carworks Corp. about asset capitalisation? Over what periods of time are assets being amortized?

8. What adjustments might management make to the financial information when preparing the annual financial statements? Consider the following categories:

    a. Current asset accounts.

    b. Non-current asset accounts.

    c. Current liability accounts.

    d. Non-current liability accounts.

    Indicate several examples in each category. Use the BDCC balance sheet and notes 3 and 5 for ideas.

9. What are the advantages of using a classified balance sheet? Why are current accounts shown before non-current ones on BDCC's balance sheet?

10. How does Big Dog Carworks Corp. make it easier to compare information from one time period to another?

11. Who is the auditor of BDCC? What does the auditor's report tell you about BDCC's financial statements? Does it raise any concerns?

12. What does the auditor's report indicate about the application of generally accepted accounting principles in BDCC's financial statements?

13. What is BDCC management's responsibility with respect to the company's financial statements? Do the financial statements belong to management? the auditor? the board of directors? shareholders?

Exercises

EXERCISE 4–1   (LO2)   Classified Balance Sheet

The following accounts and account balances are taken from the records of Joyes Enterprises Ltd. at December 31, 2016, its fiscal year-end.

	Dr.	Cr.
Accounts Receivable	$8,000	
Accounts Payable		$7,000
Accumulated Depreciation – Buildings		1,000
Accumulated Depreciation – Equipment		4,000
Bank Loan (due 2017)		5000
Buildings	25,000	
Cash	2,000	
Dividends Declared	1,000	
Equipment	20,000	
Income Tax Payable		3,000
Land	5,000	
Merchandise Inventory	19,000	
Mortgage Payable (due 2019)		5,000
Prepaid Insurance	1,000	
Share Capital		48,000
Retained Earnings, Jan. 1 2016	-0-	2,000
Totals	$81,000	$75,000
Net Income	-0-	6,000
Totals	-0-	-0-

Required:

a. Using the above information, prepare a classified balance sheet.

b. Does Joyes Enterprises Ltd. have sufficient resources to meet its obligations in the upcoming year?

c. Calculate the proportion of shareholders' to creditors' claims on the assets of Joyes.

EXERCISE 4–2   (LO2,3)   Classified Balance Sheet

The following balance sheet was prepared for Abbey Limited:

Abbey Limited
Balance Sheet
As at November 30, 2015

Assets			Liabilities		
Current			*Current*		
Cash	$1,000		Accounts Payable	$5,600	
Accounts Receivable	6,000		Notes Payable (due 2016)	2,000	
Building	12,000		Bank Loan (due 2022)	1,000	
Merchandise Inventory	3,000		Total Current Liabilities		$8,600
Total Current Assets		$22,000			
Non-current			*Non-current*		
Short-Term Investments	3,000		Mortgage Payable (due 2023)	7,000	
Equipment	1,500		Retained Earnings	1,000	
Unused Office Supplies	100		Salaries Payable	250	
Truck	1,350		Total Non-current Liabilities		8,250
Total Non-current Assets		5,950	Total Liabilities		16,850
			Equity		
			Share Capital		11,100
Total Assets		$27,950	Total Liabilities and Assets		$27,950

Required:

a. Identify the errors that exist in the balance sheet of Abbey Limited and why you consider this information incorrect.

b. Prepare a corrected, classified balance sheet.

c. Based on the balance sheet categories, what additional information should be disclosed in the notes to the financial statements?

Problems

PROBLEM 4–1   (LO2)   Classified Balance Sheet

The following list of accounts is taken from the records of the Norman Company Ltd. at December 31, 2015:

Account Title	Balance
Accounts Payable	$125
Accounts Receivable	138
Building	400
Cash	250
Share Capital	400
Equipment	140
Land	115
Mortgage Payable (due 2022)	280
Bank Loan, due within 90 days	110
Notes Receivable, due within 90 days	18
Prepaid Insurance	12
Retained Earnings	214
Salaries Payable	14
Unused Office Supplies	70

Required: Prepare a classified balance sheet.

PROBLEM 4–2   (LO2)   Classified Balance Sheet

The following adjusted trial balance has been extracted from the records of Dark Edge Sports Inc. at December 31, 2015, its second fiscal year-end.

	Account Balances	
	Dr.	Cr.
Accounts Payable		$8,350
Accounts Receivable	$18,700	
Accumulated Depreciation – Equipment		2,000
Advertising Expense	7,200	
Bank Loan, due May 31, 2016		10,000
Cash	1,500	
Depreciation Expense	1,100	
Dividends	600	
Equipment	12,500	
Income Taxes Expense	2,300	
Income Taxes Payable		4,600
Insurance Expense	1,200	
Interest and Bank Charges Expense	1,300	
Prepaid Insurance	1,300	
Prepaid Rent	600	
Retained Earnings		2,000
Rent Expense	17,950	
Revenue		80,000
Salaries Expense	39,000	
Share Capital		3,000
Telephone Expense	1,100	
Utilities Expense	3,600	
Totals	$109,950	$109,950

Note: No shares were issued during 2015.

Required:

1. Calculate net income for year ended December 31, 2015.

2. Prepare a statement of changes in equity for the year ended December 31, 2015.

3. Prepare a classified balance sheet at December 31, 2015.

4. By what amounts do total current liabilities exceed total current assets at December 31, 2015?

5. Assume a $5,000 bank loan is received, payable in six months. Will this improve the negative working capital situation calculated in (4) above? Calculate the effect on your answer to (4) above?

6. As the bank manager, what questions might you raise regarding the loan?

Chapter 5

Accounting for the Sale of Goods

To this point, examples of business operations have involved the sale of services. This chapter introduces business operations based on the purchase and resale of goods. For example, Canadian Tire and Walmart each purchase and resell goods — such businesses are known as merchandisers. The accounting transactions for merchandising companies differ from those of service-based businesses. Chapter 5 covers accounting for transactions of sales of goods on credit and related cash collections by merchandising firms, and transactions involving purchases and payments for goods sold in the normal course of business activities.

Chapter 5 Learning Objectives

LO1 – Describe merchandising and explain the financial statement components of sales, cost of goods sold, merchandise inventory, and gross profit; differentiate between the perpetual and periodic inventory systems.

LO2 – Analyze and record purchase transactions for a merchandiser.

LO3 – Analyze and record sales transactions for a merchandiser.

LO4 – Record adjustments to merchandise inventory.

LO5 – Explain and prepare a classified multiple-step income statement for a merchandiser.

LO6 – Explain the closing process for a merchandiser.

LO7 – Explain and identify the entries regarding purchase and sales transactions in a periodic inventory system.

Concept Self-Check

Use the following questions as a self-check while working through Chapter 5.

1. What is gross profit and how is it calculated?
2. How is a merchandiser different from a service company?
3. What is a perpetual inventory system?
4. How is the purchase of merchandise inventory on credit recorded in a perpetual system?

5. How is a purchase return recorded in a perpetual system?
6. What does the credit term of "1/15, n30" mean?
7. How is a purchase discount recorded in a perpetual system?
8. How is the sale of merchandise inventory on credit recorded in a perpetual system?
9. How is a sales return that is restored to inventory recorded versus a sales return that is not restored to inventory (assuming a perpetual inventory system)?
10. What is a sales discount and how is it recorded in a perpetual inventory system?
11. Why does merchandise inventory need to be adjusted at the end of the accounting period and how is this done in a perpetual inventory system?
12. What types of transactions affect merchandise inventory in a perpetual inventory system?
13. How are the closing entries for a merchandiser using a perpetual inventory system different than for a service company?
14. When reporting expenses on an income statement, how is the function of an expense reported versus the nature of an expense?
15. On a classified multiple-step income statement, what is reported under the heading 'Other revenues and expenses' and why?
16. What is the periodic inventory system?
17. How is cost of goods sold calculated under the periodic inventory system?

NOTE: The purpose of these questions is to prepare you for the concepts introduced in the chapter. Your goal should be to answer each of these questions as you read through the chapter. If, when you complete the chapter, you are unable to answer one or more the Concept Self-Check questions, go back through the content to find the answer(s). Solutions are not provided to these questions.

5.1 The Basics of Merchandising

> **LO1 – Describe merchandising and explain the financial statement components of sales, cost of goods sold, merchandise inventory, and gross profit; differentiate between the perpetual and periodic inventory systems.**

A merchandising company, or merchandiser, differs in several basic ways from a company that provides services. First, a merchandiser purchases and then sells goods whereas a service company sells services. For example, a car dealership is a merchandiser that sells cars while an airline is a service company that sells air travel. Because merchandising involves the purchase and then the resale of goods, an expense called **cost of goods sold** results. Cost of goods sold is the cost of the actual goods sold. For example, the cost of goods sold for a car dealership would be the cost of the cars purchased from manufacturers and then resold to customers. A service company does not have an expense called cost of goods sold since it does not sell goods. Because a merchandiser has cost of goods sold expense and a service business does not, the income statement for a merchandiser includes different details. A merchandising income statement highlights cost of goods sold by showing the difference between sales revenue and cost of goods sold called **gross profit** or **gross margin**. The basic income statement differences between a service business and a merchandiser are illustrated in Figure 5.1.

Service Company	*Merchandising Company*
Revenues	Sales
	Less: Cost of Goods Sold
	Equals: Gross Profit
Less: Expenses	*Less*: Expenses
Equals: Net Income	*Equals*: Net Income

Figure 5.1: Differences Between the Income Statements of Service and Merchandising Companies

Assume that Excel Cars Corporation decides to go into the business of buying used vehicles from a supplier and reselling these to customers. If Excel purchases a vehicle for $3,000 and then sells it for $4,000, the gross profit would be $1,000, as follows:

Sales................	$ 4,000
Cost of Goods Sold	3,000
Gross Profit........	$ 1,000

The word "gross" is used by accountants to indicate that other expenses incurred in running the business must still be deducted from this amount before net income is calculated. In other words, gross profit represents the amount of sales revenue that remains to pay expenses after the cost of the goods sold is deducted.

A **gross profit percentage** can be calculated to express the relationship of gross profit to sales. The sale of the vehicle that cost $3,000 results in a 25% gross profit percentage ($1,000/4,000). That is, for every $1 of sales, the company has $.25 left to cover other expenses after deducting cost of goods sold. Readers of financial statements use this percentage as a means to evaluate the performance of one company against other companies in the same industry, or in the same company from year to year. Small fluctuations in the gross profit percentage can have significant effects on the financial performance of a company because the amount of sales and cost of goods sold are often very large in comparison to other income statement items.

Another difference between a service company and a merchandiser relates to the balance sheet. A merchandiser purchases goods for resale. Goods held for resale by a merchandiser are called **merchandise inventory** and are reported as an asset on the balance sheet. A service company would not normally have merchandise inventory.

Inventory Systems

There are two types of ways in which inventory is managed: perpetual inventory system or periodic inventory system. In a **perpetual inventory system**, the merchandise inventory account and cost of goods sold account are updated immediately when transactions occur. In a perpetual system, as merchandise inventory is purchased, it is debited to the merchandise inventory account. As inventory is sold to customers, the cost of the inventory sold is removed from the merchandise inventory account and debited to the cost of goods sold account. A perpetual system means that account balances are known on a real-time basis. This chapter focuses on the perpetual system.

Some businesses still use a **periodic inventory system** in which the purchase of merchandise inventory is debited to a temporary account called Purchases. At the end of the accounting period, inventory is counted (known as a **physical count**) and the merchandise inventory account is updated and cost of goods sold is calculated. In a periodic inventory system, the real-time balances in merchandise inventory and cost of goods sold are not known. It should be noted that even in a perpetual system a physical count must be performed at the end of the accounting period to record differences between the actual inventory on hand and the account balance. The entry to record this difference is discussed later in this chapter. The periodic system is discussed in greater detail in the appendix to this chapter.

An exploration is available on the Lyryx site. Log into your Lyryx course to run Using the Information – Gross Profit Ratio.

5.2 The Purchase and Payment of Merchandise Inventory (Perpetual)

> LO2 – Analyze and record purchase transactions for a merchandiser.

As introduced in Chapter 3, a company's operating cycle includes purchases *on account* or *on credit* and is highlighted in Figure 5.2.

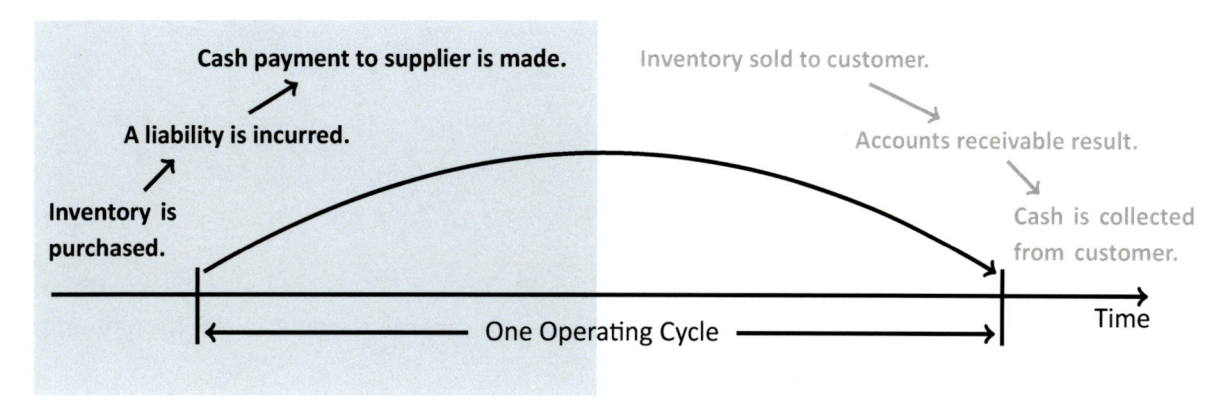

Figure 5.2: Purchase and Payment Portion of the Operating Cycle

Recording the Purchase of Merchandise Inventory (Perpetual)

When merchandise inventory is purchased, the cost is recorded in a Merchandise Inventory general ledger account. An account payable results when the merchandise inventory is acquired but will not be paid in cash until a later date. For example, recall the vehicle purchased on account by Excel for $3,000. The journal entry and general ledger T-account effects would be as follows.

Date	Account/Explanation	PR	Debit	Credit
	Merchandise Inventory		3,000	
	Accounts Payable			3,000
	To record the purchase of merchandise inventory on account.			

In addition to the purchase of merchandise inventory, there are other activities that affect the Merchandise Inventory account. For instance, merchandise may occasionally be returned to a supplier or damaged in transit, or discounts may be earned for prompt cash payment. These transactions result in the reduction of amounts due to the supplier and the costs of inventory. The purchase of merchandise inventory may also involve the payment of transportation and handling costs. These are all costs necessary to prepare inventory for sale, and all such costs are included in the Merchandise Inventory account. These costs are discussed in the following sections.

Purchase Returns and Allowances (Perpetual)

Assume that the vehicle purchased by Excel turned out to be the wrong colour. The supplier was contacted and agreed to reduce the price by $300 to $2,700. This is an example of a **purchase returns and allowances** adjustment. The amount of the allowance, or reduction, is recorded as a credit to the Merchandise Inventory account, as follows:

| General Journal ||||||
Date	Account/Explanation	PR	Debit	Credit
	Accounts Payable		300	
	Merchandise Inventory			300
	To record purchase allowance; incorrect colour.			

Note that the cost of the vehicle has been reduced to $2,700 ($3,000 – 300) as has the amount owing to the supplier. Again, the perpetual inventory system records changes in the Merchandise Inventory account each time a relevant transaction occurs.

Purchase Discounts (Perpetual)

Purchase discounts affect the purchase price of merchandise if payment is made within a time period specified in the supplier's invoice. For example, if the terms on the $3,000 invoice for one vehicle received by Excel indicates "1/15, n45", this means that the $3,000 must be paid within 45 days ('n' = net). However, if cash payment is made by Excel within 15 days, the purchase price will be reduced by 1%.

Assuming the amount is paid within 15 days, the supplier's terms entitle Excel to deduct $27 [($3,000 - $300) = $2,700 x 1% = $27]. The payment to the supplier would be recorded as:

| General Journal ||||||
Date	Account/Explanation	PR	Debit	Credit
	Accounts Payable		2,700	
	Merchandise Inventory			27
	Cash			2,673
	To record payment on account within the discount period.			

The cost of the vehicle in Excel's inventory records is now $2,673 ($3,000 – 300 – 27). If payment is made after the discount period, $2,700 of cash is paid and the entry would be:

General Journal				
Date	Account/Explanation	PR	Debit	Credit
	Accounts Payable		2,700	
	Cash.................................			2,700
	To record payment of account; no purchase discount applied.			

Trade discounts are similar to purchase discounts. A supplier advertises a **list price** which is the normal selling price of its goods to merchandisers. **Trade discounts** are given by suppliers to merchandisers that buy a large quantity of goods. For instance, assume a supplier offers a 10% trade discount on purchases of 1,000 units or more where the list price is $1/unit. If Beta Merchandiser Corp. buys 1,000 units on account, the entry in Beta's records would be:

General Journal				
Date	Account/Explanation	PR	Debit	Credit
	Merchandise Inventory		900	
	Accounts Payable			900
	To record purchase on account; 10% trade discount ($1,000 – 10% = $900).			

Note that the net amount (list price less trade discount) is recorded.

Transportation

Costs to transport goods from the supplier to the seller must also be considered when recording the cost of merchandise inventory. The shipping terms on the invoice identify the point at which ownership of the inventory transfers from the supplier to the purchaser. When the terms are **FOB shipping point**, ownership transfers at the 'shipping point' so the purchaser is responsible for transportation costs. **FOB destination** indicates that ownership transfers at the 'destination point' so the seller is responsible for transportation costs. FOB is the abbreviation for "free on board."

Assume that Excel's supplier sells with terms of FOB shipping point indicating that transportation costs are Excel's responsibility. If the cost of shipping is $125 and this amount was paid in cash to the truck driver at time of delivery, the entry would be:

General Journal				
Date	Account/Explanation	PR	Debit	Credit
	Merchandise Inventory		125	
	Cash.................................			125
	To record shipping costs on inventory purchased.			

The cost of the vehicle in the Excel Merchandise Inventory account is now $2,798 (calculated as $3,000 original cost - $300 allowance - $27 discount + $125 shipping). It is important to note that

Excel's transportation costs to deliver goods to customers are recorded as *delivery expenses* and **_do not_** affect the Merchandise Inventory account.

The next section describes how the sale of merchandise is recorded as well as the related costs of items sold.

An exploration is available on the Lyryx site. Log into your Lyryx course to run Purchases.

5.3 Merchandise Inventory: Sales and Collection (Perpetual)

LO3 – Analyze and record sales transactions for a merchandiser.

In addition to purchases on account, a merchandising company's operating cycle includes the sale of merchandise inventory *on account* or *on credit* as highlighted in Figure 5.3.

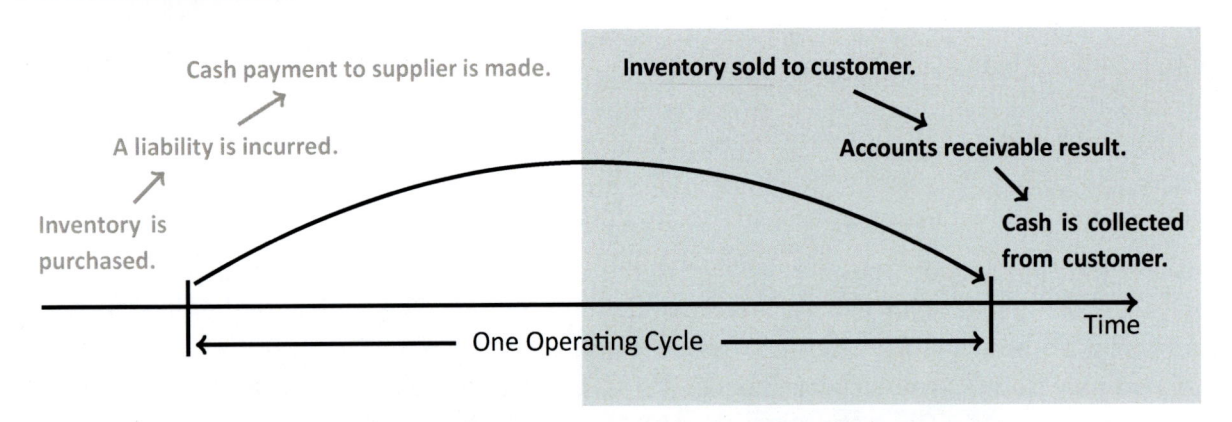

Figure 5.3: Sales and Collection Portion of the Operating Cycle

There are some slight recording differences when revenue is earned in a merchandising company. These are discussed below.

Recording the Sale of Merchandise Inventory (Perpetual)

The sale of merchandise inventory is recorded with two entries:

1. recording the sale by debiting Cash or Accounts Receivable and crediting Sales, and

2. recording the cost of the sale by debiting Cost of Goods Sold and crediting Merchandise Inventory.

Assume the vehicle purchased by Excel is sold for $4,000 on account. Recall that the cost of this vehicle in the Excel Merchandise Inventory account is $2,798, as shown below.

The entries to record the sale of the merchandise inventory are:

	General Journal			
Date	Account/Explanation	PR	Debit	Credit
	Accounts Receivable		4,000	
	Sales			4,000
	To record the sale of merchandise on account.			

	General Journal			
Date	Account/Explanation	PR	Debit	Credit
	Cost of Goods Sold		2,798	
	Merchandise Inventory...............			2,798
	To record the cost of the sale.			

The first entry records the sales revenue. The second entry is required to reduce the Merchandise Inventory account and transfer the cost of the inventory sold to the Cost of Goods Sold account. The second entry ensures that both the Merchandise Inventory account and Cost of Goods Sold account are up to date.

Sales Returns and Allowances

When merchandise inventory that has been sold is returned to the merchandiser by the customer, a **sales return and allowance** is recorded. For example, assume some damage occurs to the merchandise inventory sold by Excel while it is being delivered to the customer. Excel gives the customer a *sales allowance* by agreeing to reduce the amount owing by $100. The entry is:

	General Journal			
Date	Account/Explanation	PR	Debit	Credit
	Sales Returns and Allowances		100	
	Accounts Receivable			100
	To record allowance for damage to merchandise inventory during delivery.			

Accounts receivable is credited because the original sale was made on account and has not yet been paid. The amount owing from the customer is reduced to $3,900. If the $3,900 had already been paid, a credit would be made to Cash and $100 refunded to the customer. The Sales Returns and Allowances account is a contra revenue account and is therefore **deducted** from Sales when preparing the income statement.

If goods are returned by a customer, a *sales return* occurs. The related sales and cost of goods sold recorded on the income statement are reversed and the goods are returned to inventory. For example, assume Max Corporation sells a plastic container for $3 that it purchased for $1. The dual entry at the time of sale would be:

| General Journal ||||||
Date	Account/Explanation	PR	Debit	Credit
	Accounts Receivable		3	
	Sales			3
	To record sale on credit.			

| General Journal ||||||
Date	Account/Explanation	PR	Debit	Credit
	Cost of Goods Sold		1	
	Merchandise Inventory			1
	To record the cost of the sale.			

If the customer returns the container and the merchandise is restored to inventory, the dual journal entry would be:

| General Journal ||||||
Date	Account/Explanation	PR	Debit	Credit
	Sales Returns and Allowances		3	
	Accounts Receivable			3
	To record sales return.			

| General Journal ||||||
Date	Account/Explanation	PR	Debit	Credit
	Merchandise Inventory		1	
	Cost of Goods Sold			1
	To record sales return being restored to inventory.			

The use of a contra account to record sales returns and allowances permits management to track the amount of returned and damaged items.

Sales Discounts

Another contra revenue account, **Sales Discounts**, records reductions in sales amounts when a customer pays within a certain time period. For example, assume Excel Cars Corporation offers sales terms of "2/10, n30." This means that the amount owed must be paid by the customer within 30 days ('n' = net); however, if the customer chooses to pay within 10 days, a 2% discount may be deducted from the amount owing.

Consider the sale of the vehicle for $3,900 ($4,000 less the $100 allowance for damage). Payment within 10 days entitles the customer to a $78 discount ($3,900 x 2% = $78). If payment is made within the discount period, Excel receives $3,822 cash ($3,900 - 78) and prepares the following entry:

		General Journal			
	Date	Account/Explanation	PR	Debit	Credit
		Cash....................................		3,822	
		Sales Discounts		78	
		Accounts Receivable			3,900
		To record payment on account and sales discount applied.			

This entry reduces the accounts receivable amount to zero which is the desired result. If payment is not made within the discount period, the customer pays the full amount owing of $3,900.

As was the case for Sales Returns and Allowances, the balance in the Sales Discounts account is deducted from Sales on the income statement to arrive at Net Sales. Merchandisers often report only the net sales amount on the income statement. Details from sales returns and allowances, and sales discounts, are often omitted because they are immaterial in amount relative to total sales. However, as already stated, separate general ledger accounts for each of sales returns and allowances, and sales discounts, are useful in helping management identify potential problems that require investigation.

An exploration is available on the Lyryx site. Log into your Lyryx course to run Gross Profit.

An exploration is available on the Lyryx site. Log into your Lyryx course to run Sales.

5.4 Adjustments to Merchandise Inventory (Perpetual)

LO4 – Record adjustments to merchandise inventory.

To verify that the actual amount of merchandise inventory on hand is consistent with the balance recorded in the accounting records, a physical inventory count must be performed at the end of the accounting period. When a physical count of inventory is conducted, the costs attached to these inventory items are totalled. This total is compared to the Merchandise Inventory account balance in the general ledger. Any discrepancy is called **shrinkage**. Theft and deterioration of merchandise inventory are the most common causes of shrinkage.

The adjusting entry to record shrinkage is:

General Journal				
Date	Account/Explanation	PR	Debit	Credit
	Cost of Goods Sold		XX	
	Merchandise Inventory			XX
	To adjust for shrinkage.			

Summary of Merchandising Transactions

As the preceding sections have illustrated, there are a number of entries which are unique to a merchandiser. These are summarized below (assume all transactions were on account):

(a) To record the purchase of merchandise inventory from a supplier:

General Journal				
Date	Account/Explanation	PR	Debit	Credit
	Merchandise Inventory		XX	
	Accounts Payable			XX

(b) To record purchase return and allowances:

General Journal				
Date	Account/Explanation	PR	Debit	Credit
	Accounts Payable		XX	
	Merchandise Inventory			XX

(c) To record purchase discounts:

General Journal				
Date	Account/Explanation	PR	Debit	Credit
	Accounts Payable		XX	
	Merchandise Inventory			XX

(d) To record shipping costs from supplier to merchandiser:

General Journal				
Date	Account/Explanation	PR	Debit	Credit
	Merchandise Inventory		XX	
	Accounts Payable			XX

(e) To record sale of merchandise inventory and cost of the sale:

General Journal				
Date	Account/Explanation	PR	Debit	Credit
	Accounts Receivable		XX	
	Sales			XX

AND

General Journal				
Date	Account/Explanation	PR	Debit	Credit
	Cost of Goods Sold		XX	
	Merchandise Inventory			XX

(f) To record sales returns restored to inventory:

General Journal				
Date	Account/Explanation	PR	Debit	Credit
	Sales Returns and Allowances		XX	
	Accounts Receivable			XX

AND

General Journal				
Date	Account/Explanation	PR	Debit	Credit
	Merchandise Inventory		XX	
	Cost of Goods Sold			XX

(g) To record sales returns and allowances (where returns are not restored to inventory):

General Journal				
Date	Account/Explanation	PR	Debit	Credit
	Sales Returns and Allowances		XX	
	Accounts Receivable			XX

(h) To record discounts:

General Journal				
Date	Account/Explanation	PR	Debit	Credit
	Sales Discounts		XX	
	Cash		XX	
	Accounts Receivable			XX

(i) To record adjustment for shrinkage at the end of the accounting period:

Date	General Journal Account/Explanation	PR	Debit	Credit
	Cost of Goods Sold.................		XX	
	Merchandise Inventory..........			XX

The effect of these transactions on each of merchandise inventory and cost of goods sold is depicted below:

Merchandise Inventory (MI)	
(a) Purchase of MI	(b) Purchase Ret. & Allow.
(d) Shipping Costs	(c) Purchase Discounts
(f) Sales Return (when restored to inventory)	(e) Sale of MI
	(i) Shrinkage Adjustment
Adjusted Balance Reported on the Balance Sheet	

Cost of Goods Sold (COGS)	
(e) Cost of MI Sold	(f) Cost of sales returns restored to inventory
(i) Shrinkage Adjustment	
Adjusted Balance Reported on the Income Statement	

An exploration is available on the Lyryx site. Log into your Lyryx course to run *Merchandising Adjusting Entry*.

5.5 Merchandising Income Statement

LO5 – Explain and prepare a classified multiple-step income statement for a merchandiser.

Businesses are required to show expenses on the income statement based on either the *nature* or the *function* of the expense. The **nature of an expense** is determined by its basic characteristics (what it is). For example, when expenses are listed on the income statement as interest, depreciation, income tax, or wages, this identifies the nature of each expense. In contrast, the **function of an expense** describes the grouping of expenses based on their purpose (what they relate to). For example, an income statement that shows cost of goods sold, selling expenses, and general and administrative expenses has grouped expenses by their function. When expenses are grouped by function, additional information must be disclosed to show the nature of expenses within each group. The **full disclosure principle** is the generally accepted accounting principle that requires financial statements to report all relevant information about the operations and financial position of the entity. Information that is relevant but not included in the body of the statements is provided in the notes to the financial statements.

A merchandising income statement can be prepared in different formats. For this course, only one format will be introduced — the classified multiple-step format. This format is generally used for internal reporting because of the detail it includes. An example of a classified multiple-step income statement is shown below using assumed data for XYZ Inc. for its month ended December 31, 2015.

XYZ Inc.
Income Statement
Month Ended December 31, 2015

Sales			$100,000
Less: Sales discounts		$1,000	
Sales returns and allowances		500	1,500
Net sales			$98,500
Cost of goods sold			50,000
Gross profit from sales			$48,500
Operating expenses:			
Selling expenses:			
Sales salaries expense	$11,000		
Rent expense, selling space	9,000		
Advertising expense	5,000		
Depreciation expense, store equipment	3,000		
Total selling expenses		$28,000	
General and administrative expenses:			
Office salaries expense	$9,000		
Rent expense, office space	3,000		
Office supplies expense	1,500		
Depreciation expense, office equipment	1,000		
Insurance expense	1,000		
Total general and administrative expenses		15,500	
Total operating expenses			43,500
Income from operations			$5,000
Other revenues and expenses:			
Rent revenue		$12,000	
Interest expense		1,500	10,500
Income before tax			$15,500
Income tax expense			3,000
Net income			$12,500

Notice that the classified multiple-step income statement shows expenses by both function and nature. The broad categories that show expenses by function include operating expenses, selling expenses, and general and administrative expenses. Within each category, the nature of expenses is disclosed including sales salaries, advertising, depreciation, supplies, and insurance. Notice that Rent Expense has been divided between two groupings because it applies to more than one category or function.

The normal operating activity for XYZ Inc. is merchandising. Revenues and expenses that are not part of normal operating activities are listed under Other Revenues and Expenses. XYZ Inc. shows Rent Revenue under Other Revenues and Expenses because this type of revenue is not part of its merchandising operations. Interest earned, dividends earned, and gains on the sale of property, plant, and equipment are other examples of revenues not related to merchandising operations. XYZ Inc. deducts Interest Expense under Other Revenues and Expenses. Interest expense does not result from operating activities; it is a financing activity because it is associated with the borrowing of money. Another example of a non-operating expense is losses on the sale of property, plant, and equipment. Income tax expense is a government requirement so it is shown separately. Notice that income tax expense follows the subtotal 'Income before tax'.

5.6 Closing Entries for a Merchandiser

LO6 – Explain the closing process for a merchandiser.

The process of recording closing entries for service companies was illustrated in Chapter 3. The closing procedure for merchandising companies is the same as for service companies — all income statement accounts are transferred to the Income Summary account, the Income Summary is closed to Retained Earnings, and Dividends are closed to Retained Earnings.

When preparing closing entries for a merchandiser, the income statement accounts unique for merchandisers need to be considered — Sales, Sales Discounts, Sales Returns and Allowances, and Cost of Goods Sold. Sales is a revenue account so has a normal credit balance. To close Sales, it must be debited with a corresponding credit to the income summary. Sales Discounts and Sales Returns and Allowances are both contra revenue accounts so each has a normal debit balance. Cost of Goods Sold has a normal debit balance because it is an expense. To close these debit balance accounts, a credit is required with a corresponding debit to the income summary.

An exploration is available on the Lyryx site. Log into your Lyryx course to run Closing Entries.

5.7 Appendix A: The Periodic Inventory System

LO7 – Explain and identify the entries regarding purchase and sales transactions in a periodic inventory system.

The perpetual inventory system maintains a continuous, real-time balance in both Merchandise Inventory, a balance sheet account, and Cost of Goods Sold, an income statement account. As a result, the Merchandise inventory general ledger account balance should always equal the value of physical inventory on hand at any point in time. Additionally, the Cost of Goods Sold general ledger account balance should always equal the total cost of merchandise inventory sold for the accounting period. The accounts should perpetually agree; hence the name. An alternate system is considered below, called the *periodic* inventory system.

Description of the Periodic Inventory System

The periodic inventory system does not maintain a constantly-updated merchandise inventory balance. Instead, ending inventory is determined by a physical count and valued at the end of an accounting period. The change in inventory is recorded only periodically. Additionally, a Cost of Goods Sold account is not maintained in a periodic system. Instead, cost of goods sold is calculated at the end of the accounting period.

When goods are purchased using the periodic inventory system, the cost of merchandise is recorded in a **Purchases** account in the general ledger, rather than in the Merchandise Inventory account as is done under the perpetual inventory system. The Purchases account is an income statement account that accumulates the cost of merchandise acquired for resale.

The journal entry, assuming a purchase of merchandise on credit, is:

	General Journal			
Date	Account/Explanation	PR	Debit	Credit
	Purchases.............................		XX	
	Accounts Payable....................			XX

Purchase Returns and Allowances (Periodic)

Under the periodic inventory system, any purchase returns or purchase allowances are accumulated in a separate account called **Purchase Returns and Allowances**, an income statement account, and recorded as:

	General Journal			
Date	Account/Explanation	PR	Debit	Credit
	Accounts Payable.....................		XX	
	Purchase Returns and Allowances....			XX

Purchase Returns and Allowances is a contra expense account and the balance is deducted from Purchases when calculating cost of goods sold on the income statement.

Purchase Discounts (Periodic)

Another contra expense account, **Purchase Discounts**, accumulates reductions in the purchase price of merchandise if payment is made within a time period specified in the supplier's invoice and recorded as:

	General Journal			
Date	Account/Explanation	PR	Debit	Credit
	Accounts Payable.....................		XX	
	Purchase Discounts..................			XX

Transportation (Periodic)

Under the periodic inventory system, an income statement account called **Transportation-in** is used to accumulate transportation or freight charges on merchandise purchased for resale. The

Transportation-in account is used in calculating the cost of goods sold on the income statement. It is recorded as:

General Journal				
Date	Account/Explanation	PR	Debit	Credit
	Transportation-In		XX	
	Cash or Accounts Payable............			XX

At the end of the accounting period, cost of goods sold must be calculated which requires that the balance in Merchandise Inventory be determined. To determine the end of the period balance in Merchandise Inventory, a physical count of inventory is performed. The total value of the inventory as identified by the physical count becomes the ending balance in Merchandise Inventory. Cost of goods sold can then be calculated as follows:

Beginning Balance of Merchandise Inventory	XX
Plus: Net Cost of Goods Purchased*	XX
Less: Ending Balance of Merchandise Inventory	XX
Equals: Cost of Goods Sold	XX

*Net Cost of Goods Purchased is calculated as:

Purchases..................................	XX
Less: Purchase Returns and Allowances	XX
Less: Purchase Discounts	XX
Equals: Net Purchases........................	XX
Add: Transportation-In	XX
Equals: Net Cost of Goods Purchased	XX

Closing Entries (Periodic)

In the perpetual inventory system, the Merchandise Inventory account is continuously updated and is adjusted at the end of the accounting period based on a physical inventory count. In the periodic inventory system, the balance in Merchandise Inventory does not change during the accounting period. As a result, at the end of the accounting period, the balance in Merchandise Inventory in a periodic system is the beginning balance. In order for the Merchandise Inventory account to reflect the ending balance as determined by the physical inventory count, the beginning inventory balance must be removed by crediting Merchandise Inventory, and the ending inventory balance entered by debiting it. This is accomplished as part of the closing process. Closing entries for a merchandiser that uses a periodic inventory system are illustrated below using the adjusted trial balance information for Norva Inc.

162 — Accounting for the Sale of Goods

Norva Inc.
Adjusted Trial Balance
At December 31, 2015

	Debits	Credits
Cash	$15,000	
Merchandise inventory	1,000	
Accounts payable		$5,000
Common shares		8,000
Dividends	500	
Retained earnings		3,500
Sales		13,400
Sales discounts	200	
Purchases	5,000	
Purchase returns & allowances		800
Salaries expense	7,000	
Advertising expense	2,000	
Totals	$30,700	$30,700

Other information: The ending balance in merchandise inventory is $2,000 based on a physical count.

Step 1: Close debit balance income statement accounts plus beginning merchandise inventory:

Income Summary	15,200	
Merchandise Inventory		1,000
Sales Discounts		200
Purchases		5,000
Salaries Expense		7,000
Advertising Expense		2,000

Step 2: Close credit balance income statement accounts plus ending merchandise inventory:

Merchandise Inventory	2,000	
Sales	13,400	
Purchase Returns & Allowances	800	
Income Summary		16,200

Step 3: Close income summary to retained earnings:

Income Summary	1,000	
Retained Earnings		1,000

Step 4: Close dividends to retained earnings:

Retained Earnings	500	
Dividends		500

When the closing entries above are posted and a post-closing trial balance prepared as shown below, notice that the Merchandise Inventory account reflects the correct balance based on the physical inventory count.

Norva Inc.
Adjusted Trial Balance
At December 31, 2015

	Debits	Credits
Cash	$15,000	
Merchandise inventory	2,000	
Accounts payable		$5,000
Common shares		8,000
Retained earnings		4,500
Totals	$17,000	$17,000

An exploration is available on the Lyryx site. Log into your Lyryx course to run Journalizing Merchandise Transactions.

An exploration is available on the Lyryx site. Log into your Lyryx course to run Income Statement and Closing Entries.

Summary of Chapter 5 Learning Objectives

LO1 – Describe merchandising and explain the financial statement components of sales, cost of goods sold, merchandise inventory, and gross profit; differentiate between the perpetual and periodic inventory systems.

Merchandisers buy and resell products. Merchandise inventory, an asset, is purchased from suppliers and resold to customers to generate sales revenue. The cost of the merchandise inventory sold is an expense called cost of goods sold. The profit realized on the sale of merchandise inventory before considering any other expenses is called gross profit. Gross profit may be expressed as a dollar amount or as a percentage. To track merchandise inventory and cost of goods sold in real time, a perpetual inventory system is used; the balance in each of Merchandise Inventory and Cost of Goods Sold is always up-to-date. In a periodic inventory system, a physical count of the inventory must be performed in order to determine the balance in Merchandise Inventory and Cost of Goods Sold.

LO2 – Analyze and record purchase transactions for a merchandiser.

In a perpetual inventory system, a merchandiser debits Merchandise Inventory regarding the purchase of merchandise for resale from a supplier. Any purchase returns and allowances or purchase discounts are credited to Merchandise Inventory as they occur to keep the accounts up-to-date.

LO3 – Analyze and record sales transactions for a merchandiser.

In a perpetual inventory system, a merchandiser records two entries at the time of sale: one to record the sale and a second to record the cost of the sale. Sales returns that are returned to inventory also require to entries: one to reverse the sale by debiting a sales returns and allowances account and a second to restore the merchandise to inventory by debiting Merchandise Inventory and crediting Cost of Goods Sold. Sales returns not restored to inventory as well as sales allowances are recorded with one entry: debit sales returns and allowances and credit cash or accounts receivable. Sales discounts are recorded when a credit customer submits their payment within the discount period specified.

LO4 – Record adjustments to merchandise inventory.

A physical count of merchandise inventory is performed and the total compared to the general ledger balance of Merchandise Inventory. Discrepancies are recorded as an adjusting entry that debits cost of goods sold and credits Merchandise Inventory.

LO5 – Explain and prepare a classified multiple-step income statement for a merchandiser.

A classified multiple-step income statement for a merchandiser is for internal use because of the detail provided. Sales, less sales returns and allowances and sales discounts, results in net sales. Net sales less cost of goods sold equals gross profit. Expenses are shown based on both their function and nature. The functional or group headings are: operating expenses, selling expenses, and general and administrative expenses. Within each grouping, the nature of expenses is detailed including: depreciation, salaries, advertising, wages, and insurance. A specific expense can be divided between groupings.

LO6 – Explain the closing process for a merchandiser.

The steps in preparing closing entries for a merchandiser are the same as for a service company. The difference is that a merchandiser will need to close income statement accounts unique to merchandising such as: Sales, Sales Returns and Allowances, Sales Discounts, and Cost of Goods Sold.

LO7 – Explain and identify the entries regarding purchase and sales transactions in a periodic inventory system.

A periodic inventory system maintains a Merchandise Inventory account but does not have a Cost of Goods Sold account. The Merchandise Inventory account is updated at the end of the accounting period as a result of a physical inventory count. Because a merchandiser using a period system does not use a Merchandise Inventory account to record purchase or sales transactions during the accounting period, it maintains accounts that are different than under a perpetual system, namely, Purchases, Purchase Returns and Allowances, Purchase Discounts, and Transportation-in.

Discussion Questions

1. How does the income statement prepared for a company that sells goods differ from that prepared for a service business?

2. How is gross profit calculated? What relationships do the gross profit and gross profit percentage calculations express? Explain, using an example.

3. What are some common types of transactions that are recorded in the merchandise Inventory account?

4. Contrast and explain the sales and collection cycle and the purchase and payment cycle.

5. What contra accounts are used in conjunction with sales? What are their functions?

6. (Appendix) Compare the perpetual and periodic inventory systems. What are some advantages of each?

Exercises

EXERCISE 5–1 (LO1)

Consider the following information of Jones Corporation over four years:

	2014	2013	2012	2011
Sales	$10,000	$9,000	$?	$7,000
Cost of Goods Sold	?	6,840	6,160	?
Gross Profit	2,500	?	1,840	?
Gross Profit Percentage	?	?	?	22%

Required:

a. Calculate the missing amounts for each year.

b. What does this information indicate about the company?

EXERCISE 5–2 (LO2)

Reber Corp. uses the perpetual inventory system. Its transactions during July 2015 are as follows:

July 6   Purchased $600 of merchandise on account from Hobson Corporation for terms 1/10, net 30.
     9   Returned $200 of defective merchandise.
    15   Paid the amount owing to Hobson.

Required: Prepare journal entries to record the above transactions for Reber Corp.

EXERCISE 5–3 (LO2,3,4)

Horne Inc. and Sperling Renovations Ltd. both sell goods and use the perpetual inventory system. Horne Inc. had $3,000 of merchandise inventory at the start of its fiscal year, January 1, 2015. During the 2015, Horne Inc. had the following transactions:

May 5 Horne sold $4,000 of merchandise on account to Sperling Renovations Ltd., terms 2/10, net 30. Cost of merchandise to Horne from its supplier was $2,500.

7 Sperling returned $500 of merchandise received in error which Horne returned to inventory; Horne issued a credit memo. Cost of merchandise to Horne was $300.

15 Horne received the amount due from Sperling Renovations Ltd.

A physical count and valuation of Horne's Merchandise Inventory at May 31, the fiscal year-end, showed $700 of goods on hand.

Required: Prepare journal entries to record the above transactions and adjustment:

a. In the records of Horne Inc.

b. In the records of Sperling Renovations Ltd.

EXERCISE 5–4 (LO5)

The following information is taken from the records of Smith Corp. for the year ended June 30, 2015:

Advertising Expense	$ 1,500
Commissions Expense	4,000
Cost of Goods Sold	50,000
Delivery Expense	500
Depreciation Expense – Equipment	500
Insurance Expense	1,000
Office Salaries Expense	3,000
Rent Expense – Office	1,000
Rent Expense – Store	1,500
Sales Salaries Expense	2,000
Sales	72,000
Sales Returns and Allowances	2,000

Required:

a. Prepare a classified multi-step income statement for the year ended June 30, 2015. Assume an income tax rate of 20%.

b. Compute the gross profit percentage, rounding to two decimal places.

EXERCISE 5–5 (LO6)

Refer to the information in Exercise 5–4.

Required:

a. Prepare all closing entries. Assume cash dividends totalling $2,000 were declared during the year and recorded as a debit to Dividends Declared and a credit to Cash.

b. Calculate the June 30, 2015 post-closing balance in Retained Earnings assuming a beginning balance of $18,000.

EXERCISE 5–6   (LO7 Appendix)

Consider the information for each of the following four companies.

	A	B	C	D
Opening Inventory	$?	$ 184	$ 112	$ 750
Purchases	1415	?	840	5,860
Transportation-In	25	6	15	?
Cost of Goods Available for Sale	1,940	534	?	6,620
Ending Inventory	340	200	135	?
Cost of Goods Sold	?	?	?	5,740

Required: Calculate the missing amounts.

EXERCISE 5–7   (LO7 Appendix)

The following data pertain to Pauling Inc.

Opening Inventory	$ 375
Purchases	2930
Purchases Discounts	5
Purchases Returns and Allowances	20
Transportation-In	105

Ending inventory amounts to $440.

Required: Calculate cost of goods sold.

EXERCISE 5–8   (LO7 Appendix)

The following information is taken from the records of four different companies in the same industry:

	A	B	C	D
Sales	$300	$150	$?	$ 90
Opening Inventory	?	40	40	12
Purchases	240	?	?	63
Cost of Goods Available for Sale	320	?	190	?
Ending Inventory	?	(60)	(60)	(15)
Cost of Goods Sold	?	100	130	60
Gross Profit	$100	$?	$ 65	$?
Gross Profit percentage	?	?	?	?

Required:

a. Calculate the missing amounts.

b. Which company seems to be performing best? Why?

Problems

PROBLEM 5–1 (LO1,2,3,4)

Salem Corp. was incorporated on July 2, 2015 to operate a merchandising business. It uses the perpetual inventory system. All its sales are on account with terms: 2/10, n30. Its transactions during July 2015 are as follows:

July 2 Issued share capital for $5,000 cash.
2 Purchased $3,500 merchandise on account from Blic Pens Ltd. for terms 2/10, n30.
2 Sold $2,000 of merchandise on account to Spellman Chair Rentals Inc. (Cost to Salem: $1,200).
3 Paid Sayer Holdings Corp. $500 for July rent.
5 Paid Easton Furniture Ltd. $1,000 for equipment.
8 Collected $200 for a cash sale made today to Ethan Matthews Furniture Ltd. (Cost: $120).
8 Purchased $2,000 merchandise on account from Shaw Distributors Inc. for terms 2/15, n30.
9 Received the amount due from Spellman Chair Rentals Inc. for the July 2 sale.
10 Paid Blic Pens Ltd. for the July 2 purchase.
10 Purchased $200 of merchandise on account from Peel Products Inc. for terms n30.
15 Sold $2,000 of merchandise on account to Eagle Products Corp. (Cost: $1,300).
15 Purchased $1,500 of merchandise on account from Bevan Door Inc. for terms 2/10, n30.
15 Received a memo from Shaw Distributors Inc. to reduce accounts payable by $100 for defective merchandise included in the July 8 purchase.
16 Eagle Products Corp. returned $200 of defective merchandise which was scrapped (Cost to Salem: $150).
20 Sold $3,500 of merchandise on account to Aspen Promotions Ltd. (Cost: $2,700).
20 Paid Shaw Distributors Inc. for half the purchase made July 8.
24 Received half the amount due from Eagle Products Corp. in partial payment for the July 15 sale.
24 Paid Bevan Doors Ltd. for the purchase made July 15.
26 Sold $600 merchandise on account to Longbeach Sales Ltd. (Cost: $400).
26 Purchased $800 of merchandise on account from Silverman Co. for terms 2/10, n30.
31 Paid Speedy Transport Co. $350 for transportation to Salem's warehouse during the month (all purchases are fob shipping point).

Required:

1. Prepare journal entries to record the July transactions. Include general ledger account numbers and a brief description.

2. Calculate the unadjusted ending balance in merchandise inventory.

3. Assume the merchandise inventory is counted at July 31 and assigned a total cost of $2,400. Prepare the July 31 adjusting entry.

PROBLEM 5–2 (LO1,5,6)

The following closing entries were prepared for Whirlybird Products Inc. at December 31, 2015, the end of its fiscal year.

	General Journal			
Date	Account/Explanation	PR	Debit	Credit
Dec. 31	Sales.....................................		37,800	
	Income Summary.....................			37,800
31	Income Summary.......................		32,800	
	Cost of Goods Sold....................			26,800
	Sales Returns and Allowances.........			690
	Sales Discounts.......................			310
	Salaries Expenses.....................			5,000
31	Income Summary.......................		5,000	
	Retained Earnings.....................			5,000

Required: Calculate gross profit.

PROBLEM 5–3 (LO1,5,6)

The following alphabetized adjusted trial balance has been extracted from the records of Acme Automotive Inc. at December 31, 2015, its third fiscal year-end. All accounts have a normal balance.

Accounts Payable	9,000
Accounts Receivable	15,000
Accumulated Depreciation – Equipment	36,000
Advertising Expense	14,000
Bank Loan	14,000
Cash	2,000
Commissions Expense	29,000
Cost of Goods Sold	126,000
Delivery Expense	14,800
Depreciation Expense	12,000
Dividends	11,000
Equipment	120,000
Income Taxes Expense	4,200
Income Taxes Payable	4,200
Insurance Expense	10,400
Interest Expense	840
Merchandise Inventory	26,000
Office Supplies Expense	3,100
Rent Expense	32,400
Rent Revenue	19,200
Retained Earnings	12,440
Sales	310,000
Sales Discounts	1,300
Sales Returns and Allowances	2,900
Sales Salaries Expense	26,400
Share Capital	70,000
Supplies	3,200
Telephone Expense	1,800
Utilities Expense	4,200
Wages Expense – Office	14,300

Required:

1. Prepare a classified multi-step income statement and statement of changes in equity for the year ended December 31, 2015. Assume 40% of the Rent Expense is allocated to general and administrative expenses with the remainder allocated to selling expenses. Additionally, assume that $20,000 of shares were issued during the year ended December 31, 2015.

2. Prepare closing entries.

Chapter 6

Assigning Costs to Merchandise

Recording transactions related to the purchase and sale of merchandise inventory was introduced and discussed in Chapter 5. This chapter reviews how the cost of goods sold is calculated using various inventory cost flow assumptions. Additionally, issues related to merchandise inventory that remains on hand at the end of an accounting period are also explored.

Chapter 6 Learning Objectives

LO1 – Calculate cost of goods sold and merchandise inventory using specific identification, first-in first-out (FIFO), and weighted average cost flow assumptions — perpetual.

LO2 – Explain the impact on financial statements of inventory cost flows and errors.

LO3 – Explain and calculate lower of cost and net realizable value inventory adjustments.

LO4 – Estimate merchandise inventory using the gross profit method and the retail inventory method.

LO5 – Explain and calculate merchandise inventory turnover.

LO6 – Calculate cost of goods sold and merchandise inventory using specific identification, first-in first-out (FIFO), and weighted average cost flow assumptions — periodic.

Concept Self-Check

Use the following as a self-check while working through Chapter 6

1. What three inventory cost flow assumptions can be used in perpetual inventory systems?
2. What impact does the use of different inventory cost flow assumptions have on financial statements?
3. What is the meaning of the term *lower of cost and net realizable value*, and how is it calculated?
4. What is the effect on net income of an error in ending inventory values?
5. What methods are used to estimate ending inventory?
6. What ratio can be used to evaluate the liquidity of merchandise inventory?

7. What inventory cost flow assumptions can be used in a periodic inventory system?

NOTE: The purpose of these questions is to prepare you for the concepts introduced in the chapter. Your goal should be to answer each of these questions as you read through the chapter. If, when you complete the chapter, you are unable to answer one or more the Concept Self-Check questions, go back through the content to find the answer(s). Solutions are not provided to these questions.

6.1 Inventory Cost Flow Assumptions

> **LO1** – Calculate cost of goods sold and merchandise inventory using specific identification, first in first-out (FIFO), and weighted average cost flow assumptions — perpetual.

Determining the cost of each unit of inventory, and thus the total cost of ending inventory on the balance sheet, can be challenging. Why? We know from Chapter 5 that the cost of inventory can be affected by discounts, returns, transportation costs, and shrinkage. Additionally, the purchase cost of an inventory item can be different from one purchase to the next. For example, the cost of coffee beans could be $5.00 a kilo in October and $7.00 a kilo in November. Finally, some types of inventory flow into and out of the warehouse in a specific sequence, while others do not. For example, milk would need to be managed so that the oldest milk is sold first. In contrast, a car dealership has no control over which vehicles are sold because customers make specific choices based on what is available. So how is the cost of a unit in merchandise inventory determined? There are several methods that can be used. Each method may result in a different cost, as described in the following sections.

Assume a company sells only one product and uses the perpetual inventory system. It has no beginning inventory at June 1, 2015. The company purchased five units during June as shown in Figure 6.1.

	Purchase Transaction	
Date	Number of units	Price per unit
June 1	1	$1
5	1	2
7	1	3
21	1	4
28	1	5
	5	$15

Figure 6.1: June Purchases and Purchase Price per Unit

At June 28, there are 5 units in inventory with a total cost of $15 ($1 + $2 + $3 + $4 + $5). Assume four units are sold June 30 for $10 each on account. The cost of the four units sold could be determined based on identifying the cost associated with the specific units sold. For example, a car dealership tracks the cost of each vehicle purchased and sold. Alternatively, a business that sells perishable items would want the oldest units to move out of inventory first to minimize spoilage. Finally, if large quantities of low dollar value items are in inventory, such as pencils or hammers, an average cost might be used to calculate cost of goods sold. A business may choose one of three methods to calculate cost of goods and the resulting ending inventory based on an assumed flow. These methods are: specific identification, FIFO, and weighted average, and are discussed in the next sections.

Specific Identification

Under **specific identification**, each inventory item that is sold is matched with its purchase cost. This method is most practical when inventory consists of relatively few, expensive items, particularly when individual units can be identified with serial numbers — for example, motor vehicles.

Assume the four units sold on June 30 are those purchased on June 1, 5, 7, and 28. The fourth unit purchased on June 21 remains in ending inventory. Cost of goods sold would total $11 ($1 + $2 + $3 + $5). Sales would total $40 (4 @ $10). As a result, gross profit would be $29 ($40 − 11). Ending inventory would be $4, the cost of the unit purchased on June 21.

The general ledger T-accounts for Merchandise Inventory and Cost of Goods Sold would show:

	Merchandise Inventory			Cost of Goods Sold
Jun. 1	$1			
5	2			
7	3			
21	4			
28	5			
		11	Jun. 30 →	11
End. Bal.	4			

Figure 6.2: Cost of Goods Sold using Specific Identification

The entry to record the June 30 sale on account would be:

General Journal				
Date	Account/Explanation	PR	Debit	Credit
	Accounts Receivable		40	
	Sales			40
	To record the sale of merchandise on account.			
	Cost of Goods Sold		11	
	Merchandise Inventory			11
	To record the cost of the sale.			

176 ■ Assigning Costs to Merchandise

It is not possible to use specific identification when inventory consists of a large number of similar, inexpensive items that cannot be easily differentiated. Consequently, a method of assigning costs to inventory items based on an **assumed** flow of goods can be adopted. Two such generally accepted methods, known as cost flow assumptions, are discussed next.

The First-in, First-out (FIFO) Cost Flow Assumption

First-in, first-out (FIFO) assumes that the first goods purchased are the first ones sold. A FIFO cost flow assumption makes sense when inventory consists of perishable items such as groceries and other time-sensitive goods.

Using the information from the previous example, the first four units purchased are assumed to be the first four units sold under FIFO. The cost of the four units sold is $10 ($1 + $2 + $3 + $4). Sales still equal $40, so gross profit under FIFO is $30 ($40 – $10). The cost of the one remaining unit in ending inventory would be the cost of the fifth unit purchased ($5).

The general ledger T-accounts for Merchandise Inventory and Cost of Goods Sold as illustrated in Figure 6.3 would show:

Merchandise Inventory				Cost of Goods Sold	
Jun. 1	$1				
5	2				
7	3				
21	4				
28	5				
		10	Jun. 30 ⟶	10	
End. Bal.	5				

Figure 6.3: Cost of Goods Sold using FIFO

The entry to record the sale would be:

	General Journal			
Date	Account/Explanation	PR	Debit	Credit
	Accounts Receivable		40	
	Sales			40
	To record the sale of merchandise on account.			
	Cost of Goods Sold		10	
	Merchandise Inventory			10
	To record the cost of the sale.			

The Weighted Average Cost Flow Assumption

A **weighted average** cost flow is assumed when goods purchased on different dates are mixed with each other. The weighted average cost assumption is popular in practice because it is easy to calculate. It is also suitable when inventory is held in common storage facilities — for example, when several crude oil shipments are stored in one large holding tank. To calculate a weighted average, the total cost of all purchases of a particular inventory type is divided by the number of units purchased.

To calculate the weighted average cost in our example, the purchase prices for all five units are totaled ($1 + $2 + $3 + $4 + $5 = $15) and divided by the total number of units purchased (5). The weighted average cost for each unit is $3 ($15/5). The weighted average cost of goods sold would be $12 (4 units @ $3). Sales still equal $40 resulting in a gross profit under weighted average of $28 ($40 − $12). The cost of the one remaining unit in ending inventory is $3.

The general ledger T-accounts for Merchandise Inventory and Cost of Goods Sold are:

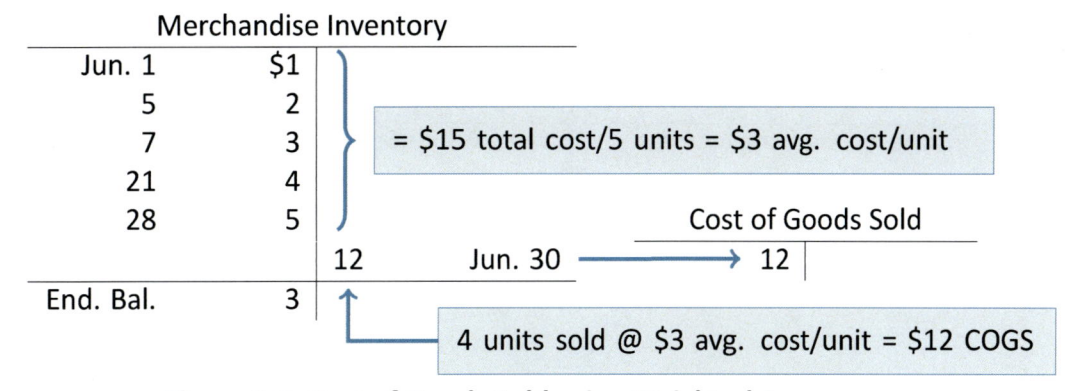

```
           Merchandise Inventory
   Jun. 1      $1  ⎫
        5        2  ⎪
        7        3  ⎬ = $15 total cost/5 units = $3 avg. cost/unit
       21        4  ⎪
       28        5  ⎭
                         Cost of Goods Sold
                12    Jun. 30  ⟶  12
   End. Bal.     3  ↑
                    └── 4 units sold @ $3 avg. cost/unit = $12 COGS
```

Figure 6.4: Cost of Goods Sold using Weighted Average

The entry to record the sale would be:

General Journal				
Date	Account/Explanation	PR	Debit	Credit
	Accounts Receivable		40	
	Sales			40
	To record the sale of merchandise on account.			
	Cost of Goods Sold		12	
	Merchandise Inventory			12
	To record the cost of the sale.			

Cost Flow Assumptions: A Comprehensive Example

Recall that under the perpetual inventory system, cost of goods sold is calculated and recorded in the accounting system at the time when sales are recorded. In our simplified example, all sales occurred on June 30 after all inventory had been purchased. In reality, the purchase and sale of merchandise is continuous. To demonstrate the calculations when purchases and sales occur continuously throughout the accounting period, let's review a more comprehensive example.

Assume the same example as above, except that sales of units occur as follows during June:

Date	Number of Units Sold
June 3	1
8	1
23	1
29	1

To help with the calculation of cost of goods sold, an *inventory record card* will be used to track the individual transactions. This card records information about purchases such as the date, number of units purchased, and purchase cost per unit. It also records cost of goods sold information: the date of sale, number of units sold, and the cost of each unit sold. Finally, the card records the balance of units on hand, the cost of each unit held, and the total cost of the units on hand. A partially-completed inventory record card is shown in Figure 6.5 below:

Date	Purchases/Shipping Costs/ (Purchase Returns/Discounts)			Cost of Goods Sold/ (Returns to Inventory)			Balance in Inventory		
	Units	Cost/Unit	Total $	Units	Cost/Unit	Total $	Units	Cost/Unit	Total $
June 1	1						1		
3				1			0		
5	1						1		
7	1						2		
8				1			1		
21	1						2		
23				1			1		
28	1						2		
29				1			1		

Ending Inventory is 1 unit.

Figure 6.5: Inventory Record Card

In Figure 6.5, the inventory at the end of the accounting period is one unit. This is the number of units on hand according to the accounting records. A *physical* inventory count must still be done, generally at the end of the fiscal year, to verify the quantities actually on hand. As discussed in Chapter 5, any discrepancies identified by the physical inventory count are adjusted for as shrinkage.

As purchases and sales are made, costs are assigned to the goods using the chosen cost flow assumption. This information is used to calculate the cost of goods sold amount for each sales transaction at the time of sale. These costs will vary depending on the inventory cost flow assumption used. As we will see in the next sections, the cost of sales may also vary depending on *when* sales occur.

Comprehensive Example—Specific Identification

To apply specific identification, we need information about which units were sold on each date. Assume that specific units were sold as detailed below.

Date of Sale	Specific Units Sold
June 3	The unit sold on June 3 was purchased on June 1
8	The unit sold on June 8 was purchased on June 7
23	The unit sold on June 23 was purchased on June 5
29	The unit sold on June 29 was purchased on June 28

Using the information above to apply specific identification, the resulting inventory record card appears in Figure 6.6.

Date	Purchases/Shipping Costs/ (Purchase Returns/Discounts)			Cost of Goods Sold/ (Returns to Inventory)			Balance in Inventory		
	Units	Cost/Unit	Total $	Units	Cost/Unit	Total $	Units	Cost/Unit	Total $
June 1	1	$1	$1				1	$1	$1
3				1	$1	$1	0	$0	$0
5	1	$2	$2				1	$2	$2
7	1	$3	$3				2	1@$2 / 1@$3	$5
8				1	$3	$3	1	$2	$2
21	1	$4	$4				2	1@$2 / 1@$4	$6
23				1	$2	$2	1	$4	$4
28	1	$5	$5				2	1@$4 / 1@$5	$9
29				1	$5	$5	1	$4	$4

Figure 6.6: Inventory Record Card using Specific Identification

Notice in Figure 6.7 that the number of units sold plus the units in ending inventory equals the total units that were available for sale. This will always be true regardless of which inventory cost flow method is used.

180 ■ Assigning Costs to Merchandise

Date	Purchases/Shipping Costs/ (Purchase Returns/Discounts) Units	Cost/Unit	Total $	Cost of Goods Sold/ (Returns to Inventory) Units	Cost/Unit	Total $	Balance in Inventory Units	Cost/Unit	Total $
June 1	1	$1	$1				1	$1	$1
3				1	$1	$1	0	$0	$0
5	1	$2	$2				1	$2	$2
7	1	$3	$3				2	1@$2 1@$3	$5
8				1	$3	$3	1	$2	$2
21	1	$4	$4				2	1@$2 1@$4	$6
23				1	$2	$2	1	$4	$4
28	1	$5	$5				2	1@$4 1@$5	$9
29				1	$5	$5	1	$4	$4

Total number of units available for sale: **5 units** = Total number of units sold: **4 units** + Total number of units in ending inventory: **1 unit**

Figure 6.7: Total Units Sold plus Total Units in Ending Inventory equals Total Units Available for Sale

Date	Purchases/Shipping Costs/ (Purchase Returns/Discounts) Units	Cost/Unit	Total $	Cost of Goods Sold/ (Returns to Inventory) Units	Cost/Unit	Total $	Balance in Inventory Units	Cost/Unit	Total $
June 1	1	$1	$1				1	$1	$1
3				1	$1	$1	0	$0	$0
5	1	$2	$2				1	$2	$2
7	1	$3	$3				2	1@$2 1@$3	$5
8				1	$3	$3	1	$2	$2
21	1	$4	$4				2	1@$2 1@$4	$6
23				1	$2	$2	1	$4	$4
28	1	$5	$5				2	1@$4 1@$5	$9
29				1	$5	$5	1	$4	$4

Total cost of goods available for sale: **$15** = Total cost of goods sold: **$11** + Total cost of ending inventory: **$4**

Figure 6.8: Total Cost of Goods Sold plus Total Cost of Units in Ending Inventory equals Total Cost of Goods Available for Sale (Specific Identification)

6.1. Inventory Cost Flow Assumptions — 181

Figure 6.8 highlights the relationship in which total cost of goods sold plus total cost of ending inventory equals total cost of goods available for sale. This relationship will always be true for each of specific identification, FIFO, and weighted average.

An exploration is available on the Lyryx site. Log into your Lyryx course to run Specific Identification.

Comprehensive Example—FIFO (Perpetual)

Using the same information, we now apply the FIFO cost flow assumption as shown in Figure 6.9.

Date	Purchases/Shipping Costs/ (Purchase Returns/Discounts) Units	Cost/Unit	Total $	Cost of Goods Sold/ (Returns to Inventory) Units	Cost/Unit	Total $	Balance in Inventory Units	Cost/Unit	Total $
June 1	1	$1	$1				1	$1	$1
3				1	$1	$1	0	$0	$0
5	1	$2	$2				1	$2	$2
7	1	$3	$3				2	1@$2 1@$3	$5
8				1	$2	$2	1	$3	$3
21	1	$4	$4				2	1@$3 1@$4	$7
23				1	$3	$3	1	$4	$4
28	1	$5	$5				2	1@$4 1@$5	$9
29				1	$4	$4	1	$5	$5

Figure 6.9: Inventory Record Card using FIFO (Perpetual)

When calculating the cost of the units sold in FIFO, the oldest unit in inventory will always be the first unit removed. For example, in Figure 6.9, on June 8, one unit is sold when the previous balance in inventory consisted of 2 units: 1 unit purchased on June 5 that cost $2 and 1 unit purchased on June 7 that cost $3. Because the unit costing $2 was in inventory first (before the June 8 unit costing $3), the cost assigned to the unit sold on June 8 is $2. Under FIFO, the first units into inventory are assumed to be the first units removed from inventory when calculating cost of goods sold. Therefore, under FIFO, ending inventory will always be the most recent units purchased. In Figure 6.9, there is one unit in ending inventory and it is assigned the $5 cost of the most recent purchase which was made on June 28.

The information in Figure 6.9 is repeated in Figure 6.10 to reinforce that goods available for sale equals the sum of goods sold and ending inventory.

182 ■ Assigning Costs to Merchandise

Date	Purchases/Shipping Costs/ (Purchase Returns/Discounts)			Cost of Goods Sold/ (Returns to Inventory)			Balance in Inventory		
	Units	Cost/Unit	Total $	Units	Cost/Unit	Total $	Units	Cost/Unit	Total $
June 1	1	$1	$1				1	$1	$1
3				1	$1	$1	0	$0	$0
5	1	$2	$2				1	$2	$2
7	1	$3	$3				2	1@$2 1@$3	$5
8				1	$2	$2	1	$3	$3
21	1	$4	$4				2	1@$3 1@$4	$7
23				1	$3	$3	1	$4	$4
28	1	$5	$5				2	1@$4 1@$5	$9
29				1	$4	$4	1	$5	$5

Total number of units available for sale: **5 units** = Total number of units sold: **4 units** + Total number of units in ending inventory: **1 unit**

Total cost of goods available for sale: **$15** = Total cost of goods sold: **$10** + Total cost of ending inventory: **$5**

Figure 6.10: Total Goods Sold plus Ending Inventory equals Total Goods Available for Sale (FIFO Perpetual)

An exploration is available on the Lyryx site. Log into your Lyryx course to run FIFO Perpetual.

Comprehensive Example—Weighted Average (Perpetual)

The inventory record card transactions using weighted average costing are detailed in Figure 6.11. *For consistency, all weighted average calculations will be rounded to two decimal places.* When a perpetual inventory system is used, the weighted average is calculated each time a purchase is made. For example, after the June 7 purchase, the balance in inventory is 2 units with a total cost of $5.00 (1 unit at $2.00 + 1 unit at $3.00) resulting in an average cost per unit of $2.50 ($5.00 ÷ 2 units = $2.50). When a sale occurs, the cost of the sale is based on the most recent average cost per unit. For example, the cost of the sale on June 3 uses the $1.00 average cost per unit from June 1 while the cost of the sale on June 8 uses the $2.50 average cost per unit from June 7.

		Purchases/Shipping Costs/ (Purchase Returns/Discounts)			Cost of Goods Sold/ (Returns to Inventory)			Balance in Inventory			Calculating AvgCost/Unit				
Date	Units	Cost/Unit	Total $	Units	Cost/Unit	Total $	Units	AvgCost/Unit	Total $	Total $	÷	Total Units	=	AvgCost/Unit
June 1	1	$1	$1				1	$1.00	$1.00	$1.00	÷	1	=	$1.00/unit
3				1	$1.00	$1.00	0	$0.00	$0.00	$0.00	÷	0	=	$0.00/unit
5	1	$2	$2				1	$2.00	$2.00	$2.00	÷	1	=	$2.00/unit
7	1	$3	$3				2	$2.50	$5.00	$5.00	÷	2	=	$2.50/unit
8				1	$2.50	$2.50	1	$2.50	$2.50	$2.50	÷	1	=	$2.50/unit
21	1	$4	$4				2	$3.25	$6.50	$6.50	÷	2	=	$3.25/unit
23				1	$3.25	$3.25	1	$3.25	$3.25	$3.25	÷	1	=	$3.25/unit
28	1	$5	$5				2	$4.13*	$8.25	$8.25	÷	2	=	$4.13*/unit
29				1	$4.13	$4.13	1	$4.12	$4.12	$4.12	÷	1	=	$4.12/unit

Rounded

Figure 6.11: Inventory Record Card using Weighted Average Costing (Perpetual)

A common error made by students when applying weighted average occurs when the unit costs are rounded. For example, on June 28, the average cost per unit is rounded to $4.13 ($8.25 ÷ 2 units = $4.125/unit rounded to $4.13). On June 29, the cost of the unit sold is $4.13, the June 28 average cost per unit. Care must be taken to recognize that the total remaining balance in inventory after the June 29 sale is $4.12, calculated as the June 28 ending inventory total dollar amount of $8.25 less the June 29 total cost of goods sold of $4.13. Students will often incorrectly use the average cost per unit, in this case $4.13, to calculate the ending inventory balance. Remember that the cost of goods sold plus the balance in inventory must equal the goods available for sale as highlighted in Figure 6.12.

6.1. Inventory Cost Flow Assumptions   185

	Purchases/Shipping Costs/ (Purchase Returns/Discounts)			Cost of Goods Sold/ (Returns to Inventory)			Balance in Inventory				Calculating AvgCost/Unit			
Date	Units	Cost/Unit	Total $	Units	Cost/Unit	Total $	Units	AvgCost/Unit	Total $	Total $	÷	Total Units	=	AvgCost/ Unit
June 1	1	$1	$1				1	$1.00	$1.00	$1.00	÷	1	=	$1.00/unit
3				1	$1.00	$1.00	0	$0.00	$0.00	$0.00	÷	0	=	$0.00/unit
5	1	$2	$2				1	$2.00	$2.00	$2.00	÷	1	=	$2.00/unit
7	1	$3	$3				2	$2.50	$5.00	$5.00	÷	2	=	$2.50/unit
8				1	$2.50	$2.50	1	$2.50	$2.50	$2.50	÷	1	=	$2.50/unit
21	1	$4	$4				2	$3.25	$6.50	$6.50	÷	2	=	$3.25/unit
23				1	$3.25	$3.25	1	$3.25	$3.25	$3.25	÷	1	=	$3.25/unit
28	1	$5	$5				2	$4.13*	$8.25	$8.25	÷	2	=	$4.13*/unit
29				1	$4.13	$4.13	1	$4.12	$4.12	$4.12	÷	1	=	$4.12/unit

Rounded

Total number of units available for sale: **5 units**

Total number of units sold: **4 units**

Total number of units in ending inventory: **1 unit**

Total cost of goods available for sale: **$15**

Total cost of goods sold: **$10.88**

Total cost of ending inventory: **$4.12**

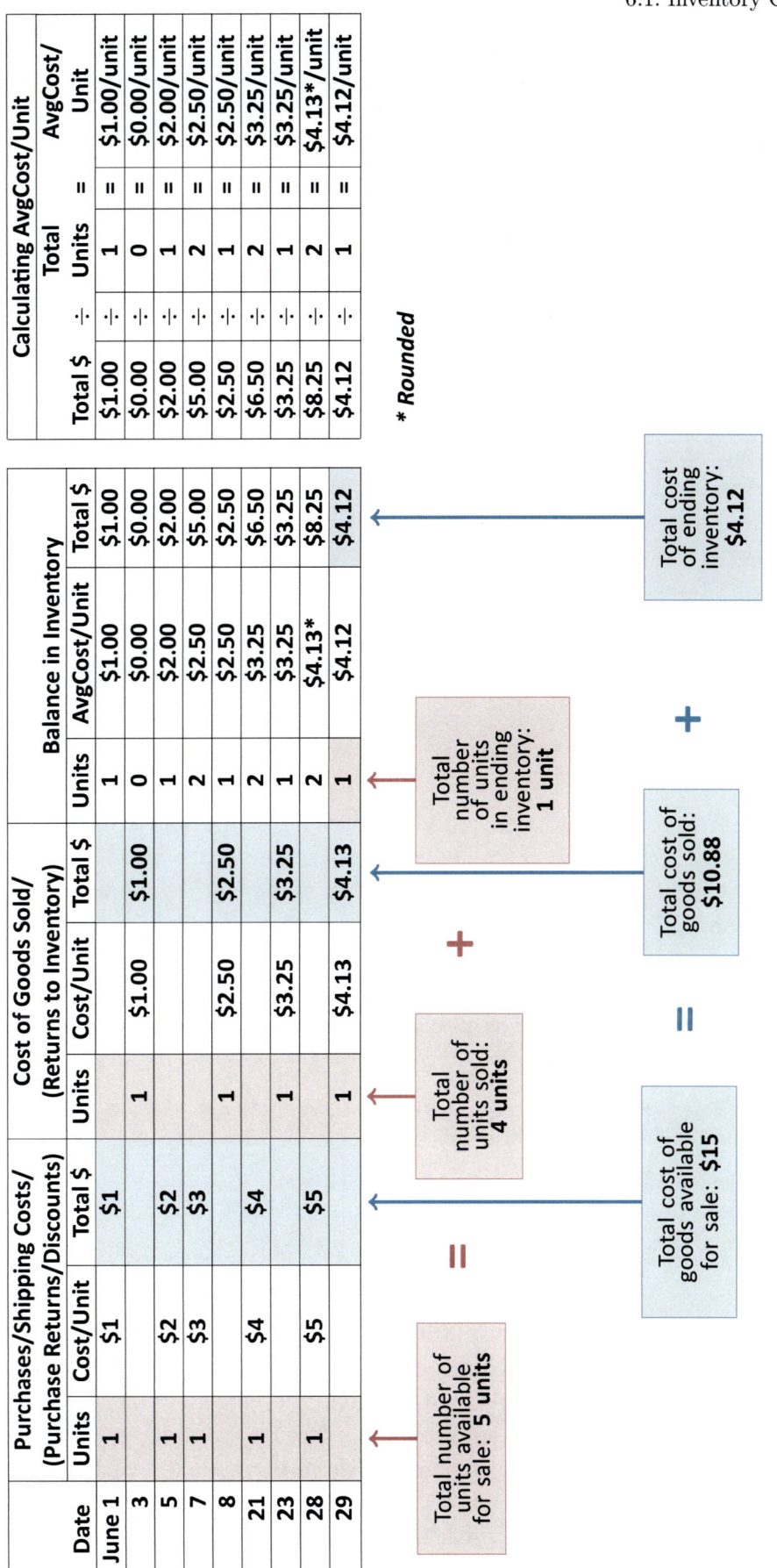

Figure 6.12: Total Goods Sold plus Ending Inventory equals Total Goods Available for Sale (Weighted Average Perpetual)

186 ■ Assigning Costs to Merchandise

An exploration is available on the Lyryx site. Log into your Lyryx course to run Weighted Average Perpetual.

Figure 6.13 compares the results of the three cost flow methods. Goods available for sale, units sold, and units in ending inventory are the same regardless of which method is used. Because each cost flow method allocates the cost of goods available for sale in a particular way, the cost of goods sold and ending inventory values are different for each method.

Cost Flow Assumption	Total Cost of Goods Available for Sale	Total Units Available for Sale	Total Cost of Goods Sold	Total Units Sold	Total Cost of Ending Inventory	Total Units in Ending Inventory
Specific Identification	$15.00	5	11.00	4	4.00	1
FIFO	15.00	5	10.00	4	5.00	1
Weighted Average	15.00	5	10.88	4	4.12	1

Figure 6.13: Comparing Specific Identification, FIFO, and Weighted Average

Journal Entries

In Chapter 5 the journal entries to record the sale of merchandise were introduced. Chapter 5 showed how the dollar value included in these journal entries is determined. We now know that the information in the inventory record is used to prepare the journal entries in the general journal. For example, the credit sale on June 23 using weighted average costing would be recorded as follows (refer to Figure 6.13).

Date	Account/Explanation	PR	Debit	Credit
	Accounts Receivable		10.00	
	Sales			10.00
	To record credit sale at a selling price of $10 per unit.			
	Cost of Goods Sold		3.25	
	Merchandise Inventory..............			3.25
	To record the cost of the sale.			

General Journal

Perpetual inventory incorporates an internal control feature that is lost under the periodic inventory method. Losses resulting from theft and error can easily be determined when the actual quantity of goods on hand is counted and compared with the quantities shown in the inventory records as being on hand. It may seem that this advantage is offset by the time and expense required to continuously update inventory records, particularly where there are thousands of different items of various sizes on hand. However, computerization makes this record keeping easier and less expensive because the inventory accounting system can be tied in to the sales system so that inventory is updated whenever a sale is recorded.

Inventory Record Card

In a company such as a large drugstore or hardware chain, inventory consists of thousands of different products. For businesses that carry large volumes of many inventory types, the general ledger merchandise inventory account contains only summarized transactions of the purchases and sales. The detailed transactions for each type of inventory would be recorded in the underlying inventory record cards. The inventory record card is an example of a *subsidiary ledger*, more commonly called a *subledger*. The **merchandise inventory subledger** provides a detailed listing of type, amount, and total cost of all types of inventory held at a particular point in time. The sum of the balances on each inventory record card in the subledger would always equal the ending amount recorded in the Mechandise Inventory general ledger account. So a subledger contains the detail for each product in inventory while the general ledger account shows only a summary. In this way, the general ledger information is streamlined while allowing for detail to be available through the subledger. There are other types of subledgers: the accounts receivable subledger and the accounts payable subledger. These will be introduced in a subsequent chapter.

6.2 Financial Statement Impact of Different Inventory Cost Flows

> LO2 – Explain the impact of inventory cost flows and errors.

When purchase costs are increasing, as in a period of inflation (or decreasing, as in a period of deflation), each cost flow assumption results in a different value for cost of goods sold and the resulting ending inventory, gross profit, and net income.

Using information from the preceding comprehensive example, the effects of each cost flow assumption on net income and ending inventory are shown in Figure 6.14.

	Spec. Ident.	FIFO	Wtd. Avg.
Sales	$ 40.00	$ 40.00	$ 40.00
Cost of goods sold	11.00	10.00	10.88
Gross profit and net income	$ 29.00	$ 30.00	$ 29.12
Ending inventory (on the balance sheet)	$ 4.00	$ 5.00	$ 4.12

Figure 6.14: Effects of Different Cost Flow Assumptions

FIFO *maximizes* net income and ending inventory amounts when costs are rising. FIFO *minimizes* net income and ending inventory amounts when purchase costs are decreasing.

Because different cost flow assumptions can affect the financial statements, GAAP requires that the assumption adopted by a company be disclosed in its financial statements (full disclosure principle). Additionally, GAAP requires that once a method is adopted, it be used every accounting period thereafter (consistency principle) unless there is a justifiable reason to change. A business that has a variety of inventory items may choose a different cost flow assumption for each item. For example, Walmart might use weighted average to account for its sporting goods items and specific identification for each of its various major appliances.

Effect of Inventory Errors on the Financial Statements

There are two components necessary to determine the inventory value disclosed on a corporation's balance sheet. The first component involves calculating the quantity of inventory on hand at the end of an accounting period by performing a physical inventory count. The second requirement involves assigning the most appropriate cost to this quantity of inventory.

An error in calculating either the quantity or the cost of ending inventory will misstate reported income for two time periods. Assume merchandise inventory at December 31, 2019, 2020, and 2021 was reported as $2,000 and that merchandise purchases during each of 2020 and 2021 were $20,000. There were no other expenditures. Assume further that sales each year amounted to $30,000 with cost of goods sold of $20,000 resulting in gross profit of $10,000. These transactions are summarized below.

Merchandise Inventory					2020	2021
Beg. Bal.	2,000			Sales	$30,000	$30,000
2020 Purch.	20,000	20,000	2020 COGS	COGS	20,000	20,000
2020 Bal.	2,000			Gross profit	$10,000	$10,000
2021 Purch.	20,000	20,000	2021 COGS			
2021 Bal.	2,000					

Assume now that ending inventory was misstated at December 31, 2020. Instead of the $2,000 that was reported, the correct value should have been $1,000. The effect of this error was to understate cost of goods sold on the income statement — cost of goods sold should have been $21,000 in 2020 as shown below instead of $20,000 as originally reported above. Because of the 2020 error, the 2021 beginning inventory was incorrectly reported above as $2,000 and should have been $1,000 as shown below. This caused the 2021 gross profit to be understated by $1,000 — cost of goods sold in 2021 should have been $19,000 as illustrated below but was originally reported above as $20,000.

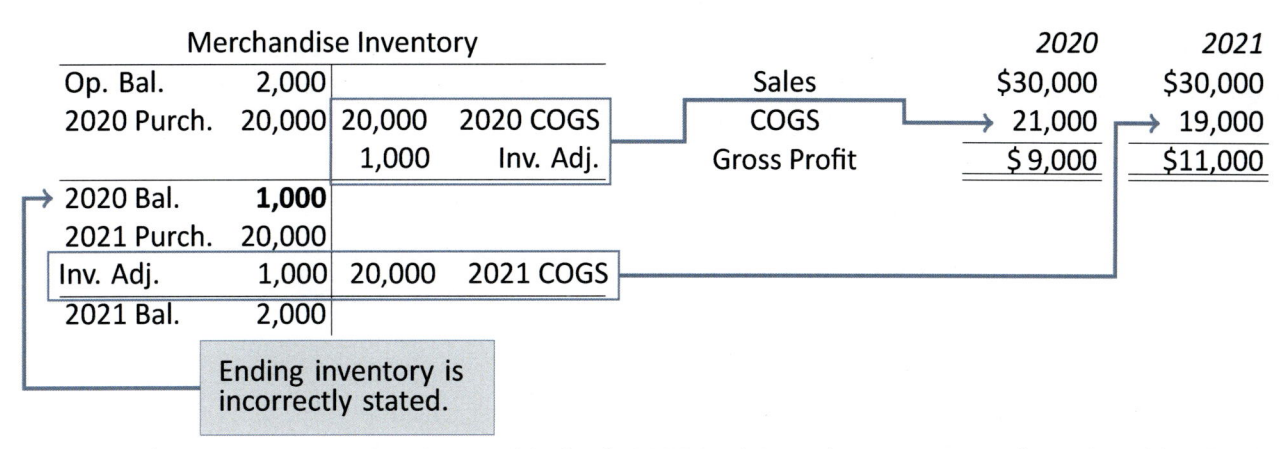

```
        Merchandise Inventory                                    2020        2021
Op. Bal.         2,000                         Sales           $30,000     $30,000
2020 Purch.     20,000  20,000   2020 COGS     COGS             21,000      19,000
                         1,000   Inv. Adj.     Gross Profit    $ 9,000     $11,000

2020 Bal.        1,000
2021 Purch.     20,000
Inv. Adj.        1,000  20,000   2021 COGS
2021 Bal.        2,000
```

Ending inventory is incorrectly stated.

As can be seen, income is misstated in both 2020 and 2021 because cost of goods sold in both years is affected by the adjustment to ending inventory needed at the end of 2020 and 2021. The opposite effects occur when inventory is understated at the end of an accounting period.

An error in ending inventory is offset in the next year because one year's ending inventory becomes the next year's opening inventory. This process can be illustrated by comparing gross profits for 2020 and 2021 in the above example. The sum of both years' gross profits is the same.

	Overstated Inventory	Correct Inventory
Gross profit for 2020	$10,000	$ 9,000
Gross profit for 2021	10,000	11,000
Total	$20,000	$20,000

An exploration is available on the Lyryx site. Log into your Lyryx course to run Inventory Errors.

6.3 Lower of Cost and Net Realizable Value (LCNRV)

LO3 — Explain and calculate lower of cost and net realizable value inventory adjustments.

In addition to the adjusting entry to record the shrinkage of merchandise inventory (discussed in Chapter 5), there is an additional adjusting entry to be considered at the end of the accounting period when calculating cost of goods sold and ending inventory values for the financial statements. Generally accepted accounting principles require that inventory be valued at the lesser amount of its *laid-down cost* and the amount for which it can likely be sold — its net realizable value (NRV). This concept is known as the lower of cost and net realizable value, or LCNRV. Note that the laid-down cost includes the invoice price of the goods (less any purchase discounts) plus transportation in, insurance while in transit, and any other expenditure made by the purchaser to get the merchandise to the place of business and ready for sale.

Assigning Costs to Merchandise

As an example, a change in consumer demand may mean that inventories become obsolete and need to be reduced in value below the purchase cost. This often occurs in the electronics industry as new and more popular products are introduced.

The lower of cost and net realizable value can be applied to individual inventory items or groups of similar items, as shown in Figure 6.15 below.

	Total Cost	Total NRV	LCNRV Unit Basis	LCNRV Group Basis
White paper	$1,250	$1,200	$1,200	
Coloured paper	1,400	1,500	1,400	
Total	$2,650	$2,700	$2,600	$2,650
Ending inventory (LCNRV)			$2,600	$2,650

Figure 6.15: LCNRV Calculations

Depending on the calculation used, the valuation of ending inventory will be either $2,600 or $2,650. Under the unit basis, the lower of cost and net realizable value is selected for each item: $1,200 for white paper and $1,400 for coloured paper, for a total LCNRV of $2,600. Because the LCNRV is lower than cost, an adjusting entry must be recorded as follows.

Date	Account/Explanation	PR	Debit	Credit
	Cost of Goods Sold....................		50	
	Merchandise Inventory.............			50
	To adjust inventory to reflect its LCNRV.			

The purpose of the adjusting entry is to ensure that inventory is not overstated on the balance sheet and that income is not overstated on the income statement.

If white paper and coloured paper are considered a similar group, the calculations in Figure 6.15 above show they have a combined cost of $2,650 and a combined net realizable value of $2700. LCNRV would therefore be $2,650. In this case, the cost is equal to the LCNRV so no adjusting entry would be required if applying LCNRV on a group basis.

An exploration is available on the Lyryx site. Log into your Lyryx course to run Lower of Cost or Net Realizable Value.

6.4 Estimating the Balance in Merchandise Inventory

LO4 – Estimate merchandise inventory using the gross profit method and the retail inventory method.

A physical inventory count determines the quantity of items on hand. When costs are assigned to these items and these individual costs are added, a total inventory amount is calculated. Is this dollar amount correct? Should it be larger? How can one tell if the physical count is accurate? Being able to estimate this amount provides a check on the reasonableness of the physical count and valuation.

The two methods used to estimate the inventory dollar amount are the *gross profit method* and the *retail inventory method*. Both methods are based on a calculation of the gross profit percentage in the income statement. Assume the following information:

Sales		$15,000	100%
Cost of Goods Sold:			
Opening Inventory	$ 4,000		
Purchases	12,000		
Cost of Goods Available for Sale	16,000		
Less: Ending Inventory	(6,000)		
Cost of Goods Sold		10,000	67%
Gross Profit		$ 5,000	33%

The gross profit percentage, rounded to the nearest whole percent, is 33% ($5,000/15,000). This means that for each dollar of sales, an average of $.33 is left to cover other expenses after deducting cost of goods sold.

Estimating ending inventory requires an understanding of the relationship of ending inventory with cost of goods sold. Review the following cost of goods sold calculations.

Cost of Goods Sold:			Cost of Goods Sold:		
Opening Inventory		$ 4,000	Opening Inventory		$ 4,000
Purchases		12,000	Purchases		12,000
Cost of Goods Available for Sale		$16,000	Cost of Goods Available for Sale		$16,000
Less: Estimated Ending Inventory		?	Less: Estimated Ending Inventory		6,000
Cost of Goods Sold		$10,000	Cost of Goods Sold		?

How much of the $16,000 of goods that the company had available to sell is still not sold at December 31 (in other words, what is ending inventory)? You can calculate this as:

Available for sale	$16,000
Less inventory that was sold	10,000
Equals what must still be on hand	$ 6,000

How much of the $16,000 of goods that were available to be sold have been sold? You use the dollar amount of ending inventory to calculate this, as:

Available for sale	$16,000
Less inventory on hand	6,000
Equals what must have been sold	$10,000

The sum of cost of goods sold and ending inventory is always equal to cost of goods available for sale. Knowing any two of these amounts enables the third amount to be calculated. Understanding this relationship is the key to estimating inventory using either the gross profit or retail inventory methods, discussed below.

Gross Profit Method

The **gross profit method** of estimating ending inventory assumes that the percentage of gross profit on sales remains approximately the same from period to period. Therefore, if the gross profit percentage is known, the dollar amount of ending inventory can be estimated. First, gross profit is estimated by applying the gross profit percentage to sales. From this, cost of goods sold can be derived, namely the difference between sales and gross profit. Cost of goods available for sale can be determined from the accounting records (opening inventory + purchases). The difference between cost of goods available for sale and cost of goods sold is the estimated value of ending inventory.

To demonstrate, assume that Pete's Products Ltd. has an average gross profit percentage of 40%. If opening inventory at January 1, 2019 was $200, sales for the six months ended June 30, 2019 were $2,000, and inventory purchased during the six months ended June 30, 2019 was $1,100, the cost of goods sold and ending inventory can be estimated as follows.

	Six Months Ended June 30, 2019
Sales (given)	$2,000
Cost of Goods Sold:	
Opening Inventory (given)	$ 200
Purchases (given)	1,100
Cost of Goods Available for Sale	1,300
Less: Estimated Ending Inventory	(100)
Cost of Goods Sold	1,200
Gross Profit	$ 800

Step 3: Ending inventory can be estimated ($1,300-1,200=100).

Step 2: Cost of goods sold can be derived ($2,000-800=$1,200).

Step 1: Gross profit is estimated at $800 ($2,000 x 40%).

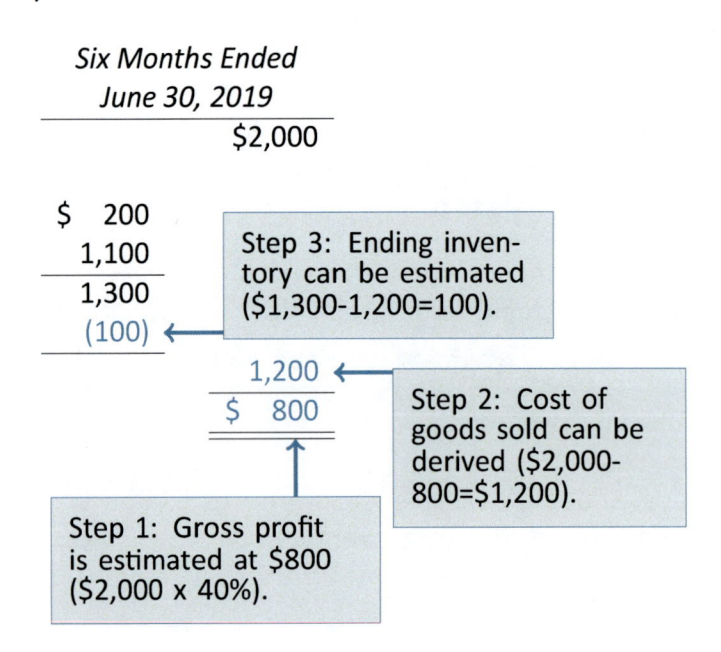

The estimated ending inventory at June 30 must be $100—the difference between the cost of goods available for sale and cost of goods sold.

The gross profit method of estimating inventory is useful in situations when goods have been stolen or destroyed by fire or when it is not cost-effective to make a physical inventory count.

An exploration is available on the Lyryx site. Log into your Lyryx course to run Gross Profit Method.

Retail Inventory Method

The **retail inventory method** is another way to estimate cost of goods sold and ending inventory. It can be used when items are consistently valued at a known percentage of cost, known as a *mark-up*. A **mark-up** is the ratio of retail value (or selling price) to cost. For example, if an inventory item had a retail value of $12 and a cost of $10, then it was marked up to 120% (12/10 x 100). Mark-ups are commonly used in clothing stores.

To apply the retail inventory method using the mark-up percentage, the cost of goods available for sale is first converted to its retail value (the selling price). To do this, the mark-up (ratio of retail to cost) must be known. Assume the same information as above for Pete's Products Ltd., except that now every item in the store is marked up to 160% of its purchase price. That is, if an item is purchased for $100, it is sold for $160. Based on this, opening inventory, purchases, and cost of goods available can be restated at retail. Cost of goods sold can then be valued at retail, meaning that it will equal sales for the period. From this, ending inventory at retail can be determined and then converted back to cost using the mark-up. These steps are illustrated below.

194 ■ Assigning Costs to Merchandise

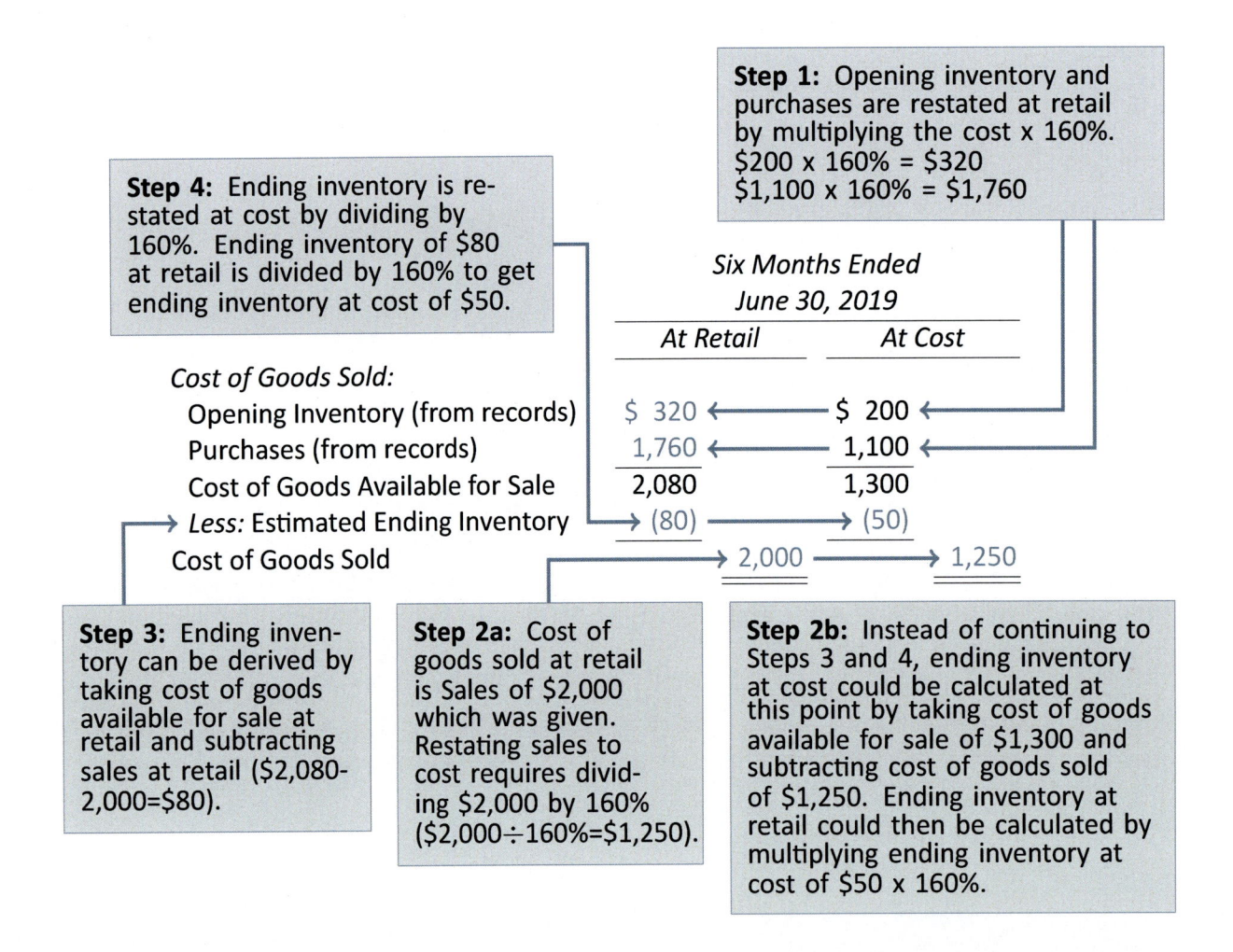

Step 1: Opening inventory and purchases are restated at retail by multiplying the cost × 160%.
$200 × 160% = $320
$1,100 × 160% = $1,760

Step 4: Ending inventory is restated at cost by dividing by 160%. Ending inventory of $80 at retail is divided by 160% to get ending inventory at cost of $50.

Six Months Ended
June 30, 2019

	At Retail	At Cost
Cost of Goods Sold:		
Opening Inventory (from records)	$ 320	$ 200
Purchases (from records)	1,760	1,100
Cost of Goods Available for Sale	2,080	1,300
Less: Estimated Ending Inventory	(80)	(50)
Cost of Goods Sold	2,000	1,250

Step 3: Ending inventory can be derived by taking cost of goods available for sale at retail and subtracting sales at retail ($2,080-2,000=$80).

Step 2a: Cost of goods sold at retail is Sales of $2,000 which was given. Restating sales to cost requires dividing $2,000 by 160% ($2,000÷160%=$1,250).

Step 2b: Instead of continuing to Steps 3 and 4, ending inventory at cost could be calculated at this point by taking cost of goods available for sale of $1,300 and subtracting cost of goods sold of $1,250. Ending inventory at retail could then be calculated by multiplying ending inventory at cost of $50 × 160%.

The retail inventory method of estimating ending inventory is easy to calculate and produces a relatively accurate cost of ending inventory, provided that no change in the average mark-up has occurred during the period.

An exploration is available on the Lyryx site. Log into your Lyryx course to run Retail Inventory Method.

6.5 Appendix A: Ratio Analysis—Merchandise Inventory Turnover

LO5 – Explain and calculate merchandise inventory turnover.

To help determine how quickly a company is able to sell its inventory, the **merchandise inventory turnover** can be calculated as:

Cost of Goods Sold ÷ Average Merchandise Inventory

The average merchandise inventory is the beginning inventory plus the ending inventory divided by two. For example, assume Company A had cost of goods sold of $3,000; beginning merchandise inventory of $500; and ending inventory of $700. The merchandise inventory turnover would be 5, calculated as:

Cost of Goods Sold ÷ Average Merchandise Inventory
$3,000 ÷ (($500+$700)/2)

The '5' means that Company A sold its inventory 5 times during the year. In contrast, assume Company B had cost of goods sold of $3,000; beginning merchandise inventory of $1,000; and ending inventory of $1,400. The merchandise inventory turnover would be 2.50 calculated as:

Cost of Goods Sold ÷ Average Merchandise Inventory
$3,000 ÷ (($1,000+$1,400)/2)

The '2.5' means that Company B sold its inventory 2.5 times during the year which is much slower than Company A. The faster a business sells its inventory, the better, because high turnover positively affects *liquidity*. **Liquidity** is the ability to convert assets, such as merchandise inventory, into cash. Therefore, Company A's merchandise turnover is more favourable than Company B's.

An exploration is available on the Lyryx site. Log into your Lyryx course to run Using the Information - Merchandise Turnover.

6.6 Appendix B: Inventory Cost Flow Assumptions Under the Periodic System

LO6 – Calculate cost of goods sold and merchandise inventory using specific identification, first-in first-out (FIFO), and weighted average cost flow assumptions periodic.

Recall from Chapter 5 that the periodic inventory system does not maintain detailed records to calculate cost of goods sold each time a sale is made. Rather, when a sale is made, the following entry is made:

	General Journal			
Date	Account/Explanation	PR	Debit	Credit
	Accounts Receivable		XX	
	Sales			XX
	To record a credit sale.			

No entry is made to record cost of goods sold and to reduce Merchandise Inventory, as is done under the perpetual inventory system. Instead, all purchases are expenses and recorded in the general ledger account "Purchases." A physical inventory count is conducted at year-end. An amount for ending inventory is calculated based on this count and the valuation of the items in inventory, and cost of goods sold is calculated in the income statement based on this total amount. The income statement format is:

Sales		$10,000
Cost of Goods Sold:		
Opening Inventory	$ 1,000	
Purchases	5,000	
Goods Available for Sale	6,000	
Less: Ending Inventory	(2,000)	
Cost of Goods Sold		4,000
Gross Profit		$6,000

Even under the periodic inventory system, however, inventory cost flow assumptions need to be made (specific identification, FIFO, weighted average) when purchase prices change over time, as in a period of inflation. Further, different inventory cost flow assumptions produce different cost of goods sold and ending inventory values, just as they did under the perpetual inventory system. These effects have been explained earlier in this chapter. *Under the periodic inventory system, cost of goods sold and ending inventory values are determined as if the sales for the period all take place at the end of the period.* These calculations were demonstrated in our earliest example in this chapter.

Our original example using units assumed there was no opening inventory at June 1, 2015 and that purchases were made as follows.

6.6. Appendix B: Inventory Cost Flow Assumptions Under the Periodic System

	Purchase Transaction	
Date	Number of units	Price per unit
June 1	1	$1
5	1	2
7	1	3
21	1	4
28	1	5
	5	$15

When recorded in the general ledger T-account "Purchases" (an income statement account), these transactions would be recorded as follows.

```
     Purchases        No. 570
Jun. 1   $1
     5    2
     7    3
    21    4
    28    5
```

Sales of four units are all assumed to take place on June 30. Ending inventory would then be counted at the end of the day on June 30. One unit should be on hand. It would be valued as follows under the various inventory cost flow assumptions, as discussed in the first part of the chapter:

Specific identification $4
FIFO   5
Weighted average   3

These values would be used to calculate cost of goods sold and gross profit on the income statement, as shown in Figure 6.16 below:

	Spec. Ident.	FIFO	Wtd. Avg.
Sales	$40	$40	$40
Cost of Goods Sold:			
Opening Inventory	-0-	-0-	-0-
Purchases	15	15	15
Goods Available for Sale	15	15	15
Less: Ending Inventory	(4)	(5)	(3)
Cost of Goods Sold	11	10	12
Gross Profit and Net Income	$29	$30	$28
Ending Inventory (Balance Sheet)	$4	$5	$3

Figure 6.16: Effects of Different Cost Flow Assumptions: Periodic Inventory System

Note that these results are the same as those calculated using the perpetual inventory method and assuming all sales take place on June 30 using specific identification (Figure 6.2), FIFO (Figure 6.3), and weighted average (Figure 6.4) cost flow assumptions, respectively.

As discussed in the appendix to Chapter 5, the ending inventory amount will be recorded in the accounting records when the income statement accounts are closed to the Income Summary at the end of the year. The amount of the closing entry for ending inventory is obtained from the income statement. Using the example above and assuming no other revenue or expense items, the closing entry to adjust ending inventory to actual under each inventory cost flow assumption would be as follows.

	Specific Identification	FIFO	Weighted Average
Merchandise Inventory (ending)	4	5	3
Sales	40	40	40
Income Summary	44	45	43

To close all income statement accounts with credit balances to the Income Summary and record ending inventory balance.

An exploration is available on the Lyryx site. Log into your Lyryx course to run Assigning Costs to Inventory - Periodic System.

Summary of Chapter 6 Learning Objectives

LO1 – Calculate cost of goods sold and merchandise inventory using specific identification, first-in first-out (FIFO), and weighted average cost flow assumptions—perpetual.

Cost of goods available for sale must be allocated between cost of goods sold and ending inventory using a cost flow assumption. Specific identification allocates cost to units sold by using the actual cost of the specific unit sold. FIFO (first-in first-out) allocates cost to units sold by assuming the units sold were the oldest units in inventory. Weighted average allocates cost to units sold by calculating a weighted average cost per unit at the time of sale.

LO2 – Explain the impact on financial statements of inventory cost flows and errors.

As purchase prices change, particular inventory methods will assign different cost of goods sold and resulting ending inventory to the financial statements. Specific identification achieves the exact matching of revenues and costs while weighted average accomplishes an averaging of price changes, or smoothing. The use of FIFO results in the current cost of inventory appearing on the balance sheet in ending inventory. The cost flow method in use must be disclosed in the notes to the financial statements and be applied consistently from period to period. An error in ending inventory in one period impacts the balance sheet (inventory and equity) and the income statement (COGS and net income) for that accounting period and the next. However, inventory errors in one period reverse themselves in the next.

LO3 – Explain and calculate lower of cost and net realizable value inventory adjustments.

Inventory must be evaluated, at minimum, each accounting period to determine whether the net realizable value (NRV) is lower than cost, known as the lower of cost and net realizable value (LCNRV) of inventory. An adjustment is made if the NRV is lower than cost. LCNRV can be applied to groups of similar items or by item.

LO4 – Estimate merchandise inventory using the gross profit method and the retail inventory method.

Estimating inventory using the gross profit method requires that estimated cost of goods sold be calculated by, first, multiplying net sales by the gross profit ratio. Estimated ending inventory at cost is then arrived at by taking goods available for sale at cost less the estimated cost of goods sold. To apply the retail inventory method, three calculations are required:

- retail value of goods available for sale less retail value of net sales equals retail value of ending inventory,

- goods available for sale at cost divided by retail value of goods available for sale equals cost to retail ratio, and

- retail value of ending inventory multiplied by the cost to retail ratio equals estimated cost of ending inventory.

LO5 – Explain and calculate merchandise inventory turnover.

The merchandise turnover is a liquidity ratio that measures how quickly inventory is sold. It is calculated as: COGS/Average Merchandise Inventory. Average merchandise inventory is the beginning inventory balance plus the ending inventory balance divided by two.

LO6 – Calculate cost of goods sold and merchandise inventory using specific identification, first-in first-out (FIFO), and weighted average cost flow assumptions—periodic.

Periodic systems assign cost of goods available for sale to cost of goods sold and ending inventory at the end of the accounting period. Specific identification and FIFO give identical results in each of periodic and perpetual. The weighted average cost, periodic, will differ from its perpetual counterpart because in periodic, the average cost per unit is calculated at the end of the accounting period based on total goods that were available for sale.

Discussion Questions

1. Explain the importance of maintaining appropriate inventory levels for
    a. management; and
    b. investors and creditors.
2. What aspects of accounting for inventory on financial statements would be of interest to accountants?
3. What is meant by the laid-down cost of inventory?
4. How does a flow of goods differ from a flow of costs? Do generally accepted accounting principles require that the flow of costs be similar to the movement of goods? Explain.
5. What two factors are considered when costing merchandise for financial statement purposes? Which of these factors is most difficult to determine? Why?
6. Why is consistency in inventory valuation necessary? Does the application of the consistency principle preclude a change from weighted average to FIFO? Explain.
7. The ending inventory of CBCA Inc. is overstated by $5,000 at December 31, 2018. What is the effect on 2018 net income? What is the effect on 2019 net income assuming that no other inventory errors have occurred during 2019?
8. When should inventory be valued at less than cost?
9. What is the primary reason for the use of the LCNRV method of inventory valuation? What does the term net *realisable value* mean?
10. When inventory is valued at LCNRV, what does cost refer to?
11. What inventory cost flow assumptions are permissible under GAAP?
12. Why is estimating inventory useful?

13. How does the estimation of ending inventory differ between the gross profit method and the retail inventory method? Use examples to illustrate.

14. When is the use of the gross profit method particularly useful?

15. Does the retail inventory method assume any particular inventory cost flow assumption?

Exercises

EXERCISE 6–1   (LO1)

Laplante Inc. uses the perpetual inventory system. The following transactions took place during January 2021.

Date		Units	Unit Cost
Jan. 1	Opening Inventory	100	$1
7	Purchase #1	10	2
9	Sale #1	80	
21	Purchase #2	20	3
24	Sale #2	40	

Required: Using the table below, calculate cost of goods sold for the January 9 and 24 sales, and ending inventory using the FIFO cost flow assumption.

	Purchased (Sold)			Balance		
Date	Units	Unit Cost	COGS	Units	Unit Cost	Total Cost
Jan. 1 Opening Inventory				100 ×	$1 =	$100
7 Purchase #1						
9 Sale #1						
21 Purchase #2						
24 Sale #2						

EXERCISE 6–2   (LO1)

Using the information from Exercise 6–1, calculate the cost of goods sold for the January 9 and 24 sales, and ending inventory using the Specific Identification cost flow assumption. Assume that:

i. on January 9, the specific units sold were 72 units from opening inventory and 8 units from the January 7 purchase and

ii. the specific units sold on January 24 were 23 units from opening inventory and 17 units from the January 21 purchase.

EXERCISE 6–3 (LO1)

ABBA uses the weighted average inventory cost flow assumption under the perpetual inventory system. The following transactions took place in January 2018.

Date		Units	Unit Selling Price/ Cost
Jan. 1	Opening Inventory	2,000	$0.50
5	Sale #1	1,200	5.00
6	Purchase #1	1,000	2.00
10	Purchase #2	500	1.00
16	Sale #2	2,000	6.00
21	Purchase #3	1,000	2.50

All sales are made on account. Round all per unit costs to two decimal places.

Required:

a. Record the journal entry for the January 5 sale. Show calculations for cost of goods sold.

b. Record the journal entry for the January 16 sale. Show calculations for cost of goods sold.

c. Calculate ending inventory in units, cost per unit, and total cost.

EXERCISE 6–4 (LO2)

Listed below are four common accounting errors.

	2016 Statements				2017 Statements			
Errors	Opening Invent.	Ending Invent.	2016 Total Assets	2016 Net Income	Opening Invent.	Ending Invent.	2017 Total Assets	2017 Net Income
1. Goods purchased in 2016 were included in the December 31, 2016 inventory, but the transaction was not recorded until early 2017.	N/E							
2. Goods purchased in 2017 were included in December 31, 2016 inventory, and the transaction was recorded in 2016.	N/E							

Required: Use N/E (No Effect), O (Overstated), or U (Understated) to indicate the effect of each error on the company's financial statements for the years ended December 31, 2016 and December 31, 2017. The opening inventory for the 2016 statements is done.

EXERCISE 6–5   (LO2)

Partial income statements of Lilydale Products Inc. are reproduced below:

	2021	2022	2023
Sales	$30,000	$40,000	$50,000
Cost of Goods Sold	20,000	23,000	25,000
Gross Profit	$10,000	$17,000	$25,000

Required:

a. Calculate the impact of the two errors listed below on the gross profit calculated for the three years:

　i. The 2021 ending inventory was understated by $2,000.

　ii. The 2023 ending inventory was overstated by $5,000.

b. What is the impact of these errors on Total Assets?

EXERCISE 6–6   (LO3)

Erndale Products Ltd. has the following items in inventory at year-end:

Item	Units	Cost/Unit	NRV/Unit
X	2	$50	$60
Y	3	150	75
Z	4	25	20

Required: Calculate the cost of ending inventory using LCNRV on

a. A unit-by-unit basis

b. A group inventory basis.

EXERCISE 6–7   (LO4)

Windy City Insurance Ltd. has received a fire-loss claim of $45,000 from Balton Corp. A fire destroyed Balton's inventory on May 25, 2015. Balton has an average gross profit of 35%. You have obtained the following information:

Inventory, May 1, 2015	$ 80,000
Purchases, May 1 - May 25	150,000
Sales, May 1 - May 25	300,000

Required:

a. Calculate the estimated amount of inventory lost in the fire.

b. How reasonable is Balton's claim?

EXERCISE 6–8   (LO5)

The following account balances for Cost of Goods Sold and Merchandise Inventory were extracted from Able Corp.'s accounting records:

	2025	2024	2023	2022	2021
Cost of Goods Sold	370,000	400,000	420,000	440,000	450,000
Merchandise Inventory	120,000	111,250	88,750	111,250	88,750

Required:

a. Calculate the Merchandise Inventory Turnover for each of the years 2022 to 2025.

b. Is the change in Able Corp.'s Merchandise Inventory Turnover ratio favourable or unfavourable? Explain.

Problems

PROBLEM 6–1   (LO1)

Southern Cross Company Limited made the following purchases and sales of Products A and B during the year ended December 31, 2020:

Product A

		Units	Unit Cost/ Selling Price
Jan. 07	Purchase #1	8,000	$12.00
Mar. 30	Sale #1	9,000	16.00
May 10	Purchase #2	12,000	12.10
Jul. 04	Sale #2	14,000	17.00

Product B

		Units	Unit Cost/ Selling Price
Jan. 13	Purchase #1	5,000	$13.81
Jul. 15	Sale #1	1,000	20.00
Oct. 23	Purchase #2	7,000	14.21
Dec. 14	Sale #2	8,000	21.00

Opening inventory at January 1 amounted to 4,000 units at $11.90 per unit for Product A and 2,000 units at $13.26 per unit for Product B.

Required:

1. Prepare inventory record cards for Products A and B for the year using the weighted average inventory cost flow assumption.

2. Calculate total cost of ending inventory at December 31, 2020.

3. Calculate the gross profit percentage earned on the sale of

   i. Product A in 2020 and

ii. Product B in 2020.

PROBLEM 6–2 (LO2)

Partial income statements of Schneider Products Inc. are reproduced below:

	2016	2017
Sales	$50,000	$50,000
Cost of Goods Sold	20,000	23,000
Gross Profit	$30,000	$27,000

The 2016 ending inventory was overstated by $2,000 during the physical count. The 2017 physical inventory count was done properly.

Required:

1. Calculate the impact of this error on the gross profit calculated for 2016 and 2017.

2. What is the impact of this error on total assets at the end of 2016 and 2017? Net assets?

PROBLEM 6–3 (LO3)

Reflex Corporation sells three products. The inventory valuation of these products is shown below for years 2017 and 2018.

	2017			2018		
	Cost	Market	Unit Basis (LCNRV)	Cost	Market	Unit Basis (LCNRV)
Product X	$14,000	$15,000	?	$15,000	$16,000	?
Product Y	12,500	12,000	?	12,000	11,500	?
Product Z	11,000	11,500	?	10,500	10,000	?
Total	?	?	?	?	?	?

Required: If Reflex values its inventory using LCNRV/unit basis, complete the 2017 and 2018 cost, net realizable value, and LCNRV calculations.

Chapter 7

Cash and Receivables

This chapter focuses on the current assets of cash and receivables. Internal control over cash involves processes and procedures that include the use of a petty cash fund and the preparation of a bank reconciliation. Receivables can be determined to be uncollectible. To match the cost of uncollectible accounts and the related revenue, uncollectible accounts, more commonly referred to as bad debts, must be estimated. Bad debts are accounted for using the allowance approach, applied using either the income statement method or balance sheet method. When uncollectible accounts are specifically identified, they are written off. Write-offs can be subsequently recovered. The journalizing of short-term notes receivable and related interest revenue is also discussed in this chapter. To help in the analysis of cash and receivables, two ratios are introduced: the acid-test and accounts receivable turnover.

Chapter 7 Learning Objectives

LO1 – Define internal control and explain how it is applied to cash.

LO2 – Explain and journalize petty cash transactions.

LO3 – Explain the purpose of and prepare a bank reconciliation, and record related adjustments.

LO4 – Explain, calculate, and record estimated uncollectible accounts receivable and subsequent write-offs and recoveries.

LO5 – Explain and record a short-term notes receivable as well as calculate related interest.

LO6 – Explain and calculate the acid-test ratio.

LO7 – Explain and calculate the accounts receivable turnover.

Concept Self-Check

Use the following as a self-check while working through Chapter 7.

1. What constitutes a good system of control over cash?

2. What is a petty cash system and how is it used to control cash?

3. How is petty cash reported on the balance sheet?

4. How does the preparation of a bank reconciliation facilitate control over cash?
5. What are the steps in preparing a bank reconciliation?
6. How does the estimation of uncollectible accounts receivable address the GAAP of matching?
7. How are uncollectible accounts disclosed on financial statements?
8. What are the different methods used for estimating uncollectible accounts receivable?
9. How is aging of accounts receivable used in estimating uncollectible accounts?
10. How are notes receivable recorded?
11. What is the acid-test ratio and how is it calculated?
12. How is the accounts receivable turnover calculated and what does it mean?

NOTE: The purpose of these questions is to prepare you for the concepts introduced in the chapter. Your goal should be to answer each of these questions as you read through the chapter. If, when you complete the chapter, you are unable to answer one or more the Concept Self-Check questions, go back through the content to find the answer(s). Solutions are not provided to these questions.

7.1 Internal Control

LO1 – Define internal control and explain how it is applied to cash.

Assets are the lifeblood of a company. As such, they must be protected. This duty falls to managers of a company. The policies and procedures implemented by management to protect assets are collectively referred to as **internal controls**. An effective internal control program not only protects assets, but also aids in accurate recordkeeping, produces financial statement information in a timely manner, ensures compliance with laws and regulations, and promotes efficient operations. Effective internal control procedures ensure that adequate records are maintained, transactions are authorized, duties among employees are divided between recordkeeping functions and control of assets, and employees' work is checked by others. The use of electronic recordkeeping systems does not decrease the need for good internal controls.

The effectiveness of internal controls is limited by human error and fraud. Human error can occur because of negligence or mistakes. Fraud is the intentional decision to circumvent internal control systems for personal gain. Sometimes, employees cooperate in order to avoid internal controls. This *collusion* is often difficult to detect, but fortunately, it is not a common occurrence when adequate controls are in place.

Internal controls take many forms. Some are broadly based, like mandatory employee drug testing, video surveillance, and scrutiny of company email systems. Others are specific to a particular type of asset or process. For instance, internal controls need to be applied to a company's accounting system to ensure that transactions are processed efficiently and correctly to produce reliable records in a timely manner. Procedures should be documented to promote good recordkeeping, and employees need to be trained in the application of internal control procedures.

Financial statements prepared according to generally accepted accounting principles are useful not only to external users in evaluating the financial performance and financial position of the company, but also for internal decision making. There are various internal control mechanisms that aid in the production of timely and useful financial information. For instance, using a chart of accounts is necessary to ensure transactions are recorded in the appropriate account. As an example, expenses are classified and recorded in applicable expense accounts, then summarized and evaluated against those of a prior year.

The design of accounting records and documents is another important means to provide financial information. Financial data is entered and summarized in records and transmitted by documents. A good system of internal control requires that these records and documents be prepared at the time a transaction takes place or as soon as possible afterward, since they become less credible and the possibility of error increases with the passage of time. The documents should also be consecutively pre-numbered, to indicate whether there may be missing documents.

Internal control also promotes the protection of assets. Cash is particularly vulnerable to misuse. A good system of internal control for cash should provide adequate procedures for protecting cash receipts and cash payments (commonly referred to as cash disbursements). Procedures to achieve control over cash vary from company to company and depend upon such variables as company size, number of employees, and cash sources. However, effective cash control generally requires the following:

- Separation of duties: People responsible for handling cash should not be responsible for maintaining cash records. By separating the custodial and record-keeping duties, theft of cash is less likely.

- Same-day deposits: All cash receipts should be deposited daily in the company's bank account. This prevents theft and personal use of the money before deposit.

- Payments made using non-cash means: Cheques or electronic funds transfer (EFT) provide a separate external record to verify cash disbursements. For example, many businesses pay their employees using electronic funds transfer because it is more secure and efficient than using cash or even cheques.

Two forms of internal control over cash will be discussed in this chapter: the use of a petty cash account and the preparation of bank reconciliations.

7.2 Petty Cash

LO2 – Explain and journalize petty cash transactions.

The payment of small amounts by cheque may be inconvenient and costly. For example, using cash to pay for postage on an incoming package might be less than the total processing cost of a cheque. A small amount of cash kept on hand to pay for small, infrequent expenses is referred to as a **petty cash fund**.

Establishing and Reimbursing the Petty Cash Fund

To set up the petty cash fund, a cheque is prepared for the amount of the fund. The custodian of the fund cashes the cheque and places the coins and currency in a locked box. Responsibility for the petty cash fund should be delegated to only one person, who should be held accountable for its contents. Cash payments are made by this petty cash custodian out of the fund as required when supported by receipts. When the amount of cash has been reduced to a pre-determined level, the receipts are compiled and submitted for entry into the accounting system. A cheque is then issued to reimburse the petty cash fund. At any given time, the petty cash amount should consist of cash and supporting receipts, all totalling the petty cash fund amount. To demonstrate the management of a petty cash fund, assume that a $200 cheque is issued for the purpose of establishing a petty cash fund.

The journal entry is:

\multicolumn{5}{c|}{General Journal}				
Date	Account/Explanation	PR	Debit	Credit
	Petty Cash.............................		200	
	Cash.............................			200
	To establish the $200 petty cash fund.			

Petty Cash is a current asset account. When reporting Cash on the financial statements, the balances in Petty Cash and Cash are added together and reported as one amount.

Assume the petty cash custodian has receipts totalling $190 and $10 in coin and currency remaining in the petty cash box. The receipts consist of the following: delivery charges $100, $35 for postage, and office supplies of $55. The petty cash custodian submits the receipts to the accountant who records the following entry and issues a cheque for $190.

\multicolumn{5}{c|}{General Journal}				
Date	Account/Explanation	PR	Debit	Credit
	Delivery Expense........................		100	
	Postage Expense........................		35	
	Office Supplies Expense[1]..............		55	
	Cash.............................			190
	To reimburse the petty cash fund.			

The petty cash receipts should be cancelled at the time of reimbursement in order to prevent their reuse for duplicate reimbursements. The petty cash custodian cashes the $190 cheque. The $190 plus the $10 of coin and currency in the locked box immediately prior to reimbursement equals the $200 total required in the petty cash fund.

Sometimes, the receipts plus the coin and currency in the petty cash locked box do not equal the required petty cash balance. To demonstrate, assume the same information above except that the coin and currency remaining in the petty cash locked box was $8. This amount plus the receipts for $190 equals $198 and not $200, indicating a shortage in the petty cash box. The entry at the time of reimbursement reflects the shortage and is recorded as:

	General Journal			
Date	Account/Explanation	PR	Debit	Credit
	Delivery Expense..........................		100	
	Postage Expense..........................		35	
	Office Supplies Expense..................		55	
	Cash Over/Short Expense...............		2	
	Cash.................................			192
	To reimburse the petty cash fund and account for the $2.00 shortage.			

Notice that the $192 credit to Cash plus the $8 of coin and currency remaining in the petty cash box immediately prior to reimbursement equals the $200 required total in the petty cash fund.

Assume, instead, that the coin and currency in the petty cash locked box was $14. This amount plus the receipts for $190 equals $204 and not $200, indicating an overage in the petty cash box. The entry at the time of reimbursement reflects the overage and is recorded as:

	General Journal			
Date	Account/Explanation	PR	Debit	Credit
	Delivery Expense..........................		100	
	Postage Expense..........................		35	
	Office Supplies Expense..................		55	
	Cash Over/Short Expense.............			4
	Cash.................................			186
	To reimburse the petty cash fund and account for the $4.00 overage.			

Again, notice that the $186 credit to Cash plus the $14 of coin and currency remaining in the petty cash box immediately prior to reimbursement equals the $200 required total in the petty cash fund.

What happens if the petty cash custodian finds that the fund is rarely used? In such a case, the size of the fund should be decreased to reduce the risk of theft. To demonstrate, assume the petty cash custodian has receipts totalling $110 and $90 in coin and currency remaining in the

---

[1]An expense is debited instead of Office Supplies, an asset, because the need to purchase supplies through petty cash assumes the immediate use of the items.

petty cash box. The receipts consist of the following: delivery charges $80 and postage $30. The petty cash custodian submits the receipts to the accountant and requests that the petty cash fund be reduced by $75. The following entry is recorded and a cheque for $35 is issued.

General Journal				
Date	Account/Explanation	PR	Debit	Credit
	Delivery Expense.........................		80	
	Postage Expense		30	
	Petty Cash			75
	Cash.................................			35
	To reimburse the petty cash fund and reduce it by $75.			

The $35 credit to Cash plus the $90 of coin and currency remaining in the petty cash box immediately prior to reimbursement equals the $125 new balance in the petty cash fund ($200 original balance less the $75 reduction).

In cases when the size of the petty cash fund is too small, the petty cash custodian could request an increase in the size of the petty cash fund at the time of reimbursement. Care should be taken to ensure that the size of the petty cash fund is not so large as to become a potential theft issue. Additionally, if a petty cash fund is too large, it may be an indicator that transactions that should be paid by cheque are not being processed in accordance with company policy. Remember that the purpose of the petty cash fund is to pay for infrequent expenses; day-to-day items should not go through petty cash.

An exploration is available on the Lyryx site. Log into your Lyryx course to run Petty Cash.

7.3 Cash Collections and Payments

LO3 – Explain the purpose of and prepare a bank reconciliation, and record related adjustments.

The widespread use of banks facilitates cash transactions between entities and provides a safeguard for the cash assets being exchanged. This involvement of banks as intermediaries between entities has accounting implications. At any point in time, the cash balance in the accounting records of a particular company usually differs from the bank cash balance of that company. The difference is usually because some cash transactions recorded in the accounting records have not yet been recorded by the bank and, conversely, some cash transactions recorded by the bank have not yet been recorded in the company's accounting records.

The use of a bank reconciliation is one method of internal control over cash. The reconciliation process brings into agreement the company's accounting records for cash and the **bank statement** issued by the company's bank. A bank reconciliation explains the difference between the balances reported by the company and by the bank on a given date.

A bank reconciliation proves the accuracy of both the company's and the bank's records, and reveals any errors made by either party. The bank reconciliation is a tool that can help detect attempts at theft and manipulation of records. The preparation of a bank reconciliation is discussed in the following section.

The Bank Reconciliation

The bank reconciliation is a report prepared by a company at a point in time. It identifies discrepancies between the cash balance reported on the bank statement and the cash balance reported in a business's Cash account in the general ledger, more commonly referred to as the *books*. These discrepancies are known as *reconciling items* and are added or subtracted to either the book balance or bank balance of cash. Each of the reconciling items is added or subtracted to the business's cash balance. The business's cash balance will change as a result of the reconciling items. The cash balance prior to reconciliation is called the *unreconciled* cash balance. The balance after adding and subtracting the reconciling items is called the *reconciled* cash balance. The following is a list of potential reconciling items and their impact on the bank reconciliation.

Book reconciling items	Bank reconciling items
Collection of notes receivable (added)	Outstanding deposits (added)
NSF cheques (subtracted)	Outstanding cheques (subtracted)
Bank charges (subtracted)	
Book errors (added or subtracted, depending on the nature of the error	Bank errors (added or subtracted, depending on the nature of the error)

Book Reconciling Items

The collection of notes receivable may be made by a bank on behalf of the company. These collections are often unknown to the company until they appear as an addition on the bank statement, and so cause the general ledger cash account to be understated. As a result, the collection of a notes receivable is added to the unreconciled book balance of cash on the bank reconciliation.

Cheques returned to the bank because there were not sufficient funds (NSF) to cover them appear on the bank statement as a reduction of cash. The company must then request that the customer pay the amount again. As a result, the general ledger cash account is overstated by the amount of the NSF cheque. NSF cheques must therefore be subtracted from the unreconciled book balance of cash on the bank reconciliation to reconcile cash.

Cheques received by a company and deposited into its bank account may be returned by the customer's bank for a number of reasons (e.g., the cheque was issued too long ago, known as a stale-dated cheque, an unsigned or illegible cheque, or the cheque shows the wrong account number). Returned cheques cause the general ledger cash account to be overstated. These cheques are therefore subtracted on the bank statement, and must be deducted from the unreconciled book balance of cash on the bank reconciliation.

Bank service charges are deducted from the customer's bank account. Since the service charges have not yet been recorded by the company, the general ledger cash account is overstated. Therefore, service charges are subtracted from the unreconciled book balance of cash on the bank reconciliation.

A business may incorrectly record journal entries involving cash. For instance, a deposit or cheque may be recorded for the wrong amount in the company records. These errors are often detected when amounts recorded by the company are compared to the bank statement. Depending on the nature of the error, it will be either added to or subtracted from the unreconciled book balance of cash on the bank reconciliation. For example, if the company recorded a cheque as $520 when the correct amount of the cheque was $250, the $270 difference would be added to the unreconciled book balance of cash on the bank reconciliation. Why? Because the cash balance reported on the books is understated by $270 as a result of the error. As another example, if the company recorded a deposit as $520 when the correct amount of the deposit was $250, the $270 difference would be subtracted from the unreconciled book balance of cash on the bank reconciliation. Why? Because the cash balance reported on the books is overstated by $270 as a result of the error. Each error requires careful analysis to determine whether it will be added or subtracted in the unreconciled book balance of cash on the bank reconciliation.

Bank Reconciling Items

Cash receipts are recorded as an increase of cash in the company's accounting records when they are received. These cash receipts are deposited by the company into its bank. The bank records an increase in cash only when these amounts are actually deposited with the bank. Since not all cash receipts recorded by the company will have been recorded by the bank when the bank statement is prepared, there will be outstanding deposits, also known as **deposits in transit**. Outstanding deposits cause the bank statement cash balance to be understated. Therefore, outstanding deposits are a reconciling item that must be added to the unreconciled bank balance of cash on the bank reconciliation.

On the date that a cheque is prepared by a company, it is recorded as a reduction of cash in a company's books. A bank statement will not record a cash reduction until a cheque is presented and accepted for payment (or *clears* the bank). Cheques that are recorded in the company's books but are not paid out of its bank account when the bank statement is prepared are referred to as **outstanding cheques**. Outstanding cheques mean that the bank statement cash balance is overstated. Therefore, outstanding cheques are a reconciling item that must be subtracted from the unreconciled bank balance of cash on the bank reconciliation.

Bank errors sometimes occur and are not revealed until the transactions on the bank statement are compared to the company's accounting records. When an error is identified, the company notifies the bank to have it corrected. Depending on the nature of the error, it is either added to or subtracted from the unreconciled bank balance of cash on the bank reconciliation. For example, if the bank cleared a cheque as $520 that was correctly written for $250, the $270 difference would be added to the unreconciled bank balance of cash on the bank reconciliation. Why? Because the cash balance reported on the bank statement is understated by $270 as a result of this error. As another example, if the bank recorded a deposit as $520 when the correct amount was actually $250, the $270 difference would be subtracted from the unreconciled bank balance of cash on the bank reconciliation. Why? Because the cash balance reported on the bank statement is overstated by $270 as a result of this specific error. Each error must be carefully analyzed to determine how it will be treated on the bank reconciliation.

An exploration is available on the Lyryx site. Log into your Lyryx course to run Bank Reconciliation.

Illustrative Problem—Bank Reconciliation

Assume that a bank reconciliation is prepared by Big Dog Carworks Corp. (BDCC) at April 30. At this date, the Cash account in the general ledger shows a balance of $21,929 and includes the cash receipts and payments shown in Figure 7.1.

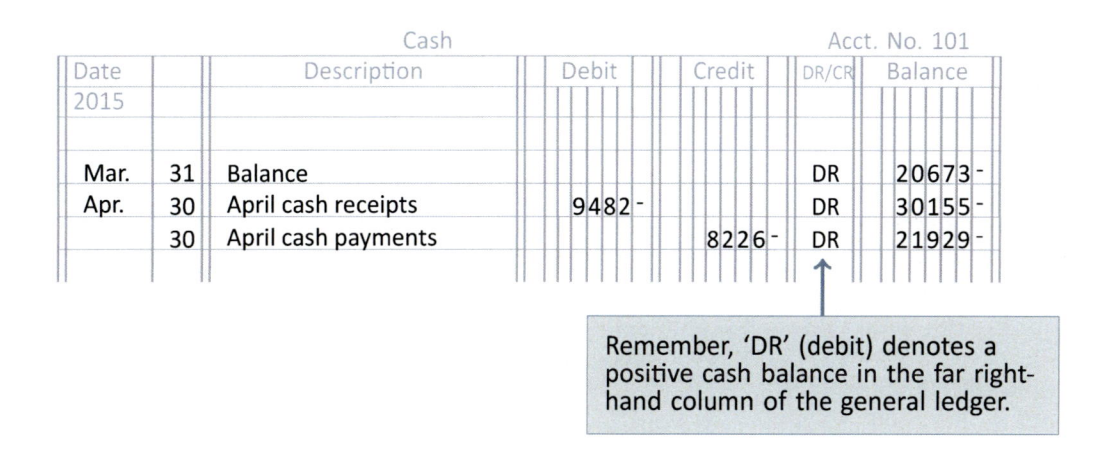

Cash   Acct. No. 101

Date 2015		Description	Debit	Credit	DR/CR	Balance
Mar.	31	Balance			DR	20,673
Apr.	30	April cash receipts	9,482		DR	30,155
	30	April cash payments		8,226	DR	21,929

Remember, 'DR' (debit) denotes a positive cash balance in the far right-hand column of the general ledger.

Figure 7.1: Big Dog's General Ledger 'Cash' Account at April 30

Extracts from BDCC's accounting records are reproduced with the bank statement for April in Figure 7.2.

PER COMPANY RECORDS

Outstanding cheques at March 31:

Cheque No.	Amount
580	$4,051 x
599	196 x
600	7 x

Cheques written during month of April:

Cheque No.	Amount
601	$ 24 x
602	1,720 x
603	230 x
604	200 x
605	2,220 x
606	287
607	1,364
608	100
609	40
610	1,520
611	124 x
612	397 x
	$8,226

Deposits made for the month of April:

Date	Amount
April 5	$1,570 x
10	390 x
23	5,000 x
28	1,522 x
30	1,000
	$9,482

Step 1a: March 31 outstanding cheques are compared with cheques cashed to see if any are still outstanding at April 30. Cleared items are marked with an 'x'.

Step 1b: Cheques written are compared with the cleared cheques on the bank statement to identify which ones have not cleared the bank (outstanding cheques). Cleared items are marked with an 'x'.

Step 2: Other charges made by the bank are identified (SC=service charge; NSF=not sufficient funds).

Step 3: Deposits made by the company are compared with deposits on the bank statement to determine outstanding deposits at April 30. Cleared items are marked with an 'x'.

PER BANK RECORDS

The BDCC bank statement for the month of April is as follows:

Second Chartered Bank
Bank Statement
for Big Dog Carworks Corp.
For the Month Ended April 30, 2015

Cheques/Charges/Debits			Deposits/Credits	Balance
				24,927
4,051 x			1,570	22,446
196 x	24 x	230 x	390	22,386
200 x				22,186
124 x	397 x	7 x		21,658
2,220 x	180 NSF		5,000	24,258
1,720 x	31		1,522	24,029
6 SC				24,023

Step 5: Remaining items are identified and resolved with the bank.

Step 4: Outstanding deposits from March 31 are compared with the bank statement to see if they are still outstanding at April 30. (There were no outstanding deposits at March 31.)

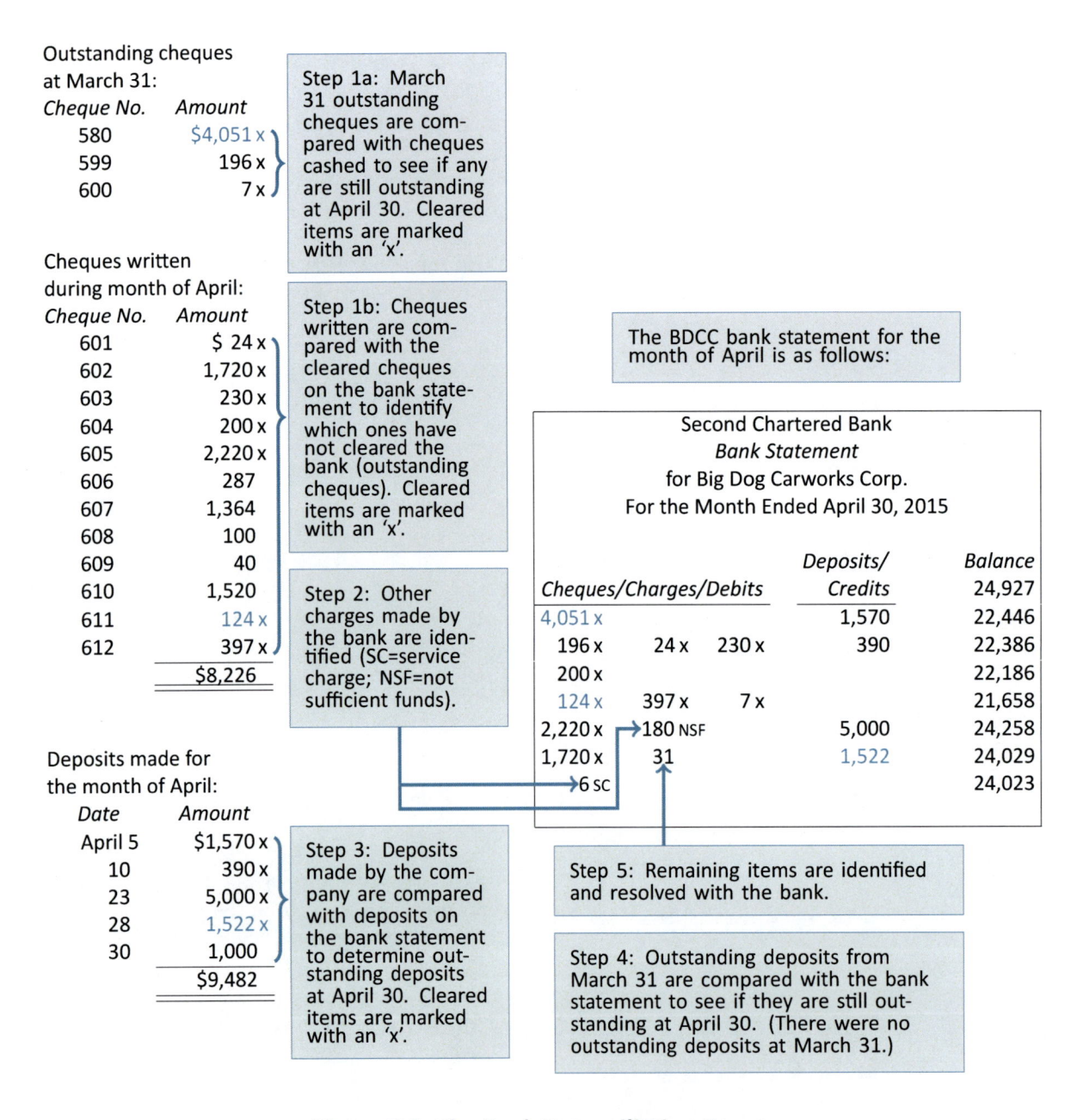

Figure 7.2: The Bank Reconciliation Process

For each entry in BDCC's general ledger Cash account, there should be a matching entry on its bank statement. Items in the general ledger Cash account but not on the bank statement must be reported as a reconciling item on the bank reconciliation. For each entry on the bank statement, there should be a matching entry in BDCC's general ledger Cash account. Items on the bank statement but not in the general ledger Cash account must be reported as a reconciling item on the bank reconciliation.

There are nine steps to follow in preparing a bank reconciliation for BDCC at April 30, 2015:

Step 1

Identify the ending general ledger cash balance ($21,929 from Figure 7.1) and list it on the bank reconciliation as the book balance on April 30 as shown in Figure 7.3. This represents the unreconciled book balance.

Step 2

Identify the ending cash balance on the bank statement ($24,023 from Figure 7.2) and list it on the bank reconciliation as the bank statement balance on April 30 as shown in Figure 7.3. This represents the unreconciled bank balance.

Step 3

Cheques written that have cleared the bank are returned with the bank statement. These cheques are said to be *cancelled* because, once cleared, the bank marks them to prevent them from being used again. Cancelled cheques are compared to the company's list of cash payments. Outstanding cheques are identified using two steps:

a. Any outstanding cheques listed on the BDCC's March 31 bank reconciliation are compared to the cheques listed on the April 30 bank statement.

For BDCC, all of the March outstanding cheques (nos. 580, 599, and 600) were paid by the bank in April. Therefore, there are no reconciling items to include in the April 30 bank reconciliation. If one of the March outstanding cheques had not been paid by the bank in April, it would be subtracted as an outstanding cheque from the unreconciled bank balance on the bank reconciliation.

b. The cash payments listed in BDCC's accounting records are compared to the cheques on the bank statement. This comparison indicates that the following cheques are outstanding.

Cheque No.	Amount
606	$ 287
607	1,364
608	100
609	40
610	1,520

Outstanding cheques must be deducted from the bank statement's unreconciled ending cash balance of $24,023 as shown in Figure 7.3.

Step 4

Other payments made by the bank are identified on the bank statement and subtracted from the unreconciled book balance on the bank reconciliation.

a. An examination of the April bank statement shows that the bank had deducted the NSF cheque of John Donne for $180. This is deducted from the unreconciled book balance on the bank reconciliation as shown in Figure 7.3.

b. An examination of the April 30 bank statement shows that the bank had also deducted a service charge of $6 during April. This amount is deducted from the unreconciled book balance on the bank reconciliation as shown in Figure 7.3.

Step 5

Last month's bank reconciliation is reviewed for outstanding deposits at March 31. There were no outstanding deposits at March 31. If there had been, the amount would have been added to the unreconciled bank balance on the bank reconciliation.

Step 6

The deposits shown on the bank statement are compared with the amounts recorded in the company records. This comparison indicates that the April 30 cash receipt amounting to $1,000 was deposited but it is not included in the bank statement. The outstanding deposit is added to the unreconciled bank balance on the bank reconciliation as shown in Figure 7.3.

Step 7

Any errors in the company's records or in the bank statement must be identified and reported on the bank reconciliation.

An examination of the April bank statement shows that the bank deducted a cheque issued by another company for $31 from the BDCC bank account in error. Assume that when notified, the bank indicated it would make a correction in May's bank statement.

The cheque deducted in error must be added to the bank statement balance on the bank reconciliation as shown in Figure 7.3.

Step 8

Total both sides of the bank reconciliation. The result must be that the book balance and the bank statement balance are equal or reconciled. These balances represent the adjusted balance.

The bank reconciliation in Figure 7.3 is the result of completing the preceding eight steps.

7.3. Cash Collections and Payments

Big Dog Carworks Corp.
Bank Reconciliation
At April 30, 2015

Book balance at Apr. 30		$21,929	Bank statement balance at Apr. 30			$24,023
			Add: Outstanding deposit			1,000
			Cheque deducted in error			31
						25,054
Less: Bank charges	$ 6		Less: Outstanding cheques			
NSF Cheque – J. Donne	180	186	Cheque No.	Amount		
			606	$ 287		
			607	1,364		
			608	100		
			609	40		
			610	1,520	3,311	
Adjusted book balance at Apr. 30		$21,743	Adjusted bank balance at Apr. 30			$21,743

These balances must agree.

Reconciling items in this section require journal entries to be made in the general journal to correct the unreconciled Cash balance of $21,929 in the general ledger to the reconciled balance of $21,743.

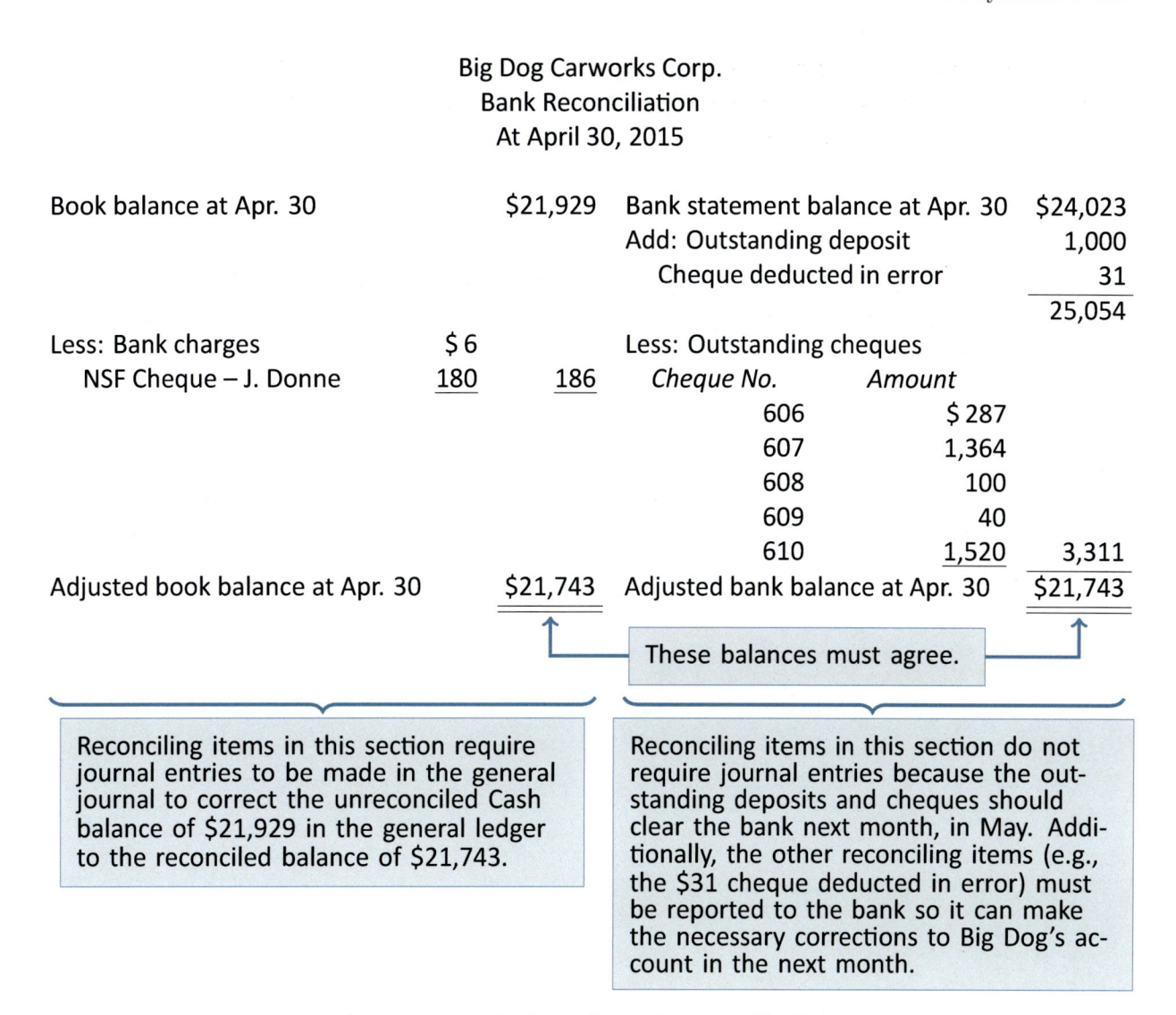

Reconciling items in this section do not require journal entries because the outstanding deposits and cheques should clear the bank next month, in May. Additionally, the other reconciling items (e.g., the $31 cheque deducted in error) must be reported to the bank so it can make the necessary corrections to Big Dog's account in the next month.

Figure 7.3: BDCC's April Bank Reconciliation

Step 9

For the adjusted balance calculated in the bank reconciliation to appear in the accounting records, an adjusting entry(s) must be prepared.

The adjusting entry(s) is based on the reconciling item(s) used to calculate the adjusted book balance. The book balance side of BDCC's April 30 bank reconciliation is copied to the left below to clarify the source of the following April 30 adjustments.

220 ■ Cash and Receivables

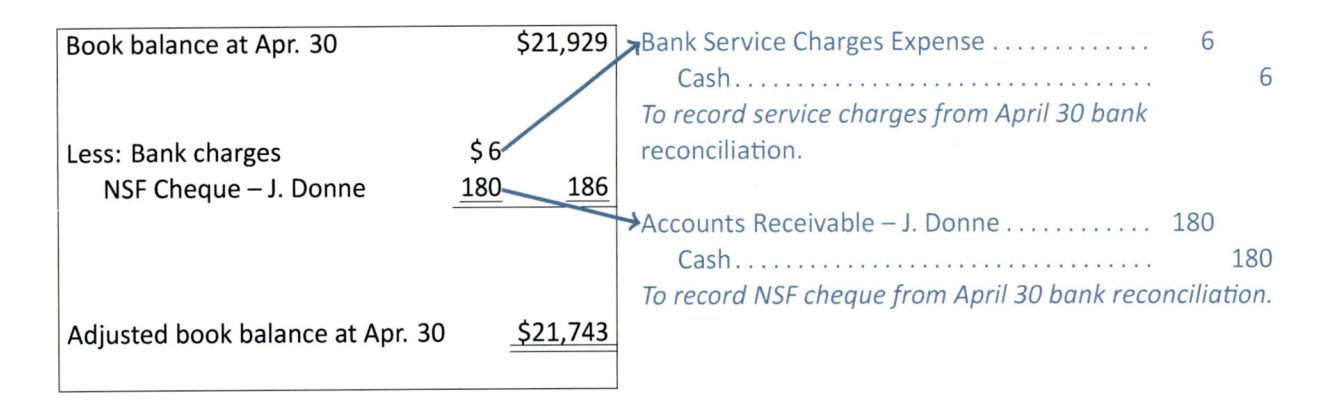

Book balance at Apr. 30		$21,929
Less: Bank charges	$6	
NSF Cheque – J. Donne	180	186
Adjusted book balance at Apr. 30		$21,743

Bank Service Charges Expense 6
    Cash. 6
To record service charges from April 30 bank reconciliation.

Accounts Receivable – J. Donne 180
    Cash. 180
To record NSF cheque from April 30 bank reconciliation.

It is common practice to use one compound entry to record the adjustments resulting from a bank reconciliation as shown below for BDCC.

Once the adjustment is posted, the Cash general ledger account is up to date, as illustrated in Figure 7.4.

Bank Service Charges Expense 6
Accounts Receivable – J. Donne 180
    Cash. 186

To record reconciling items from April 30 bank reconciliation.

Cash   Acct. No. 101

Date 2015		Description	Debit	Credit	DR/CR	Balance
Mar.	31	Balance			DR	20673-
Apr.	30	April cash receipts	9482-		DR	30155-
	30	April cash payments		8226-	DR	21929-
	30	Bank charge expense		6-	DR	21923-
	30	NSF cheque		180-	DR	21743-

This adjusted cash balance now agrees with the bank reconciliation.

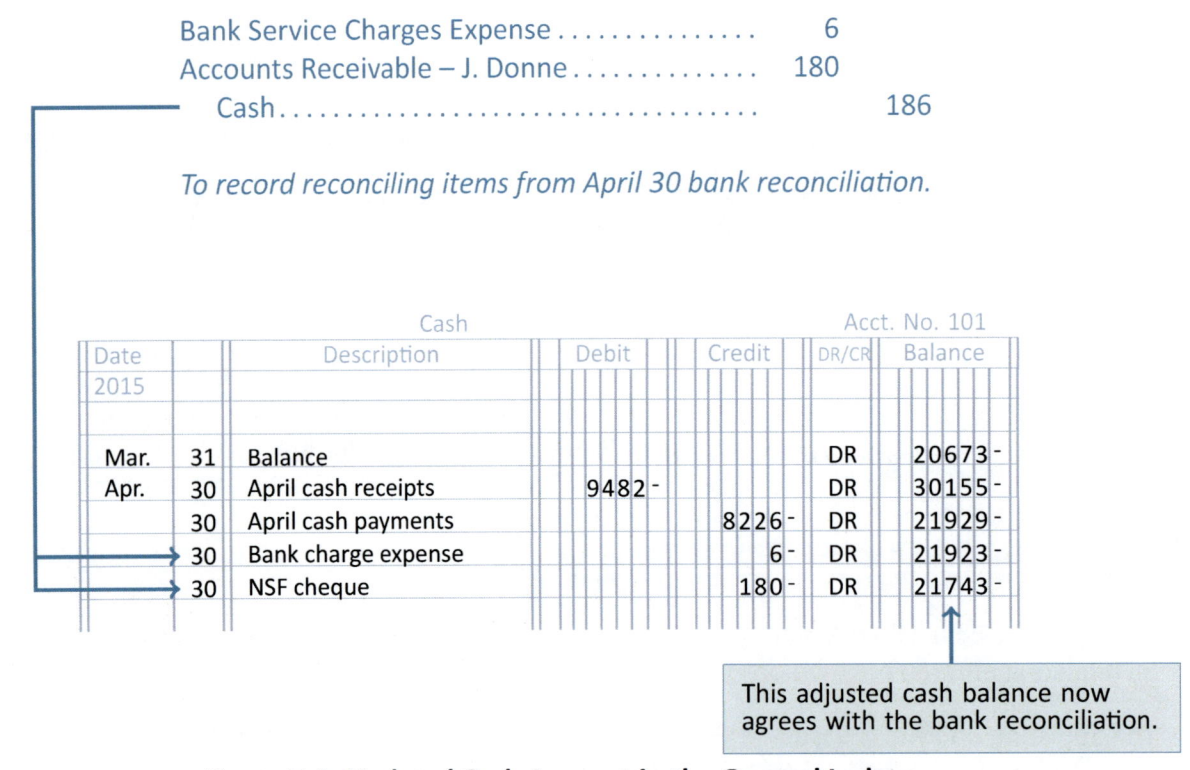

Figure 7.4: Updated Cash Account in the General Ledger

Note that the balance of $21,743 in the general ledger Cash account is the same as the adjusted book balance of $21,743 on the bank reconciliation. Big Dog does not make any adjusting entries for the reconciling items on the bank side of the bank reconciliation since these will eventually clear the bank and appear on a later bank statement. Bank errors will be corrected by the bank.

Debit and Credit Card Transactions

Debit and credit cards are commonly accepted by companies when customers make purchases. Because the cash is efficiently and safely transferred directly into a company's bank account by the debit or credit card company, such transactions enhance internal control over cash. However, the seller is typically charged a fee for accepting debit and credit cards. For example, assume BDCC makes a $1,000 sale to a customer who uses a credit card that charges BDCC a fee of 2%; the cost of the sale is $750. BDCC would record:

Date	Account/Explanation	PR	Debit	Credit
	Cash....................................		980	
	Credit Card Expense.....................		20	
	Sales			1,000
	To record sale and related credit card fee.			
	Cost of Goods Sold		750	
	Merchandise Inventory..............			750
	To record cost of sales.			

The credit card fee is calculated as the $1,000 sale X 2% = $20. This means that BDCC collects net cash proceeds of $980 ($1,000 - $20). The use of debit cards also involves fees and these would be journalized in the same manner.

An exploration is available on the Lyryx site. Log into your Lyryx course to run Bank Credit Cards.

7.4 Accounts Receivable

LO4 – Explain, calculate, and record estimated uncollectible accounts receivable and subsequent write-offs and recoveries.

Recall from Chapter 5 that the revenue portion of the operating cycle, as copied in Figure 7.5, begins with a sale on credit and is completed with the collection of cash. Unfortunately, not all receivables are collected. This section discusses issues related to accounts receivable and their collection.

Cash payment to supplier is made.

Inventory sold to customer.

A liability is incurred.

Accounts receivable result.

Inventory is purchased.

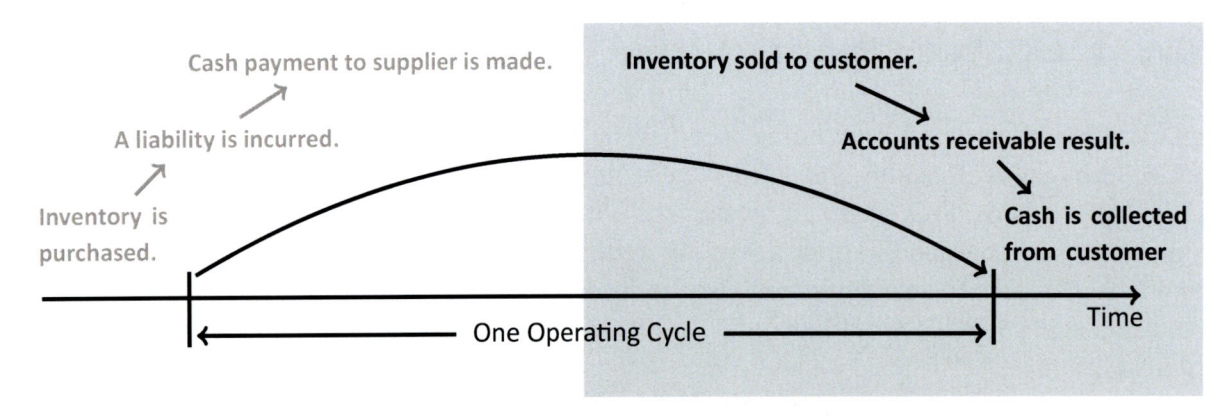

Cash is collected from customer

One Operating Cycle

Time

Figure 7.5: Revenue Portion of Operating Cycle

An exploration is available on the Lyryx site. Log into your Lyryx course to run Accounts Receivable Transactions.

Uncollectible Accounts Receivable

Extending credit to customers results in increased sales and therefore profits. However, there is a risk that some accounts receivable will not be collected. A good internal control system is designed to minimize bad debt losses. One such control is to permit sales on account only to credit-worthy customers; this can be difficult to determine in advance. Companies with credit sales realize that some of these amounts may never be collected. **Uncollectible accounts**, commonly known as **bad debts**, are an expense associated with selling on credit.

Bad debt expenses must be matched to the credit sales of the same period. For example, assume BDCC recorded a $1,000 credit sale to XYA Company in April, 2015. Assume further that in 2016 it was determined that the $1,000 receivable from XYA Company would never be collected. The bad debt arising from the credit sale to XYA Company should be matched to the period in which the sale occurred, namely, April, 2015. But how can that be done if it is not known which receivables will become uncollectible? A means of estimating and recording the amount of sales that will not be collected in cash is needed. This is done by establishing a contra current asset account called **Allowance for Doubtful Accounts (AFDA)** in the general ledger to record estimated uncollectible receivables. This account is a contra account to accounts receivable and is disclosed on the balance sheet as shown below using assumed values.

Accounts receivable	$25,000	
Less: Allowance for doubtful accounts	1,400	23,600
OR		
Accounts receivable (net of $1,400 AFDA)		$ 23,600

The Allowance for Doubtful Accounts contra account reduces accounts receivable to the amount that is expected to be collected — in this case, $23,600.

Estimating Uncollectible Accounts Receivable

The AFDA account is used to reflect how much of the total Accounts Receivable is estimated to be uncollectible. To record estimated uncollectible accounts, the following adjusting entry is made.

General Journal				
Date	Account/Explanation	PR	Debit	Credit
	Bad Debts Expense.....................		XXX	
	Allowance for Doubtful Accounts.....			XXX
	To record the adjustment estimating un-collectible accounts receivable.			

The bad debt expense is shown on the income statement. AFDA appears on the balance sheet and is subtracted from accounts receivable resulting in the estimated net realizable accounts receivable.

Two different methods can be used to estimate uncollectible accounts. One method focuses on estimating Bad Debt Expense on the income statement, while the other focuses on estimating the desired balance in AFDA on the balance sheet.

The Income Statement Method

The objective of the **income statement method** is to estimate bad debt expense based on credit sales. Bad debt expense is calculated by applying an estimated loss percentage to credit sales for the period. The percentage is typically based on actual losses experienced in prior years. For instance, a company may have the following history of uncollected sales on account:

Year	Credit Sales	Amounts Not Collected
2012	$150,000	$1,000
2013	200,000	1,200
2014	250,000	800
	$600,000	$3,000

The average loss over these years is $\frac{\$3,000}{\$600,000}$, or $\frac{1}{2}$ of 1%. If management anticipates that similar losses can be expected in 2015 and credit sales for 2015 amount to $300,000, bad debts expense would be estimated as $1,500 ($300,000 x 0.005). Under the income statement method, the $1,500 represents estimated bad debt expense and is recorded as:

This estimated bad debt expense is calculated without considering any existing balance in the AFDA account.

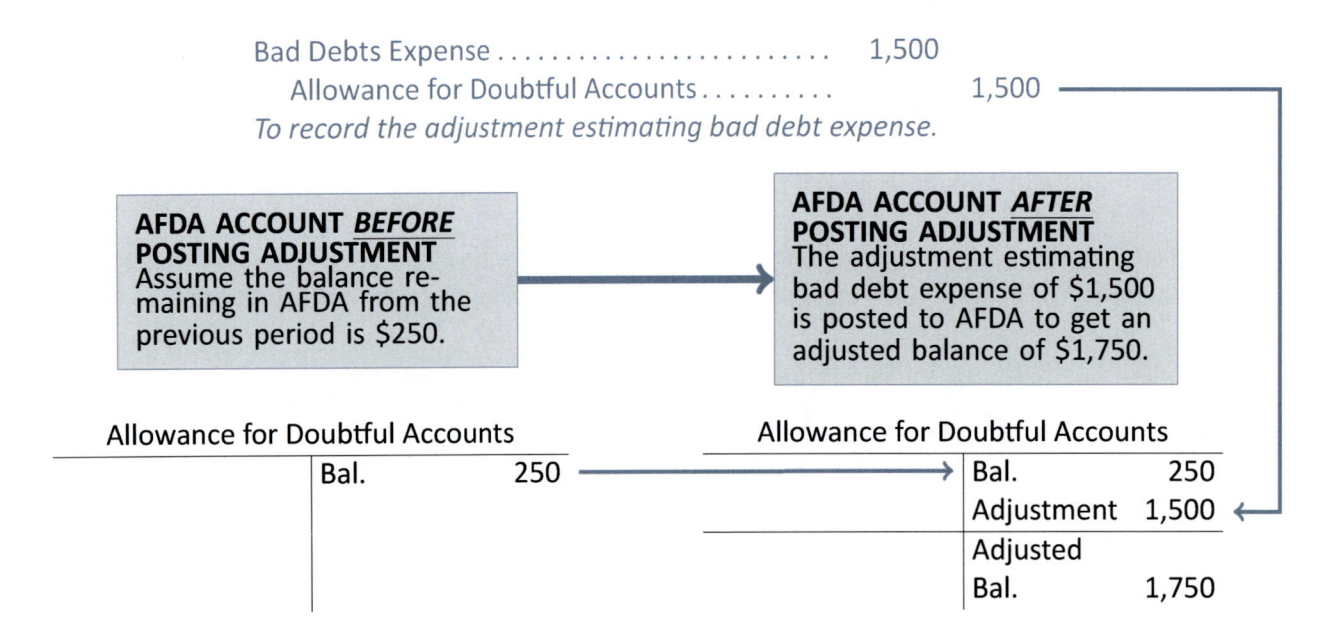

```
Bad Debts Expense . . . . . . . . . . . . . . . . . . . . . . .    1,500
      Allowance for Doubtful Accounts . . . . . . . . . .         1,500
   To record the adjustment estimating bad debt expense.
```

AFDA ACCOUNT *BEFORE* POSTING ADJUSTMENT
Assume the balance remaining in AFDA from the previous period is $250.

AFDA ACCOUNT *AFTER* POSTING ADJUSTMENT
The adjustment estimating bad debt expense of $1,500 is posted to AFDA to get an adjusted balance of $1,750.

Allowance for Doubtful Accounts

	Bal. 250

Allowance for Doubtful Accounts

	Bal. 250
	Adjustment 1,500
	Adjusted Bal. 1,750

An exploration is available on the Lyryx site. Log into your Lyryx course to run Income Statement Method.

The Balance Sheet Method

Estimated uncollectible accounts can also be calculated by using the **balance sheet method** where a process called **aging of accounts receivable** is used. At the end of the period, the total of estimated uncollectible accounts is calculated by analyzing accounts receivable according to how long each account has been outstanding. An aging analysis approach assumes that the longer a receivable is outstanding, the less chance there is of collecting it. This process is illustrated in the following schedule.

Aging of Accounts Receivable
December 31, 2015

			Number of Days Past Due				
Customer	Total	Not Yet Due	1–30	31–60	61–90	91–120	Over 120
Bendix Inc.	$ 1,000						$ 1,000
Devco Marketing Inc.	6,000		$ 1,000	$3,000	$2,000		
Horngren Corp	4,000		2,000	1,000		$ 1,000	
Perry Co. Ltd.	5,000		3,000	1,000		1,000	
Others	9,000		4,000			5,000	
Totals	$25,000	$ 0	$10,000	$5,000	$2,000	$ 7,000	$ 1,000

In this example, accounts receivable total $25,000 at the end of the period. These are classified into six time periods: those receivables that are not yet due; 1–30 days past due; 31–60 days past due; 61–90 days past due; 91–120 days past due; and over 120 days past due.

Based on past experience, assume management estimates a bad debt percentage, or rate of uncollectibility, for each time period as follows:

Number of Days Outstanding	Not Yet Due	1–30	31–60	61–90	91–120	Over 120
Rate of Uncollectibility	0.5%	1%	3%	5%	10%	40%

The calculation of expected uncollectible accounts receivable at December 31, 2015 would be as follows:

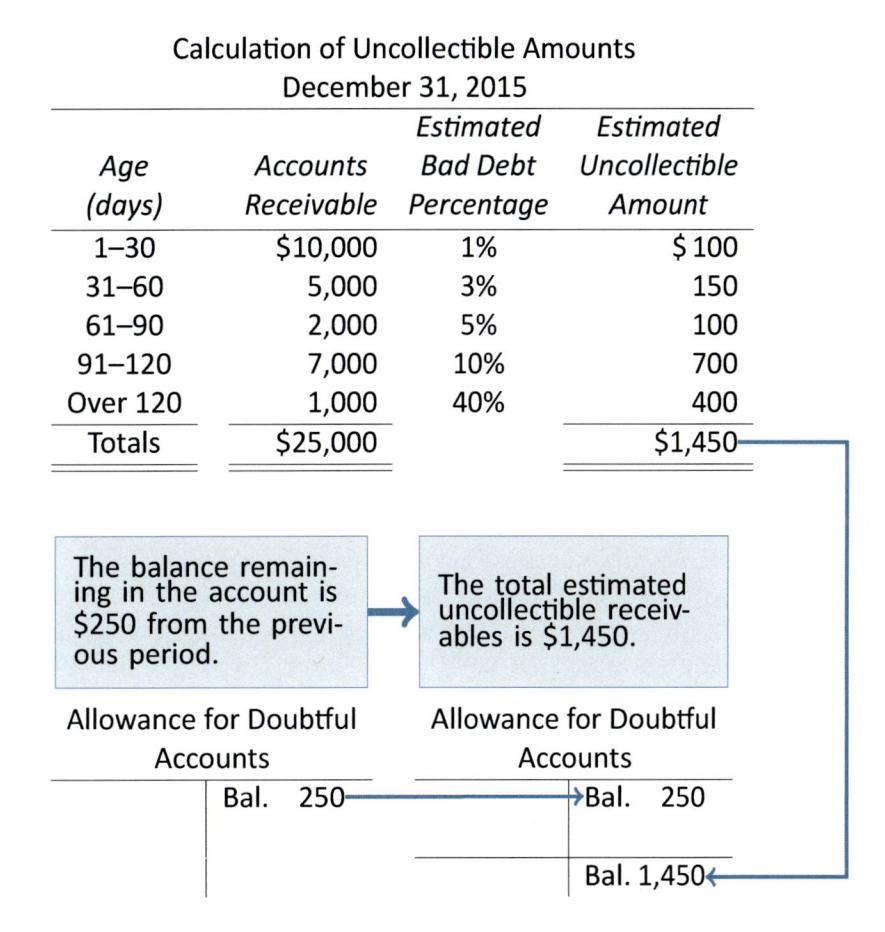

Calculation of Uncollectible Amounts
December 31, 2015

Age (days)	Accounts Receivable	Estimated Bad Debt Percentage	Estimated Uncollectible Amount
1–30	$10,000	1%	$ 100
31–60	5,000	3%	150
61–90	2,000	5%	100
91–120	7,000	10%	700
Over 120	1,000	40%	400
Totals	$25,000		$1,450

The balance remaining in the account is $250 from the previous period.

The total estimated uncollectible receivables is $1,450.

Allowance for Doubtful Accounts
Bal. 250

Allowance for Doubtful Accounts
Bal. 250
Bal. 1,450

A total of $1,450 of accounts receivable is estimated to be uncollectible at December 31, 2015.

Under the balance sheet method, the estimated bad debt expense consists of the *difference* between the opening AFDA balance ($250, as in the prior example) and the estimated uncollectible receivables ($1,450) required at year-end.

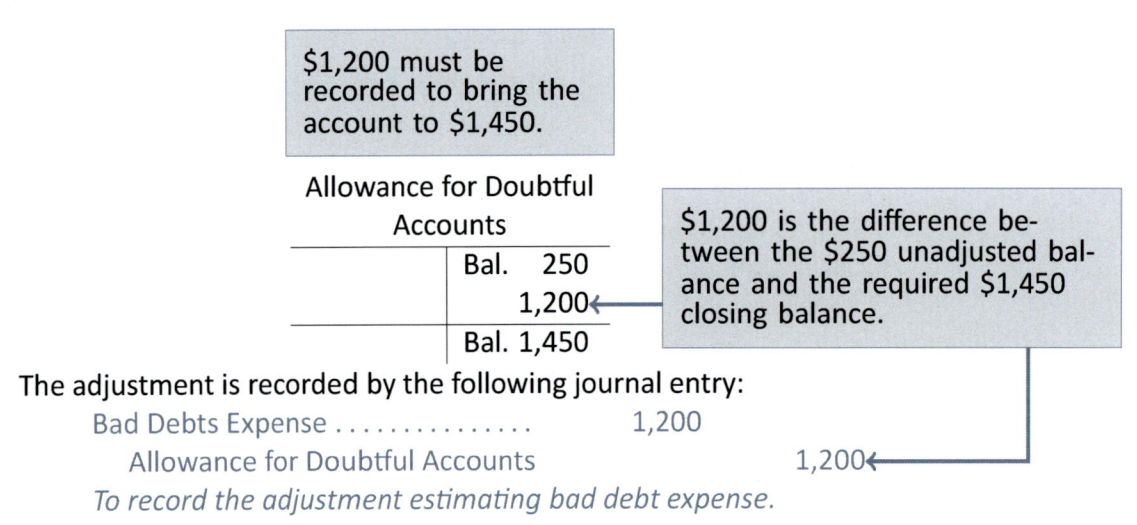

> $1,200 must be recorded to bring the account to $1,450.

Allowance for Doubtful Accounts

	Bal. 250
	1,200
	Bal. 1,450

> $1,200 is the difference between the $250 unadjusted balance and the required $1,450 closing balance.

The adjustment is recorded by the following journal entry:

    Bad Debts Expense   1,200
        Allowance for Doubtful Accounts   1,200
    To record the adjustment estimating bad debt expense.

As an alternative to using an aging analysis to estimate uncollectible accounts, a simplified balance sheet method can be used. The **simplified balance sheet method** calculates the total estimated uncollectible accounts as a percentage of the outstanding accounts receivables balance. For example, assume an unadjusted balance in AFDA of $250 as in the preceding example. Also assume the accounts receivable balance at the end of the period was $25,000 as in the previous illustration. If it was estimated that 6% of these would be uncollectible based on historical data, the adjustment would be:

	General Journal			
Date	Account/Explanation	PR	Debit	Credit
	Bad Debts Expense		1,250	
	Allowance for Doubtful Accounts			1,250
	To record the adjustment estimating bad debt expense.			

The total estimated uncollectible accounts was $1,500 ($25,000 × 0.06). Given an unadjusted balance in AFDA of $250, the adjustment to AFDA must be a credit of $1,250 ($1,500 − $250).

Regardless of whether the income statement method or balance sheet method is used, the amount estimated as an allowance for doubtful accounts seldom agrees with the amounts that actually prove uncollectible. A credit balance remains in the allowance account if fewer bad debts occur during the year than are estimated. There is a debit balance in the allowance account if more bad debts occur during the year than are estimated. By monitoring the balance in the Allowance for Doubtful Accounts general ledger account at each year-end, though, management can determine whether the estimates of uncollectible amounts are accurate. If not, they can adjust these estimates going forward.

An exploration is available on the Lyryx site. Log into your Lyryx course to run Balance Sheet Method.

Writing Off Accounts Receivable

When recording the adjusting entry to estimate uncollectible accounts receivable at the end of the period, it is not known which specific receivables will become uncollectible. When an account is determined to be uncollectible, it must be removed from the accounts receivable account. This process is known as a **write-off**. To demonstrate the write-off of an account receivable, assume that on January 15, 2016 the $1,000 credit account for customer Bendix Inc. is identified as uncollectible because of the company's bankruptcy. The receivable is removed by:

\multicolumn{5}{c	}{General Journal}
Date	Account/Explanation	PR	Debit	Credit
	AFDA		1,000	
	Accounts Receivable – Bendix Inc.			1,000
	To record write-off of Bendix Inc.'s account receivable.			

The $1,000 write-off reduces both the accounts receivable and AFDA accounts. The write-off does not affect net realizable accounts receivable as demonstrated below.

	Before Write-Off	Write-Off	After Write-Off
Accounts receivable	$25,000	Cr 1,000	$24,000
Less: Allowance for doubtful accounts	1,450	Dr 1,000	450
Net accounts receivable	$23,550		$23,550

Additionally, a write-off does not affect bad debt expense. This can be a challenge to understand. To help clarify, recall that the adjusting entry to estimate uncollectibles was:

\multicolumn{5}{c	}{General Journal}
Date	Account/Explanation	PR	Debit	Credit
	Bad Debts Expense		XXX	
	AFDA			XXX
	To record the adjustment estimating bad debt expense.			

This adjustment was recorded because GAAP requires that the bad debt expense be matched to the period in which the sales occurred even though it is not known which receivables will become uncollectible. Later, when an uncollectible receivable is identified, it is written off as:

\multicolumn{5}{c	}{General Journal}
Date	Account/Explanation	PR	Debit	Credit
	AFDA		XXX	
	Accounts Receivable			XXX
	To record write-off of account receivable.			

Notice that the AFDA entries cancel each other out so that the net effect is a debit to bad debt expense and a credit to accounts receivable. The use of the AFDA contra account allows us to estimate uncollectible accounts in one period and record the write-off of bad receivables as they become known in a later period.

Recovery of a Write-Off

When Bendix Inc. went bankrupt, its debt to Big Dog Carworks Corp. was written off in anticipation that there would be no recovery of the amount owed. Assume that later, an announcement was made that 25% of amounts owed by Bendix would be paid. This new information indicates that BDCC will be able to recover a portion of the receivable previously written off. A recovery requires two journal entries. The first entry reinstates the amount *expected* to be collected by BDCC—$250 ($1,000 × 25%) in this case and is recorded as:

	General Journal			
Date	Account/Explanation	PR	Debit	Credit
	Accounts Receivable – Bendix Inc.		250	
	AFDA			250
	To reverse write-off and reinstate collectible portion of account.			

This entry reverses the collectible part of the receivable previously written off. The effect of the reversal is shown below.

Accounts Receivable				Allowance for Doubtful Accounts			
Bal.	$25,000					Bal.	1,450
		Write-off	1,000	Write-off	1,000		
Recovery	250					Recovery	250

The second entry records the collection of the reinstated amount as:

	General Journal			
Date	Account/Explanation	PR	Debit	Credit
	Cash		250	
	Accounts Receivable – Bendix Inc.			250
	To record recovery of collectible portion of account previously written off.			

The various journal entries related to accounts receivable are summarized below.

Sale on account.	Accounts Receivable	XXX	
	Sales		XXX
	COGS...........................	XXX	
	Merchandise Inventory.........		XXX
Adjusting entry estimating uncollectible accounts.	Bad Debts Expense	XXX	
	AFDA		XXX
Write-off of uncollectible account.	AFDA...........................	XXX	
	Accounts Receivable		XXX
Recovery of account previously written off.	Accounts Receivable	XXX	
	AFDA		XXX
	Cash	XXX	
	Accounts Receivable		XXX

7.5 Short-Term Notes Receivable

> **LO5** – Explain and record a short-term notes receivable as well as calculate related interest.

Short-term notes receivable are current assets, since they are due within the greater of 12 months or the business's operating cycle. A note receivable is a *promissory note*. A **promissory note** is a signed document where the **debtor**, the person who owes the money, promises to pay the *creditor* the *principal* and *interest* on the *due date*. The **principal** is the amount owed. The **creditor**, or **payee**, is the entity owed the principal and interest. **Interest** is the fee for using the principal and is calculated as: Principal × Annual Interest Rate × Time. The **time** or **term** of the note is the period from the *date of the note* to the due date. The **due date**, also known as the **maturity date**, is the date on which the principal and interest must be paid. The **date of the note** is the date the note begins accruing interest.

Short-term notes receivable can arise at the time of sale or when a customer's account receivable becomes overdue. To demonstrate the conversion of a customer's account to a short-term receivable, assume that BDCC's customer Bendix Inc. is unable to pay its $5,000 account within the normal 30-day period. The receivable is converted to a 5%, 60-day note dated December 5, 2015 with the following entry:

230 ■ Cash and Receivables

General Journal				
Date	Account/Explanation	PR	Debit	Credit
Dec 5	Notes Receivable - Bendix...............		5,000	
	Accounts Receivable - Bendix.........			5,000
	To record the conversion of a customer's account to a 5%, 60-day note dated December 5, 2015.			

The note is due on February 3, 2016 calculated as:

Days in December	31
Less: December 5 date of the note	5
Subtotal number of days	26
Add: Days in January	31
Subtotal number of days	57
Add: Days in February to total 60 days	**3**
Total term of the note in days	60

Assuming a December 31, year-end for BDCC, the adjusting entry to accrue interest on December 31 would be:

General Journal				
Date	Account/Explanation	PR	Debit	Credit
Dec 31	Interest Receivable......................		17.81	
	Interest Revenue			17.81
	To record the accrual of interest from December 5 to December 31.			

The interest of $17.81 was calculated as: $5,000 × 5% × 26/365[2] = $17.80822 rounded to $17.81. **All interest calculations in this textbook are rounded to two decimal places.**

At maturity, February 3, 2016, BDCC collects the note plus interest and records:

General Journal				
Date	Account/Explanation	PR	Debit	Credit
Feb 3	Cash.....................................		5,041.10	
	Note Receivable - Bendix............			5,000.00
	Interest Receivable..................			17.81
	Interest Revenue			23.29
	To record the collection of the principal and interest.			

The total interest realized on the note was $41.10 ($5,000 × 5% × 60/365 = $41.0959 rounded to $41.10). Part of the $41.10 total interest revenue was realized in 2015 ($17.81) and the rest in

---
[2] When calculating interest based on days, use 365 days per year.

2016 ($41.10 - $17.81 = $23.29). Therefore, care must be taken to correctly allocate the interest between periods. The total cash received by BDCC on February 3 was the sum of the principal and interest: $5,000.00 + $41.10 = $5,041.10.

When the term of a note is expressed in months, the calculations are less complex. For example, assume that BDCC sold customer Woodlow a $4,000 service on August 1, 2015. On that date, the customer signed a 4%, 3-month note. The term of the note is based on months and not days therefore the maturity date is October 31, 2015. BDCC would record the collection on October 31 as:

	General Journal			
Date	Account/Explanation	PR	Debit	Credit
Oct 31	Cash....................................		4,040	
	Note Receivable - Woodlow...........			4,000
	Interest Revenue			40
	To record the collection of the principal and interest.			

The total interest realized on the note was $40 ($4,000 × 4% × 3/12[3] = $40.00)

An exploration is available on the Lyryx site. Log into your Lyryx course to run Notes Receivable.

7.6 Appendix A: Ratio Analysis—Acid Test

LO6 — Explain and calculate the acid-test ratio.

The **acid-test ratio**, also known as the **quick ratio**, is a liquidity ratio that is a strict measure of a business's availability of cash to pay current liabilities as they come due. It is considered a strict measure because it includes only *quick current assets*. **Quick current assets** are those current assets that are one step away from becoming cash. For example, accounts receivable are a quick current asset because collection of receivables results in cash. However, inventory is not a quick current asset because it is two steps from cash — it has to be sold which creates an account receivable and the receivable then has to be collected. Prepaids are not a quick current asset because the intent in holding prepaids is not to convert them into cash but, instead, to use them (e.g., prepaid insurance becomes insurance expense as it is used). Quick current assets include only cash, short-term investments, and receivables.

The acid-test ratio is calculated as:

---

[3] When calculating interest based on months, use 12 months per year.

Quick current assets ÷ Current liabilities

The acid-test ratios for three companies operating in a similar industry are shown below:

	Acid-Test Ratios		
Year	Company A	Company B	Company C
2014	0.56	1.3	8.6
2015	0.72	1.2	8.7

In 2014, Company A's acid-test ratio shows that it has only $0.56 to cover each $1.00 of current liabilities as they come due. Company A therefore has a liquidity issue. Although Company A's acid-test ratio is still unfavourable in 2015, the change is favourable because the liquidity improved. So a company can have an unfavourable acid-test ratio but show a favourable change.

Company B's 2014 acid-test shows that it has favourable liquidity: $1.30 to cover each $1.00 of current liabilities as they come due. However, the change from 2014 to 2015 shows a decrease in the acid-test ratio which is unfavourable although Company B's acid-test still shows favourable liquidity. So a company can have a favourable acid-test ratio but an unfavourable change.

Company C's 2014 acid-test ratio indicates that it has favourable liquidity: $8.60 to cover each $1.00 of current liabilities as they come due. However, this is actually unfavourable because a company can have an acid-test ratio that is too high. If the acid-test ratio is too high, it is a reflection that the company has idle assets. Idle assets do not typically generate the most optimum levels of revenue. Remember that the purpose of holding assets is to generate revenue. In 2015, Company C's acid-test ratio increased a bit and it is still excessive which is unfavourable. So the change was favourable but because the ratio is too high, it reflects an unfavourable liquidity position, though for different reasons than Company A.

An exploration is available on the Lyryx site. Log into your Lyryx course to run Using the Information - Acid-Test Ratio.

7.7 Appendix B: Ratio Analysis—Accounts Receivable Turnover

LO7 – Explain and calculate the accounts receivable turnover.

The accounts receivable turnover not only measures the liquidity of receivables but also the efficiency of collection, referred to as turnover (i.e., accounts receivable *turnover* into cash). A low turnover indicates high levels of accounts receivable which has an unfavourable impact on liquidity since cash is tied up in receivables. A low turnover means management might need to review credit granting policies and/or strengthen collection efforts.

The accounts receivable turnover is calculated as:

Net credit sales (or revenues) ÷ **Average net accounts receivable**[4]

Average accounts receivable is calculated by taking the beginning of the period balance plus the end of the period balance and dividing the sum by two.

The accounts receivable turnover ratios for two companies operating in a similar industry are shown below:

	Accounts Receivable Turnover	
Year	Company A	Company B
2015	5.8	6.9

Company B is more efficient at collecting receivables than is Company A. The higher the ratio, the more favourable.

An exploration is available on the Lyryx site. Log into your Lyryx course to run Accounts Receivable Turnover Ratio.

Summary of Chapter 7 Learning Objectives

LO1 – Define internal control and explain how it is applied to cash.

The purpose of internal controls is to safeguard the assets of a business. Since cash is a particularly vulnerable asset, policies and procedures specific to cash need to be implemented, such as the use of cheques and electronic funds transfer for payments, daily cash deposits into a financial institution, and the preparation of bank reconciliations.

LO2 – Explain and journalize petty cash transactions.

A petty cash fund is used to pay small, irregular amounts for which issuing a cheque would be inefficient. A petty cash custodian administers the fund by obtaining a cheque from the cash payments clerk. The cheque is cashed and the coin and currency placed in a locked box. The petty cash custodian collects receipts and reimburses individuals for the related amounts. When the petty cash fund is replenished, the receipts are compiled and submitted for entry in the accounting records so that a replacement cheque can be issued and cashed.

---

[4]Short-term notes receivable from customers would be included in this amount.

LO3 – Explain the purpose of and prepare a bank reconciliation, and record related adjustments.

A bank reconciliation is a form of internal control that reconciles the bank statement balance to the general ledger cash account, also known as the book balance. Reconciling items that affect the bank statement balance are outstanding deposits, outstanding cheques, and bank errors. Reconciling items that affect the book balance are collections made by the bank on behalf of the company, NSF cheques, bank service charges, and errors. Once the book and bank statement balances are reconciled, an adjusting entry is prepared based on the reconciling items affecting the book balance.

LO4 – Explain, calculate, and record estimated uncollectible accounts receivable and subsequent write-offs and recoveries.

Not all accounts receivable are collected, resulting in uncollectible accounts. Because it is not known which receivables will become uncollectible, the allowance approach is used to match the cost of estimated uncollectible accounts to the period in which the related revenue was generated. The adjusting entry to record estimated uncollectibles is a debit to Bad Debt Expense and a credit to Allowance for Doubtful Accounts (AFDA). The income statement method and the balance sheet method are two ways to estimate and apply the allowance approach. The income statement method calculates bad debt expense based on a percentage of credit sales while the balance sheet method calculates total estimated uncollectible accounts (aka the balance in AFDA) using an aging analysis. When receivables are identified as being uncollectible, they are written off. If write-offs subsequently become collectible, a recovery is recorded using two entries: by reversing the write-off (or the portion that is recoverable) and then journalizing the collection.

LO5 – Explain and record a short-term notes receivable as well as calculate related interest.

A short-term notes receivable is a promissory note that bears an interest rate calculated over the term of the note. Short-term notes receivable are current assets that mature within 12 months from the date of issue or within a business's operating cycle, whichever is longer. Notes can be issued to a customer at the time of sale, or a note receivable can replace an overdue receivable.

LO6 – Explain and calculate the acid-test ratio.

The acid-test ratio is a strict measure of liquidity. It is calculated as quick current assets divided by current liabilities. Quick assets include cash, short-term investments, and accounts receivable.

LO7 – Explain and calculate the accounts receivable turnover.

The accounts receivable turnover is a measure of liquidity and demonstrates how efficiently receivables are being collected. It is calculated as net sales divided by average accounts receivable. Average accounts receivable are the sum of the beginning accounts receivable, including short-term notes receivable from customers, plus ending receivables, divided by two.

Discussion Questions

1. What is internal control?
2. How does the preparation of a bank reconciliation strengthen the internal control of cash?
3. What are some reconciling items that appear in a bank reconciliation?
4. What are the steps in preparing a bank reconciliation?
5. What is an NSF cheque?
6. What is a petty cash system?
7. What is the difference between establishing and replenishing the petty cash fund?
8. How does use of allowance for doubtful accounts match expenses with revenue?
9. How does the income statement method calculate the estimated amount of uncollectible accounts?
10. What is an ageing schedule for bad debts, and how is it used in calculating the estimated amount of uncollectible accounts?
11. How are credit balances in accounts receivable reported on the financial statements?

Exercises

EXERCISE 7–1   (LO2)

The following transactions were made by Landers Corp. in March 2017.

Mar. 1 Established a petty cash fund of $200
12 Reimbursed the fund for the following:

Postage	$10
Office supplies	50
Maintenance	35
Meals (selling expenses)	25
	$120

18 Increased the fund by an additional $200
25 Reimbursed the fund for the following:

Office supplies	$75
Delivery charges	30
	$105

28 Reduced the amount of the fund to $350.

Required: Prepare journal entries to record the petty cash transactions.

EXERCISE 7–2 (LO3)

The following information pertains to Ferguson Corp. at December 31, 2016, its year-end:

Cash per company records		$5,005
Cash per bank statement		7,000
Bank service charges not yet recorded in company records		30
Note collected by bank not yet recorded in company records:		
Amount of note receivable	$1,300	
Amount of interest	25	1,325
Fluet inc. cheque deducted in error by bank		200
December cheques not yet paid by bank in December:		
#631	$354	
#642	746	
#660	200	
#661	300	1,600
December deposit recorded by the bank January 3, 2017		700

Required: Prepare a bank reconciliation and all necessary adjusting entries at December 31, 2016.

EXERCISE 7–3 (LO3)

The Cash general ledger account balance of Gladstone Ltd. was $2,531 at March 31, 2018. On this same date, the bank statement had a balance of $1,500. The following discrepancies were noted:

a. A deposit of $1,000 made on March 30, 2018 was not yet recorded by the bank on the March statement.

b. A customer's cheque amounting to $700 and deposited on March 15 was returned NSF with the bank statement.

c. Cheque #4302 for office supplies expense, correctly made out for $125 and cleared the bank for this amount, was recorded in the company records incorrectly as $152.

d. $20 for March service charges were recorded on the bank statement but not in the company records.

e. A cancelled cheque for $250 belonging to Global Corp. but charged by the bank to Gladstone Ltd. was included with the cancelled cheques returned by the bank.

f. There were $622 of outstanding cheques at March 31.

g. The bank collected a net amount of $290: $250 regarding a note receivable, interest revenue of $50, and a $10 service charge that also is not included in the company records.

Required: Prepare a bank reconciliation and record all necessary adjusting entries at March 31, 2018.

EXERCISE 7–4   (LO4)

Sather Ltd. had the following unadjusted account balances at December 31, 2015 (assume normal account balances):

Accounts Receivable	$147,000
Allowance for Doubtful Accounts	3,000
Sales	750,000

Required:

a. Assume that Sather Ltd. estimated its uncollectible accounts at December 31, 2015 to be two per cent of sales.

   i. Prepare the appropriate adjusting entry to record the estimated uncollectible accounts at December 31, 2015.

   ii. Calculate the balance in the Allowance for Doubtful Accounts account after posting the adjusting entry.

b. Assume that Sather Ltd. estimated its uncollectible accounts at December 31, 2015 to be ten per cent of the unadjusted balance in accounts receivable.

i. Prepare the appropriate adjusting entry to record the estimated uncollectible accounts at December 31, 2015.

ii. Calculate the balance in the Allowance for Doubtful Accounts account after posting the adjusting entry.

c. Why is there a difference in the calculated estimates of doubtful accounts in parts **a.** and **b.**?

d. Which calculation provides better matching: that made in part **a.** or in part **b.**? Why?

EXERCISE 7–5   (LO4)

The following information is taken from the records of Salzl Corp. at its December 31 year-end:

	2019	2020
Accounts written off		
During 2019	$2,400	
During 2020		$1,000
Recovery of accounts written off		
Recovered in 2020		300
Allowance for doubtful accounts (adjusted balance)		
At December 31, 2018	8,000	
At December 31, 2019	9,000	

Salzl had always estimated its uncollectible accounts at two per cent of sales. However, because of large discrepancies between the estimated and actual amounts, Hilroy decided to estimate its December 31, 2020 uncollectible accounts by preparing an ageing of its accounts receivable. An amount of $10,000 was considered uncollectible at December 31, 2020.

Required:

a. Calculate the amount of bad debt expense for 2019.

b. What adjusting entry was recorded at December 31, 2019 to account for bad debts?

c. Calculate the amount of bad debt expense for 2020.

d. What adjusting entry was recorded at December 31, 2020 to account for bad debts?

EXERCISE 7–6   (LO5)

Following are notes receivable transactions of Vilco Inc. whose year-end is March 31:

Mar. 1	Accepted a $40,000, 90-day, 3% note receivable dated today in granting a time extension to West Corp. on its past-due accounts receivable.
Mar. 31	Made an adjusting entry to record the accrued interest on West Corp.'s note receivable.
May 30	Received West Corp.'s payment for the principal and interest on the note receivable dated March 1.
Jun. 15	Accepted a $50,000, 45-day, 3% note receivable dated today in granting a time extension to Jill Monte on her past-due accounts receivable.
???	Received Jill Monte's payment for the principal and interest on her note dated June 15.

Required:

a. Prepare journal entries to record Vilco Inc.'s transactions (round all calculations to two decimal places).

b. Assume instead that on May 30 West Corp. dishonoured (did not pay) its note when presented for payment. How would Vilco Inc. record this transaction on May 30?

EXERCISE 7–7 (LO6,7)

The following comparative information is taken from the records of Salzl Corp. at its December 31 year-ends from 2016 to 2018:

	2018	2017	2016
Cash	$42,000	$30,000	$21,000
Accounts receivable	25,000	20,000	14,000
Merchandise inventory	36,000	25,000	17,500
Prepaid insurance	6,000	4,000	2,800
Plant and equipment	160,000	160,000	112,000
Accumulated depreciation – plant and equipment	68,000	54,000	37,800
Accounts payable	14,000	12,000	8,400
Salaries payable	9,000	8,000	5,600
Income tax payable	11,000	9,000	6,300
Bank loan, due in 3 months	17,000	0	0
Bank loan, due in 24 months	48,000	0	0
Share capital	50,000	50,000	35,000
Retained earnings	15,000	12,000	8,400
Dividends	15,000	15,000	10,500
Sales	375,000	367,000	256,900
Cost of goods sold	190,000	152,000	106,400
Operating expenses	120,000	96,000	67,200
Income tax expense	13,000	10,000	7,000

Required:

a. Calculate the acid-test and accounts receivable turnover ratios for each of 2017 and 2018 (round final calculations to two decimal places).

b. Was the change in each ratio from 2017 to 2018 favourable or unfavourable? Explain.

Problems

PROBLEM 7–1   (LO3)

The reconciliation of the cash balance per bank statement with the balance in the Cash account in the general ledger usually results in one of five types of adjustments. These are

a. Additions to the reported general ledger cash balance.

b. Deductions from the reported general ledger cash balance.

c. Additions to the reported cash balance per the bank statement.

d. Deductions from the reported cash balance per the bank statement.

e. Information that has no effect on the current reconciliation.

Required: Using the above letters a to e from the list, indicate the appropriate adjustment for each of the following items that apply to Goertzen Ltd. for December, 2019:

_____ The company has received a $3,000 loan from the bank that was deposited into its bank account but was not recorded in the company records.

_____ A $250 cheque was not returned with the bank statement though it was paid by the bank.

_____ Cheques amounting to $4,290 shown as outstanding on the November reconciliation still have not been returned by the bank.

_____ A collection of a note receivable for $1,000 made by the bank has not been previously reported to Goertzen. This includes interest earned of $50.

_____ The bank has erroneously charged Goertzen with a $1,100 cheque, which should have been charged to Gagetown Ltd.

_____ A $350 cheque made out by Fynn Company and deposited by Goertzen has been returned by the bank marked NSF; this is the first knowledge Goertzen has of this action.

_____ An $840 cheque from customer Abe Dobbs was incorrectly recorded as $730 in the company records.

_____ A $600 bank deposit of December 31 does not appear on the bank statement.

_____ Bank service charges amounting to $75 were deducted from the bank statement but not yet from the company records.

PROBLEM 7–2   (LO4)

Tarpon Inc. made $1,000,000 in sales during 2018. Thirty per cent of these were cash sales. During 2018, $25,000 of accounts receivable were written off as being uncollectible. In addition, $15,000 of the accounts that were written off in 2017 were unexpectedly collected in 2018. The December 31, 2017 adjusted balance in AFDA was a credit of $15,000. At its December 31, 2018 year-end, Tarpon had the following accounts receivable:

Age (days)	Accounts Receivable
1-30	$100,000
31-60	50,000
61-90	25,000
91-120	60,000
Over 120	15,000
Total	$250,000

Required:

1. Prepare journal entries to record the following 2018 transactions:

    (a) The write-off of $25,000.

    (b) The recovery of $15,000.

2. Calculate the unadjusted balance in AFDA at December 31, 2018.

3. Prepare the adjusting entry required at December 31, 2018 for each of the following scenarios:

    (a) Bad debts at December 31, 2018 is based on three per cent of credit sales.

    (b) Estimated uncollectible accounts at December 31, 2018 is estimated at five per cent of accounts receivable.

    (c) Estimated uncollectible accounts at December 31, 2018 is calculated using the following aging analysis:

Age (days)	Estimated Loss Percentage
2015-01-30	2%
31-60	4%
61-90	5%
91-120	10%
Over 120	50%

4. Calculate the December 31, 2018 adjusted balance in AFDA based on the adjustments prepared in 3(a), 3(b), and 3(c) above.

Chapter 8

Long-lived Assets

Long-lived assets or *property, plant, and equipment (PPE)* assets are used in the normal operating activities of the business and are expected to provide benefits for a period in excess of one year. Long-lived assets covered in this chapter consist of three types: property, plant, and equipment (PPE), intangible assets, and goodwill. Also discussed are *depreciation* and *amortization*, techniques to allocate the cost of most long-lived assets over their estimated useful lives.

Chapter 8 Learning Objectives

LO1 – Describe how the cost of property, plant, and equipment (PPE) is determined, and calculate PPE.

LO2 – Explain, calculate, and record depreciation using the units-of-production, straight-line, and double-declining balance methods.

LO3 – Explain, calculate, and record depreciation for partial years.

LO4 – Explain, calculate, and record revised depreciation for subsequent capital expenditures.

LO5 – Explain, calculate, and record the impairment of long-lived assets.

LO6 – Account for the derecognition of PPE assets.

LO7 – Explain and record the acquisition and amortization of intangible assets.

LO8 – Explain goodwill and identify where on the balance sheet it is reported.

LO9 – Describe the disclosure requirements for long-lived assets in the notes to the financial statements.

Concept Self-Check

Use the following as a self-check while working through Chapter 8.

1. What is the distinction between capital expenditures and revenue expenditures?

2. How do generally accepted accounting principles prescribe what amount should be capitalized?

3. How is partial period depreciation recorded?
4. What is the formula for calculating revised depreciation?
5. What is the difference between a tangible and intangible long-lived asset?
6. What different methods can be used to calculate depreciation for property, plant, and equipment?
7. How are disposals of property, plant, and equipment recorded in the accounting records?
8. How is the impairment of a long-lived asset accounted for?
9. How are intangible assets amortized?
10. What is goodwill and what is its accounting treatment?

NOTE: The purpose of these questions is to prepare you for the concepts introduced in the chapter. Your goal should be to answer each of these questions as you read through the chapter. If, when you complete the chapter, you are unable to answer one or more the Concept Self-Check questions, go back through the content to find the answer(s). Solutions are not provided to these questions.

8.1 Establishing the Cost of Property, Plant, and Equipment (PPE)

LO1 – Describe how the cost of property, plant, and equipment (PPE) is determined, and calculate PPE.

Property, plant, and equipment (PPE) are *tangible* long-lived assets that are acquired for the purpose of generating revenue either directly or indirectly. They are held for use in the production or supply of goods and services, have been acquired for use on a continuing basis, and are not intended for sale in the ordinary course of business. Because PPE assets are long-lived or have a life greater than one year, they are non-current in nature, also known as long-term assets. Examples of PPE assets include land, office and manufacturing buildings, production machinery, trucks, ships or aircraft used to deliver goods or transport passengers, salespersons' automobiles owned by a company, or a farmer's production machinery like tractors and field equipment. PPE assets are **tangible assets** because they can be physically touched. There are other types of non-current assets that are *intangible* – existing only as legal concepts – like copyrights and patents. These will be discussed later in this chapter.

Capital Expenditures

Any cash disbursement is referred to as an **expenditure**. A **capital expenditure** results in the acquisition of a non-current asset, including any additional costs involved in preparing the asset for its intended use. Examples of various costs that may be incurred to prepare PPE for use are listed below.

	Capital Expenditures		
	Land	Building	Equipment
Costs to Acquire PPE	Purchase price Commission to real estate agent Legal fees	Purchase price Commission to real estate agent Legal fees	Invoice cost Transportation Insurance (during transportation)
Costs to Prepare PPE for Use	Costs of draining, clearing, and landscaping; demolition Assessments for streets and sewage system	Repair and remodelling costs before use Payments to tenants for premature termination of lease	Assembly Installation (including wages paid to company employees) Special floor foundations or supports Wiring Inspection Test run costs

To demonstrate, assume that equipment is purchased for $20,000. Additional costs include transportation costs $500, installation costs $1,000, construction costs for a cement foundation $2,500, and test run(s) costs to debug the equipment $2,000. The total capitalized cost of the asset to put it into use is $26,000.

Determining whether an outlay is a capital expenditure or a *revenue expenditure* is a matter of judgment. A **revenue expenditure** does not have a future benefit beyond one year. The concept of materiality enters into the distinction between capital and revenue expenditures. As a matter of expediency, an expenditure of $20 that has all the characteristics of a capital expenditure would probably be expensed rather than capitalized, because the time and effort required by accounting staff to capitalize and then depreciate the item over its estimated useful life is so much greater than the benefits derived from doing so. Capitalization policies are established by many companies to resolve the problem of distinguishing between capital and revenue expenditures. For example, one company's capitalization policy may state that all capital expenditures equal to or greater than $1,000 will capitalized, while all capital expenditures under $1,000 will be expensed when incurred. Another company may have a capitalization policy limit of $500. Additionally, a company may have a different capitalization policy for different types of plant and equipment assets – hand tools may have a capitalization policy limit of $200 while the limit might be $1,000 for furniture.

Not all asset-related expenditures incurred after the purchase of an asset are capitalized. An expenditure made to maintain PPE in satisfactory working order is a revenue expenditure and recorded as a debit to an expense account. Examples of these expenditures include: (a) the cost of replacing small parts of an asset that normally wear out (in the case of a truck, for example: new tires, new muffler, new battery); (b) continuing expenditures for maintaining the asset in good working order (for example, oil changes, antifreeze, transmission fluid changes); and (c) costs of renewing structural parts of an asset (for example, repairs of collision damage, repair or replacement of rusted parts).

Although some expenditures for repair and maintenance may benefit more than one accounting period, they may not be material in amount or they may have uncertain future benefits. They are therefore treated as expenses. These three criteria must all be met for an expenditure to be considered capital in nature.

1. Will it benefit more than one accounting period?

2. Will it enhance the service potential of the asset, or make it more valuable or more adaptable?

3. Is the dollar amount material?

Regardless of when an expenditure is incurred, if it meets the three criteria above it will always be a capital expenditure and debited to the appropriate asset account. If the expenditure does not meet all three criteria, then it is a revenue expenditure and is expensed.

An exploration is available on the Lyryx site. Log into your Lyryx course to run Revenue and Capital Expenditures.

Land

The purchase of land is a capital expenditure when land is used in the operation of a business. In addition to the costs listed in the schedule above, the cost of land should be increased by the cost of removing any unwanted structures on it. This cost is reduced by the proceeds, if any, obtained from the sale of the scrap. For example, assume that the purchase price of land is $100,000 before an additional $15,000 cost to raze an old building: $1,000 is expected to be received for salvaged materials. The cost of the land is $114,000 ($100,000 + $15,000 - $1,000).

Frequently, land and useful buildings are purchased for a *lump sum*. That is, one price is negotiated for their entire purchase. A lump sum purchase price must be apportioned between the PPE assets acquired on the basis of their respective market values, perhaps established by a municipal assessment or a professional land appraiser. Assume that a lump sum of $150,000 cash is paid for land and a building, and that the land is appraised at 25% of the total purchase price. The Land account would be debited for $37,500 ($150,000 x 25%) and the Building account would be debited for the remaining 75% or $112,500 ($150,000 x 75% = $112,500 or $150,000 - $37,500 = $112,500) as shown in the following journal entry.

8.1. Establishing the Cost of Property, Plant, and Equipment (PPE) ■ 247

General Journal				
Date	Account/Explanation	PR	Debit	Credit
	Land...............................		37,500	
	Building............................		112,500	
	Cash...............................			150,000
	To record the purchase of land and building for a lump sum of $150,000; $150,000 x 25% = $37,500; $150,000 x 75% = $112,500.			

An exploration is available on the Lyryx site. Log into your Lyryx course to run Lump Sum Purchases.

Building and Equipment

When a capital asset is purchased, its cost includes the purchase price plus all costs to prepare the asset for its intended use. However, a company may construct its own building or equipment. In the case of a building, for example, costs include those incurred for excavation, building permits, insurance and property taxes during construction, engineering fees, the cost of labour incurred by having company employees supervise and work on the construction of the building, and the cost of any interest incurred to finance the construction during the construction period.

An exploration is available on the Lyryx site. Log into your Lyryx course to run Cost of Property, Plant and Equipment (PPE).

Property, Plant, and Equipment (PPE) Subsidiary Ledger

The accounts receivable and accounts payable subsidiary ledgers (more commonly referred to as subledgers) were introduced in Chapter 5 and the merchandise inventory subledger was introduced in Chapter 6. To review, a subledger lists individual accounts that fall under a common account, also known as the controlling account. For example, the accounts receivable controlling account for ABC Inc. shows a balance of $4,000 on the December 31, 2015 balance sheet. The accounts receivable subledger shows that the $4,000 is made up of three receivables: $800 for Ducker Inc.; $2,200 for Zest Inc.; and $1,000 for Frank Corporation. Since the controlling account is a summary of the subledger, their balances must be identical. Subledgers allow details to be maintained in a separate record.

In a PPE subledger, an account would exist for each piece of land, each piece of machinery, each vehicle, and so on. The subledger account would include information regarding the date of purchase, cost, residual value, estimated useful life, depreciation, and other relevant information.

An exploration is available on the Lyryx site. Log into your Lyryx course to run *Preparing the PPE Section of a Balance Sheet*.

8.2 Depreciation

LO2 – Explain, calculate, and record depreciation using the units-of-production, straight-line, and double-declining balance methods.

The role of **depreciation** is to allocate the cost of a PPE asset (except land) over the accounting periods expected to receive benefits from its use. Depreciation begins when the asset is in the location and condition necessary for it to be put to use. Depreciation continues even if the asset becomes idle or is retired from use, unless it is fully depreciated. Land is not depreciated, as it is assumed to have an unlimited life.

Depreciation is an application of the matching principle.

According to generally accepted accounting principles, a company should select a method of depreciation that represents the way in which the asset's future economic benefits are estimated to be used up.

There are many different ways to calculate depreciation. The most frequently used methods are usage-based and time-based. Regardless of depreciation method, there are three factors necessary to calculate depreciation:

- cost of the asset
- residual value
- estimated useful life or productive output.

Residual value is the estimated worth of the asset at the end of its estimated useful life.

Useful life is the length of time that a long-lived asset is estimated to be of benefit *to the current owner*. This is not necessarily the same as the asset's economic life. If a company has a policy of replacing its delivery truck every two years, its useful life is two years even though it may be used by the next owner for several more years.

Productive output is the amount of goods or services expected to be provided. For example, it may be measured in units of output, hours used, or kilometres driven.

Usage-Based Depreciation Method – Units-of-Production

Usage-based depreciation methods, such as the Units-of-Production Method, are used when the output of an asset varies from period to period.

> Usage methods assume that the asset will contribute to the earning of revenues in relation to the amount of output during the accounting period. Therefore, the depreciation expense will vary from year to year.

To demonstrate, assume that Big Dog Carworks Corp. purchased a $20,000 piece of equipment on January 1, 2015 with a $2,000 residual value and estimated productive life of 10,000 units. If 1,500 units were produced during 2015, the depreciation expense for the year ended December 31, 2015 would be calculated using the following formula:

$$\frac{\text{Cost} - \text{Residual value}}{\text{Estimated units of output}} = \text{Depreciation per unit} \times \text{Number of units produced} = \text{Depreciation expense}$$

$$\frac{\$20{,}000 - \$2{,}000}{10{,}000 \text{ units}} = \$1.80 \text{ depreciation per unit} \times 1{,}500 \text{ units produced} = \$2{,}700 \text{ depreciation expense for 2015}$$

The following adjusting entry would be made on December 31, 2015:

Date	Account/Explanation	PR	Debit	Credit
Dec 31	Depreciation Expense		2,700	
	Accumulated Depreciation...........			2,700
	To record depreciation expense using the Units-of-Production method; ($20,000 - $2,000)/10,000 units = $1.80/unit; $1.80/unit x 1,500 units = $2,700.			

The **carrying amount** or **net book value** of the asset (cost less accumulated depreciation) on the December 31, 2015 balance sheet would be $17,300 ($20,000 - 2,700).

> Note that the residual value is only used to calculate depreciation expense. It is not recorded in the accounts of the company or included as part of the carrying amount (net book value) on the balance sheet.

If 2,000 units were produced during 2016, depreciation expense for that year would be $3,600 ($1.80 per unit $\times$ 2,000 units). At December 31, 2016, the following adjusting entry would be recorded:

Date	Account/Explanation	PR	Debit	Credit
Dec 31	Depreciation Expense		3,600	
	Accumulated Depreciation............			3,600
	To record depreciation expense using the Units-of-Production method; ($20,000 - $2,000)/10,000 units = $1.80/unit; $1.80/unit x 2,000 units = $3,600.			

The carrying amount (or net book value) at December 31, 2016 would be $13,700 ($20,000 – 2,700 – 3,600). If the equipment produces 1,000 units in 2017, 2,500 units in 2018, and 3,000 units in 2019, depreciation expense and carrying amounts would be as follows each year:

(a)	(b)	(c)	(d)	(e)	(f)
Year	Carrying amount at start of year	Usage (units)	Rate	Dep'n expense	Carrying amount at end of year (b) – (e)
2015	$20,000	1,500	$1.80	$2,700	$17,300
2016	17,300	2,000	1.80	3,600	13,700
2017	13,700	1,000	1.80	1,800	11,900
2018	11,900	2,500	1.80	4,500	7,400
2019	7,400	3,000	1.80	5,400	2,000
		10,000		$18,000	

If the equipment produces exactly 10,000 units over its useful life and is then retired, depreciation expense over all years will total $18,000 (10,000 × $1.80) and the carrying amount will equal residual value of $2,000.

It is unlikely that the equipment will produce exactly 10,000 units over its useful life. Assume instead that 4,800 units were produced in 2019. Depreciation expense and carrying amounts would be as follows each year:

(a) Year	(b) Carrying amount at start of year	(c) Usage (units)	(d) Rate	(e) Dep'n expense	(f) Carrying amount at end of year (b) – (e)
2015	$20,000	1,500	$1.80	$2,700	$17,300
2016	17,300	2,000	1.80	3,600	13,700
2017	13,700	1,000	1.80	1,800	11,900
2018	11,900	2,500	1.80	4,500	7,400
2019	7,400	4,800	1.80	5,400	2,000 ←
		11,800		$18,000	

Carrying amount (or net book value) cannot be less than residual value

Notice that the depreciation expense for 2019 is **not** $8,640 (calculated as the 4,800 units x $1.80/unit = $8,640). The depreciation expense for 2019 cannot exceed $5,400 because the remaining carrying amount must be equal to or greater than the residual value. In other words, the **maximum allowable accumulated depreciation** cannot exceed cost less residual. A PPE asset cannot be depreciation below its residual value.

An exploration is available on the Lyryx site. Log into your Lyryx course to run Units-of-Production Method.

Time-Based Depreciation Method - Straight-Line

The **straight-line method of depreciation** – introduced in Chapter 3 – assumes that the asset will contribute to the earning of revenues equally each time period. Therefore, equal amounts of depreciation are recorded during each year of the asset's useful life. Straight-line depreciation is based on time – the asset's estimated useful life.

Straight-line depreciation is calculated as:

$$\frac{\text{Cost} - \text{Estimated residual value}}{\text{Estimated useful life in years}} = \text{Depreciation expense/year}$$

To demonstrate, assume the same $20,000 piece of equipment used earlier, with an estimated useful life of five years and an estimated residual value of $2,000. Straight-line depreciation would be $3,600 per year calculated as:

$$\frac{\$20,000 - \$2,000}{5 \text{ years}} = \$3,600 \text{ depreciation expense/year}$$

Over the five-year useful life of the equipment, depreciation expense and carrying amounts will be as follows:

(a)	*(b)*	*(c)*	*(d)*
Year	*Carrying amount at start of year*	*Dep'n expense*	*Carrying amount at end of year (b) – (c)*
2015	$20,000	$3,600	$16,400
2016	16,400	3,600	12,800
2017	12,800	3,600	9,200
2018	9,200	3,600	5,600
2019	5,600	3,600	2,000
		$18,000	

The carrying amount at December 31, 2019 will be the residual value of $2,000 ($20,000 – 18,000).

Under the straight-line method, depreciation expense for each accounting period remains the same dollar amount over the useful life of the asset.

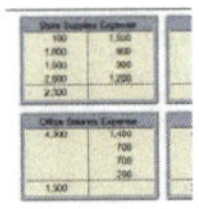

An exploration is available on the Lyryx site. Log into your Lyryx course to run Straight-Line Method.

Accelerated Time-Based Depreciation Method – Double-Declining Balance (DDB)

An **accelerated depreciation** method assumes that a plant and equipment asset will contribute more to the earning of revenues in the earlier stages of its useful life than in the later stages. This means that more depreciation is recorded in earlier years with the depreciation expense decreasing each year. This approach is most appropriate where assets experience a high degree of obsolescence (such as computers) or where the value of the asset is highest in the first year when it is new and efficient and declines significantly each year as it is used and becomes worn (such as equipment).

Under an accelerated depreciation method, depreciation expense decreases each year over the useful life of the asset.

One type of accelerated depreciation is the **double-declining balance (DDB)** method. It is calculated as:

$$\text{Carrying Amount (or Net Book Value)} \times (2/n)$$

where n = estimated useful life. $2/n$ is the rate of depreciation and it remains constant over the asset's estimated useful life (unless there is a change in the useful life which is discussed in a later section of this chapter). The DDB rate of depreciation can also be described as twice the straight-line rate. For example, if the straight-line rate of depreciation is 15%, the DDB rate will be 30% (calculated as 2 × 15%).

To demonstrate DDB depreciation calculations, assume the same $20,000 equipment with an estimated useful life of five years. The DDB rate of depreciation is calculated as $2/n = 2/5 = 0.40$ or 40%. Alternatively, given that we know the straight-line rate is 20%, doubling it is 40%.

The declining balance rate is applied to the carrying amount of the asset *without regard to residual value*. Regardless of which depreciation method is used, remember that the asset cannot be depreciated below its carrying amount (or net book value) which in this case is $2,000. The DDB depreciation for the five years of the asset's useful life follows.

(a) Year	(b) Carrying amount at start of year	(c) DDB rate	(d) Dep'n expense (b) x (c)	(e) Carrying amount at end of year (b) – (d)
2015	$20,000	40%	$8,000	$12,000
2016	12,000	40%	4,800	7,200
2017	7,200	40%	2,880	4,320
2018	4,320	40%	1,728	2,592
2019	2,592	40%	592	2,000
			$18,000	

> Although for 2019 the depreciation expense would be calculated as $1,037 ($2,592 x 40%), only $592 is recorded to bring the carrying amount of the asset down to its residual value of $2,000.

At the end of five years, the carrying amount is once again equal to the residual value of $2,000.

An exploration is available on the Lyryx site. Log into your Lyryx course to run Double-Declining Balance.

A comparison of the three depreciation methods is shown in Figure 8.1.

254 ■ Long-lived Assets

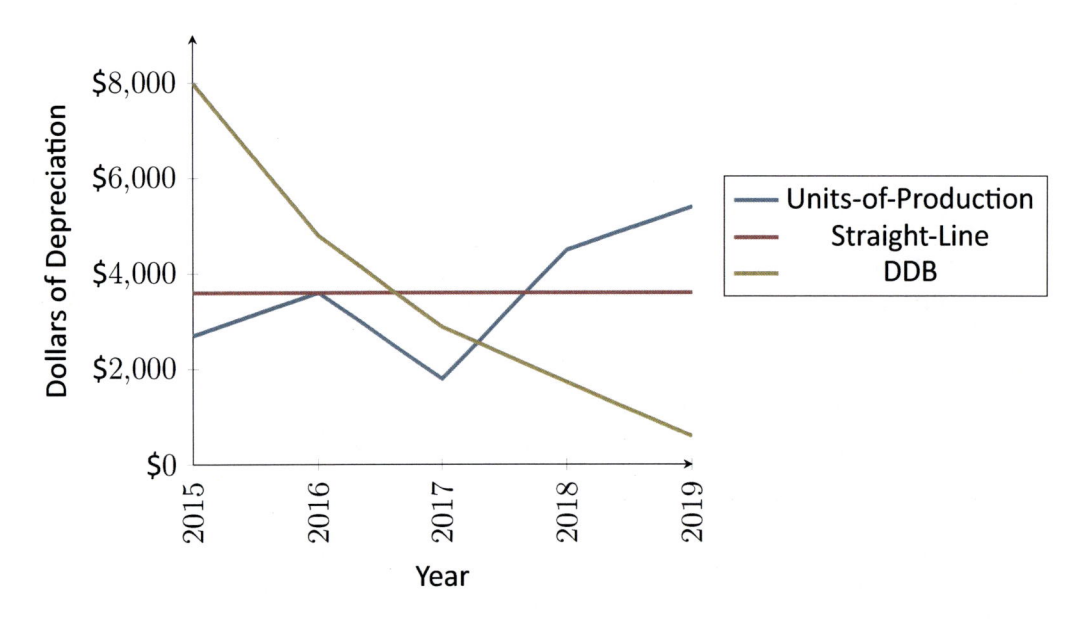

Figure 8.1: Comparing Three Depreciation Methods

8.3 Partial Year Depreciation

LO3 – Explain, calculate, and record depreciation for partial years.

Assets may be purchased or sold at any time during a fiscal year. Should depreciation be calculated for a whole year in such a case? The answer depends on corporate accounting policy. There are many alternatives. One is to calculate depreciation to the nearest whole month. Another, often called the **half-year rule**, records half a year's depreciation regardless of when an asset purchase or disposal occurs during the year.

To demonstrate the half-year approach to calculating depreciation for partial periods, assume again that Big Dog Carworks Corp. purchases equipment for $20,000 with an estimated useful life of five years and a residual value of $2,000. Recall that depreciation expense for 2015 was $3,600 using the straight-line method. Because of the half-year rule, depreciation expense for 2015 would be $1,800 ($3,600 x .5) even though the asset was purchased on the first day of the fiscal year. Using the double-declining balance method, depreciation expense for 2015 under the half-year rule would be $4,000 ($8,000 × .5). Applying the half-year rule to the units-of-production depreciation for 2015, would result in no change because the method is usage-based and not time-based (presumably usage would be less if the asset is purchased partway through the year, so this depreciation method already takes this into account).

An exploration is available on the Lyryx site. Log into your Lyryx course to run Partial Periods.

8.4 Revising Depreciation

LO4 – Explain, calculate, and record revised depreciation for subsequent capital expenditures.

Both the useful life and residual value of a depreciable asset are estimated at the time it is purchased. As time goes by, these estimates may change for a variety of reasons. In these cases, the depreciation expense is recalculated from the date of the change in the accounting estimate and applied going forward. *No change is made to depreciation expense already recorded.*

Consider the example of the equipment purchased for $20,000 on January 1, 2015, with an estimated useful life of five years and residual value of $2,000. If the straight-line depreciation method is used, the yearly depreciation expense is $3,600. After two years, the carrying amount at the end of 2016 is $12,800 ($20,000 - 3,600 - 3,600). Assume that on January 1, 2017, management estimates the remaining useful life of the equipment to be six years, and the residual value to be $5,000.

Depreciation expense for the remaining six years would be calculated as:

$$= \frac{(\text{Remaining carrying amount} - \text{Revised residual value})}{\text{Estimated remaining useful life}}$$

$$= \frac{(\$12{,}800 - 5{,}000)}{6 \text{ years}}$$

$$= \$1{,}300 \text{ per year}$$

An exploration is available on the Lyryx site. Log into your Lyryx course to run Revised Dep. - Change in Life/Residual.

Subsequent Capital Expenditures

As noted earlier, normal, recurring expenditures that relate to day-to-day servicing of depreciable assets are not capitalized, but rather are expensed when incurred. Oil changes and new tires for vehicles are examples of recurring expenditures that are expensed. Expenditures that are material, can be reliably measured, and enhance the future economic benefit provided by the asset, are added to the cost of the asset rather than being expensed when incurred. A subsequent capital expenditure can take one of two forms:

1. Addition (e.g., adding a garage to the back of an existing building or adding a skywalk in a factory)

2. Replacement (e.g., replacing the refrigeration unit in a long-haul truck or replacing the windows in a building).

To demonstrate the accounting for an addition, recall our original example where equipment was purchased on January 1, 2015 for $20,000; the estimated useful life and residual value were five years and $2,000, respectively. Assume that on January 4, 2016, a heat exchanger was added to the equipment that allowed it to produce a new product in addition to the existing product line. This $12,000 addition, paid in cash, had an estimated life of ten years with no residual value. The useful life and residual value of the original equipment did not change as a result of the addition. The entry to record the addition on January 4 is:

\multicolumn{5}{c	}{General Journal}
Date	Account/Explanation	PR	Debit	Credit
Jan 4	Equipment – Heat Exchanger............		12,000	
	Cash.................................			12,000
	To record the addition of a heat exchanger to the equipment.			

The entry to record revised depreciation on December 31, 2016 is:

\multicolumn{5}{c	}{General Journal}
Date	Account/Explanation	PR	Debit	Credit
Dec 31	Depreciation Expense - Equipment.......		4,800	
	Accumulated Depreciation - Equipment.................................			4,800
	To record revised straight-line depreciation; ($20,000 - $2,000)/5 years = $3,600/year; ($12,000 - $0)/10 years = $1,200/year; $3,600 + $1,200 = $4,800.			

An exploration is available on the Lyryx site. Log into your Lyryx course to run Revised Dep. - Addition.

The accounting for a replacement is more involved. The cost of the replaced item and its related accumulated depreciation must be removed from the accounting records when the replacement is capitalized recording any resulting gain or loss *as well as* calculating revised depreciation. Let's demonstrate, again using the $20,000 equipment purchased on January 1, 2015 with a five-year life and $2,000 residual value. Assume that on January 5, 2018 the engine in the equipment burned out and needed to be replaced. The PPE subledger showed that the engine had an original cost of $8,000, useful life of five years, and residual value of $1,000 resulting in a carrying amount as at January 5, 2018 of $3,800 ($8,000 cost – $4,200 accumulated depreciation). The entry to dispose of the old engine and remove it from the accounting records is (the old engine was scrapped and not sold because it was burned out):

8.4. Revising Depreciation

General Journal				
Date	Account/Explanation	PR	Debit	Credit
Jan 5	Accum. Dep. – Equip. – Engine		4,200	
	Loss on Disposal		3,800	
	Equipment – Engine.................			8,000
	To record the scrapping of the burned out equipment engine; ($8,000 - $1,000)/5 years = $1,400/year depreciation X 3 years = $4,200 accumulated depreciation.			

Notice in the entry above that the cost of the old engine and the accumulated depreciation must be individually removed from the accounting records. Since the asset is not completely depreciated and was scrapped, the $3,800 carrying amount represents a loss. If the engine had been sold, the gain or loss would have been calculated as the difference between its carrying value and the cash proceeds. Losses (as well as gains) are reported on the income statement under *Other Revenues and Expenses*. **A common error made by students is to debit loss on disposal and credit equipment–engine for the carrying amount; this is incorrect.** After posting the entry to dispose of the old engine, the account balances in the Equipment account and its related Accumulated Depreciation account would be as follows.

Equipment			
Jan. 1, 2015 20,000	8,000 Jan. 5, 2018
Balance 12,000	

Accumulated Depreciation – Equipment	
	3,600 Dec. 31, 2015
	3,600 Dec. 31, 2016
	3,600 Dec. 31, 2017
Jan. 5, 2018 4,200	
	6,600 Balance

The entry to record the new engine purchased for $12,000 cash (estimated life 8 years; estimated zero residual value) is:

General Journal				
Date	Account/Explanation	PR	Debit	Credit
Jan 5	Equipment - Engine		12,000	
	Cash...........................			12,000
	To record the new engine with estimated useful life of 8 years and estimated residual value of zero.			

Alternatively, the entries to dispose of the old engine and record the addition of the new engine can be combined into one compound entry as follows:

General Journal				
Date	Account/Explanation	PR	Debit	Credit
Jan 5	Accum. Dep. – Equip. – Engine (old)		4,200	
	Loss on Disposal		3,800	
	Equipment – Engine (new)		12,000	
	Equipment – Engine (old)			8,000
	Cash			12,000
	To record the scrapping of the burned out equipment engine and its replacement with a new engine.			

Assuming the useful life and residual value of the equipment did not change and the new engine had an estimated useful life of eight years and an estimated residual value of zero, the entry to record revised depreciation on December 31, 2018 is:

General Journal				
Date	Account/Explanation	PR	Debit	Credit
Dec 31	Depreciation Expense - Equipment		3,200	
	Accum. Dep. - Equipment			3,200
	To record revised straight-line depreciation; Remaining carrying amount of equipment = $12,000 remaining cost - $6,600 remaining balance in accumulated depreciation = $5,400; Revised depreciation on equipment = ($5,400 remaining carrying amount - $2,000 residual)/2 years remaining useful life = $1,700 depreciation/year; Depreciation on new engine = ($12,000 - $0)/8 years = $1,500/year; Total depreciation = $1,700 + $1,500 = $3,200.			

The previous example emphasizes the importance of maintaining a PPE subledger in order to apply the concept of *componentization*. **Componentization** requires each *major component* that has a different estimated useful life than the rest of an asset to be recorded and depreciated separately. For instance, assume a commercial airliner is purchased for $100 million ($100M) on January 1, 2015 with the following components: airframe, engines, landing gear, interior, and other parts. Original cost, estimated residual value, estimated useful lives, depreciation method to be used, serial numbers where applicable, and other relevant information are recorded in the PPE subledger.

An exploration is available on the Lyryx site. Log into your Lyryx course to run Revised Dep. - Replacement.

8.5 Impairment of Long-lived Assets

LO5 – Explain, calculate, and record the impairment of long-lived assets.

Under generally accepted accounting principles, management must compare the **recoverable amount** of a long-lived asset with its carrying amount (cost less accumulated depreciation) at the end of each reporting period. The recoverable amount is the fair value of the asset at the time less any estimated costs to sell it. If the recoverable amount is lower than the carrying amount, an **impairment loss** must be recorded.

An impairment loss may occur because of a variety of reasons such as technological obsolescence, an economic downturn, or a physical disaster. When an impairment is recorded, subsequent years' depreciation expense must also be revised.

Recall again our $20,000 equipment purchased January 1, 2015 with an estimated useful life of five years and a residual value of $2,000. Assume straight-line depreciation has been recorded for 2015 and 2016 at $3,600 per year. At December 31, 2016, the carrying amount of the equipment is $12,800 ($20,000 – 3,600 – 3,600). At that point management determines that new equipment with equivalent capabilities can be purchased for much less than the old equipment due to technological changes. As a result, the recoverable value of the original equipment at December 31, 2016 is estimated to be $7,000. Because the recoverable amount is less than its carrying amount of $12,800, an impairment loss of $5,800 ($12,800 – 7,000) is recorded in the accounting records of BDCC as follows:

General Journal				
Date	Account/Explanation	PR	Debit	Credit
Dec 31	Impairment Loss		5,800	
	Equipment			5,800
	To record impairment loss on equipment.			

This reduces the carrying amount of the equipment to $7,000 so that revised depreciation expense of $1,667 per year would be recorded at the end of 2017, 2018, and 2019, calculated as follows (assume no change to original useful life and residual value):

$$\frac{(\text{Revised carrying amount} - \text{Revised residual value})}{\text{Remaining useful life}}$$
$$= \frac{(\$7,000 - \$2,000)}{3 \text{ years remaining useful life}}$$
$$= \$1,667 \text{ per year}$$

Impairment losses can be reversed in subsequent years if the recoverable amount of the asset exceeds the carrying amount. Also, if the fair value of a PPE asset can be reliably measured, it can be revalued to more than its original cost. However, the revaluation process needs to be conducted thereafter on a regular basis. These topics are not dealt with here, as they are beyond the scope of introductory financial accounting.

An exploration is available on the Lyryx site. Log into your Lyryx course to run Impairment Loss.

8.6 Derecognition of Property, Plant, and Equipment

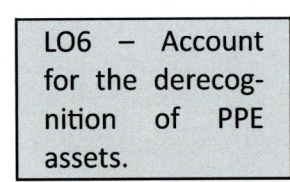

LO6 – Account for the derecognition of PPE assets.

Property, Plant, and Equipment is *derecognized* (that is, the cost and any related accumulated depreciation are removed from the accounting records) when it is sold or when no future economic benefit is expected. To account for the disposal of a PPE asset, the following must occur:

1. If the disposal occurs part way through the accounting period, depreciation must be updated to the date of disposal by

	General Journal			
Date	Account/Explanation	PR	Debit	Credit
	Depreciation Expense		XXX	
	Accumulated Depreciation...........			XXX
	To update depreciation for partial period.			

2. Record the disposal including any resulting gain or loss by

	General Journal			
Date	Account/Explanation	PR	Debit	Credit
	Cash (if any, or other assets received)....		XXX	
	Accumulated Depreciation...............		XXX	
	Loss on Disposal.......................		XXX	
	OR Gain on Disposal			XXX
	PPE Asset (such as Equipment).......			XXX
	To record disposal of PPE asset.			

A loss results when the carrying amount of the asset is greater than the proceeds received, if any. A gain results when the carrying amount is less than any proceeds received.

Sale or Retirement of PPE

When a PPE asset has reached the end of its useful life it can be either sold or retired. In either case, the asset's cost and accumulated depreciation must be removed from the records, after depreciation expense has been recorded up to the date of disposal or retirement.

8.6. Derecognition of Property, Plant, and Equipment

Recall the calculation of straight-line depreciation for the equipment purchased for $20,000 with an estimated useful life of five years and a residual value of $2,000. Assume that the general ledger T-accounts of equipment and accumulated depreciation contain the following entries for the last five years:

Equipment		Accumulated Depreciation Equipment	
2015 20,000		2015	3,600
		2016	3,600
		2017	3,600
		2018	3,600
		2019	3,600
			18,000

Assume that the equipment is sold at the end of 2019, when accumulated depreciation totals $18,000. The carrying amount at this date is $2,000 ($20,000 cost – $18,000 accumulated depreciation). Three different situations are possible.

1. **Sale at carrying amount**

    Assume the equipment is sold for its residual value of $2,000. No gain or loss on disposal would occur.

Cost	$	20,000
Accumulated depreciation		(18,000)
Carrying amount		2,000
Proceeds of disposition		(2,000)
Gain on disposal	$	-0-

    General Journal

Date	Account/Explanation	PR	Debit	Credit
Dec 31	Cash....................................		2,000	
	Accumulated Dep. – Equipment..........		18,000	
	Equipment...........................			20,000
	To record the disposal of equipment sold for $2,000 cash.			

2. **Sale above carrying amount**

    Assume the equipment is sold for $3,000. A gain of $1,000 would occur.

Cost	$	20,000
Accumulated depreciation		(18,000)
Carrying amount		2,000
Proceeds of disposition		(3,000)
Gain on disposal	$	(1,000)

General Journal

Date	Account/Explanation	PR	Debit	Credit
Dec 31	Cash..............................		3,000	
	Accumulated Dep. – Equipment..........		18,000	
	Gain on Disposal.....................			1,000
	Equipment..........................			20,000
	To record the disposal of equipment sold for $3,000 cash.			

3. **Sale below carrying amount**

    Assume the equipment is sold for $500. A loss on disposal of $1,500 would occur.

Cost	$	20,000
Accumulated depreciation		(18,000)
Carrying amount		2,000
Proceeds of disposition		(500)
Loss on disposal	$	1,500

General Journal

Date	Account/Explanation	PR	Debit	Credit
Dec 31	Cash..............................		500	
	Accumulated Dep. – Equipment..........		18,000	
	Loss on Disposal.....................		1,500	
	Equipment..........................			20,000
	To record the disposal of equipment sold for $500 cash.			

In each of these cases, the cash proceeds must be recorded (by a debit) and the cost and accumulated depreciation must be removed from the accounts. A credit difference represents a gain on disposal while a debit difference represents a loss.

Disposal Involving Trade-In

It is a common practice to exchange a used PPE asset for a new one. This is known as a **trade-in**. The value of the trade-in agreed by the purchaser and seller is called the **trade-in allowance**. This amount is applied to the purchase price of the new asset, and the purchaser pays the difference. For instance, if the cost of a new asset is $10,000 and a trade-in allowance of $6,000 is given for the old asset, the purchaser will pay $4,000 ($10,000 – 6,000).

Sometimes as an inducement to the purchaser, the trade-in allowance is higher than the fair value of the used asset on the open market. Regardless, the cost of the new asset must be recorded at its fair value, calculated as follows:

$$\text{Cost of new asset} = \text{Cash paid} + \text{Fair value of asset traded}$$

8.6. Derecognition of Property, Plant, and Equipment

If there is a difference between the fair value of the old asset and its carrying value, a gain or loss results. For example, assume again that equipment was purchased by BDCC for $20,000 and has accumulated depreciation of $18,000 at the end of 2019. It is traded on January 1, 2020 for new equipment with a list price of $25,000. A trade-in allowance of $2,500 is given on the old equipment, which has a fair value of only $1,800. In this case, the cost of the new asset is calculated as follows:

Cash paid	+	Fair value of asset traded	=	Cost of new asset
$22,500	+	1,800	=	$24,300

Cash paid will equal the difference between the selling price of the new equipment less the trade-in allowance, or $22,500 ($25,000 - 2,500). The fair value of the asset traded-in is $1,800. The cost of the new asset is therefore $24,300 ($22,500 + 1,800). There will be a loss on disposal of $200 on the old equipment, calculated as follows:

Cost	$	20,000
Accumulated depreciation		(18,000)
Carrying amount		2,000
Fair value		(1,800)
Loss on disposal	$	200

The journal entry on January 1, 2020 to record the purchase of the new equipment and trade-in of the old equipment is:

	General Journal			
Date	Account/Explanation	PR	Debit	Credit
Jan 1	Equipment (new)		24,300	
	Accumulated Dep. – Equipment (old)		18,000	
	Loss on Disposal		200	
	Equipment (old)			20,000
	Cash...............................			22,500
	To record trade-in.			

By this entry, the cost of the new equipment ($24,300) is entered into the accounts, the accumulated depreciation and cost of the old equipment is removed from the accounts, and the amount of cash paid is recorded. The debit difference of $200 represents the loss on disposal of the old equipment.

An exploration is available on the Lyryx site. Log into your Lyryx course to run Exchange of PPE Assets.

8.7 Intangible Assets

> LO7 – Explain and record the acquisition and amortization of intangible assets.

Another major category of long-lived assets that arises from legal rights and does not have physical substance is that of **intangible assets**. The characteristics of various types of intangible assets are discussed below.

Patents

A **patent** is an intangible asset that is granted when a company has an exclusive legal privilege to produce and sell a product or use a process for a specified period. This period varies depending on the nature of the product or process patented, and on the legislation in effect. Modifications to the original product or process can result in a new patent being granted, in effect extending the life of the original patent.

Patents are recorded at cost. If purchased from an inventor, the patent's cost is easily identified; if developed internally, the patent's cost includes all expenditures incurred in the development of the product or process, including salaries and benefits of staff involved.

Copyrights

A **copyright** is another intangible asset that confers on the holder an exclusive legal privilege to publish a literary or artistic work. In this case, the state grants control over a published or artistic work for the life of the copyright holder (often the original artist) and for a specified period afterward. This control extends to the reproduction, sale, or other use of the copyrighted material.

Trademarks

A **trademark** is a symbol or a word used by a company to identify itself or one of its products in the marketplace. Symbols are often logos printed on company stationery or displayed at company offices, on vehicles, or in advertising. A well-known example is Coke®. The right to use a trademark can be protected by registering it with the appropriate agency. The symbol '®' denotes that a trademark is registered.

Franchises

A **franchise** is a legal right granted by one company (the franchisor) to another company (the franchisee) to sell particular products or to provide certain services in a given region using a specific trademark or trade name. In return, the franchisee pays a fee to the franchisor. McDonald's® is an example of a franchised fast-food chain.

Another example of a franchise is one granted by government for the provision of certain services within a given geographical location: for example, television stations and telephone services authorized by the telecommunications branch of the state, or garbage collection authorized within a given community.

In addition to the payment of an initial franchise fee, which is capitalized, a franchise agreement usually requires annual payments. These payments are considered operating expenses.

Computer Software

Computer software programs may be developed by a company, patented, and then sold to customers for use on their computers. Productivity software like Microsoft Office® is an example. The cost of acquiring and developing computer software programs is recorded as an intangible asset, even if it is stored on a physical device like a computer. However, computer software that is integral to machinery – for instance, software that is necessary to control a piece of production equipment – is included as the cost of the equipment and classified as PPE.

Capitalization of Intangible Assets

Normally, intangible assets are measured at cost at the time of acquisition and are reported in the asset section of a company's balance sheet under the heading "Intangible Assets." The cost of an acquired intangible asset includes its purchase price and any expenditures needed to directly prepare it for its intended use.

There are special rules regarding intangible assets with a finite life and an indefinite life. Detailed discussion of these topics is beyond the scope of this textbook. It will be assumed that all intangibles being discussed in this textbook have a finite life.

Amortization of Intangible Assets

Plant and equipment assets are depreciated. Intangible assets are also depreciated but the term used is *amortization* instead of depreciation. **Amortization** (of intangible assets) is the systematic process of allocating the cost of intangible assets over their estimated useful lives using the straight-line, double-declining-balance, units-of-production or other method deemed appropriate.

Like PPE considerations, useful life and residual value of intangible assets are estimated by management and must be reviewed annually for reasonableness. Any effects on amortization expense because of changes in estimates are accounted for prospectively. That is, prior accounting periods' expenses are not changed.

To demonstrate the accounting for intangibles, assume a patent is purchased for $20,000 on July 1, 2015. The entry to record the purchase is:

General Journal				
Date	Account/Explanation	PR	Debit	Credit
July 1	Patent		20,000	
	Cash....................................			20,000
	To record the purchase of a patent, an intangible asset.			

Assuming the patent will last 40 years with no residual value, and amortization is calculated to the nearest whole month, amortization expense will be recorded at the December 31, 2015 year end as:

General Journal				
Date	Account/Explanation	PR	Debit	Credit
Dec 31	Amortization Expense - Patent		250	
	Accumulated Amortization - Patent...			250
	To record amortization on the patent; ($20,000 – 0)/40 years = $500/year; $500 x 6/12 = $250.			

Notice that an accumulated amortization account[1] is credited and not accumulated depreciation.

Impairment losses, and gains and losses on disposal of intangible assets, are calculated and recorded in the same manner as for property, plant, and equipment.

An exploration is available on the Lyryx site. Log into your Lyryx course to run Intangible Assets.

8.8 Goodwill

LO8 – Explain goodwill and identify where on the balance sheet it is reported.

Assume that Big Dog Carworks Corp. purchases another company for $10 million ($10M). BDCC takes over all operations, including management and staff. There are no liabilities. The fair values of the purchased assets consist of the following:

Patents	$2M
Machinery	$7M
Total	$9M

---

[1]IFRS 2014, IAS 38, para. 98; effective January 1, 2016 but can be applied sooner.

Why would BDCC pay $10M for assets with a fair value of only $9M? The extra $1M represents *goodwill*. **Goodwill** is the excess paid over the fair value of the net assets when one company buys another, and represents the value of the purchasee's ability to generate superior earnings compared to other companies in the same industry.

Goodwill is the combination of a company's assets which cannot be separately identified – such as a well-trained workforce, better retail locations, superior products, or excellent senior managers – the value of which is recognized only when a significant portion of the business is purchased by another company.

Recall that among other characteristics, intangible assets must be separately identifiable. Because components of goodwill are not separately identifiable, goodwill is not considered an intangible asset. However, it does have future value and therefore is recorded as a long-lived asset under its own heading of "Goodwill" on the balance sheet.

The detailed discussion of goodwill is an advanced accounting topic and beyond the scope of this textbook.

8.9 Disclosure

LO9 – Describe the disclosure requirements for long-lived assets in the notes to the financial statements.

When long-lived assets are presented on the balance sheet, the notes to the financial statements need to disclose the following:

- details of each class of assets (e.g., land; equipment including separate parts; patents; goodwill)
- measurement basis (usually historical cost)
- type of depreciation and amortization methods used, including estimated useful lives
- cost and accumulated depreciation at the beginning and end of the period, including additions, disposals, and impairment losses
- whether the assets are constructed by the company for its own use (if PPE) or internally developed (if intangible assets).

Examples of appropriate disclosure of long-lived assets were shown in notes 3(d) and 4 of BDCC's financial statements in Chapter 4.

Summary of Chapter 8 Learning Objectives

LO1 – Describe how the cost of property, plant, and equipment (PPE) is determined, and calculate PPE.

Property, plant and equipment (PPE) are tangible, long-lived assets that are acquired for the purpose of generating revenue either directly or indirectly. A capital expditure is debited to a PPE asset account because it results in the acquisition of a non-current asset and includes any additional costs involved in preparing the asset for its intended use at or after initial acquisition. A revenue expenditure does not have a future benefit beyond one year so is expensed. The details regarding a PPE asset are maintained in a PPE subsidiary ledger.

LO2 – Explain, calculate, and record depreciation using the units-of-production, straight-line, and double-declining balance methods.

Depreciation, an application of matching, allocates the cost of a PPE asset (except land) over the accounting periods expected to receive benefits from its use. A PPE asset's cost, residual value, and useful life or productive output are used to calculate depreciation. There are different depreciation methods. Units-of-production is a usage-based method. Straight-line and double-declining balance are time-based methods. The formulas for calculating depreciation using these methods are:

Units-of-Production	Straight-Line	Double-Declining Balance
$\dfrac{\text{Cost} - \text{Estimated Residual Value}}{\text{Estimated Total Units of Production}}$	$\dfrac{\text{Cost} - \text{Estimated Residual Value}}{\text{Estimated Total Useful Life}}$	Carrying Amount $\times\ 2/n$ where n = estimated useful life
= Depreciation Expense/Unit	= Depreciation Expense/Period	= Depreciation Expense/Period

Maximum accumulated depreciation is equal to cost less residual. The carrying amount of a PPE asset, also known as the net book value, equals the cost less accumulated depreciation.

LO3 – Explain, calculate, and record depreciation for partial years.

When assets are acquired or derecognized partway through the accounting period, partial period depreciation is recorded. There are several ways to account for partial period depreciation. Two common approaches are to calculate depreciation to the nearest whole month or to apply the half-year rule. The half-year rule assumes six months of depreciation in the year of acquisition and year of derecognition regardless of the actual date these occurred.

LO4 – Explain, calculate, and record revised depreciation for subsequent capital expenditures.

When there is a change that impacts depreciation (such as a change in the estimated useful life or estimated residual value, or a subsequent capital expenditure) revised depreciation is calculated prospectively. It is calculated as:

$$\frac{\text{Remaining Carrying Amount} - \text{Estimated Residual Value}*}{\text{Estimated Remaining Useful Life}*}$$

* where the residual value and/or useful life may have changed

LO5 – Explain, calculate, and record the impairment of long-lived assets.

The **recoverable amount** of a long-lived asset must be compared with its carrying amount (cost less accumulated depreciation) at the end of each reporting period. The recoverable amount is the fair value of the asset at the time less any estimated costs to sell it. If the recoverable amount is lower than the carrying amount, an **impairment loss** must be recorded as:

	General Journal			
Date	Account/Explanation	PR	Debit	Credit
	Impairment Loss....................		XXX	
	Equipment.....................			XXX
	To record impairment loss.			

Impairment losses can be reversed in subsequent years if the recoverable amount of the asset exceeds the carrying amount. Also, if the fair value of a PPE asset can be reliably measured, it can be revalued to more than its original cost.

LO6 – Account for the derecognition of PPE assets.

Property, plant, and equipment is *derecognized* (that is, the cost and any related accumulated depreciation are removed from the accounting records) when it is sold or when no future economic benefit is expected. To account for the disposal of a PPE asset, the following must occur:

1. If the disposal occurs part way through the accounting period, depreciation must be updated to the date of disposal by

	General Journal			
Date	Account/Explanation	PR	Debit	Credit
	Depreciation Expense		XXX	
	Accumulated Depreciation...........			XXX
	To update depreciation for partial period.			

2. Record the disposal including any resulting gain or loss by

Date	Account/Explanation	PR	Debit	Credit
	Cash (if any, or other assets received)		XXX	
	Accumulated Depreciation		XXX	
	Loss on Disposal		XXX	
	OR Gain on Disposal			XXX
	PPE Asset (such as Equipment)			XXX
	To record disposal of PPE asset.			

A loss results when the carrying amount of the asset is greater than the proceeds received, if any. A gain results when the carrying amount is less than any proceeds received.

It is a common practice to exchange a used PPE asset for a new one, known as a **trade-in**. The value of the trade-in is called the **trade-in allowance** and is applied to the purchase price of the new asset so that the purchaser pays the difference. Sometimes the trade-in allowance is higher than the fair value of the used asset. The cost of the new asset must be recorded at its fair value, calculated as:

$$\text{Cost of new asset} = \text{Cash paid} + \text{Fair value of asset traded}$$

If there is a difference between the fair value of the old asset and its carrying value, a gain or loss results.

LO7 – Explain and record the acquisition and amortization of intangible assets.

Intangible assets are long-lived assets that arise from legal rights and do not have physical substance. Examples include patents, copyrights, trademarks, and franchises. Intangibles are amortized using the straight-line method. The entry to record amortization is a debit to amortization expense and a credit to the intangible asset – there is no accumulated amortization account.

LO8 – Explain goodwill and identify where on the balance sheet it is reported.

Goodwill is a long-lived asset that does not have physical substance but it is NOT an intangible. When one company buys another company, goodwill is the excess paid over the fair value of the net assets purchased and represents the value of the purchasee's ability to generate superior earnings compared to other companies in the same industry. Goodwill appears in the asset section of the balance sheet under its own heading of "Goodwill".

LO9 – Describe the disclosure requirements for long-lived assets in the notes to the financial statements.

When long-lived assets are presented on the balance sheet, the notes to the financial statements need to disclose the following:

- details of each class of assets (e.g., land; equipment including separate parts; patents; goodwill)
- measurement basis (usually historical cost)
- type of depreciation and amortization methods used, including estimated useful lives
- cost and accumulated depreciation at the beginning and end of the period, including additions, disposals, and impairment losses

whether the assets are constructed by the company for its own use (if PPE) or internally developed (if intangible assets).

Discussion Questions

1. The cost of a long-lived asset is said to be *capitalized*. What does this mean?

2. How does a capital expenditure differ from a revenue expenditure?

3. Assume that you have purchased a computer for business use. Illustrate, using examples, capital and revenue expenditures associated with its purchase.

4. A company purchases land and buildings for a lump sum. What does this mean? What is the acceptable manner of accounting for a lump sum purchase?

5. How does the concept of materiality affect the recording of an expenditure as a capital or revenue item?

6. List the three criteria used to determine whether a replacement part for equipment is considered a capital or revenue expenditure.

7. When one long-lived asset is exchanged for another, how is the cost of the newly-acquired asset determined?

8. What is depreciation?

9. Long-lived assets can be considered future benefits to be used over a period of years. The value of these benefits in the first years may not be the same as in later years. Using a car as an example, indicate whether you agree or disagree.

10. Assume that you have recently purchased a new sports car. Is a usage or a time-based method preferable for recording depreciation? Why?

11. Why is residual value ignored when depreciation is calculated using the declining balance method but not the straight-line method? Is this inconsistent? Why or why not?

12. What is the formula for calculating the declining balance method of depreciation? ...the straight-line method?

13. What is the double-declining balance rate of depreciation for an asset that is expected to have a ten-year useful life?

14. Explain two types of partial-year depreciation methods.

15. What changes in estimates affect calculation of depreciation expense using the straight-line method? Explain the appropriate accounting treatment when there is a revision of an estimate that affects the calculation of depreciation expense.

16. Explain the effect on the calculation of depreciation expense for capital expenditures made subsequent to the initial purchase of plant or equipment.

17. Explain the process for determining whether the value of a long-lived asset has been impaired, and the required adjustments to the accounting records.

18. Your friend is concerned that the calculation of depreciation and amortization relies too much on the use of estimates. Your friend believes that accounting should be precise. Do you agree that the use of estimates makes accounting imprecise? Why or why not?

19. Why are the significant parts of property, plant, and equipment recorded separately?

20. When does the disposal of PPE not result in a gain or loss?

21. What is a trade-in? Explain whether a trade-in is the same as the sale of an asset.

22. Why might a trade-in allowance, particularly in the case of a car, be unrealistic? Why would a dealer give more trade-in allowance on a used car than it is worth?

23. How is the cost of a new capital asset calculated when a trade-in is involved?

24. How are intangible assets different from property, plant, and equipment? the same?

25. What is a patent? Assume a patent's legal life is twenty years. Does a patent's useful life correspond to its legal life? Why or why not? Support your answer with an example.

26. How does a copyright differ from a trademark? Give an example of each.

27. What is goodwill? Why is a company's internally-generated goodwill usually not recorded in its accounting records?

28. How are intangible assets valued, and what are their financial statement disclosure requirements?

Exercises

EXERCISE 8–1   (LO1)

For all expenditures, accountants identify them as either capital or revenue expenditures. The entries for such transactions can be made to any one of the following accounts:

Capital expenditures are recorded in an asset account on the balance sheet such as:

- **a.** Land
- **b.** Buildings
- **c.** Equipment
- **d.** Trucks
- **e.** Automobiles

Revenue expenditures are recorded in an income statement account:

- **f.** An expense account

Required: For each transaction below, indicate the account to be adjusted. Assume all expenditures are material in amount. Explain your answers.

Example:

    b   Architect fees to design building.

_____ Battery purchased for truck.
_____ Commission paid to real estate agent to purchase land.
_____ Cost of equipment test runs.
_____ Cost to remodel building.
_____ Cost to replace manual elevator with automatic elevator.
_____ Cost of sewage system.
_____ Equipment assembly expenditure.
_____ Expenditures for debugging new equipment and getting it ready for use.
_____ Installcation of air-conditioner in automobile.
_____ Insurance paid during construction of building.
_____ Legal fees associated with purchase of land.
_____ Oil change for truck.
_____ Payment for landscaping.
_____ Expenditures for removal of derelict structures.
_____ Repair made to building after moving in.
_____ Repair of collision damage to truck.
_____ Repair of torn seats in automobile.
_____ Replacement of engine in automobile.
_____ Special floor foundations for installation of new equipment.
_____ Tires purchased for truck.
_____ Transportation expenditures to bring newly purchased equipment to plant.

EXERCISE 8–2 (LO1)

Glasgo Holdings Inc. purchased a property including land and a building for $300,000. The market values of the land and building were $100,000 and $300,000, respectively.

Required: Using these market values, prepare a journal entry to record the lump sum purchase.

EXERCISE 8–3 (LO1,2)

Ekman Corporation purchased a new laser printer to be used in its business. The printer had a list price of $4,000, but Ekman was able to purchase it for $3,575. The company expects it to have a useful life of five years, with an estimated residual value of $250. Ekman is paying the delivery costs of $100 along with the set-up and debugging costs of $350.

Required:

    a. Calculate the total cost of the laser printer.

    b. Ekman management asks you whether the straight-line or double-declining balance method of depreciation would be most appropriate for the printer. Provide calculations to support your answer.

EXERCISE 8–4   (LO2)

Willow Inc. began a business on January 1, 2019. It purchased equipment for its factory on this date for $240,000. The equipment is expected to have an estimated useful life of five years with a residual value of $40,000. Willow's year-end is December 31.

Required: Compute the depreciation for 2019, 2020, 2021, 2022 and 2023 using

a. The straight-line method

b. The double-declining balance method.

EXERCISE 8–5   (LO2)

Mayr Inc. began a business on January 1, 2019. It purchased a machine for its factory on this date for $110,000. The machine is expected to have an estimated useful life of four years with a residual value of $40,000.

Required: Compute the depreciation for 2019, 2020, 2021, and 2022 using

a. The straight-line method

b. The double-declining balance method.

EXERCISE 8–6   (LO2,3)

Penny Corp. purchased a new car on March 1, 2019 for $25,000. The estimated useful life of the car was five years or 500,000 kms. Estimated residual value was $5,000. The car was driven 120,000 kms. in 2019 and 150,000 kms. in 2020. Penny Corp.'s year end is December 31.

Required:

a. Applying the half-year rule, calculate depreciation for 2019 and 2020 using

   i. The straight-line method

   ii. Units-of-production method

   iii. Double-declining-balance method

276 ■ Long-lived Assets

b. Assuming Penny Corp. calculates depreciation to the nearest whole month, determine depreciation for 2019 and 2020 using

   i. The straight-line method
   ii. Units-of-production method
   iii. Double-declining-balance method

EXERCISE 8–7   (LO4)

Global Flow Inc. purchased machinery on January 1, 2019 for $60,000 cash. It had an estimated useful life of three years, with no residual value, and depreciation is calculated using the straight-line method. During 2021, Global Flow determined that the estimated useful life should be revised to a total of five years and the residual value changed to $10,000.

Required: Prepare the entry to record revised depreciation for the year ended December 31, 2021.

EXERCISE 8–8   (LO4)

Denton Inc. purchased machinery on January 1, 2019 for $140,000 cash. It had an estimated useful life of five years and no residual value. On January 1, 2020, Denton purchased a specialized component for $50,000 that was attached to the machinery to significantly increase its productivity. The estimated useful life of the component was four years with no residual value. The life and residual value of the original machinery was not affected by the new component.

Required:

a. Prepare the entry to record depreciation for the year ended December 31, 2019.

b. Prepare the entry to record revised depreciation for the year ended December 31, 2020.

EXERCISE 8–9   (LO5)

As part of its December 31, 2019 year end procedures, Beltore Inc. is evaluating its assets for impairment. It has recorded no impairment losses for previous years. Following is the Property, Plant and Equipment schedule showing adjusted balances as at December 31, 2019:

Asset	Date of Purchase	Depreciation Method	Cost	Estimated Residual	Estimated Useful life	Accumulated Depreciation	Recoverable Amount
Land	Sept. 1/2018	N/A	$100,000	N/A	N/A	N/A	$115,000
Building	Dec. 1/2018	SL	890,000	$250,000	20	$34,667	870,000
Machinery	Dec. 1/2018	SL	400,000	150,000	10	27,083	350,000

DDB = Double-declining-balance; SL = Straight-line; U = Units-of-production; N/A = Not applicable

Required:

a. Record any impairment losses at December 31, 2019.

b. Record depreciation expense for the year ended December 31, 2020 assuming no changes in the estimated residual values or estimated useful lives of the assets.

EXERCISE 8–10   (LO6)

Freeman Inc. purchased a piece of agricultural land several years ago for $125,000. The land has a fair value of $200,000 now. The company plans to exchange this land for equipment owned by a land developer that has a fair value of $240,000. The equipment was originally purchased for $325,000, and $80,000 of depreciation has been recorded to the date of the exchange.

Required:

a. Prepare the journal entry on the books of

   i. Freeman

   ii. the developer.

b. Why would the developer give up an asset with a fair value of $240,000 in exchange for an asset with a fair value of only $200,000?

EXERCISE 8–11   (LO6)

Mayr Inc. showed the following selected adjusted trial balance information at June 30, 2019:

	Debits	Credits
Equipment	$60,000	
Accumulated Depreciation – Equipment		$40,000

Required: Mayr Inc. is planning on selling the equipment. Using the information provided above, prepare the journal entry to record the sale assuming

a. The equipment was sold for $20,000.

b. The equipment was sold for $30,000.

c. The equipment was sold for $5,000.

EXERCISE 8–12   (LO7)

On March 1, 2019, Willis Publishing purchased the copyright from the author of a new book for cash of $50,000. It is expected that the book will have a shelf life of about 5 years with no expected residual value. On October 1, 2021, Willis sold the copyright to a movie producer for $100,000. Willis Publishing uses the straight-line method to amortize copyrights.

Required: Prepare Willis Publishing's journal entries at

a. March 1, 2019 to record the purchase of the copyright.

b. December 31, 2019, Willis's year-end, to record amortization of the copyright.

c. October 1, 2021.

Problems

PROBLEM 8–1   (LO1)

Arrow Construction Company Ltd. purchased a farm from K. Jones. Arrow and Jones completed the transaction under the following terms: a cheque from Arrow to Jones for $140,000; bank loan assumed by Arrow, $100,000. Legal, accounting, and brokerage fees amounted to $20,000.

It was Arrow's intention to build homes on the property after sub-dividing. Crops on the farm were sold for $6,000; a house, to be moved by the buyer, was sold for $1,600; barns were razed at a cost of $6,000, while salvaged lumber was sold for $4,400. The property was cleared and levelled at a cost of $10,000.

The necessary property was turned over to the township for roads, schools, churches, and playgrounds. Riverside still expected to secure a total of 500 identical lots from the remaining land.

Required: Prepare a schedule showing the cost to Arrow of the 500 lots.

PROBLEM 8–2   (LO2,6)

Janz Corporation purchased a piece of machinery on January 1, 2019. The company's year-end is December 31. The following information is available regarding the machinery:

Cost	Estimated Useful Life	Estimated Residual Value	Depreciation Method
$95,000	9,000 units	$5,000	Units-of-Production

Assume actual output was:

Year	Actual Units Produced
2019	2,000
2020	3,000
2021	2,800
2022	2,900

The machinery was sold on January 15, 2023 for $12,000.

Required:

1. Calculate the depreciation expense for each of 2019 through to 2022 inclusive.

2. What is the balance of accumulated depreciation at the end of 2022?

3. What is the carrying amount of the machinery shown on the balance sheet at the end of 2022?

4. Prepare the entry on January 15, 2023 to record the sale of the machinery.

Chapter 9

Debt Financing: Current and Long-term Liabilities

A corporation often has liabilities. These liabilities must be classified on the balance sheet as current or long-term. Current liabilities can include known liabilities such as payroll liabilities, interest payable, and other accrued liabilities. Short-term notes payable and estimated liabilities, including warranties and income taxes, are also classified as current. Long-term debt is used to finance operations and may include a bond issue or long-term bank loan.

Chapter 9 Learning Objectives

LO1 – Identify and explain current versus long-term liabilities.

LO2 – Record and disclose known current liabilities.

LO3 – Record and disclose estimated current liabilities.

LO4 – Identify, describe, and record bonds.

LO5 – Explain, calculate, and record long-term loans.

Concept Self-Check

Use the following as a self-check while working through Chapter 9.

1. What is the difference between a current and long-term liability?
2. What are some examples of known current liabilities?
3. How are known current liabilities different from estimated current liabilities?
4. What are some examples of estimated current liabilities?
5. How is an estimated current liability different from a contingent liability?
6. What are bonds, and what rights are attached to bond certificates?
7. What are some characteristics of bonds?
8. When a bond is issued at a premium, is the market interest rate higher or lower than the contract interest rate on the bond?

9. When a bond is issued at a discount, is the market interest rate higher or lower than the contract interest rate on the bond?

10. How are bonds and related premiums or discounts recorded in the accounting records and disclosed on the balance sheet?

11. How is a loan payable similar to a bond issue? How is it different?

12. How are payments on a loan recorded, and how is a loan payable presented on the balance sheet?

NOTE: The purpose of these questions is to prepare you for the concepts introduced in the chapter. Your goal should be to answer each of these questions as you read through the chapter. If, when you complete the chapter, you are unable to answer one or more the Concept Self-Check questions, go back through the content to find the answer(s). Solutions are not provided to these questions.

9.1 Current versus Long-term Liabilities

LO1 – Identify and explain current versus long-term liabilities.

Current or **short-term liabilities** are a form of debt that is expected to be paid within the longer of one year of the balance sheet date or one operating cycle. Examples include accounts payable, wages or salaries payable, unearned revenues, short-term notes payable, and the current portion of long-term debt.

Long-term liabilities are forms of debt expected to be paid beyond one year of the balance sheet date or the next operating cycle, whichever is longer. Mortgages, long-term bank loans, and bonds payable are examples of long-term liabilities.

Current and long-term liabilities must be shown separately on the balance sheet. For example, assume the following adjusted trial balance at December 31, 2015 for Waterton Inc.:

Waterton Inc.
Adjusted Trial Balance
December 31, 2015

Account	Debits	Credits
Cash	$80,000	
Accounts receivable	140,000	
Equipment	570,000	
Accumulated depreciation – equipment		$40,000
Accounts payable		39,000
Unearned revenue		15,000
Wages payable		7,000
Notes payable, due November 30, 2016		20,000
Notes payable, due March 31, 2018		75,000
Mortgage payable (Note 1)		115,797
Share capital		300,000
Retained earnings		178,203
	$790,000	$790,000

Note 1: A 4-year, 6%, $150,000 mortgage was dated January 1, 2015. Waterton makes monthly payments of $3,523. The principal balances at the end of each year are:
- December 31, 2015 – $ 115,797
- December 31, 2016 – $ 79,484
- December 31, 2017 – $ 40,931
- December 31, 2018 – $ -0-

Based on this information, the liabilities section of the December 31, 2015 balance sheet would appear as follows:

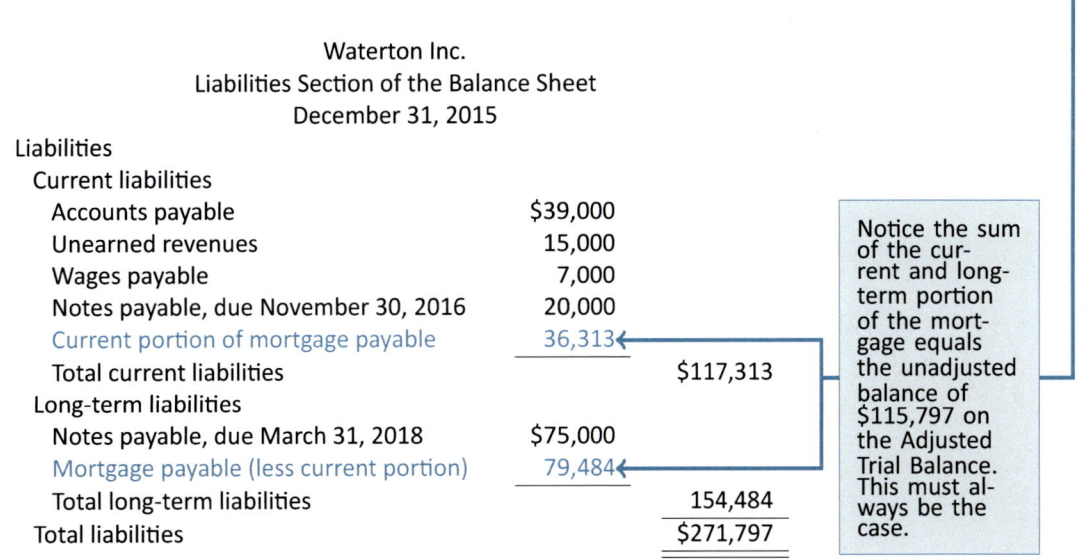

Waterton Inc.
Liabilities Section of the Balance Sheet
December 31, 2015

Liabilities
  Current liabilities
Accounts payable	$39,000	
Unearned revenues	15,000	
Wages payable	7,000	
Notes payable, due November 30, 2016	20,000	
Current portion of mortgage payable	36,313	
Total current liabilities		$117,313
Long-term liabilities		
Notes payable, due March 31, 2018	$75,000	
Mortgage payable (less current portion)	79,484	
Total long-term liabilities		154,484
Total liabilities		$271,797

Notice the sum of the current and long-term portion of the mortgage equals the unadjusted balance of $115,797 on the Adjusted Trial Balance. This must always be the case.

The $20,000 notes payable, due November 30, 2016 is a current liability because its maturity date is within one year of the balance sheet date, a characteristic of a current liability. The $75,000 notes payable, due March 31, 2018 is a long-term liability since it is to be repaid beyond one year of the balance sheet date.

It is important to classify liabilities correctly otherwise decision makers may make incorrect conclusions regarding, for example, the organization's liquidity position.

An exploration is available on the Lyryx site. Log into your Lyryx course to run Current and Long-Term Liabilities.

9.2 Known Current Liabilities

LO2 – Record and disclose known current liabilities.

Known current liabilities are those where the payee, amount, and timing of payment are known. Examples include accounts payable, unearned revenues, and payroll liabilities. These are different from **estimated current liabilities** where the amount is not known and must be estimated. Estimated current liabilities are discussed later in this chapter.

Payroll Liabilities

Accounts payable and unearned revenues were introduced and discussed in previous chapters. Payroll liabilities are amounts owing to employees. Employee income taxes, Canada Pension Plan (CPP, or Quebec Pension Plan in Quebec), Employment Insurance (EI), union dues, health insurance, and other amounts are deducted by the employer from an employee's salary or wages. These withheld amounts are remitted by the employer to the appropriate agencies. An employee's gross earnings, less the deductions withheld by the employer, equals the net pay. To demonstrate the journal entries to record a business's payroll liabilities for its two employees, assume the following payroll record:

	Deductions					Payment	Distribution	
							Sales	Office
	Income	Health		Union	Total		Salaries	Salaries
EI	Taxes	Ins.	CPP	Dues	Deductions	Net Pay	Expense	Expense
25.84	285.00	55.00	62.16	105.00	533.00	1,027.00	1,560.00	
16.50	114.00	55.00	51.50	75.00	312.00	663.00		975.00
42.34	399.00	110.00	113.66	180.00	845.00	1,690.00	1,560.00	975.00

The employer's journal entries would be:

General Journal				
Date	Account/Explanation	PR	Debit	Credit
	Sales Salaries Expense....................		1,560.00	
	Office Salaries Expense...................		975.00	
	EI Payable...........................			42.34
	Employee Income Taxes Payable.......			399.00
	Employee Health Insurance Payable..			110.00
	CPP Payable.........................			113.66
	Employee Union Dues Payable.......			180.00
	Salaries Payable.....................			1,690.00
	To record payroll.			

General Journal				
Date	Account/Explanation	PR	Debit	Credit
	EI Expense............................		59.28	
	CPP Expense...........................		113.66	
	EI Payable...........................			59.28
	CPP Payable.........................			113.66
	To record the employer's portions of EI and CPP calculated as 1.4 times (42.34 x 1.4) and 1 times (113.66 x 1) the employees' portion.			

For EI and CPP, both the employee and employer are responsible for making payments to the government. At the time of writing, the employer's portion of EI was calculated as 1.4 times the employee's EI amount. For CPP, the employer is required to pay the same amount as the employee. EI, CPP, and federal/provincial income tax amounts payable are based on rates applied to an employee's gross earnings. The rates are subject to change each tax year. The actual rates for EI, CPP, and federal/provincial income tax can be viewed online at Canada Revenue Agency's website: http://www.cra-arc.gc.ca.

Sales Taxes

Sales taxes are also classified as known current liabilities. There are two types of sales taxes in Canada: federal *Goods and Services Tax (GST)* and *Provincial Sales Tax (PST)*. The **Goods and Services Tax (GST)** is calculated as 5% of the selling price of *taxable supplies*. For example, if a business is purchasing supplies with a selling price of $1,000, the GST is $50 (calculated as $1,000 x 5%). **Taxable supplies** are the goods or services on which GST applies. GST is not applied to **zero-rated supplies** (prescription drugs, groceries, and medical supplies) or **exempt supplies** (services such as education, health care, and financial). Sellers of taxable supplies are **registrants**, businesses registered with Canada Revenue Agency that sell taxable supplies and collect GST on behalf of the *Receiver General for Canada*. The **Receiver General for Canada** is the federal government body to which all taxes, including federal income tax, are remitted. Registrants also pay GST on the purchase of taxable supplies recording an **input tax credit** for the GST paid. Total input tax credits, or GST receivable, less GST payable is the amount to be remitted/refunded.

Provincial Sales Tax (PST) is the provincial sales tax paid by the *final* consumers of products. The PST rate is determined provincially. PST is calculated as a percentage of the selling price. Quebec's equivalent to PST is called the **Quebec Sales Tax (QST)**.

The **Harmonized Sales Tax (HST)** is a combination of GST and PST that is used in some Canadian jurisdictions. Figure 9.1 summarizes sales taxes across Canada.

	GST	PST	QST	HST
Alberta	5%	-	-	-
British Columbia	5%	7%	-	-
Manitoba	5%	7%	-	-
Northwest Territories	5%	-	-	-
Nunavut	5%	-	-	-
Saskatchewan	5%	5%	-	-
Yukon	5%	-	-	-
Quebec	5%	-	9.975%	-
Newfoundland and Labrador	-	-	-	13%
New Brunswick	-	-	-	13%
Nova Scotia	-	-	-	15%
Ontario	-	-	-	13%
Prince Edward Island	-	-	-	14%

Figure 9.1: Sales Taxes in Canada[1]

To demonstrate how sales taxes are recorded, let us review an example. Assume Perry Sales, out of Saskatchewan, purchased $2,400 of merchandise inventory on account from a supplier, Carmen Inc., also in Saskatchewan. Perry Sales then sold this merchandise inventory to a customer for cash of $3,600. Perry Sales' entries for the purchase, subsequent sale of merchandise, and remittance of sales taxes are:

---

[1] These were the sales tax rates in effect at the time of writing, July 2014.

GST receivable is debited. Because Perry Sales is a merchandiser and therefore not the final consumer, there is no PST.	Merchandise Inventory............	2,400.00	
	GST Receivable...................	120.00	
	Accounts Payable – Carmen Inc.		2,520.00
	To record purchase of merchandise inventory on account.		
The previous $120 debit to GST receivable plus the $180 credit to GST payable in this entry result in a balance owing to the government of $60.	Cash...........................	3,960.00	
	Sales.......................		3,600.00
	PST Payable..................		180.00
	GST Payable..................		180.00
	To record cash sale.		
	Cost of Goods Sold..............	2,400.00	
	Merchandise Inventory........		2,400.00
	To record the cost of the sale.		
PST and GST are remitted to the appropriate government authority.	PST Payable.....................	180.00	
	GST Payable.....................	180.00	
	GST Receivable...............		120.00
	Cash.........................		240.00
	To record remittance of sales taxes.		

Short-term Notes Payable

Short-term notes receivable were discussed in Chapter 7. A short-term note payable is identical to a note receivable except that it is a current liability instead of an asset. In Chapter 7, BDCC's customer Bendix Inc. was unable to pay its $5,000 account within the normal 30-day period. The receivable was converted to a 5%, 60-day note receivable dated December 5, 2015. The following example contrasts the entries recorded by BDCC for the note receivable to the entries recorded by Bendix Inc. for its note payable.

288 ■ Debt Financing: Current and Long-term Liabilities

Entries in BDCC's records for the note receivable:

Notes Receivable – Bendix	5,000	
Accounts Receivable – Bendix		5,000

To record the conversion of a customer's account to a 5%, 60-day note dated December 5, 2015.

Interest Receivable	17.81	
Interest Revenue		17.81

To record the adjusting entry on December 31 to accrue interest from December 5 to December 31.

Cash	5,041.10	
Note Receivable – Bendix		5,000.00
Interest Receivable		17.81
Interest Revenue		23.29

To record the collection of the principal and interest at maturity on February 3, 2016.

Entries in Bendix Inc.'s records for the note payable:

Accounts Payable – BDCC	5,000	
Notes Payable – BDCC		5,000

To record the conversion of a supplier's account to a 5%, 60-day note dated December 5, 2015.

Interest Expense	17.81	
Interest Payable		17.81

To record the adjusting entry on December 31 to accrue interest from December 5 to December 31.

Notes Payable – BDCC	5,000.00	
Interest Expense	23.29	
Interest Payable	17.81	
Cash		5,041.10

To record the payment of the principal and interest at maturity on February 3, 2016.

Notice that the dollar amounts in the entries for BDCC are identical to those for Bendix. The difference is that BDCC is recognizing a receivable from Bendix while Bendix is recognizing a payable to BDCC.

An exploration is available on the Lyryx site. Log into your Lyryx course to run Known (Determinable) Liabilities.

9.3 Estimated Current Liabilities

LO3 – Record and disclose estimated current liabilities.

An **estimated liability** is known to exist where the amount, although uncertain, can be estimated. Two common examples of estimated liabilities are warranties and income taxes.

Warranty Liabilities

A **warranty** is an obligation incurred by the seller of a product or service to replace or repair defects. Warranties typically apply for a limited period of time. For example, appliances are often sold with a warranty for a specific time period. The seller does not know which product/service will require warranty work, when it might occur, or the amount. To match the warranty expense to the period in which the revenue was realized, the following entry that estimates the amount of warranty expense and related liability must be recorded:

General Journal				
Date	Account/Explanation	PR	Debit	Credit
	Warranty Expense....................		XXX	
	Estimated Warranty Liability.........			XXX
	To record estimated warranty expense and related liability.			

When the warranty work is actually performed, assuming both parts and labour, the following is recorded:

General Journal				
Date	Account/Explanation	PR	Debit	Credit
	Estimated Warranty Liability............		XXX	
	Parts Inventory.....................			XXX
	Wages Payable.....................			XXX
	To record the actual costs of parts and labour for warranty work.			

An exploration is available on the Lyryx site. Log into your Lyryx course to run Estimated Liabilities.

Income Tax Liabilities

A corporation is taxed on the taxable income it earns. As for any entity, corporations must file a tax return annually. However, the government typically requires the corporation to make advance monthly payments based on an estimated amount. When the total actual amount of income tax is known at the end of the accounting period, the corporation will record an adjustment to reconcile any difference between the total actual tax and the total monthly tax accrued in the accounting records. For example, assume it is estimated that the total income tax for the year ended December 31, 2015 will be $300,000. This translates into $25,000 of income tax to be accrued at the end of each month ($300,000 ÷ 12 months = $25,000/month). Assume further that the government requires payments to be made by the 15th of the following month. The entries at the end of each month from January through to November would be:

General Journal				
Date	Account/Explanation	PR	Debit	Credit
	Income Tax Expense....................		25,000	
	Income Tax Payable..................			25,000
	To record estimated income tax expense.			

On the 15th of each month beginning February 15th to December 15th, the following entry would be recorded:

General Journal				
Date	Account/Explanation	PR	Debit	Credit
	Income Tax Payable		25,000	
	Cash................................			25,000
	To record payment of income tax.			

Assume that at the end of December, the corporation's actual income tax was determined to be $297,000 instead of the originally estimated $300,000. The entry at December 31 would be:

General Journal				
Date	Account/Explanation	PR	Debit	Credit
Dec 31	Income Tax Expense		22,000	
	Income Tax Payable			22,000
	To record income tax expense; ($25,000 x 11 months = $275,000; $297,000 - $275,000 = $22,000).			

Contingent Liabilities

Recall that an estimated liability is recorded when the liability is probable and the amount can be reliably estimated. A **contingent liability** exists when one of the following two criteria are satisfied:

1. it is not probable or

2. it cannot be reliably estimated.

A liability that is determined to be contingent is not recorded, rather it is disclosed in the notes to the financial statements except when there is a remote likelihood of its existence. An example of a contingent liability is a lawsuit where it is probable there will be a loss but the amount cannot be reliably determined. A brief description of the lawsuit must be disclosed in the notes to the financial statements; it would not be recorded until the amount of the loss could be reliably estimated. Great care must be taken with contingencies — if an organization intentionally withholds information, it could cause decision makers, such as investors, to make decisions they would not otherwise have made.

Contingent assets, on the other hand, are not recorded until actually realized. If a contingent asset is probable, it is disclosed in the notes to the financial statements.

9.4 Long-Term Liabilities—Bonds Payable

LO4 – Identify, describe, and record bonds.

Corporations generally acquire long-lived assets like property, plant, and equipment through the issue of shares or long-term debt that is repayable over many years. Chapter 10 addresses the ways in which a corporation can raise funds by issuing shares, known as equity financing. This chapter discusses corporate financing by means of issuing long-term debt, known as debt financing. Types of long-term debt are typically classified according to their means of repayment.

1. **Bonds** pay *only interest* at regular intervals to investors. The original investment is repaid to bondholders when the bond *matures* (or comes due), usually after a number of years. Bonds are generally issued to many individual investors.

2. **Loans** are repaid in equal payments on a regular basis. The payments represent both *interest and principal* paid to creditors. Such payments are said to be *blended*. That is, each payment contains repayment of a certain amount of the original amount of the loan (the principal), as well as interest on the remaining principal balance.

Bonds are discussed in this section. Loans are expanded upon in the next section. Other types of debt, such as leases, are left for study in a more advanced accounting textbook.

Rights of Bondholders

As noted above, a **bond** is a debt instrument, generally issued to many investors, that requires future repayment of the original amount at a fixed date, as well as periodic interest payments during the intervening period. A contract called a **bond indenture** is prepared between the corporation and the future bondholders. It specifies the terms with which the corporation will comply, such as how much interest will be paid and when. Another of these terms may be a restriction on further borrowing by the corporation in the future. A **trustee** is appointed to be an intermediary between the corporation and the bondholder. The trustee administers the terms of the indenture.

Ownership of a bond certificate carries with it certain rights. These rights are printed on the actual certificate and vary among bond issues. The various characteristics applicable to bond issues are the subject of more advanced courses in finance and are not covered here. However, individual bondholders always acquire two rights.

1. The right to receive the face value of the bond at a specified date in the future, called the *maturity date*.

2. The right to receive periodic interest payments at a specified percent of the bond's face value.

Bond Authorization

Every corporation is legally required to follow a well-defined sequence in authorizing a bond issue. The bond issue is presented to the board of directors by management and must be approved by shareholders. Legal requirements must be followed and disclosure in the financial statements of the corporation is required.

Shareholder approval is an important step because bondholders are creditors with a prior claim on the corporation's assets if liquidation occurs. Further, dividend distributions may be restricted during the life of the bonds, and those shareholders affected usually need to approve this. These restrictions are typically reported to the reader of financial statements through note disclosure.

Assume that Big Dog Carworks Corp. decides to issue $30 million of 12% bonds to finance its expansion. The bonds are repayable three years from the date of issue, January 1, 2015. The amount of authorized bonds, their interest rate, and their maturity date can be shown in the accounts as follows:

GENERAL LEDGER
Bonds Payable –
Long-Term
Due Jan. 1, 2018

Acct. No. 272

Date		Description	Debit	Credit	DR/CR	Balance
2015						
Jan.	1	Authorized to issue $30,000,000 of 12%, 3-year bonds, due January 1, 2018.				

Bonds in the Financial Statement

Each bond issue is disclosed separately in the notes to the financial statements because each issue may have different characteristics. The descriptive information disclosed to readers of financial statements includes the interest rate and maturity date of the bond issue. Also disclosed in a note are any restrictions imposed on the corporation's activities by the terms of the bond indenture and the assets pledged, if any.

Other Issues Related to Bond Financing

There are several additional considerations related to the issue of bonds.

1. **Cash Required in the Immediate and the Foreseeable Future**

    Most bond issues are sold in their entirety when market conditions are favourable. However, more bonds can be authorized in a particular bond issue than will be immediately sold. Authorized bonds can be issued whenever cash is required.

2. **Time Periods Associated with Bonds**

    The interest rate of bonds is associated with time, their maturity date is based on time, and other provisions — such as convertibility into share capital and restrictions on future dividend distributions of the corporation — are typically activated at a given point in time. These must also be considered, as the success of a bond issue often depends on the proper combination of these and other similar features.

3. **Assets of the Corporation to Be Pledged**

    Whether or not long-lived assets like property, plant, and equipment are pledged as security is an important consideration for bondholders because doing so helps to safeguard their investments. This decision is also important to the corporation because pledging all these assets may restrict future borrowings. The total amount of authorized bonds is usually a fraction of the pledged assets, such as 50%. The difference represents a margin of safety to bondholders. The value of these assets can shrink substantially but still permit reimbursement of bondholders should the company be unable to pay the bond interest or principal, and need to sell the pledged assets.

Bond Characteristics

Each corporation issuing bonds has unique financing needs and attempts to satisfy various borrowing situations and investor preferences. Many types of bonds have been created to meet these varying needs.

Secured bonds are backed by physical assets of the corporation. These are usually long-lived assets. When real property is legally pledged as security for the bonds, they are called **mortgage bonds**.

Unsecured bonds are commonly referred to as **debentures**. A debenture is a formal document stating that a company is liable to pay a specified amount with interest. The debt is not backed by any collateral. As such, debentures are usually only issued by large, well-established companies. Debenture holders are ordinary creditors of the corporation. These bonds usually command a higher interest rate because of the added risk for investors.

Registered bonds require the name and address of the owner to be recorded by the corporation or its trustee. The title to **bearer bonds** passes on delivery of the bonds to new owners and is not tracked. Payment of interest is made when the bearer clips coupons attached to the bond and presents these for payment. Bearer bonds are becoming increasingly rare.

When **serial bonds** Serial bondsare issued, the bonds have differing maturity dates, as indicated on the bond contract. Investors are able to choose bonds with a term that agrees with their investment plans. For example, in a $30 million serial bond issue, $10 million worth of the bonds may mature each year for three years.

The issue of bonds with a **call provision** permits the issuing corporation to redeem, or call, the bonds before their maturity date. The bond indenture usually indicates the price at which bonds are callable. Corporate bond issuers are thereby protected in the event that market interest rates decline below the bond contract interest rate. The higher interest rate bonds can be called to be replaced by bonds bearing a lower interest rate.

Some bonds allow the bondholder to exchange bonds for a specified type and amount of the corporation's share capital. Bonds with this feature are called **convertible bonds**. This feature permits bondholders to enjoy the security of being creditors while having the option to become shareholders if the corporation is successful.

When **sinking fund bonds** are issued, the corporation is required to deposit funds at regular intervals with a trustee. This feature ensures the availability of adequate cash for the redemption of the bonds at maturity. The fund is called "sinking" because the transferred assets are tied up or "sunk," and cannot be used for any purpose other than the redemption of the bonds.

The corporation issuing bonds may be required to restrict its retained earnings. The **restriction of dividends** means that dividends declared cannot exceed a specified balance in retained earnings. This protects bondholders by limiting the amount of dividends that can be paid.

Investors consider the interest rates of bonds as well as the quality of the assets, if any, that are pledged as security. The other provisions in a bond contract are of limited or no value if the issuing corporation is in financial difficulties. A corporation in such difficulties may not be able to sell its bonds, regardless of the attractive provisions attached to them.

Recording the Issuance of Bonds at Face Value (at Par)

Each bond has an amount printed on the face of the bond certificate. This is called the **face value** of the bond; it is also referred to as the **par-value** of the bond. When the cash received is the same as a bond's face value, the bond is said to be issued at *par*. A common face value of bonds is $1,000, although bonds of other denominations exist. A $30 million bond issue can be divided into 30,000 bonds, for example. This permits a large number of individuals and institutions to participate in corporate financing.

If a bond is sold at face value, the journal entry is:

\multicolumn{5}{c|}{General Journal}				
Date	Account/Explanation	PR	Debit	Credit
	Cash............................		1,000	
	Bonds Payable.....................			1,000
	To record the issue of 8% bonds at par.			

Recording the Issuance of Bonds at a Premium

A $1,000 bond is sold at a **premium** when it is sold for more than its face value. This results when the bond interest rate is higher than the market interest rate. For instance, assume Big Dog Carworks Corp. issues a bond on January 1, 2015 with a face value of $1,000, a maturity date of one year, and a stated or contract interest rate of 8% per year, at a time when the market interest rate is 7%. Potential investors will bid up the bond price to $1,009.34 based on present value calculations where FV = $1,000; PMT = $80; i = 7 (the market rate); and n = 1.[2] We will round the $1,009.34 to $1,009 to simplify the demonstration.

The premium is the $9 difference between the $1,009 selling price of the bond and the $1,000 face value. The journal entry to record the sale of the bond on January 1, 2015 is:

	General Journal			
Date	Account/Explanation	PR	Debit	Credit
Jan 1	Cash....................................		1,009	
	Bonds Payable......................			1,000
	Premium on Bonds Payable..........			9
	To record the issue of 8% bonds at a premium.			

The Premium on Bonds Payable account is a contra liability account that is added to the value of the bonds on the balance sheet. Because the bonds mature in one year, the bond appears in the current liabilities section of the balance sheet as follows:

Liabilities

Current
   Bonds payable $1,000
   Add: Premium on bonds payable   9 $1,009

On the maturity date of December 31, 2015, the interest expense of $80 is paid, bondholders are repaid, and the premium is written off as a reduction of interest expense.

These three journal entries would be made:

	General Journal			
Date	Account/Explanation	PR	Debit	Credit
Dec 31	Interest Expense.......................		80	
	Cash.................................			80
	To record interest paid on bonds.			

	General Journal			
Date	Account/Explanation	PR	Debit	Credit
Dec 31	Bonds Payable........................		1,000	
	Cash.................................			1,000
	To record payment of bonds.			

---

[2] Present Value (PV) calculations can be done using tables or a business calculator. Table values are rounded causing results to be less accurate. Since business calculators have PV functionality, all PV calculations should be done using a calculator. PV calculations are reviewed in Section 9.6. Given the variety of calculators on the market, students should take responsibility for knowing how to do PV calculations using their own calculator.

General Journal				
Date	Account/Explanation	PR	Debit	Credit
Dec 31	Premium on Bonds Payable		9	
	Interest Expense			9
	To record write-off of premium against interest.			

Alternatively, a single entry would be preferable as follows:

General Journal				
Date	Account/Explanation	PR	Debit	Credit
Dec 31	Interest Expense		71	
	Premium on Bonds Payable		9	
	Bonds Payable		1,000	
	Cash			1,080
	To record payment of bond and interest on maturity date.			

Note that the interest expense recorded on the income statement would be $71 ($80 – 9). This is equal to the market rate of interest at the time of bond issue.

Recording the Issuance of Bonds at a Discount

If the bond is sold for less than $1,000, then the bond has been sold at a **discount**. This results when the bond interest rate is lower than the market interest rate. To demonstrate the journal entries, assume a $1,000, one-year, 8% bond is issued by BDCC when the market interest rate is 9%. The selling amount will be $990.83 using PV calculations where FV = $1,000; PMT = $80; i = 9 (the market rate); and n = 1. We will round the $990.83 to $991 to simplify the demonstration.

The difference between the face value of the bond ($1,000) and the selling price of the bond ($991) is $9. This is the *discount*.

The journal entry to record the transaction on January 1, 2015 is:

General Journal				
Date	Account/Explanation	PR	Debit	Credit
Jan 1	Cash		991	
	Discount on Bonds Payable		9	
	Bonds Payable			1,000
	To record issue of bonds at a discount.			

The $9 amount is a contra liability account and is *deducted* from the face value of the bonds on the balance sheet as follows:

Liabilities

Current

Bonds payable	$1,000	
Less: Discount on bonds payable	(9)	$991

On December 31, 2015, when the bonds mature, the following entries would be recorded:

General Journal				
Date	Account/Explanation	PR	Debit	Credit
Dec 31	Interest Expense..........................		80	
	Cash................................			80
	To record interest paid on bonds.			

General Journal				
Date	Account/Explanation	PR	Debit	Credit
Dec 31	Bonds Payable........................		1,000	
	Cash................................			1,000
	To record payment of bonds.			

General Journal				
Date	Account/Explanation	PR	Debit	Credit
Dec 31	Interest Expense..........................		9	
	Discount on Bonds Payable............			9
	To record write-off of discount against interest.			

Alternatively, a single entry would be preferable as follows:

General Journal				
Date	Account/Explanation	PR	Debit	Credit
Dec 31	Interest Expense..........................		89	
	Bonds Payable........................		1,000	
	Discount on Bonds Payable............			9
	Cash................................			1,080
	To record payment of bond and interest on maturity date.			

The interest expense recorded on the income statement would be $89 ($80 + 9). This is equal to the market rate of interest at the time of bond issue.

These are simplified examples, and the amounts of bond premiums and discounts in these examples are insignificant. In reality, bonds may be outstanding for a number of years, and related premiums and discounts can be substantial when millions of dollars of bonds are issued. These premiums and discounts are *amortized* using the effective interest method over the same number of periods as the related bonds are outstanding. The amortization of premiums and discounts is an intermediate financial accounting topic and is not covered here.

An exploration is available on the Lyryx site. Log into your Lyryx course to run Issuance of bond at par.

An exploration is available on the Lyryx site. Log into your Lyryx course to run Recording payment of Bond Interest.

An exploration is available on the Lyryx site. Log into your Lyryx course to run Pricing Bonds Using a Calculator.

An exploration is available on the Lyryx site. Log into your Lyryx course to run Issuing Bonds at a Discount.

An exploration is available on the Lyryx site. Log into your Lyryx course to run Issuing Bonds at a Premium.

9.5 Long-term Liabilities—Loans Payable

LO5 – Explain, calculate, and record long-term loans.

A *loan* is another form of long-term debt that a corporation can use to finance its operations. Like bonds, loans can be *secured*, giving the lender the right to specified assets of the corporation if the debt cannot be repaid. For instance a mortgage is a loan secured by specified real estate of the company, usually land with buildings on it.

Unlike a bond, a loan is typically obtained from one lender such as a bank. Also, a loan is repaid in equal *blended* payments over a period time. These payments contain both interest payments and some repayment of principal. As well, a loan does not give rise to a premium or discount because it is obtained at the market rate of interest in effect at the time.

To demonstrate the journal entries related to long-term loans, assume BDCC obtained a three-year, $100,000, 10% loan on January 1, 2015 from First Bank to acquire a piece of equipment. When the loan proceeds are deposited into BDCC's bank account, the following entry is recorded:

9.5. Long-term Liabilities—Loans Payable

	General Journal			
Date	Account/Explanation	PR	Debit	Credit
Jan 1	Cash.............................		100,000	
	Long-Term Note Payable.............			100,000
	To record 10%, 3-year, $100,000 bank loan.			

The loan is repayable in three annual blended payments. To calculate the payments, PV analysis is used whereby the following keystrokes are entered into a business calculator:

PV = 100000 (the cash received from the bank),

i = 10 (the interest rate),

n = 3 (the term of the loan is three years), and

Compute PMT.

The PMT (or payment) is -40211.48. The result is negative because payments are cash outflows. While the payments remain the same each year, the amount of interest paid decreases and the amount of principal increases. Figure 9.2 illustrates this effect.

Year Ended Dec. 31	(a) Beginning Loan Balance (e)	(b) Periodic Interest Expense (a) x 10%	(c) Reduction of Loan Payable (d) - (b)	(d) Total Loan Payment	(e) Ending Loan Balance (a) - (c)
2015	$100,000	$10,000	$30,211	$40,211	$69,789
2016	69,789	6,979	33,232	40,211	36,557
2017	36,557	3,654	36,557	40,211	-0-
			$100,000		

Interest expense and the principal balance decrease with each loan payment.

Figure 9.2: Effect of Blended Interest and Principal Payments

Figure 9.2 can be used to construct the journal entries to record the loan payments at the end of each year:

300 ■ Debt Financing: Current and Long-term Liabilities

\multicolumn{5}{c	}{General Journal}
Date	Account/Explanation	PR	Debit	Credit
Dec. 31, 2015	Interest Expense............................		10,000	
	Loan Payable		30,211	
	Cash.....................................			40,211
Dec. 31, 2016	Interest Expense............................		6,979	
	Loan Payable		33,232	
	Cash.....................................			40,211
Dec. 31, 2017	Interest Expense............................		3,654	
	Loan Payable		36,557	
	Cash.....................................			40,211

The amounts in Figure 9.2 can also be used to present the related information on the financial statements of BDCC at each year end. Recall that assets and liabilities need to be classified as current and non-current portions on the balance sheet. Current liabilities are amounts paid within one year of the balance sheet date. That part of the loan payable to First Bank to be paid in the upcoming year needs to be classified as a current liability on the balance sheet. The amount of the total loan outstanding at December 31, 2015, 2016, and 2017 and the current and non-current portions are shown in Figure 9.3:

A	B	C	D
Year ended Dec. 31	Ending loan balance per general ledger (Fig 9.2, Col. E)	Current portion (Fig. 9.2, Col. C)	(B – C) Long-term portion
2015	$69,788	$33,232	$36,557
2016	36,557	36,557	-0-
2017	-0-	-0-	-0-

Figure 9.3: Current and Long-term Portions of Loan Principal

Balance sheet presentation would be as follows at the end of 2015, 2016, and 2017:

	2015	2016	2017
Current liabilities			
Current portion of bank loan	$33,232	$36,557	$ -0-
Long-term liabilities			
Bank loan (Note X)	36,557	-0-	-0-

Details of the loan would be disclosed in a note to the financial statements. Only the *principal* amount of the loan is reported on the balance sheet. The *interest* expense portion is reported on the income statement as an expense. Because these loan payments are made at BDCC's year end, no interest payable is accrued or reported on the balance sheet.

An exploration is available on the Lyryx site. Log into your Lyryx course to run Equal Payments.

9.6 Appendix A: Present Value Calculations

Interest is the time value of money. If you borrow $1 today for one year at 10% interest, its future value in one year is $1.10 ($1 × 110% = $1.10). The increase of 10 cents results from the interest on $1 for the year. Conversely, if you are to pay $1.10 one year from today, the *present value* is $1 — the amount you would need to invest today at 10% to receive $1.10 in one year's time ($1.10/110% = $1). The exclusion of applicable interest in calculating present value is referred to as *discounting*.

If the above $1.10 amount at the end of the first year is invested for an additional year at 10% interest, its future value would be $1.21 ($1.10 x 110%). This consists of the original $1 investment, $.10 interest earned in the first year, and $.11 interest earned during the second year. Note that the second year's interest is earned on both the original $1 and on the 10 cents interest earned during the first year. This increase provides an example of *compound interest* — interest earned on interest.

The following formula can be used to calculate this:

$$FV = PV \times (1+i)^n$$

where FV = future value, PV = present value, i = the interest rate, and n = number of periods.

Substituting the values of our example, the calculation would be $FV = \$1[(1+.1)^2]$, or $1.21.

If the *future* value of today's $1 at 10% interest compounded annually amounts to $1.21 at the end of two years, the *present* value of $1.21 to be paid in two years, discounted at 10%, is $1. The formula to calculate this is just the inverse of the formula shown above, or

$$PV = \frac{FV}{(1+i)^n}$$

Substituting the values of our example,

$$PV = \frac{\$1.21}{(1+.1)^2}$$

That is, the present value of $1.21 received two years in the future is $1. The present value is always less than the future value, since an amount received today can be invested to earn a return (interest) in the intervening period. Calculating the present value of amounts payable or receivable over several time periods is explained more thoroughly below.

Instead of using formulas to calculate future and present values, a business calculator can be used where:

PV = present value

FV = future value

i = interest rate per period (for a semi-annual period where the annual interest rate is 8%, for example, i = 4% and would be entered into the calculator as '4' – not .04)

PMT = dollar amount of interest per period

n = number of periods.

The following three scenarios demonstrate how PV analysis is used to determine the issue price of a $100,000 bond.

1. Big Dog Carworks Corp. issues $100,000 of 3-year, 12% bonds on January 1, 2015 when the market rate of interest is 12%. Interest is paid semi-annually.

2. BDCC's bonds are issued at a premium because the market rate of interest is 8% at the date of issue.

3. BDCC's bonds are issued at a discount because the market rate of interest is 16% at the date of issue.

In each scenario, the bond *principal* of $100,000 will be repaid at the end of three years, and *interest* payments of $6,000 (calculated as $100,000 x 12% x 6/12) will be received every six months for three years.

Scenario 1: The Bond Contract Interest Rate is 12% and the Market Interest Rate Is 12%

The market interest rate is the same as the bond interest rate, therefore the bond is selling at par. The present value will be $100,000, the face value of the bond, which can be confirmed by entering the following into a business calculator:

FV = -100000 (we enter this as a negative because it is a cash outflow — it is being paid and not received when the bond matures)

i = 6 (calculated as 12%/year ÷ 2 periods per year)

PMT = -6000 (we enter this as a negative because it is a cash outflow — it is being paid and not received each semi-annual interest period)

n = 6 (3-year bond × 2 periods per year)

Compute PV

The PV = 100000. This result confirms that the bond is being issued at par or face value.

Scenario 2: The Bond Contract Interest Rate is 12% and the Market Interest Rate Is 8%

The market interest rate is less than the bond interest rate, therefore the bond is selling at a premium. The present value can be determined by entering the following into a business calculator:

FV = -100000 (we enter this as a negative because it is a cash outflow — it is being paid and not received when the bond matures)

i = 4 (calculated as 8%/year ÷ 2 periods per year)

PMT = -6000 (we enter this as a negative because it is a cash outflow — it is being paid and not received each semi-annual interest period)

n = 6 (3-year bond × 2 periods per year)

Compute PV

The PV = 110484.27. This confirms that the bond is being issued at a premium. The premium is $10,484.27 calculated as the difference between the present value of $110,484.27 and the face value of $100,000.

Scenario 3: The Bond Contract Interest Rate is 12% and the Market Interest Rate Is 16%

The market interest rate is more than the bond interest rate, therefore the bond is selling at a discount. The present value can be determined by entering the following into a business calculator:

FV = -100000 (we enter this as a negative because it is a cash outflow — it is being paid and not received when the bond matures)

i = 8 (calculated as 16%/year ÷ 2 periods per year)

PMT = -6000 (we enter this as a negative because it is a cash outflow — it is being paid and not received each semi-annual interest period)

n = 6 (3-year bond × 2 periods per year)

Compute PV

The PV = 90754.24. This confirms that the bond is being issued at a discount. The discount is $9,245.76 calculated as the difference between the present value of $90,754.24 and the face value of $100,000.

9.7 Appendix B: Additional Payroll Transactions

Net pay calculations

A business maintains a **Payroll Register** that summarizes the hours worked for each employee per pay period. The payroll register details an employee's regular pay plus any overtime pay *before* deductions, known as **gross pay**. An employee is paid their **net pay** (gross pay less total deductions). **Payroll deductions** are amounts subtracted by the employer from an employee's gross pay. Deductions are also known as withholdings or withheld amounts. Deductions can vary depending on the employer. Some deductions are optional and deducted by the employer based on directions made by the employee. Examples of optional deductions include an employee's charitable donations or Canada Savings Bonds contributions.

Certain payroll deductions are required by law. Deductions legally required to be deducted by the employer from an employee's gross pay are income tax, Employment Insurance (EI), and Canada Pension Plan (CPP or QPP in Quebec). The amount of legally required deductions is prescribed and based on an employee's income. For more detailed information regarding the calculation of these deductions, go to: http://www.cra-arc.gc.ca/tx/bsnss/tpcs/pyrll/clcltng/menu-eng.html

Other deductions that are often withheld by employers include union dues and health care premiums.

All deductions withheld by employers must be paid to the appropriate authority. For example, income tax, EI, and CPP must be paid to the Receiver General for Canada. Charitable donations withheld by an employer would be paid to the charity as directed by the employee.

An exploration is available on the Lyryx site. Log into your Lyryx course to run Net Pay Calculations.

Recording Payroll

The entry made by the employer to record payroll would debit the appropriate salary or wage expense category and credit:

1. Salaries Payable or Wages Payable for the net pay and

2. Each deduction such as EI Payable, CPP Payable, etc.

To demonstrate, assume the following payroll information for Wil Stavely and Courtney Dell:

		Deductions				Distribution	
	Gross Pay	Income Tax	EI	CPP	Net Pay	Exec Salaries	Office Wages
Dell, Courtney	5,800	1,160	106	280	4,254	5,800	
Stavely, Will	3,500	700	70	170	2,560		3,500

The payroll journal entry would be:

General Journal				
Date	Account/Explanation	PR	Debit	Credit
	Exec Salaries Expense		5,800	
	Office Wages Expense		3,500	
	Employee Income Tax Payable			1,860
	EI Payable..........................			176
	CPP (or QPP) Payable................			450
	Salaries Payable			6,814
	To record payroll.			

An exploration is available on the Lyryx site. Log into your Lyryx course to run Recording Payroll.

Recording Employer's CPP and EI Amounts

As already indicated, employers are legally required to deduct/withhold an employee's amount for each of the following from an employee's gross pay:

1. the employee's amount for Canada Pension Plan (CPP or QPP in Quebec) and
2. the employee's amount for Employment Insurance (EI).

The employer is required by law to pay Employment Insurance (EI) at the rate of 1.4 times the EI withheld from each employee. For example, if the employer withheld $100 of EI from Employee A's gross pay, the employer would have to pay EI of $140 (calculated as $100 x 1.4). Therefore, the total amount of EI being paid to the government regarding Employee A is $240 (calculated as the employee's portion of $100 plus the employer's portion of $140).

The employer is also required by law to pay CPP (or QPP in Quebec) of an amount that equals the employee amount. For example, if the employer withheld $50 of CPP from Employee A's gross pay, the employer would have to pay CPP of $50. Therefore, the total amount of CPP being paid to the government regarding Employee A is $100 (calculated as the employee's portion of $50 plus the employer's portion of $50).

The journal entry to record the employer's amounts above for EI and CPP would be:

General Journal				
Date	Account/Explanation	PR	Debit	Credit
	EI Expense		140	
	CPP (or QPP) Expense		50	
	EI Payable			140
	CPP (or QPP) Payable			50
	To record employer's EI and CPP amounts.			

An exploration is available on the Lyryx site. Log into your Lyryx course to run Journalizing Liability for Employer Payroll Amounts.

Employer's Entries to Pay the Payroll Deductions

Employers are required by law to pay/remit to the Receiver General for Canada all income tax, EI, and CPP amounts deducted/withheld from employees along with the employer's portion of EI and CPP. Any other amounts deducted/withheld from employees such as union dues, health care premiums, or charitable donations must also be paid/remitted to the appropriate organizations. The journal entry to record these payments/remittances by the employer would debit the respective liability account and credit cash. For example, using the information from our previous example, we know that the employer withheld from the employee's gross pay $100 of EI and $50 of CPP. Additionally, the employer recorded its share of the EI ($140) and CPP ($50) amounts. The total EI to be paid is therefore $240 and the total CPP $100. The payment by the employer would be:

General Journal				
Date	Account/Explanation	PR	Debit	Credit
	EI Payable[3]		240	
	CPP (or QPP[4]) Payable		100	
	Cash			340
	To record employer's EI and CPP amounts.			

An exploration is available on the Lyryx site. Log into your Lyryx course to run Journalizing Payment of Employer Amounts.

Fringe Benefits and Vacation Benefits

Some employers pay for an employee's benefits such as health insurance. The journal entry to record benefits would be:

---

[3] Employee's $100 portion + Employer's $140 portion
[4] Employee's $50 portion + Employer's $50 portion

General Journal				
Date	Account/Explanation	PR	Debit	Credit
	Benefits Expense....................		XX	
	Health Insurance Payable............			XX
	To record health insurance benefits.			

Employers are also required to pay for vacation time equal to 4% of gross income. The entry to accrue vacation benefits would be:

General Journal				
Date	Account/Explanation	PR	Debit	Credit
	Benefits Expense....................		XX	
	Estimated Vacation Liability..........			XX
	To record accrual of vacation benefits.			

When vacation benefits are realized by the employee, the Estimated Vacation Liability account is debited and the appropriate liability accounts to record deductions/withholdings and net pay are credited.

An exploration is available on the Lyryx site. Log into your Lyryx course to run Recording Employee Benefits.

Summary of Chapter 9 Learning Objectives

LO1 – Identify and explain current versus long-term liabilities.

Current or short-term liabilities are a form of debt that is expected to be paid within the longer of one year of the balance sheet date or one operating cycle. Long-term liabilities are a form of debt that is expected to be paid beyond one year of the balance sheet date or the next operating cycle, whichever is longer. Current and long-term liabilities must be shown separately on the balance sheet.

LO2 – Record and disclose known current liabilities.

Known current liabilities are those where the payee, amount, and timing of payment are known. Payroll liabilities are a type of known current liability. Employers are responsible for withholding from employees amounts including Employment Insurance (EI), Canada Pension Plan (CPP), and income tax, and then remitting the amounts to the appropriate authority. Sales taxes, including the Goods and Services Tax (GST) and Provincial Sales Tax (PST), must be collected by registrants and subsequently remitted to the Receiver General for Canada. Short-term notes payable, also a known current liability, can involve the accrual of interest if the maturity date falls in the next accounting period.

LO3 – Record and disclose estimated current liabilities.

An estimated liability is known to exist where the amount, although uncertain, can be estimated. Warranties and income taxes are examples of estimated liabilities. Contingent liabilities are neither a known liability nor an estimated liability and are not recorded if they are determined to exist. A contingent liability exists when it is not probable or it cannot be realiably estimated. A contingent liability is disclosed in the notes to the financial statements.

LO4 – Identify, describe, and record bonds.

Bonds pay interest at regular intervals to bondholders. The original investment is repaid to bondholders when the bonds mature. There are different types of bonds: secured or unsecured, as well as registered or bearer bonds. Bonds can have a variety of characteristics, including: varying maturity dates, call provisions, conversion privileges, sinking fund requirements, or dividend restrictions. Bonds are issued: (a) at par (also known as the face value) when the market interest rate is the same as the bond (or contract) interest rate; (b) at a discount when the market interest rate is higher than the bond interest rate; or (c) at a premium when the market interest rate is lower than the bond interest rate.

LO5 – Explain, calculate, and record long-term loans.

A loan is a form of long-term debt that can be used by a corporation to finance its operations. Bonds can be secured and are typically obtained from a bank. Loans are often repaid in equal blended payments containing both interest and principal.

Discussion Questions

1. What is the difference between a current and long-term liability?
2. What are some examples of known current liabilities?
3. How are known current liabilities different from estimated current liabilities?
4. What are some examples of estimated current liabilities?
5. How is an estimated current liability different from a contingent liability?

6. What is a bond? ...a bond indenture? Why might a trustee by used to administer a bond indenture?

7. List and explain some bondholder rights.

8. How are different bond issues reported in the financial statements of a corporation?

9. What are three reasons why bonds might be redeemed before their maturity date?

10. Why would investors pay a premium for a corporate bond? Why would a corporation issue its bonds at a discount? Explain, using the relationship between the bond contract interest rate and the prevailing market interest rate.

11. How is an unamortised bond premium or discount disclosed in accordance with GAAP?

12. If the bond contract interest rate is greater than that required in the market on the date of issue, what is the effect on the selling price of the bond? Why?

13. What method is used to amortise premiums and discounts?

14. How is a loan payable similar to a bond? How is it different?

15. Distinguish between future value and present value. What is the time value of money? Why is it important?

16. How is the actual price of a bond determined?

Exercises

EXERCISE 9–1 (LO1)

Ajam Inc. shows the following selected adjusted account balances at March 31, 2019:

Accounts Payable	$ 58,000
Wages Payable	102,000
Accumulated Depreciation – Machinery	69,000
Income Taxes Payable	92,000
Note Payable, due May 15, 2021	108,000
Note Payable, due November 30, 2019	64,000
Mortgage Payable	320,000
Accounts Receivable	71,000

Note: $240,000 of the mortgage payable balance is due one year beyond the balance sheet date; the remainder will be paid within the next 12 months.

Required: Prepare the liability section of Ajam's March 31, 2019 balance sheet.

EXERCISE 9–2   (LO2)

On June 7, 2019, Dilby Mechanical Corp. completed $50,000 of servicing work for a client and billed them for that amount plus GST of $2,500 and PST of $3,500; terms are n20.

Required:

a. Prepare the journal entry as it would appear in Dilby's accounting records.

b. Assume the receivable established on June 7 was collected on June 27. Record the entry.

EXERCISE 9–3   (LO2)

Libra Company borrowed $300,000 by signing a 3.5%, 45-day note payable on July 1, 2019. Libra's year-end is July 31. Round all calculations to two decimal places.

Required:

a. Prepare the entry to record the issuance of the note on July 1, 2019.

b. Prepare the entry to accrue interest on July 31, 2019.

c. On what date will this note mature?

d. Prepare the entry to record the payment of the note on the due date.

EXERCISE 9–4   (LO3)

On January 23, 2019, Zenox Company sold $105,000 of furniture on account that had a cost of $82,000. All of Zenox's sales are covered by an unconditional 24-month replacement warranty. Historical data indicates that warranty costs average 2% of the cost of sales. On January 29, 2019, Zenox replaced furniture with a cost of $2,000 that was covered by warranty.

Required:

a. Prepare the journal entry to record the estimated warranty liability for January.

b. Prepare the entry to record the warranty expense incurred in January.

c. Assuming the Estimated Warranty Liability account had a credit balance of $740 on January 1, 2019, calculate the balance at January 31, 2019 after the entries above were posted.

EXERCISE 9–5   (LO4)

Required: Complete the following by responding either *premium* or *discount*.

a. If the market rate of interest is 15 per cent and the bond interest rate is 10 per cent, the bonds will sell at a _____.

b. If a bond's interest rate is 10 per cent and the market rate of interest is 8 per cent, the bonds will sell at a _____.

c. In computing the carrying amount of a bond, unamortised _____ is subtracted from the face value of the bond.

d. In computing the carrying amount of a bond, unamortised _____ is added to the face value of the bond.

e. If a bond sells at a _____, an amount in excess of the face value of the bond is received on the date of issuance.

f. If a bond sells at a _____, an amount less than the face value of the bond is received on the date of issuance.

EXERCISE 9–6   (LO4)

On January 1, 2019, the date of bond authorization, Nevada Inc. issued a 3-year, 12-per cent bond with a face value of $100,000 at 94. Semi-annual interest is payable on June 30 and December 31.

Required: Prepare the journal entry to record the issuance of the bonds on January 1, 2019.

EXERCISE 9–7   (LO4)

On January 1, 2019, the date of bond authorization, Sydney Corp. issued 3-year, 12-per cent bonds with a face value of $200,000 at 112. Semi-annual interest is payable on June 30 and December 31.

Required: Prepare the journal entry to record the issuance of the bonds on January 1, 2019.

EXERCISE 9–8   (LO5)   Long Term Loan Payable

Rosedale Corp. obtained a $50,000 loan from Second Capital Bank on January 1, 2019. It purchases a piece of heavy equipment for $48,000 on the same day. The loan bears interest at 6%

per year on the unpaid balance and is repayable in three annual blended payments of $18,705 on December 31 each year.

Required:

a. Prepare the journal entries to record the following transactions:

　　i. Receipt of loan proceeds from the bank.

　　ii. Purchase of the equipment.

b. Prepare the loan repayment schedule.

c. Prepare the journal entry to record the first loan payment.

Problems

PROBLEM 9–1　(LO5)

Zinc Corp. obtained a $100,000 loan from First Capital Bank on December 31, 2015. It purchased a piece of heavy equipment for $95,000 on January 2, 2016. The loan bears interest at 8% per year on the unpaid balance and is repayable in four annual blended payments of $30,192 on December 31 each year, starting in 2016.

Required:

1. Prepare the journal entries to record the following transactions:

　　(a) Receipt of loan proceeds from the bank.

　　(b) Purchase of the equipment.

2. Prepare the loan repayment schedule in the following format:

Zinc Corp.
Loan Repayment Schedule

Year Ended Dec. 31	A Beginning Loan Balance	B Interest Expense	C (D − B) Reduction of Loan Payable	D Total Loan Payment	E (A − C) Ending Loan Balance
2016					
2017					
2018					
2019					

3. Prepare the journal entry to record the last loan payment.

4. Prepare a partial balance sheet showing the loan liability at December 31, 2017

Chapter 10

Equity Financing

Corporations sometimes finance a large portion of their operations by issuing equity in the form of shares. This chapter discusses in detail the nature of the corporate form of organization, the different types of shares used to obtain funds for business activities, and how these transactions are recorded. It also expands on the concept of dividends.

Chapter 10 Learning Objectives

LO1 – Identify and explain characteristics of the corporate form of organization and classes of shares.

LO2 – Record and disclose preferred and common share transactions including share splits.

LO3 – Record and disclose cash dividends.

LO4 – Record and disclose share dividends.

LO5 – Calculate and explain the book value per share ratio.

Concept Self-Check

Use the following as a self-check while working through Chapter 10.

1. What are the characteristics of a corporation?
2. What types of shares can a corporation issue to investors?
3. What are the rights of common shareholders in a corporation?
4. How are the rights of common shareholders different from those of preferred shareholders?
5. How are share transactions recorded?
6. When both preferred and common shares are issued by a corporation, how is this disclosed in the equity section of the balance sheet?
7. What is meant by *authorized* shares?
8. How do *issued* shares differ from *outstanding* shares?

9. What is a share split?

10. How does a share split affect equity?

11. How are cash dividends recorded?

12. What is a share dividend and how is it recorded?

13. How does a share dividend affect equity?

14. What is book value and how is it calculated?

NOTE: The purpose of these questions is to prepare you for the concepts introduced in the chapter. Your goal should be to answer each of these questions as you read through the chapter. If, when you complete the chapter, you are unable to answer one or more the Concept Self-Check questions, go back through the content to find the answer(s). Solutions are not provided to these questions.

10.1 The Corporate Structure

LO1 – Identify and explain characteristics of the corporate form of organization and classes of shares.

The accounting equation expresses the relationship between assets owned by a corporation and the claims against those assets by creditors and shareholders. Accounting for equity in a corporation requires a distinction between the two main sources of shareholders' equity: share capital and retained earnings. Their relationship to the accounting equation is shown in Figure 10.1.

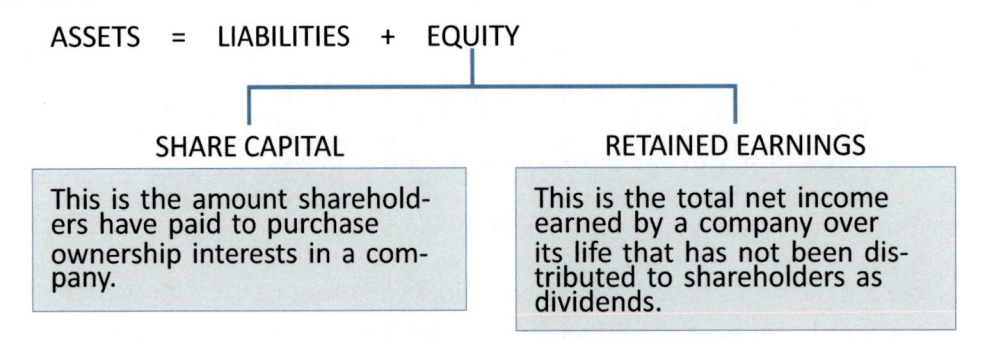

ASSETS = LIABILITIES + EQUITY

SHARE CAPITAL
This is the amount shareholders have paid to purchase ownership interests in a company.

RETAINED EARNINGS
This is the total net income earned by a company over its life that has not been distributed to shareholders as dividends.

Figure 10.1: Share Capital Versus Retained Earnings

Corporate Characteristics

A unique characteristic of corporations is that they are legally separate from their owners, who are called **shareholders**. Each unit of ownership of a corporation is called a **share**. If a corporation issues 1,000 shares and you own 100 of them, you own 10% of the company. Corporations can be *privately-held* shares or *publicly-held* shares. A privately-held corporation's shares are not issued for sale to the general public. A publicly-held corporation offers its shares for sale to the general public, sometimes on a stock market like the Toronto Stock Exchange or the New York Stock Exchange.

A corporation has some of the same rights and obligations as individuals. For instance, it pays income taxes on its earnings, can enter into legal contracts, can own property, and can sue and be sued. A corporation also has distinctive features. It is separately regulated by law, has an indefinite life, its owners have limited liability, and it can usually acquire capital more easily than an individual. These features are discussed below.

- **Creation by law**

A corporation is formed under legislation enacted by a country or a political jurisdiction within it. For instance, in Canada a corporation can be formed under either federal or provincial laws. Although details may vary among jurisdictions, a legal document variously described as *articles of incorporation*, a *memorandum of association*, or *letters patent* is submitted for consideration to the appropriate government by prospective shareholders. The document lists the **classes** or types of shares that will be issued as well as the total number of shares of each class that can be issued, known as the **authorized** number of shares.

When approved, the government issues a certificate of incorporation. Investors then purchase shares from the corporation. They meet and elect a board of directors. The board formulates corporation policy and broadly directs the affairs of the corporation. This includes the appointment of a person in charge of day-to-day operations, often called a president, chief executive officer, or similar title. This person in turn has authority over the employees of the corporation.

A shareholder or group of shareholders who control more than 50% of the voting shares of a corporation are able to elect the board of directors and thus direct the affairs of the company. In a large public corporation with many shareholders, minority shareholders with similar ideas about how the company should be run sometimes delegate their votes to one person who will vote on their behalf by signing a **proxy** statement. This increases their relative voting power, as many other shareholders may not participate in shareholders' meetings.

Shareholders usually meet annually to vote for a board of directors — either to re-elect the current directors or to vote in new directors. The board meets regularly, perhaps monthly or quarterly, to review the operations of the corporation and to set policies for future operations. The board may decide to distribute some assets of the corporation as a dividend to shareholders. It may also decide that some percentage of the assets of the corporation legally available for dividends should be made unavailable; in this case, a *restriction* is created. Accounting for such restrictions is discussed later in this chapter.

Wherever it is incorporated, a company is generally subject to the following regulations:

1. It must provide timely financial information to investors.

2. It must file required reports with the government.

3. It cannot distribute profits arbitrarily but must treat all shares of the same class alike.

4. It is subject to special taxes and fees.

Despite these requirements, a corporation's advantages usually outweigh its disadvantages when compared to other forms of business such as a proprietorship or partnership. These features of a corporation are described further below. Proprietorships and partnerships are discussed in more detail in Chapter 13.

- **Indefinite life**

A corporation has an existence separate from that of its owners. Individual shareholders may die, but the corporate entity continues. The life of a corporation comes to an end only when it is dissolved, becomes bankrupt, or has its charter revoked for failing to follow laws and regulations.

- **Limited liability**

The corporation's owners are liable only for the amount that they have invested in the corporation. If the corporation fails, its assets are used to pay creditors. If insufficient assets exist to pay all debts, there is no further liability on the part of shareholders. This situation is in direct contrast to a proprietorship or a partnership. In these forms of organization, creditors have full recourse to the personal assets of the proprietorship or partners if the business is unable to fulfil its financial obligations. For the protection of creditors, the limited liability of a corporation must be disclosed in its name. The words "Limited," "Incorporated," or "Corporation" (or the abbreviations Ltd., Inc., or Corp.) are often used as the last word of the name of a company to indicate this corporate form.

- **Ease of acquiring capital**

Issuing shares allows many individuals to participate in the financing of a corporation. Both small and large investors are able to participate because of the relatively small cost of a share, and the ease with which ownership can be transferred — shares are simply purchased or sold. Large amounts of capital can be raised by a corporation because the risks and rewards of ownership can be spread among many investors.

A corporation only receives money when shares are first issued. Once a share is issued, it can be bought and sold a number of times by various investors. These subsequent transactions between investors do not affect the corporation's balance sheet.

Income Taxes on Earnings

Because corporations are considered separate legal entities, they pay income taxes on their earnings. To encourage risk-taking and entrepreneurial activity, certain types of corporations may be taxed at rates that are lower than other corporations and individual shareholders' income tax rates. This can encourage research and development activity or small-company start-ups, for instance.

Classes of Shares

There are many types of shares, with differences related to voting rights, dividend rights, liquidation rights, and other preferential features. The rights of each shareholder depend on the class or type of shares held.

Every corporation issues **common shares**. The rights and privileges usually attached to common shares are outlined below.

- The right to participate in the management of the corporation by voting at shareholders' meetings (this participation includes voting to elect a board of directors; each share normally corresponds to one vote).

- The right to receive dividends when they are declared by the corporation's board of directors.

- The right to receive assets upon liquidation of the corporation.

- The right to appoint auditors through the board of directors.

For other classes of shares, some or all of these rights are usually restricted. The articles of incorporation may also grant the shareholders the **pre-emptive** right to maintain their proportionate interests in the corporation if additional shares are issued.

If the company is successful, common shareholders may receive dividend payments. As well, the value of common shares may increase. Common shareholders can submit a proposal to raise any matter at an annual meeting and have this proposal circulated to other shareholders at the corporation's expense. If the corporation intends to make fundamental changes in its business, these shareholders can often require the corporation to buy their shares at their fair value. In addition, shareholders can apply to the courts for an appropriate remedy if they believe their interests have been unfairly disregarded by the corporation.

Some corporations issue different classes of shares in order to appeal to as large a group of investors as possible. This permits different risks to be assumed by different classes of shareholders in the same company. For instance, a corporation may issue common shares but divide these into different classes like class A and class B common shares. When dividends are declared, they might only be paid to holders of class A shares.

Preferred shares is a class of share where the shareholders are entitled to receive dividends before common shareholders. These shares usually do not have voting privileges. Preferred shareholders typically assume less risk than common shareholders. In return, they receive only a limited amount of dividends. Issuing preferred shares allows a corporation to raise additional capital without requiring existing shareholders to give up control. Preferred shares are listed before common shares in the equity section of the balance sheet. Other characteristics of preferred shares and dividend payments are discussed later in this chapter.

The shares of a corporation can have a different status at different points in time. They can be **unissued** or **issued**, issued and **outstanding**, or issued and reacquired by the corporation (called **treasury shares**). The meaning of these terms is summarized in Figure 10.2:

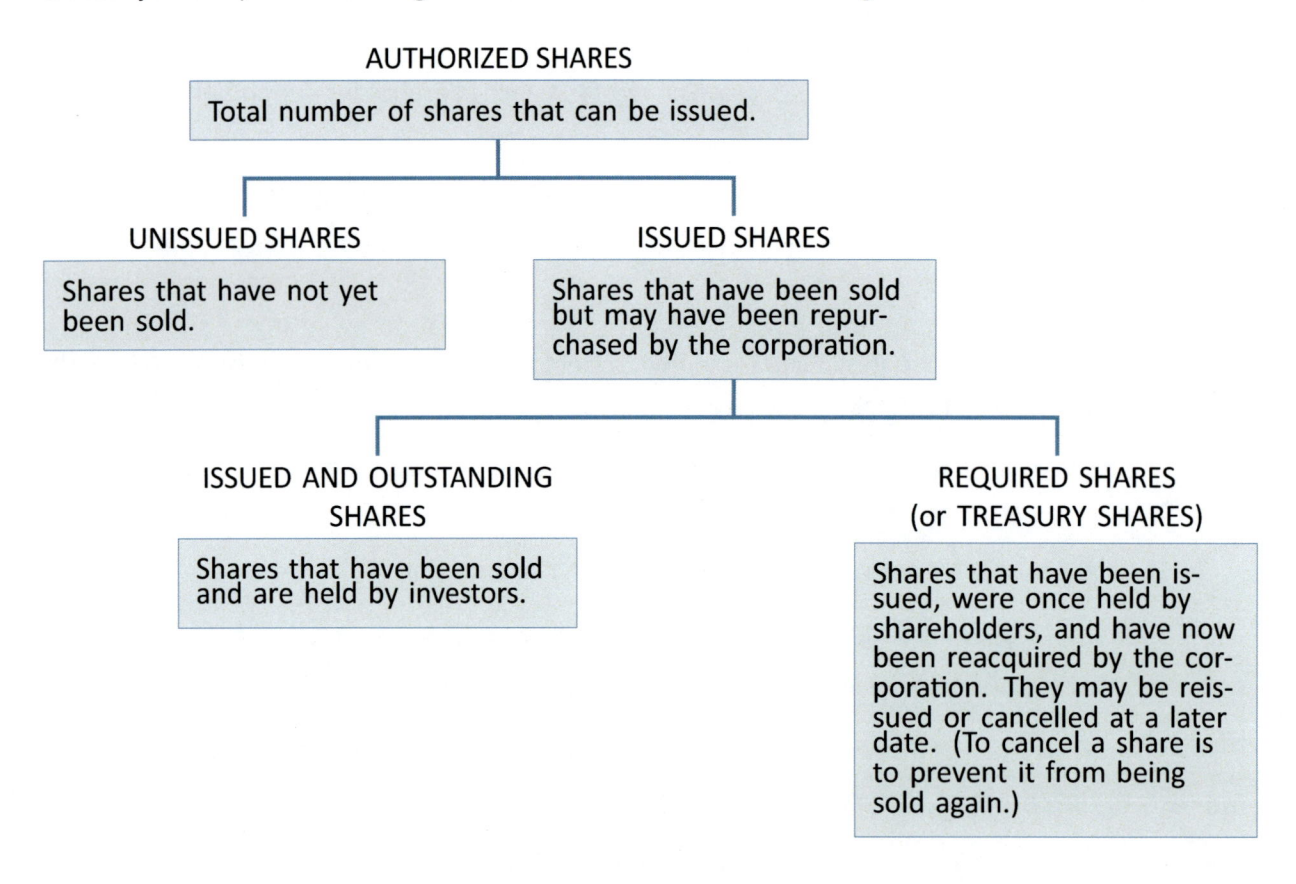

AUTHORIZED SHARES
Total number of shares that can be issued.

UNISSUED SHARES
Shares that have not yet been sold.

ISSUED SHARES
Shares that have been sold but may have been repurchased by the corporation.

ISSUED AND OUTSTANDING SHARES
Shares that have been sold and are held by investors.

REQUIRED SHARES (or TREASURY SHARES)
Shares that have been issued, were once held by shareholders, and have now been reacquired by the corporation. They may be reissued or cancelled at a later date. (To cancel a share is to prevent it from being sold again.)

Figure 10.2: Status of Shares

The Debt Versus Equity Financing Decision

Many factors influence management in its choice between the issue of debt and the issue of share capital. One of the most important considerations is the potential effect of each of these financing methods on the present shareholders.

Consider the example of Old World Corporation, which has 100,000 common shares outstanding, is a growth company, and is profitable. Assume Old World requires $30 million in cash to finance a new plant. Management is currently reviewing three financing options:

1. Issue 12% debt, due in three years
2. Issue 300,000 preferred shares (dividend $8 per share annually)
3. Issue an additional 200,000 common shares at $30 each.

Management estimates that the new plant should result in income before interest and tax of $6 million. Management has prepared the following analysis to compare and evaluate each financing option.

	Plan 1: Issue Debt	Plan 2: Issue Preferred Shares	Plan 3: Issue Common Shares
Income before interest and income taxes	$ 6,000,000	$ 6,000,000	$ 6,000,000
Less: Interest expense ($30M x 12%)	(3,600,000)	-0-	-0-
Income before taxes	$ 2,400,000	$ 6,000,000	$ 6,000,000
Less: Income taxes assumed to be 50%	(1,200,000)	(3,000,000)	(3,000,000)
Net income	1,200,000	3,000,000	3,000,000
Less: Preferred dividends (300,000 x $8 per share)	-0-	(2,400,000)	-0-
Net income available to common shareholders	$ 1,200,000	$ 600,000	$ 3,000,000
Number of common shares outstanding	100,000	100,000	300,000
Earnings per common share[1]	$ 12	$ 6	$ 10

Plan 1, the issue of debt, has several advantages for existing common shareholders.

- **Advantage 1: Earnings per share**

If the additional long-term financing were acquired through the issue of debt, the corporate earnings per share (EPS) on each common share would be $12. This EPS is greater than the EPS earned through financing with either preferred shares or additional common shares. On this basis alone, the issue of debt is more financially attractive to existing common shareholders.

- **Advantage 2: Control of the corporation**

---

[1] The amount of net income earned in a year can be divided by the number of common shares outstanding to establish how much return has been earned for each outstanding share. EPS is calculated as:

$$\frac{\text{Net income}}{\text{Number of common shares outstanding}}$$

EPS is quoted in financial markets and is disclosed on the income statement of publicly-traded companies. It is discussed in more detail in Chapter 12.

Creditors have no vote in the affairs of the corporation. If additional common shares were issued, there might be a loss of corporate control by existing shareholders because ownership would be distributed over a larger number of shareholders, or concentrated in the hands of one or a few new owners. In the Old World case, issuing common shares would increase the number threefold from 100,000 to 300,000 shares.

- **Advantage 3: Income taxes expense**

Interest expense paid on debt is deductible from income for income tax purposes. Dividend payments are distributions of retained earnings, which is after-tax income. Thus, dividends are not deductible again for tax purposes. With a 50% income tax rate, the after-tax interest expense to the corporation is only 6% (12% x 50%). The effective interest rate on preferred shares in this example is much higher, at 40% ($8/$20).

Debt Financing Disadvantages

There are also some disadvantages in long-term financing with debt that must be carefully reviewed by management and the board of directors. The most serious disadvantage is the possibility that the corporation might earn less than $6 million before interest expense and income taxes. The interest expense is a fixed amount. It must be paid to creditors at specified times, unlike dividends.

Another disadvantage is the fact that debt must be repaid at maturity, whether or not the corporation is financially able to do so. Shares do not have to be repaid.

An exploration is available on the Lyryx site. Log into your Lyryx course to run Debt vs Equity Financing.

10.2 Recording Share Transactions

LO2 – Record and disclose preferred and common share transactions including share splits.

Shares have a **stated (or *nominal*) value**—the amount for which they are issued. Alternatively, but rarely, shares will have a **par-value** which is the amount stated in the corporate charter below which shares cannot be sold upon initial offering. For consistency, we will assume all shares have a stated value.

To demonstrate the issuance and financial statement presentation of shares, assume that New World Corporation is authorized to issue share capital consisting of an unlimited number of voting common shares and 100,000 non-voting preferred shares.

Transaction 1: On January 1, 2015, New World sells 1,000 common shares to its first shareholders for $10 per share, or $10,000 cash. New World records the following entry:

	General Journal			
Date	Account/Explanation	PR	Debit	Credit
Jan 1	Cash.....................................		10,000	
	Common Shares.....................			10,000
	To record the issuance of 1,000 common shares at $10 per share.			

Transaction 2: On February 1, 2015, 2,500 preferred shares are issued to the owner of land and buildings that have a fair value of $35,000 and $50,000, respectively. The journal entry to record this transaction is:

	General Journal			
Date	Account/Explanation	PR	Debit	Credit
Feb 1	Land.....................................		35,000	
	Building................................		50,000	
	Preferred Shares....................			85,000
	To record the issuance of 2,500 preferred shares in exchange for land and buildings.			

Usually, one or more individuals decide to form a corporation and before the corporation is created, may then use their own funds to pay for legal and government fees, travel and promotional costs, and so on. When the corporation is legally formed, it is not unusual for the corporation to issue shares to these organizers for these amounts. These expenditures are referred to as **organization costs (start-up costs)** and are expensed.

Transaction 3: On March 1, 2015, 500 common shares are issued to the organizers of New World to pay for their services, valued at $5,000. The journal entry to record this transaction is:

	General Journal			
Date	Account/Explanation	PR	Debit	Credit
Mar 1	Organization Expense		5,000	
	Common Shares.....................			5,000
	To record the issuance of 500 common shares in exchange for organization efforts.			

Assuming no further share transactions and a retained earnings balance of $480,000, the equity section of the New World Corporation balance sheet would show the following at December 31, 2015:

Heading required when there is more than one share capital account on a classified balance sheet.

Equity Section of the Balance Sheet

Contributed capital
    Preferred shares, 100,000 shares authorized,
        2,500 shares issued and outstanding $85,000
    Common shares, unlimited shares authorized,
        1,500 shares issued and outstanding 15,000
        Total contributed capital $100,000
    Retained earnings 480,000
    Total equity $580,000

100,000 shares authorized means there are 100,000 shares available for sale.

1,500 shares issued means 1,500 shares have been sold.

1,500 shares outstanding means 1,500 shares are held by shareholders (shares that have been issued but are not outstanding means the corporation purchased its own shares).

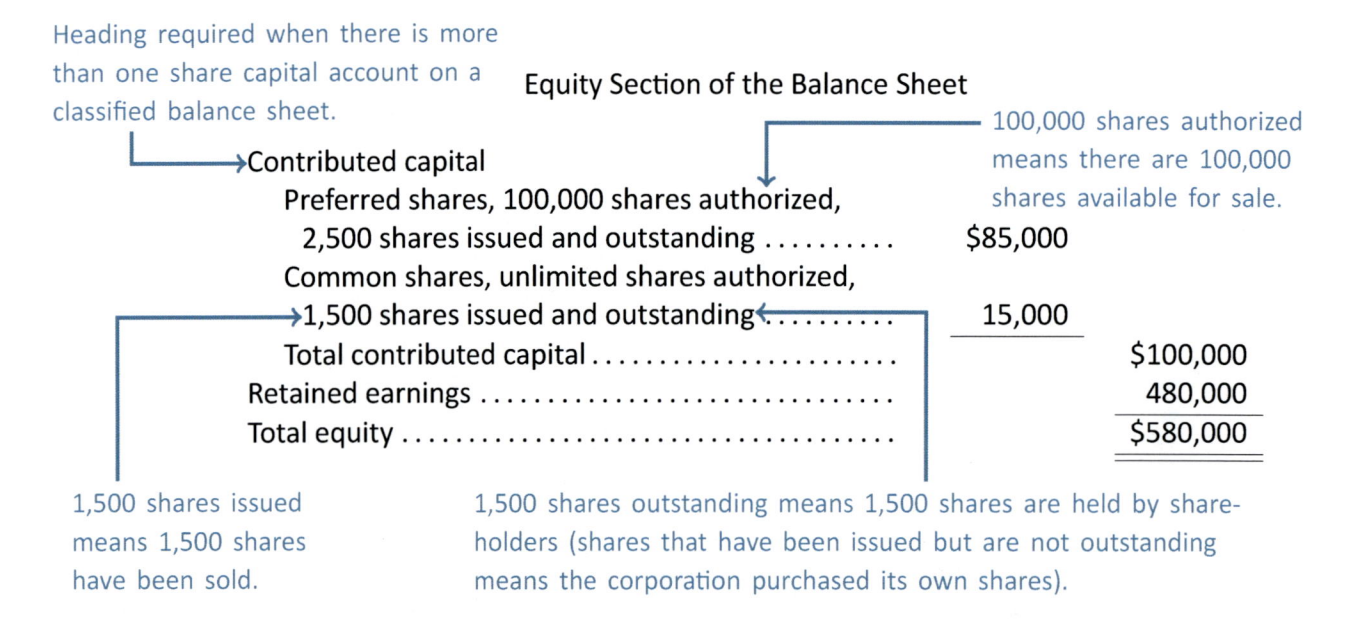

Transaction 4: Corporate legislation permits a company to reacquire some of its shares, provided that the purchase does not cause insolvency. A company can repurchase and then cancel the repurchased shares. When repurchased shares are cancelled, they are no longer issued and no longer outstanding. A company can also repurchase shares and then hold them in treasury. Treasury shares are issued but not outstanding. A company can use treasury shares for purposes such as giving to employees as an incentive or bonus.

Assume that New World Corporation decides to repurchase 200 common shares on December 1, 2016 and hold them in treasury. Assume that the price of each share is the average issue price of the outstanding common shares, or $10. The journal entry to record the repurchase is:

General Journal

Date	Account/Explanation	PR	Debit	Credit
Dec 1	Common Shares		2,000	
	Cash...............................			2,000
	To record the repurchase of 200 common shares at $10 per share to be held in treasury.			

Assuming no further transactions, the equity section of the New World Corporation balance sheet would show the following at December 31, 2016:

Equity Section of the Balance Sheet

Contributed capital
    Preferred shares, 100,000 shares authorized,
        2,500 shares issued and outstanding $85,000
    Common shares, unlimited shares authorized,
        1,500 shares issued; 1,300 shares outstanding 13,000
    Total contributed capital $98,000
    Retained earnings 480,000
    Total equity $578,000

Notice that the repurchase of shares caused a decrease in both the paid-in capital for the common shares ($2,000 decrease) and in the number of shares outstanding decreased (decreased by 200 shares). If the 200 shares had been cancelled, both the number of shares issued and outstanding would have decreased by 200 shares.

An exploration is available on the Lyryx site. Log into your Lyryx course to run Issuing Share Capital.

Share Splits

A corporation may find its shares are selling at a high price on a stock exchange, perhaps putting them beyond the reach of many investors. To increase the marketability of a corporation's shares, management may opt for a **share split**. A share split increases the number of shares issued and outstanding, and lowers the cost of each new share. The originally-issued shares are exchanged for a larger number of new shares.

Assume that on December 1, 2017 New World Corporation declares a 3-for-1 common share split. This results in three new common shares replacing each currently-issued and outstanding common share. The number of issued and outstanding shares has now been tripled. The market price of each share will decrease to about one-third of its former market price. Since there is no change in the dollar amount of common shares, no debit-credit entry is required to record the share split. Instead, a memorandum entry would be recorded in the general ledger indicating the new number of shares issued and outstanding, as follows:

		Common Shares				Acct. No. 320
Date		Description	Debit	Credit	DR/CR	Balance
2017						
Dec.	1	Memorandum Entry: Because of a 3-for-1 share split, the issued and outstanding common shares increased, respectively, from 1,500 and 1,300 to 4,500 and 3,900.				

The dollar amount shown on the balance sheet and statement of changes in equity will not change. The only change is an increase in the number of issued and outstanding common shares. After the share split, the equity section of the New World Corporation would appear as follows:

Equity Section of the Balance Sheet

The number of common shares issued changed from 1,500 shares before the share split to 4,500 after the share split.

The paid-in capital is not affected by a share split.

Contributed capital
  Preferred shares, 100,000 shares authorized,
    2,500 shares issued and outstanding $85,000
  Common shares, unlimited shares authorized,
    4,500 shares issued; 3,900 shares outstanding.. 13,000
  Total contributed capital $98,000
  Retained earnings 480,000
  Total equity $578,000

The number of common shares outstanding changed from 1,300 shares before the share split to 3,900 after the share split.

An exploration is available on the Lyryx site. Log into your Lyryx course to run Share Splits.

10.3 Cash Dividends

LO3 – Record and disclose cash dividends.

Both creditors and shareholders are interested in the amount of assets that can be distributed as dividends. Dividends The paid-in share capital is not available for distribution as dividends. This helps protect creditors by preventing shareholders from withdrawing assets as dividends to the point where remaining assets become insufficient to pay creditors. For example, assume total assets are $40,000; total liabilities $39,000; and total equity $1,000, consisting of $900 in common shares and $100 of retained earnings. The maximum dividends that could be declared in this situation is $100, the balance in retained earnings.

Dividend Policy

Sometimes the board of directors may choose not to declare any dividends. There may be financial conditions in the corporation that make the payment impractical.

- **Consideration 1: There may not be adequate cash**

Corporations regularly reinvest their earnings in assets in order to make more profits. In this way, growth occurs and reliance on creditor financing can be minimized. As a result, there may not be enough cash on hand to declare and pay a cash dividend. The assets of the corporation may be tied up in property, plant, and equipment, for instance.

- **Consideration 2: A policy of the corporation may preclude dividend payments**

Some corporations pay no dividends. Instead, they reinvest their earnings in the business. Shareholders generally benefit through increased earnings, reflected in increased market price for the corporation's shares. A stated policy to this effect can apprise investors. This type of dividend policy is often found in growth-oriented corporations.

- **Consideration 3: No legal requirement that dividends have to be paid**

The board of directors may decide that no dividends should be paid. Legally, there is no requirement to do so. If shareholders are dissatisfied, they can elect a new board of directors or sell their shares.

- **Consideration 4: Dividends may be issued in shares of the corporation rather than in cash**

Share dividends may be issued to conserve cash or to increase the number of shares to be traded on the stock market. Shares dividends are discussed in Section 10.4.

Dividend Declaration

Dividends can be paid only if they have been officially declared by the board of directors. The board must pass a formal resolution authorizing the dividend payment. Notices of the dividend are then published. Once a dividend declaration has been made public, the dividend becomes a liability and must be paid. An example of a dividend notice is shown in Figure 10.3.

New World Corporation
Dividend Notice

On May 25, 2016 the board of directors of New World Corporation declared a dividend of $0.50 per share on common shares outstanding (3,900). The dividend will be paid on June 26, 2016 to shareholders of record on June 7, 2016.

By order of the board

[signed]
Lee Smith
Secretary
May 25, 2016

Figure 10.3: An Example of a Dividend Notice

There are three dates associated with a dividend. Usually dividends are declared on one date, the **date of declaration** (May 25, 2016 in this case); they are payable to shareholders on a second date, the date of record (June 7, 2016); and the dividend is paid on a third date, the **date of payment** (June 26, 2016).

Date of Declaration

The dividend declaration provides an official notice of the dividend. It specifies the amount of the dividend as well as which shareholders will receive the dividend. The liability for the dividend is recorded in the books of the corporation at its declaration date.

The following entry would be made in the general ledger of New World Corporation on May 25, 2016, the date of declaration:

	General Journal			
Date	Account/Explanation	PR	Debit	Credit
May 25	Cash Dividends Declared................		1,950	
	Dividends Payable			1,950
	To record $0.50 per common share cash dividend declared; 3,900 shares x $0.50/share = $1,950.			

OR

	General Journal			
Date	Account/Explanation	PR	Debit	Credit
May 25	Retained Earnings......................		1,950	
	Dividends Payable			1,950
	To record $0.50 per common share cash dividend declared; 3,900 shares x $0.50/share = $1,950.			

If, as shown in the second entry above, retained earnings is debited instead of cash dividends declared, a closing entry is not required for dividends during the closing process.

Date of Record

Shareholders who own shares on the date of record will receive the dividend even if they have sold the shares before the dividend is actually paid. No journal entry is made in the accounting records for the date of record.

Date of Payment

The dividend is paid on this date and recorded as:

	General Journal			
Date	Account/Explanation	PR	Debit	Credit
	Dividends Payable....................		1,950	
	Cash...............................			1,950
	To record payment of dividend.			

An exploration is available on the Lyryx site. Log into your Lyryx course to run Dividends.

Preferred Shareholder Dividends

Preferred shares are offered to attract investors who have lower tolerance for risk than do common shareholders. Preferred shareholders are content with a smaller but more predictable share of a corporation's profits. For instance, preferred shareholders are entitled to dividends before any dividends are distributed to common shareholders. Also, most preferred shares specifically state what amount of dividends their holders can expect each year. For example, owners of $8 preferred shares would be paid $8 per share held each year. These dividends are often paid even if the corporation experiences a net loss in a particular year.

Preferred shares may also have other dividend preferences, depending on what rights have been attached to preferred shares at the date of incorporation. One such preference is the accumulation of undeclared dividends from one year to the next — referred to as *cumulative dividends*. Discussion of other preferences is beyond the scope of this introductory textbook. Cumulative dividends are discussed in the next section.

Cumulative Dividend Preferences

Cumulative preferred shares require that any unpaid dividends accumulate from one year to the next and are payable from future earnings when a dividend is eventually declared by a corporation. These accumulated dividends must be paid before any dividends are paid on common shares. The unpaid dividends are called **dividends in arrears**. Dividends in arrears are not recorded as a liability on the balance sheet of the company until they have been declared by the board of directors. However, disclosure of dividends in arrears must be made in a note to the financial statements.

If a preferred share is **non-cumulative**, a dividend not declared by the board of directors in any one year is never paid to shareholders.

An exploration is available on the Lyryx site. Log into your Lyryx course to run Allocating Dividends.

10.4 Share Dividends

LO4 – Record and disclose share dividends.

A **share dividend** is a dividend given to shareholders in the form of shares rather than cash. In this way, the declaring corporation is able to retain cash in the business and reduce the need to finance its activities through borrowing. Like a cash dividend, a share dividend reduces retained earnings. However, a share dividend does not cause assets to change. Instead, it simply transfers an amount from retained earnings to contributed capital. Total assets, total liabilities, and total equity remain unchanged when there is a share dividend. Like a cash dividend, there are three dates regarding a share dividend: date of declaration, date of record, and date of distribution. Notice that there is no 'date of payment' as there was for a cash dividend. This is because there is no cash payment involved for a share dividend. Instead, shares are distributed, or given, to the shareholders.

Accounting for Share Dividends

To demonstrate a share dividend, assume that the Sherbrooke Corporation declares a 10% share dividend to common shareholders. The share dividend is declared on December 15, 2015 payable to shareholders of record on December 20, 2015. The share dividend is distributed on January 10, 2016. At the time of the dividend declaration, the shares were trading on the stock exchange at $4 per share and the equity of the corporation consisted of the following:

Common shares; 20,000 shares authorized; 5,000 shares issued and outstanding	$25,000
Retained earnings	100,000
Total equity	$125,000

The 10% share dividend equals 500 shares (calculated as 5,000 outstanding shares x 10% share dividend). The market price on the date of declaration is used to record a share dividend. On the declaration date, the journal entry to record the share dividend is:

10.4. Share Dividends

General Journal				
Date	Account/Explanation	PR	Debit	Credit

Dec 15	Share Dividends Declared...............
	     Common Share Dividends Distributable............................
	     To record declaration of share dividend; 5,000 shares x 10% = 500 shares; 500 shares x $4 = $2,000.
			2,000	2,000

OR

General Journal				
Date	Account/Explanation	PR	Debit	Credit

Dec 15	Retained Earnings......................
	     Common Share Dividends Distributable.............................
	     To record declaration of share dividend; 5,000 shares x 10% = 500 shares; 500 shares x $4 = $2,000.
			2,000	2,000

If, as shown in the second entry above, retained earnings is debited instead of share dividends, a closing entry is not required for dividends during the closing process. Common Share Dividends Distributable is an equity account, specifically, a share capital account.

On the share dividend distribution date, the following entry is recorded:

General Journal				
Date	Account/Explanation	PR	Debit	Credit

Jan 10	Common Share Dividends Distributable ..
	     Common Shares.....................
	     To record distribution of share dividend.
			2,000	2,000

The effect of these entries is to transfer $2,000 from retained earnings to share capital. No assets are paid by the corporation when the additional shares are issued as a share dividend, and therefore the total equity remains unchanged.

Is There Any Change in the Investor's Percentage of Corporate Ownership Because of a Share Dividend?

Since a share dividend is issued to all shareholders of a particular class, as a result of a share dividend, each shareholder has a larger number of shares. However, ownership percentage of the company remains the same for each shareholder, as illustrated below, for the four shareholders of Sherbrooke Corporation.

Each shareholder has received a 10% share dividend but their ownership percentage of the company remains constant. Since total equity does not change when there is a share dividend, the proportion owned by each shareholder does not change.

	Corporate ownership			
	Before share dividend		After share dividend	
Shareholder	Shares	Percent	Shares	Percent
1	1,000	20%	1,100	20%
2	500	10%	550	10%
3	2,000	40%	2,200	40%
4	1,500	30%	1,650	30%
	5,000	100%	5,500	100%

An exploration is available on the Lyryx site. Log into your Lyryx course to run Share Dividends.

10.5 Book Value

LO5 – Calculate and explain the book value per share ratio.

The **book value** of a share is the amount of net assets represented by one share. When referring to common shares, book value represents the amount of net assets not claimed by creditors and preferred shareholders. When referring to preferred shares, book value represents the amount that preferred shareholders would receive if the corporation were liquidated.

Book value per preferred share =

$$\frac{\text{Paid-in capital for preferred shares plus dividends in arrears}}{\text{Number of preferred shares outstanding}}$$

Book value per common share =

$$\frac{\text{Total equity less (paid-in capital for preferred shares plus dividends in arrears)}}{\text{Number of common shares outstanding}}$$

Calculation of the Book Value of Shares

The calculation of the book value of preferred and common shares can be illustrated by using the following data:

Equity Section of the Balance Sheet

Contributed capital		
Preferred shares; 5,000 shares authorized;		
1,000 shares issued and outstanding ..	$10,000	
Common shares; 200,000 shares authorized;		
60,000 shares issued and outstanding..	20,000	
Total contributed capital.........		$30,000
Retained earnings.............		105,000
Total equity................		$135,000

Book value is calculated as:

Preferred shares		Common shares	
Dividends in arrears	$ 5,000	Total equity	$135,000
Plus: Paid-in capital	10,000	*Less:* Preferred claims	15,000
Balance	$15,000	Balance	$120,000
Shares outstanding	1,000	Shares outstanding	60,000
Book value per share	$15	Book value per share	$2

Comparison of book value with market value provides insight into investors' evaluations of the corporation. For instance, if the book value of one common share of Corporation A is $20 and its common shares are traded on a public stock exchange for $40 per share (market value), it is said to be trading for "two times book value." If Corporation B is trading for three times book value, investors are indicating that the future profit prospects for corporation B are higher than those for Corporation A. They are willing to pay proportionately more for shares of Corporation B than Corporation A, relative to the underlying book values.

Some shares regularly sell for less than their book value on various stock exchanges. This does not necessarily mean they are a bargain investment. The market price of a share is related to such factors as general economic outlook and perceived potential of the company to generate earnings.

An exploration is available on the Lyryx site. Log into your Lyryx course to run Book Value per Share.

Summary of Chapter 10 Learning Objectives

LO1 – Identify and explain characteristics of the corporate form of organization and classes of shares.

A corporation is a legal entity that is separate from its owners, known as shareholders. The board of directors is responsible for corporate policy and broad direction of the corporation, including hiring the person in charge of day-to-day operations. A corporation has an indefinite life, its shareholders have limited liability, it can acquire capital more easily than a sole proprietorship or partnership, and it pays income taxes on its earnings since it is a separate legal entity. A corporation can issue common and preferred shares. Common shares have voting rights while preferred shares do not. Preferred shares are listed before common shares in the equity section of the balance sheet. Preferred shareholders are entitled to receive dividends before common shareholders. Authorized shares are the total number of shares that can be issued or sold. Shares that have been issued can be repurchased by the corporation and either held in treasury for subsequent sale/distribution or cancelled. Outstanding shares are those that have been issued and are held by shareholders. Shares repurchased by a corporation are not outstanding shares.

LO2 – Record and disclose preferred and common share transactions including share splits.

Common and preferred shares can be issued for cash or other assets. Organization costs are expensed when incurred and organizers sometimes accept shares in lieu of cash for their work in organizing the corporation. When more than one type of share has been issued, the equity section of the balance sheet must be classified by including a Contributed Capital section. When a corporations shares are selling at a high price, a share split may be declared to increase the marketability of the shares. There is no journal entry for a share split. Instead, a memorandum entry is entered into the records detailing the split. A share split increases the number of shares but does not change any of the dollar amounts on the financial statements.

LO3 – Record and disclose cash dividends.

Cash dividends are a distribution of earnings to the shareholders and are declared by the board of directors. On the declaration date, cash dividends declared (or retained earnings) is debited and dividends payable is credited. On the date of record, no journal entry is recorded. Shareholders who hold shares on the date of record are eligible to receive the declared dividend. On the date of payment, dividends payable is debited and cash is credited. Preferred shares may have a feature known as cumulative or non-cumulative. Cumulative preferred shares accumulate undeclared dividends from one year to the next. These unpaid dividends are called dividends in arrears. When dividends are subsequently declared, dividends in arrears must be paid before anything is paid to the other shareholders. Non-cumulative preferred shares do not accumulate undeclared dividends.

LO4 – Record and disclose share dividends.

Share dividends distribute additional shares to shareholders and are declared by the board of directors. On the declaration date, share dividends declared (or retained earnings) is debited and common share dividends distributable, a share capital account, is credited. When the share dividend is distributed to shareholders, the Common Share Dividends Distributable account is debited and common shares is credited. Share dividends cause an increase in the number of shares issued and outstanding but do not affect account balances. Share dividends simply transfer an amount from retained earnings to share capital within the equity section of the balance sheet.

LO5 – Calculate and explain the book value per share ratio.

The book value of a share is the amount of net assets represented by one share. Book value per common share is the amount of net assets not claimed by creditors and preferred shareholders. Preferred book value per share is the net assets that preferred shareholders would receive if the corporation were liquidated.

Discussion Questions

1. What are some advantages of the corporate form of organization?

2. What is meant by *limited liability* of a corporation?

3. What rights are attached to common shares? Where are these rights indicated?

4. What is a board of directors and whom does it represent? Are the directors involved in the daily management of the entity?

5. Describe:
    a. two main classes of shares that can be issued by a corporation; and
    b. the different terms relating to the status of a corporation's shares.

6. In what ways can shares be "preferred"? In which ways are they similar to common shares? Different from common shares?

7. Why do corporations sometimes opt for a share split?

8. Identify the major components of the equity section of a balance sheet. Why are these components distinguished?

9. How can retained earnings be said to be reinvested in a corporation?

10. What are the main issues a board of directors considers when making a dividend declaration decision?

11. Even if a corporation is making a substantial net income each year, why might the board of directors decide to not pay any cash dividends?

12. Distinguish among the date of dividend declaration, the date of record, and the date of payment.

13. What is the difference in accounting between cash dividends and share dividends?

14. Explain the different dividend preferences that may be attached to preferred shares. Why would preferred shares have these preferences over common shares? Does it mean that purchasing preferred shares is better than purchasing common shares?

15. What are dividends in arrears? Are they a liability of the corporation?

16. How does a share dividend differ from a share split?

17. Does a share dividend change an investor's percentage of corporate ownership? Explain, using an example.

Exercises

EXERCISE 10–1   (LO1,2)

Bagan Corporation, a profitable growth company with 200,000 shares of common shares outstanding, is in need of $40 million in new funds to finance a required expansion. Management has three options:

(1) Sell $40 million of 12% bonds at face value.

(2) Sell preferred shares: 400,000, $10 shares at $100 per share.

(3) Sell an additional 200,000 common shares at $200 per share.

Operating income (before interest and income taxes) upon completion of the expansion is expected to average $12 million per year; assume an income tax rate of 50 per cent.

Required:

a. Complete the schedule below.

	12% Bonds	Preferred Shares	Common Shares
Income before interest and income taxes			
Less: Interest expense			
Income before taxes			
Less: Income taxes at 50%			
Net income			
Less: Preferred dividends			
Net income available to common shareholders			
Number of common shares outstanding			
Earnings per common share			

b. Which financing option is most advantageous to the common shareholders? Why?

EXERCISE 10–2 (LO2)

A tract of land valued at $50,000 has been given to a corporation in exchange for 1,000 preferred shares.

Required:

a. Prepare the journal entry to record the transaction.

b. Where would the transaction be classified in the balance sheet?

EXERCISE 10–3 (LO1,2)

The equity section of Gannon Oilfield Corporation's balance sheet at December 31, 2019 is shown below.

Preferred Shares
    Authorized – 100 shares
    Issued and Outstanding – 64 Shares $3,456
Common Shares
    Authorized – 2,000 Shares
    Issued and Outstanding – 800 Shares   1680
Retained Earnings   600

Required:

a. What is the average price received for each issued preferred share?

b. What is the average price received for each issued common share?

c. What is the total contributed capital of the company?

EXERCISE 10–4   (LO3)

Strada Controls Inc. has 100,000 common shares outstanding on January 1, 2019. On May 25, 2019, the board of directors declared a semi-annual cash dividend of $1 per share. The dividend will be paid on June 26, 2019 to shareholders of record on June 7, 2019.

Required: Prepare journal entries for

a. The declaration of the dividend.

b. The payment of the dividend.

EXERCISE 10–5   (LO1,3)

Landers Flynn Inc. has 1,000, $5 cumulative preferred shares outstanding. Dividends were not paid last year. The corporation also has 5,000 common shares outstanding. Landers Flynn declared a $14,000 cash dividend to be paid in the current year.

Required:

a. Calculate the dividends received by the preferred and common shareholders

b. If the preferred shares were non-cumulative, how would your answers to part a. above change?

EXERCISE 10–6 (LO1,3)

The following note appeared on the balance sheet of Sabre Rigging Limited:

> As of December 31, 2019, dividends on the 1,000 issued and outstanding shares of cumulative preferred shares were in arrears for three years at the rate of $5 per share per year or $15,000 in total.

Required:

a. Does the $15,000 of dividends in arrears appear as a liability on the December 31, 2019 balance sheet? Explain your answer.

b. Why might the dividends be in arrears?

c. The comptroller of Sabre Rigging projects net income for the 2020 fiscal year of $35,000. When the company last paid dividends, the directors allocated 50 per cent of current year's net income for dividends. If dividends on preferred shares are declared at the end of 2020 and the established policy of 50 per cent is continued, how much will be available for dividends to the common shareholders if the profit projection is realized?

EXERCISE 10–7 (LO1,2,3,4)

The December 31, 2018 balance sheet for Arrow Streaming Corporation shows that as of that date it issued a total of 10,000 common shares for $140,000. On April 1, 2019 Arrow Streaming declared a 10 per cent share dividend, payable on April 15 to shareholders of record on April 10. The market value of Arrow's shares on April 1 was $15. On June 1, the company declared a $2 cash dividend per share to common shareholders of record on June 10, and paid the dividend on June 30. Assume the year end of the corporation is December 31.

Required: Prepare journal entries for the above transactions, including closing entries.

EXERCISE 10–8 (LO2,5)

The equity section of Pembina Valley Manufacturing Limited's balance sheet at December 31, 2019 is shown below.

Share Capital

Preferred Shares, Cumulative	
Authorized – 500 shares	
Issued and Outstanding – 300 Shares	$300
Common Shares	
Authorized – 100 Shares	
Issued and Outstanding – 20 Shares	500
Total Contributed Capital	800
Retained Earnings	192
Total Equity	$992

Note: There were $30 of dividends in arrears on the preferred shares at December 31, 2019.

Required:

a. Calculate the December 31, 2019 book value per share of

 i. the preferred shares; and

 ii. the common shares.

b. Assume that the common shares were split 2 for 1 on January 2, 2020 and that there was no change in any other account at that time. Calculate the new book value of common shares immediately following the share split.

Problems

PROBLEM 10–1 (LO2)

Following is the equity section of Critter Contracting Inc. shown before and after the board of directors authorized a 5 for 1 share split on April 15, 2019.

Before split		After split	
Equity		*Equity*	
Common Shares		Common Shares	
Authorized – 5,000 Shares		Authorized – ? Shares	
Issued and Outstanding		Issued and Outstanding	
– 1,000 Shares	$100,000	– ? Shares	$?

Required:

1. Complete the equity section of the balance sheet after the split.

2. Record a memorandum indicating the new number of shares.

3. If the market value per share was $40 before the split, what would be the market value after the split? Why?

PROBLEM 10–2 (LO3,4)

The equity section of TWR Contracting Inc.'s December 31, 2018 balance sheet showed the following:

Equity

Share Capital	
Preferred Shares, $0.60, Cumulative,	
Issued and Outstanding – 40 Shares	
Common Shares,	$ 400
Issued and Outstanding – 2,000 Shares	2,000
Total Contributed Capital	2,400
Retained Earnings	900
Total Equity	$3,300

The following transactions occurred during 2019:

Feb. 15 Declared the regular $0.30 per share semi-annual dividend on its preferred shares and a $0.05 per share dividend on the common shares to holders of record March 5, payable April 1.

Apr. 1 Paid the dividends declared on February 15.

May 1 Declared a 10 per cent share dividend to common shareholders of record May 15 to be issued June 15, 2016. The market value of the common shares at May 1 was $2 per share.

June 15 Distributed the dividends declared on May 1.

Aug. 15 Declared the regular semi-annual dividend on preferred shares and a dividend of $0.05 on the common shares to holders of record August 31, payable October 1.

Oct. 1 Paid the dividends declared on August 15.

Dec. 15 Declared a 10 per cent share dividend to common shareholders of record December 20 to be issued on December 27, 2019. The market value of the common shares at December 15 was $3 per share.

Dec. 27 Distributed the dividends declared on December 15.

Dec. 31 Net income for the year ended December 31, 2019 was $1,400.

Required:

1. Prepare journal entries to record the 2019 transactions, including closing entries for the December 31 year end date. Show calculations. Descriptive narrative is not needed.

2. Prepare the statement of changes in equity for the year ended December 31, 2019.

PROBLEM 10–3 (LO1,2,3,4)

The equity section of Wondra Inc.'s December 31, 2018 balance sheet showed the following:

Contributed Capital	
Preferred Shares; $0.50 cumulative; unlimited shares authorized; 30,000 shares issued and outstanding	$ 480,000
Common Shares; unlimited shares authorized; 70,000 shares issued and outstanding	560,000
Total contributed capital	$1,040,000
Retained Earnings	95,000
Total Equity	$1,135,000

At December 31, 2018 there were $15,000 of dividends in arrears.

The following transactions occurred during 2019:

Feb. 10 Declared a total dividend of $32,000 to shareholders of record on February 15, payable March 1.
Mar. 1 Paid dividends declared February 10.
    5 Issued for cash 2,000 preferred shares at $18 each.
Apr. 15 The Board of Directors declared a 2:1 split on the preferred and common shares.
Jun. 22 Issued for cash 20,000 common shares at $4.00 per share.
Nov. 10 Declared a 20% share dividend to common shareholders of record on Nov. 14, distributable Dec. 15. The market price of the shares on Nov. 10 was $3.50.
Dec. 15 Distributed share dividend declared on November 10.
Dec. 31 Closed the Income Summary account which had a credit balance of $290,000.
    31 Closed the dividend accounts.

Required:

1. Journalize the 2019 transactions.

2. Prepare the equity section of the December 31, 2019 balance sheet.

PROBLEM 10–4 (LO1,2,5)

The following is the equity section of the balance sheet of Tridon Construction Limited at December 31, 2019.

Equity

Share Capital	
Common Shares	
Authorized – 500 shares	
Issued and Outstanding – 300 Shares	$3,070
Retained Earnings	500
Total Equity	$3,570

Required:

1. What is the paid-in capital per common share? ...the book value per common share? Round calculations to two decimal places.

2. On December 31, the Tridon Construction common shares traded at $24. Why is the market value different from the book value of commons shares?

Chapter 11

The Statement of Cash Flows

Details about the amount of cash received and paid out during an accounting period are not shown on the balance sheet, income statement, or statement of changes in equity. This information is disclosed on the statement of cash flows (SCF). This chapter discusses the purpose of the statement of cash flows, the steps in preparing the SCF, as well as how to interpret various sections of the statement of cash flows.

Chapter 11 Learning Objectives

LO1 – Explain the purpose of the statement of cash flows.

LO2 – Prepare a statement of cash flows.

LO3 – Interpret a statement of cash flows.

Concept Self-Check

Use the following as a self-check while working through Chapter 11.

1. What is the definition of cash and cash equivalents?

2. Why is a statement of cash flows prepared?

3. What are the three sections of a statement of cash flows?

4. What two methods can be used to prepare the operating activities section of the statement of cash flows?

5. Why is depreciation expense an adjustment in the operating activities section of the statement of cash flows?

6. Where are dividend payments listed on the statement of cash flows?

7. In what section of the statement of cash flows are the cash proceeds resulting from the sale of a non-current asset listed?

8. Where on the statement of cash flows is a long-term bank loan payment identified?

NOTE: The purpose of these questions is to prepare you for the concepts introduced in the chapter. Your goal should be to answer each of these questions as you read through the chapter. If, when you complete the chapter, you are unable to answer one or more the Concept Self-Check questions, go back through the content to find the answer(s). Solutions are not provided to these questions.

11.1 Financial Statement Reporting

LO1 – Explain the purpose of the statement of cash flows.

Cash flow is an important factor in determining the success or failure of a corporation. It is quite possible for a profitable business to be short of cash. As discussed in Chapter 7, a company can have liquidity issues because of large amounts of cash tied up in inventory and accounts receivable, for instance. Conversely, an unprofitable business might have sufficient cash to pay its bills if it has access to enough financing from loans or by issuing share capital.

We know that the financial activities of a corporation are reported through four financial statements: a balance sheet, an income statement, a statement of changes in equity, and a statement of cash flows (SCF). Statement of cash flowsThis chapter discusses the statement of cash flows in detail.

The SCF identifies the sources (inflows) and uses (outflows) of cash during the accounting period. It explains why the cash balance at the end of the accounting period is different from that at the beginning of the period by describing the enterprise's *financing*, *investing*, and *operating* activities.

Cash flow information is useful to management when making decisions such as purchasing equipment, plant expansion, retiring long-term debt, or declaring dividends. The SCF is useful to external users when evaluating a corporation's financial performance.

The SCF, together with the income statement, provides a somewhat limited means of assessing future cash flows because these statements are based on historical, not prospective data. Nevertheless, the ability to generate cash from past operations is often an important indication of whether the enterprise will be able to meet obligations as they become due, pay dividends, pay for recurring operating costs, or survive adverse economic conditions.

For SCF purposes, cash includes cash and cash equivalents — assets that can be quickly converted into a known amount of cash, such as short-term investments that are not subject to significant risk of changes in value. For our purposes, an investment will be considered a cash equivalent when it has a maturity of three months or less from the date of acquisition.

Because of differences in the nature of each entity and industry, management judgment is required to determine what assets constitute cash and cash equivalents for a particular firm. This decision needs to be disclosed on the SCF or in a note to the financial statements as shown in the following example:

Note X
Cash and cash equivalents consist of cash on deposit and short-term investments held for the purposes of meeting cash commitments within three months from the balance sheet date. Cash and cash equivalents consist of the following:

	($000s)		
	2019	2018	2017
Cash on Deposit	$20	$30	$50
Short-term Investments	36	31	37
	$56	$61	$87

For simplicity, examples throughout this chapter involving cash and cash equivalents will include only cash.

Cash flows result from a wide variety of a corporation's activities as cash is received and disbursed over a period of time. Because the income statement is based on accrual accounting that matches expenses with revenues, net income most often does not reflect cash receipts and disbursements during the time period they were made. As we will see, the statement of cash flows converts accrual net income to a cash basis net income.

11.2 Preparing the Statement of Cash Flows

> LO2 – Prepare a statement of cash flows.

The general format for a SCF is shown in Figure 11.1. The SCF details the cash inflows and outflows that caused the beginning of the period cash account balance to change to its end of period balance.

Name of Company
Statement of Cash Flows
For the Period Ended

Cash flows from operating activities:
  [Each operating inflow/outflow is listed]
  Net cash inflow/outflow from operating activities $ XX
Cash flows from investing activities:
  [Each investing inflow/outflow is listed]
  Net cash inflow/outflow from investing activities   XX
Cash flows from financing activities:
  [Each financing inflow/outflow is listed]
  Net cash inflow/outflow from financing activities   XX
Net increase/decrease in cash $ XX
Cash at beginning of period   XX
Cash at end of period $ XX

Figure 11.1: General Format for a Statement of Cash Flows

Notice that the cash flows in Figure 11.1 are separated into three groups: cash flows from operating, investing, and financing activities. Grouping or classifying cash flows is a key component of preparing a SCF.

Classifying Cash Flows—Operating Activities

Cash flow from operating activities represents cash flows generated from the principal activities that produce revenue for a corporation, such as selling products, and the related expenses reported on the income statement. Because of accrual accounting, the net income reported on the income statement includes noncash transactions. For example, revenue earned on account is included in accrual net income but it does not involve cash (debit accounts receivable and credit revenue). Therefore, the operating activities section of the SCF must convert accrual net income to a cash basis net income. There are two generally accepted methods for preparing the operating activities section of the SCF, namely the direct method and the indirect method. This chapter illustrates the indirect method because it is more commonly used in Canada. The direct method is addressed in a different textbook. Both methods result in the same cash flows from operating activities — it is the way in which the number is calculated that differs. The method used has an impact on only the operating activities section and not on the investing or financing activities sections.

In using the indirect method for preparing the operating activities section, the accrual net income is adjusted for changes in current assets (except cash), current liabilities (except dividends payable), depreciation expense, and gains/losses on the disposition of non-current assets. Figure 11.2 illustrates the effect of these items on the SCF.

Cash flows from operating activities:

Net income/net loss	$ XX
Adjustments to reconcile net income/loss to cash provided/used by operating activities:	
Add: Decreases in current assets (except Cash)	XX
Subtract: Increases in current assets (except Cash)	XX
Add: Increases in current liabilities (except Dividends payable)	XX
Subtract: Decreases in current liabilities (except Dividends payable)	XX
Add: Depreciation expense	XX
Add: Losses on disposal of non-current assets	XX
Subtract: Gains on disposal of non-current assets	XX
Net cash inflow/outflow from operating activities	$ XX

Figure 11.2: Detailed Adjustments to Convert Accrual Net Income to a Cash Basis

Decreases in current assets are added back as an adjustment to net income because, for example, a decrease in accounts receivable indicates that cash was collected from credit customers (debit cash and credit accounts receivable) yet it is not part of accrual net income, so the cash collected must be added. An increase in accounts receivable indicates that sales on account were recorded (debit accounts receivable and credit sales) so it is part of accrual net income. However, since no cash was collected, this must be subtracted from accrual net income to adjust it to a cash basis.

Increases in current liabilities are added back as an adjustment to net income because, for example, an increase in accounts payable indicates that a purchase/expense was made on account (debit expense and credit accounts payable) so it was subtracted in calculating accrual net income. However, since no cash was paid, this must be added back to accrual net income to adjust it to a cash basis. A decrease in accounts payable indicates that a payment was made to a creditor (debit accounts payable and credit cash) yet it is not part of accrual net income so the cash paid must be subtracted.

Depreciation expense is subtracted in calculating accrual net income. However, an analysis of the journal entry shows that no cash was involved (debit depreciation expense and credit accumulated depreciation), so it must be added back to adjust the accrual net income to a cash basis.

A loss on the disposal of a non-current asset is added back as an adjustment to net income because, in analyzing the journal entry when losses occur (e.g., debit cash, debit loss, credit land), the loss represents the difference between the cash proceeds and the book value of the non-current asset. Since a loss is subtracted on the income statement and does not represent a cash outflow, it is added back to adjust the accrual net income to a cash basis. The same logic applies for a gain on the disposal of a non-current asset.

Classifying Cash Flows—Investing Activities

Cash flows from investing activities involve increases and decreases in long-term asset accounts. These include outlays for the acquisition of property, plant, and equipment, as well as proceeds from their disposal. Figure 11.3 illustrates the effect of these items on the SCF.

Cash flows from investing activities:
Cash proceeds from sale of non-current assets	XX
Cash paid to purchase non-current assets	XX
Net cash inflow/outflow from investing activities	XX

Figure 11.3: Detail of Inflows/(Outflows) From Investing Activities

Classifying Cash Flows—Financing Activities

Cash flows from financing activities result when the composition of the debt and equity capital structure of the entity changes. This category is generally limited to increases and decreases in long-term liability accounts and share capital accounts such as common and preferred shares. These include cash flows from the issue and repayment of debt, and the issue and repurchase of share capital. Dividend payments are generally considered to be financing activities, since these represent a return to shareholders on the original capital they invested. Figure 11.4 illustrates the effect of these items on the SCF.

Cash flows from financing activities:
Cash proceeds from issuance of shares	XX
Cash paid for repurchase of shares	XX
Cash proceeds from borrowings	XX
Cash repayments of borrowings	XX
Cash paid for dividends	XX
Net cash inflow/outflow from financing activities	XX

Figure 11.4: Detail of Inflows/(Outflows) From Financing Activities

Classifying Cash Flows—Noncash Investing and Noncash Financing Activities

There are some transactions that involve the direct exchange of non-current balance sheet items so that cash is not affected. For example, noncash investing and noncash financing activities would include the purchase of a non-current asset by issuing debt or share capital, the declaration and issuance of a share dividend, retirement of debt by issuing shares, or the exchange of noncash assets for other noncash assets. Although noncash investing and noncash financing activities do not appear on the SCF, the full disclosure principle requires that they be disclosed either in a note to the financial statements or in a schedule on the SCF.

An exploration is available on the Lyryx site. Log into your Lyryx course to run Cash Flow Statement Categories.

Now, let us demonstrate the preparation of a SCF using the balance sheet, income statement, and statement of changes in equity of Example Corporation shown below.

Example Corporation
Balance Sheet
At December 31
($000s)

	2016	2015
Assets		
Current assets		
Cash	$ 27	$ 150
Accounts receivable	375	450
Merchandise inventory	900	450
Prepaid expenses	20	10
Total current assets	1,322	1,060
Property, plant, and equipment		
Land	70	70
Buildings	1,340	620
Less: Accumulated depreciation - buildings	(430)	(280)
Machinery	1,130	920
Less: Accumulated depreciation - machinery	(250)	(240)
Total property, plant, and equipment	1,860	1,090
Total assets	$ 3,182	$ 2,150
Liabilities		
Current liabilities		
Accounts payable	$ 235	$ 145
Dividends payable	25	30
Income taxes payable	40	25
Total current liabilities	300	200
Long-term loan payable	1,000	500
Total liabilities	1,300	700
Equity		
Common shares	1,210	800
Retained earnings	672	650
Total equity	1,882	1,450
Total liabilities and equity	$ 3,182	$ 2,150

Example Corporation
Income Statement
For the Year Ended December 31, 2016
($000s)

Sales		$ 1,200
Cost of goods sold		674
Gross profit		526
Operating expenses		
Selling, general, and administration	$ 115	
Depreciation	260	375
Income from operations		151
Other revenues and expenses		
Interest expense	26	
Loss on disposal of machinery	10	36
Income before income taxes		115
Income taxes		35
Net Income		$ 80

Example Corporation
Statement of Changes in Equity
For the Year Ended December 31, 2016
($000s)

	Share Capital	Retained Earnings	Total Equity
Opening balance	$ 800	$ 650	$ 1,450
Common shares issued	410	-	410
Net income	-	80	80
Dividends declared	-	(58)	(58)
Ending balance	$ 1,210	$ 672	$ 1,882

The SCF can be prepared from an analysis of transactions recorded in the Cash account. Accountants summarize and classify these cash flows on the SCF for the three major activities noted earlier, namely operating, investing, and financing. To aid our analysis, the following list of additional information from the records of Example Corporation will be used.

Additional Information

1. A building was purchased for $720 cash.

2. Machinery was purchased for $350 cash.

3. Machinery costing $140 with accumulated depreciation of $100 was sold for $30 cash.

4. Total depreciation expense of $260 was recorded during the year; $150 on the building and $110 on the machinery.

5. Example Corporation received $500 cash from issuing a long-term loan with the bank.

6. Shares were issued for $410 cash.

7. $58 of dividends were declared during the year.

Analysis of Cash Flows

There are different ways to analyze cash flows and then prepare the SCF; only one of those techniques will be illustrated here using the following steps.

1. Set up a cash flow table.

2. Calculate the changes in each balance sheet account.

3. Calculate and analyze the changes in retained earnings and dividends payable (if there is a Dividends Payable account).

4. Calculate and analyze the changes in the noncash current assets and current liabilities (excluding Dividends Payable account).

5. Calculate and analyze changes in non-current asset accounts

6. Calculate and analyze changes in Long-term Liability and Share Capital accounts.

7. Reconcile the analysis.

8. Prepare a statement of cash flows.

Step 1: Set up a cash flow table

Set up a table as shown below with a row for each account shown on the balance sheet. Enter amounts for each account for 2015 and 2016. Show credit balances in parentheses. Total both columns and ensure they equal zero. The table should appear as follows after this step has been completed:

Account	Balance ($000s) 2016 Dr. (Cr.)	2015 Dr. (Cr.)
Cash	27	150
Accounts receivable	375	450
Merchandise inventory	900	450
Prepaid expenses	20	10
Land	70	70
Buildings	1,340	620
Accum. dep.- buildings	(430)	(280)
Machinery	1,130	920
Accum. dep.- machinery	(250)	(240)
Accounts payable	(235)	(145)
Dividends payable	(25)	(30)
Income taxes payable	(40)	(25)
Long-term loan payable	(1,000)	(500)
Share capital	(1,210)	(800)
Retained earnings	(672)	(650)
Total	-0-	-0-

Step 2: Calculate the change in cash

Add two columns to the cash flow table. Calculate the net debit or net credit change in cash and insert this change in the appropriate column. This step is shown below.

354 ■ The Statement of Cash Flows

	Balance ($000s)		Step 2 Change	
Account	2016 Dr. (Cr.)	2015 Dr. (Cr.)	Dr.	Cr.
Cash	27	150		123
Accounts receivable	375	450		
Merchandise inventory	900	450		
Prepaid expenses	20	10		
Land	70	70		
Buildings	1,340	620		
Accum. dep. – buildings	(430)	(280)		
Machinery	1,130	920		
Accum. dep. – machinery	(250)	(240)		
Accounts payable	(235)	(145)		
Dividends payable	(25)	(30)		
Income taxes payable	(40)	(25)		
Long-term loan payable	(1,000)	(500)		
Share capital	(1,210)	(800)		
Retained earnings	(672)	(650)		
Total	-0-	-0-		

> Cash has decreased by $123k. This is the amount that the SCF analysis must reconcile to.

An exploration is available on the Lyryx site. Log into your Lyryx course to run Cash Balance.

Step 3: Calculate and analyze the changes in retained earnings and dividends payable (if there is a Dividends Payable account)

When we calculate the changes for each of retained earnings and dividends payable, the net difference may not always reflect the causes for change in these accounts. For example, the net difference between the beginning and ending balances in retained earnings is an increase of $22 thousand. However, two things occurred to cause this net change: a net income of $80 thousand (a debit to income summary and a credit to retained earnings) and dividends of $58 thousand that were declared during the year per the additional information (a debit to retained earnings of $58k and a credit to dividends payable of $58k). **The net income of $80 thousand is the starting position in the operating activities section of the SCF (see Figure 11.5).**

The change in the dividends payable balance was also caused by two transactions — the dividend declaration of $58 thousand (a debit to retained earnings and a credit to dividends payable) and a $63 thousand payment of dividends (a debit to dividends payable and a credit to cash). **The $63 thousand cash payment is subtracted in the financing activities section of the SCF (see**

Figure 11.5). Dividends payable can change because of two transactions, as in this example, or because of one transaction, which could be either a dividend declaration with no payment of cash, or a payment of the dividend payable and no dividend declaration. Step 3 as it applies to Example Corporation is detailed below.

During 2016, dividends of $58k were declared (this information was given). The beginning balance of $30k plus $58k means $63k were paid, creating the ending balance of $25k (the $63k was not given so had to be calculated and results in a debit to dividends payable). The payment of $63k of dividends is a financing activity.

Step 3

	Balance ($000s)		Change	
	2016	2015		
	Dr.	Dr.		
Account	(Cr.)	(Cr.)	Dr.	Cr.
Cash	27	150		123
Accounts receivable	375	450		75
Merchandise inventory	900	450	450	
Prepaid expenses	20	10	10	
Land	70	70		
Buildings	1,340	620		
Accum. dep. – buildings	(430)	(280)		
Machinery	1,130	920		
Accum. dep. – machinery	(250)	(240)		
Accounts payable	(235)	(145)		90
→Dividends payable	(25)	(30)	63	58
Income taxes payable	(40)	(25)		15
Long-term loan payable	(1,000)	(500)		
Share capital	(1,210)	(800)		
Retained earnings	(672)	(650)	58	80←
Total	-0-	-0-		

During 2016, net income of $80k was earned. The beginning balance in retained earnings of $650k plus net income of $80 means $58k of dividends were declared, creating the $672k ending retained earnings balance.

An exploration is available on the Lyryx site. Log into your Lyryx course to run Net income/loss and Dividends Paid.

Step 4: Calculate and analyze the changes in the noncash current assets and current liabilities (excluding Dividends Payable account)

Calculate the net debit or net credit changes for each current asset and current liability account on the balance sheet and insert these changes in the appropriate column. Step 4 as it applies to Example Corporation is detailed below. **The $75 thousand decrease in accounts receivable is added in the operating activities section of the SCF, the $450 thousand increase in merchandise inventory is subtracted, the $10 thousand increase in prepaid expenses is subtracted, the $90 thousand increase in accounts payable is added, and the $15 thousand increase in income taxes payable is added (see Figure 11.5).**

	Balance ($000s)		Step 4 Change		
Account	2016 Dr. (Cr.)	2015 Dr. (Cr.)	Dr.	Cr.	
Cash	27	150		123	The net change in each of accounts receivable, merchandise inventory, and prepaid expenses are classified as operating activities.
Accounts receivable	375	450		75 ←
Merchandise inventory	900	450	450 ←	
Prepaid expenses	20	10	10 ←	
Land	70	70		
Buildings	1,340	620		
Accum. dep. – buildings	(430)	(280)		
Machinery	1,130	920			The net change in each of accounts payable and income taxes payable are classified as operating activities.
Accum. dep. – machinery	(250)	(240)		
Accounts payable	(235)	(145)		90 ←
Dividends payable	(25)	(30)		
Income taxes payable	(40)	(25)		15 ←
Long-term loan payable	(1,000)	(500)		
Share capital	(1,210)	(800)		
Retained earnings	(672)	(650)		
Total	-0-	-0-		

An exploration is available on the Lyryx site. Log into your Lyryx course to run Cash Flows from Operating Activities.

Step 5: Calculate and analyze changes in non-current asset accounts

Changes in non-current assets are classified as investing activities. There was no change in the Land account. We know from the additional information provided that buildings and machinery were purchased and that machinery was sold.

Buildings were purchased for $720 thousand (a debit to buildings and a credit to cash). *The cash payment of $720 thousand is shown in the investing activities section (see Figure 11.5)*.

Accumulated depreciation–buildings is a non-current asset account and it increased by $150 thousand. This change was caused by a debit to depreciation expense and a credit to accumulated depreciation–building. We know from an earlier discussion that depreciation expense is an adjustment in the operating activities section of the SCF therefore *the $150 thousand is added in the operating activities section (see Figure 11.5)*.

Two transactions caused machinery to change. First, the purchase of $350 thousand of machinery (debit machinery and credit cash); **the $350 thousand cash payment is shown in the investing activities section (see Figure 11.5)**. Second, machinery costing $140 thousand with accumulated depreciation of $100 thousand was sold for cash of $30 thousand resulting in a loss of $10 thousand. **The cash proceeds of $30 thousand is shown in the investing activities section of the SCF and the $10 thousand loss is added in the operating activities section (see Figure 11.5)**.

Accumulated depreciation–machinery not only decreased $100 thousand because of the sale of machinery but it increased by $110 thousand because of depreciation (debit depreciation expense and credit accumulated depreciation–machinery). **The $110 thousand of depreciation expense is added in the operating activities section of the SCF (see Figure 11.5)**.

	Balance ($000s)		Change	
	2016	2015		
	Dr.	Dr.		
Account	(Cr.)	(Cr.)	Dr.	Cr.
Cash	27	150		123
Accounts receivable	375	450		75
Merchandise inventory	900	450	450	
Prepaid expenses	20	10	10	
Land	70	70	-0-	
Buildings	1,340	620	720	
Accum. dep. – buildings	(430)	(280)		150
Machinery	1,130	920	350	140
Accum. dep. – machinery	(250)	(240)	100	110
Accounts payable	(235)	(145)		90
Dividends payable	(25)	(30)	5	
Income taxes payable	(40)	(25)		15
Long-term loan payable	(1,000)	(500)		
Share capital	(1,210)	(800)		
Retained earnings	(672)	(650)		
Total	-0-	-0-		

Step 5

Total depreciation expense of $260k was recorded during the year; $150k on the building and $110k on the machinery, an adjustment under operating activities on the SCF.

A building was purchased for cash of $720k, an investing activity.

Machinery costing $140k with accum. dep. of $100k was sold for cash of $30k, an investing activity.

An exploration is available on the Lyryx site. Log into your Lyryx course to run Investing Activities.

Step 6: Calculate and analyze changes in Long-term Liability and Share Capital accounts

Changes in Long-term Liability and Share Capital accounts result from financing activities. We know from the additional information provided earlier that Example Corporation received cash of $500k from a bank loan (debit cash and credit long-term loan payable) and issued shares for $410k cash (debit cash and credit share capital). ***The $500 thousand cash proceeds from the bank loan and $410 thousand cash proceeds from the issuance of shares are listed in the financing section of the SCF (see Figure 11.5).***

		Balance ($000s)		Step 6 Change	
Account		2016 Dr. (Cr.)	2015 Dr. (Cr.)	Dr.	Cr.
Cash		27	150		123
Accounts receivable		375	450		75
Merchandise inventory		900	450	450	
Prepaid expenses		20	10	10	
Land		70	70	-0-	
Buildings		1,340	620	720	
Accum. dep. – buildings		(430)	(280)		150
Machinery		1,130	920	350	140
Accum. dep. – machinery		(250)	(240)	100	110
Accounts payable		(235)	(145)		90
Dividends payable		(25)	(30)	5	
Income taxes payable		(40)	(25)		15
Long-term loan payable		(1,000)	(500)		500
Share capital		(1,210)	(800)		410
Retained earnings		(672)	(650)	58	80
Total		-0-	-0-		

Shares were issued for cash of $410k, a financing activity.

$500k of cash was received because of an additional bank loan, a financing activity.

An exploration is available on the Lyryx site. Log into your Lyryx course to run Financing Activities.

Step 7: Reconcile the analysis

The analysis is now complete. Add the debit and credit changes, excluding the change in cash. The total debits of $1,693 less the total credits of $1,570 equal a difference of $123 which reconciles to the decrease in cash calculated in Step 2.

11.2. Preparing the Statement of Cash Flows

	Balance ($000s)		Step 7 Change		
Account	2016 Dr. (Cr.)	2015 Dr. (Cr.)	Dr.	Cr.	
Cash	27	150		123 ←	The change in cash calculated in Step 2...
Accounts receivable	375	450		75	
Merchandise inventory	900	450	450		
Prepaid expenses	20	10	10		
Land	70	70	-0-		
Buildings	1,340	620	720		
Accum. dep. – buildings	(430)	(280)		150	
Machinery	1,130	920	350	140	
Accum. dep. – machinery	(250)	(240)	100	110	
Accounts payable	(235)	(145)		90	
Dividends payable	(25)	(30)	5		
Income taxes payable	(40)	(25)		15	
Long-term loan payable	(1,000)	(500)		500	...must agree to the change in cash resulting from the analysis.
Share capital	(1,210)	(800)		410	
Retained earnings	(672)	(650)	58	80	
Total	-0-	-0-	1,693	1,570	
Change in cash				123 ←	

The information in the completed analysis can be used to prepare the statement of cash flows shown in Figure 11.5.

Example Corporation
Statement of Cash Flows
For the Year Ended December 31, 2016
($000s)

Cash flows from operating activities:

Net income		$ 80
Adjustments to reconcile net income cash provided by operating activities:		
Decrease in accounts receivable		75
Increase in merchandise inventory		(450)
Increase in prepaid expenses		(10)
Increase in accounts payable		90
Increase in income taxes payable		15
Depreciation expense		260
Loss on disposal of machinery		10
Net cash inflow from operating activities		$ 70
Cash flows from investing activities:		
Proceeds from sale of machinery	30	
Purchase of building	(720)	
Purchase of machinery	(350)	
Net cash outflow from investing activities		(1,040)
Cash flows from financing activities:		
Payment of dividends	(63)	
Proceeds from bank loan	500	
Issuance of shares	410	
Net cash inflow from financing activities		847
Net decrease in cash		$ (123)
Cash at beginning of year		150
Cash at end of year		$ 27

Figure 11.5: Statement of Cash Flows for Example Corporation

11.3 Interpreting the Statement of Cash Flows

LO3 – Interpret a statement of cash flows.

Readers of financial statements need to know how cash has been used by the enterprise. The SCF provides external decision makers such as creditors and investors with this information. The statement of cash flows provides information about an enterprise's financial management policies and practices. It also may aid in predicting future cash flows, which is an important piece of information for investors and creditors.

The *quality* of earnings as reported on the income statement can also be assessed with the information provided by the SCF. The measurement of net income depends on a number of accruals and allocations that may not provide clear information about the cash-generating power of a company. Users will be more confident in a company with a high correlation between cash provided by operations and net income measured under the accrual basis. Recall, for instance, that although Example Corporation has net income of $80,000 during 2016, its net cash inflow from operations is only $70,000, chiefly due to the large increase in inventory levels. Although net cash flow from operations is still positive, this discrepancy between net income and cash flow from operations may indicate looming cash flow problems, particularly if the trend continues over time.

Example Corporation's SCF also reveals that significant net additions to plant and equipment assets occurred during the year ($1,070,000), financed in part by cash flow from operating activities but primarily by financing activities. These activities included the assumption of loans and issue of shares that amounted to $847,000, net of dividend payments ($500,000 from issuing a long-term loan plus $410,000 from issuing shares less $63,000 for payment of dividends).

It appears that a significant plant and equipment asset acquisition program may be underway, which may affect future financial performance positively. This expansion has been financed mainly by increases in long-term debt and the issuance of common shares. However, the magnitude of the plant and equipment asset purchases, coupled with the payment of the dividends to shareholders, has more than offset cash inflows from operating and financing activities, resulting in a net overall decrease in cash of $123,000. Though the current cash expenditure on long-term productive assets may be a prudent business decision, it has resulted in (hopefully temporary) adverse effects on overall cash flow.

The SCF is not a substitute for an income statement prepared on the accrual basis. Both statements should be used to evaluate a company's financial performance. Together, the SCF and income statement provide a better basis for determining the enterprise's ability to generate funds from operations and thereby meet current obligations when they fall due (liquidity), pay dividends, meet recurring operating costs, survive adverse economic conditions, or expand operations with internally-generated cash.

The SCF highlights the amount of cash available to a corporation, which is important. Excess cash on hand is unproductive. Conversely, inadequate cash decreases liquidity. Cash is the most liquid asset, and its efficient use is one of the most important tasks of management. Cash flow information, interpreted in conjunction with other financial statement analyses, is useful in assessing the effectiveness of the enterprise's cash management policies.

Readers who wish to evaluate the financial position and results of an enterprise's operations also require information on cash flows produced by investing and financing activities. The SCF is the only statement that explicitly provides this information. By examining the relationship among the various sources and uses of cash during the year, readers can also focus on the effectiveness of management's investing and financing decisions and how these may affect future financial performance.

Summary of Chapter 11 Learning Objectives

LO1 – Explain the purpose of the statement of cash flows.

The statement of cash flows is one of the four financial statements. It highlights the net increase or decrease in the cash and cash equivalents balance during the accounting period, and details the sources and uses of cash that caused that change.

LO2 – Prepare a statement of cash flows.

The operating activities section of the statement of cash flows can be prepared using the direct or indirect method. This textbook focuses only on the indirect method. The result of both methods is identical; it is only how the calculations are performed that differs. The operating activities section begins with accrual net income and, by adjusting for changes in current assets, current liabilities, adding back depreciation expense, and adding back/subtracting losses/gains on disposal of non-current assets, arrives at net income on a cash basis. The investing activities section analyzes cash inflows and outflows from the sale and purchase of non-current assets. The finance activities section details the cash inflows and outflows resulting from the issue and payment of loans, issue and repurchase of shares, and payment of dividends.

LO3 – Interpret a statement of cash flows.

A statement of cash flows contributes to the decision-making process by explaining the sources and uses of cash. The operating activities section can signal potential areas of concern by focusing on differences between accrual net income and cash basis net income. The investing activities section can highlight if cash is being used to acquire assets for generating revenue, while the financing activities section can identify where the cash to purchase those assets might be coming from. Those who use financial statements can focus on the effectiveness of management's investing and financing decisions and how these may affect future financial performance.

Discussion Questions

1. Using an example, explain in your own words the function of a statement of cash flows. Why is it prepared? What does it communicate to the reader of financial statements? What is its advantage over a balance sheet? over an income statement?

2. Why are financing and investing activities of a corporation important to financial statement readers?

3. How does an increase in accounts receivable during the year affect the cash flow from operating activities?

4. What effect does the declaration of a cash dividend have on cash flow? the payment of a dividend declared and paid during the current year? the payment of a dividend declared in the preceding year?

5. Why may a change in the Short-term investments account not affect the amount of cash provided by operations?

6. Why is it possible that cash may have decreased during the year, even though there has been a substantial net income during the same period?

7. Describe common transactions affecting balance sheet accounts that use cash. Explain how these items are analysed to identify cash flows that have occurred during the year.

Exercises

EXERCISE 11–1   (LO1,2)

The following transactions were carried out by Crozier Manufacturing Limited.

Required: Indicate into which category each transaction or adjustment is placed in the statement of cash flows: operating (O), financing (F), or investing (I) activities. For non-cash investing/financing activities that are disclosed in a note to the financial statements, indicate (NC).

_____ A payment of $5,000 was made on a bank loan.
_____ Depreciation expense for equipment was $1,000.
_____ $10,000 of share capital was issued for cash.
_____ Cash dividends of $2,500 were declared and paid to shareholders.
_____ Bonds were issued in exchange for equipment costing $7,000.
_____ Land was purchased for $25,000 cash.
_____ $750 of accrued salaries was paid.
_____ $10,000 of accounts receivable was collected.
_____ A building was purchased for $80,000: $30,000 was paid in cash and the rest was borrowed.
_____ A long-term investment in shares of another company was sold for $50,000 cash.
_____ Equipment was sold for $6,000. The related accumulation depreciation was $3,000 with an original cost of $10,000.
_____ $1,200 was paid for a 12-month insurance policy in effect next year.
_____ A patent was amortized for $500.
_____ Bonds were issued for $50,000 cash.

EXERCISE 11–2   (LO2)

Assume the following selected income statement and balance sheet information for Larriet Inc.:

Larriet Inc.
Balance Sheet Information
(000's)

	December 31, Year 5	Year 4
Cash	$40	$22
Accounts receivable	34	39
Merchandise inventory	150	146
Prepaid expenses	3	2
Machinery	125	138
Accumulated depreciation	55	42
Accounts payable	29	31
Dividends payable	1	5
Bonds payable	15	38
Common shares	208	150
Retained earnings	44	81

Larriet Inc.
Income Statement
Year Ended December 31, Year 5
(000's)

Sales revenue		$385
Cost of goods sold	$224	
Other operating expenses	135	
Depreciation expense	25	
Loss on sale of machinery	3	(387)
Net loss		$2

Additional information:

i. Machinery costing $20 thousand was sold for cash.

ii. Machinery was purchased for cash.

iii. The change in retained earnings was caused by the net loss and the declaration of dividends.

Required:

a. Reconstruct the journal entry regarding the sale of the machinery.

b. Reconstruct the entry regarding the purchase of machinery.

c. Reconstruct the entry regarding the declaration of dividends.

d. Reconstruct the entry regarding the payment of dividends.

e. Prepare the statement of cash flows for the year ended December 31, Year 5.

Problems

PROBLEM 11–1 (LO2)

Assume the following income statement information:

Sales (all cash)	$35
Operating Expenses	
Depreciation	10
Income before Other Item	25
Other Item	
Gain on Sale of Equipment	8
Net Income	$33

Required:

1. Assume the equipment that was sold for a gain of $8 originally cost $20, had a book value of $4 at the date of disposal, and was sold for $12. Prepare the journal entry to record the disposal. What is the cash effect of this entry?

2. Calculate cash flow from operating activities.

PROBLEM 11–2 (LO2)

Assume the following selected income statement and balance sheet information for the year ended December 31, 2019:

Sales	$200
Cost of Goods Sold	120
Gross Profit	80
Operating Expenses	
Rent	30
Net Income	$50

	2019 Dr. (Cr.)	2018 Dr. (Cr.)
Cash	$100	$86
Accounts Receivable	60	40
Inventory	36	30
Prepaid Rent	10	-0-
Retained Earnings	(206)	(156)

Required:

1. Reconcile the change in retained earnings from December 31, 2018 to December 31, 2019.
2. Calculate cash flow from operating activities.

PROBLEM 11–3   (LO2)

Assume the following income statement and balance sheet information:

Revenue	$-0-
Depreciation Expense	(100)
Net Loss	$(100)

	2019 Dr. (Cr.)	2018 Dr. (Cr.)
Cash	$350	$650
Machinery	500	200
Accumulated Depreciation – Machinery	(250)	(150)
Retained Earnings	(600)	(700)

No machinery was disposed during the year. All machinery purchases were paid in cash.

Required:

1. Prepare a journal entry to record the depreciation expense for the year. Determine the cash effect.
2. Prepare a journal entry to account for the change in the Machinery balance sheet account. What is the cash effect of this entry?
3. Prepare a statement of cash flows for the year ended December 31, 2019.

PROBLEM 11–4   (LO2)

Assume the following income statement and balance sheet information:

Service Revenue (all cash)	$175
Operating Expenses	
Salaries (all cash)	85
Net Income	$90

	2019 Dr. (Cr.)	2018 Dr. (Cr.)
Cash	$1,350	$1,800
Borrowings	(800)	(1,300)
Retained Earnings	(550)	(500)

Other information: All dividends were paid in cash.

Required:

1. Calculate cash flow from operating activities.

2. Calculate the amount of dividends paid during the year.

3. Calculate cash flow used by financing activities.

PROBLEM 11–5   (LO2)

The following transactions occurred in the Hubris Corporation during the year ended December 31, 2019.

(a)	Net income for the year (accrual basis)	$800
(b)	Depreciation expense	120
(c)	Increase in wages payable	20
(d)	Increase in accounts receivable	40
(e)	Decrease in merchandise inventory	50
(f)	Amortization of patents	5
(g)	Payment of non-current borrowings	250
(h)	Issuance of common shares for cash	500
(i)	Payment of cash dividends	30

Other information: Cash at December 31, 2019 was $1,200.

Required: Prepare a statement of cash flows.

PROBLEM 11–6   (LO2,3)

During the year ended December 31, 2019, the Wheaton Co. Ltd. reported $95,000 of revenues, $70,000 of operating expenses, and $5,000 of income taxes expense. Following is a list of transactions that occurred during the year:

(a) Depreciation expense, $3,000 (included with operating expenses)

(b) Increase in wages payable, $500

(c) Increase in accounts receivable, $900

(d) Decrease in merchandise inventory, $1,200

(e) Amortisation of patent, $100

(f) Non-current borrowings paid in cash, $5,000

(g) Issuance of common shares for cash, $12,500

(h) Equipment, cost $10,000, acquired by issuing common shares

(i) At the end of the fiscal year, a $5,000 cash dividend was declared but not paid.

(j) Old machinery sold for $6,000 cash; it originally cost $15,000 (one-half depreciated). Loss reported on income statement as ordinary item and included in the $70,000 of operating expenses.

(k) Decrease in accounts payable, $1,000.

(l) Cash at January 1, 2019 was $1,000; increase in cash during the year, $37,900

(m) There was no change in income taxes owing.

Required:

1. Prepare a statement of cash flows.

2. Explain what this statement tells you about Wheaton Co. Ltd.

Chapter 12

Financial Statement Analysis

Financial statements can be used by shareholders, creditors, and other interested parties to analyze a corporation's liquidity, profitability, and financial structure compared to prior years and other similar companies. As part of this analysis, financial evaluation tools are used. Some of these tools are discussed in this chapter.

Chapter 12 Learning Objectives

LO1 – Describe ratio analysis, and explain how the liquidity, profitability, leverage, and market ratios are used to analyze and compare financial statements.

LO2 – Describe horizontal and vertical trend analysis, and explain how they are used to analyze financial statements.

Concept Self-Check

Use the following as a self-check while working through Chapter 12.

1. What is working capital?
2. What is meant by *liquidity*?
3. What are some ratios commonly used to evaluate liquidity?
4. What is a company's revenue operating cycle and how is it measured?
5. What profitability ratios can be used to evaluate a corporation?
6. How is the amount of shareholder claims against a corporation's assets compared to the amount of creditor claims?
7. What are the relative advantages of short-term and long-term debt?
8. What are some measures used to evaluate the future financial prospects of a company for investors?
9. What is a *horizontal analysis*? How does it differ from a *vertical analysis*?
10. What is a common-size analysis?

NOTE: The purpose of these questions is to prepare you for the concepts introduced in the chapter. Your goal should be to answer each of these questions as you read through the chapter. If, when you complete the chapter, you are unable to answer one or more the Concept Self-Check questions, go back through the content to find the answer(s). Solutions are not provided to these questions.

12.1 Introduction to Ratio Analysis

LO1 – Describe ratio analysis, and explain how the liquidity, profitability, leverage, and market ratios are used to analyze and compare financial statements.

A common way to evaluate financial statements is through **ratio analysis**. A *ratio* is a relationship between two numbers of the same kind. For example, if there are two apples and three oranges, the ratio of the number of apples to the number of oranges is 2:3 (read as "two to three"). A *financial ratio* is a measure of the relative magnitude of two selected numerical values taken from a company's financial statements. For instance, the gross profit percentage studied in Chapter 6, also known as the gross profit ratio, expresses the numerical relationship between gross profit and sales. If a company has a gross profit ratio of 0.25:1, this means that for every $1 of sales, the company earns, on average, $0.25 to cover expenses other than cost of goods sold. Another way of stating this is to say that the gross profit ratio is 25%.[1]

Financial ratios are effective tools for measuring the financial performance of a company because they provide a common basis for evaluation — for instance, the amount of gross profit generated by each dollar of sales for different companies. Numbers that appear on financial statements need to be evaluated in context. It is their relationship to other numbers and the relative changes of these numbers that provide some insight into the financial health of a business. One of the main purposes of ratio analysis is to highlight areas that require further analysis and investigation. Ratio analysis alone will not provide a definitive financial evaluation. It is used as one analytic tool, which, when combined with informed judgment, offers insight into the financial performance of a business.

For example, one business may have a completely different product mix than another company even though both operate in the same broad industry. To determine how well one company is doing relative to others, or to identify whether key indicators are changing, ratios are often compared to *industry averages*. To determine trends in one company's performance, ratios are often compared to past years' ratios of the same company.

To perform a comprehensive analysis, qualitative information about the company as well as ratios should be considered. For example, although a business may have sold hundreds of refrigerators last year and all of the key financial indicators suggest growth, qualitative information from trade publications and consumer reports may indicate that the trend will be towards refrigerators us-

---

[1] Any ratio in the form X:1 can be expressed as a percentage by multiplying both the numerator and denominator by 100. For example, a 0.25:1 ratio would equal 25% [$(0.25 \times 100)/(1 \times 100) = 25/100 = 25\%$]

ing significantly different technologies in the next few years. If the company does not have the capacity or necessary equipment to produce these new appliances, the present positive financial indicators may not accurately reflect the likely future financial performance of the company.

An examination of qualitative factors provides valuable insights and contributes to the comprehensive analysis of a company. An important source of qualitative information is also found in the notes to the financial statements, which are an integral part of the company's financial statements.

In this chapter, financial ratios will be used to provide insights into the financial performance of Big Dog Carworks Corp. (BDCC). The ratios will focus on financial information contained within the income statement, statement of changes in equity, and balance sheet of BDCC for the three years 2019, 2020, and 2021. This information is shown below. Note that figures in these statements are reported in thousands of dollars (000s). **For consistency, all final calculations in this chapter are rounded to two decimal places.**

Big Dog Carworks Corp.
Balance Sheet
At December 31
($000s)

Assets

	2021	2020	2019
Current			
Cash	$ 20	$ 30	$ 50
Short-term Investments	36	31	37
Accounts Receivable	544	420	257
Inventories	833	503	361
	1,433	984	705
Property, Plant, and Equipment, net	1,053	1,128	712
Total Assets	$ 2,486	$ 2,112	$ 1,417

Liabilities

Current			
Borrowings	$ 825	$ 570	$ 100
Accounts Payable	382	295	$ 219
Income Taxes Payable	48	52	$ 50
	1,255	917	369

Equity

Share Capital	1,063	1,063	963
Retained Earnings	168	132	85
	1,231	1,195	1,048
Total Liabilities and Equity	$ 2,486	$ 2,112	$ 1,417

Big Dog Carworks Corp.
Income Statement
For the Year Ended December 31
($000s)

	2021	2020	2019
Sales (net)	$ 3,200	$ 2,800	$ 2,340
Cost of Goods Sold	2,500	2,150	1,800
Gross Profit	700	650	540
Operating Expenses			
Selling, General, and Administration	212	183	154
Employee Benefits	113	109	119
Depreciation	75	84	63
	400	376	336
Income from Operations	300	274	204
Financing Costs			
Interest	89	61	-0-
Income Before Income Taxes	211	213	204
Income Taxes	95	96	92
Net Income	$ 116	$ 117	$ 112

Big Dog Carworks Corp.
Statement of Changes in Equity
For the Year Ended December 31
($000s)

	2021			2020	2019
	Share Capital	Retained Earnings	Total Equity	Total Equity	Total Equity
Opening Balance	$1,063	$132	$1,195	$1,148	$143
Common Shares Issued					953
Net Income		116	116	117	112
Dividends Declared		(80)	(80)	(70)	(60)
Ending Balance	$1,063	$168	$1,231	$1,195	$1,148

Assume that 100,000 common shares are outstanding at the end of 2019, 2020, and 2021.

There are four major types of financial ratios: a) *liquidity ratios* that measure the ability of a corporation to satisfy demands for cash as they arise in the near-term (such as payment of current liabilities); b) *profitability ratios* that measure various levels of return on sales, total assets employed, and shareholder investment; c) *leverage ratios* that measure the financial structure of a corporation, its amount of relative debt, and its ability to cover interest expense; and d) *market ratios* that measure financial returns to shareholders, and perceptions of the stock market about the corporation's value.

Initial insights into the financial performance of BDCC can be derived from an analysis of relative amounts of current and non-current debt. This analysis is addressed in the following sections.

12.2 Liquidity Ratios: Analyzing Short-term Cash Needs

Current (Short-term) versus Non-current (Long-term) Debt

Short-term and long-term financing strategies both have their advantages. The advantage of some short-term debt (repayable within one year of the balance sheet date) is that it often does not require interest payments to creditors. For example, accounts payable may not require payment of interest if they are paid within the first 30 days they are outstanding. Short-term debt also has its disadvantages; payment is required within at least one year, and often sooner. Interest rates on short-term debt are often higher than on long-term debt. An increase in the proportion of short-term debt is more risky because it must be renewed and therefore renegotiated more frequently.

The advantages of long-term debt are that payment may be made over an extended period of time. Risk may be somewhat reduced through the use of a formal contractual agreement that is often lacking with short-term debt. The disadvantages of long-term debt are that interest payments must be made at specified times and the amounts owing may be secured by assets of the company.

Analyzing Financial Structure

As a general rule, long-term financing should be used to finance long-term assets. Note that in BDCC's case, property, plant, and equipment assets amount to $1,053,000 at December 31, 2021 yet the firm has no long-term liabilities. This is unusual. An analysis of the company's balance sheet reveals the following:

	(000s)		
	2021	2020	2019
Current Liabilities	$1,255	$917	$369
Non-current Liabilities	-0-	-0-	-0-

2021 information indicates that BDCC's management relies solely on short-term creditor financing, part of which is $382,000 of accounts payable that may bear no interest and $825,000 of borrowings that also need to be repaid within one year. The risk is that management will likely need to replace current liabilities with new liabilities. If creditors become unwilling to do this, the ability of BDCC to pay its short-term creditors may be compromised. As a result, the company may experience a liquidity crisis — the inability to pay its current liabilities as they come due. The ratios used to evaluate liquidity of a corporation are discussed below.

Even though a company may be earning net income each year (as in BDCC's case), it may still be unable to pay its current liabilities as needed because of a shortage of cash. This can trigger various problems related to current and non-current liabilities and equity.

Current Liabilities

- Creditors can refuse to provide any further goods or services on account.
- Creditors can sue for payment.
- Creditors can put the company into receivership or bankruptcy.

Non-current Liabilities

- Long-term creditors can refuse to lend additional cash.
- Creditors can demand repayment of their long-term debts, under some circumstances.

Equity

- Shareholders may be unwilling to invest in additional share capital of the company.
- Shareholders risk the loss of their investments if the company declares bankruptcy.

There are several ratios that can be used to analyze the liquidity of a company.

Working Capital

Working capital is the difference between a company's current assets and current liabilities at a point in time. BDCC's working capital calculation is as follows:

(000s)

	2021	2020	2019
Current Assets			
Cash	$ 20	$ 30	$ 50
Short-term Investments	36	31	37
Accounts Receivable	544	420	257
Inventories	833	503	361
Total Current Assets (a)	1,433	984	705
Current Liabilities			
Borrowings	825	570	100
Accounts Payable	382	295	219
Income Taxes Payable	48	52	50
Total Current Liabilities (b)	1,255	917	369
Net Working Capital (a−b)	$ 178	$ 67	$ 336

In the schedule above, working capital amounts to $178,000 at December 31, 2021. Between 2019 and 2021, working capital decreased by $158,000 ($336,000 − 178,000). BDCC is less liquid in 2021 than in 2019, though its liquidity position has improved since 2020 when it was only $67,000.

In addition to calculating an absolute amount of working capital, ratio analysis can also be used. The advantage of a ratio is that it is usually easier to interpret.

An exploration is available on the Lyryx site. Log into your Lyryx course to run Working Capital.

Current Ratio

Is BDCC able to repay short-term creditors? The **current ratio** can help answer this question. It expresses working capital as a proportion of current assets to current liabilities and is calculated as:

$$\frac{\text{Current assets}}{\text{Current liabilities}}$$

The relevant BDCC financial data required to calculate this ratio is taken from the balance sheet, as follows:

		(000s)		
		2021	2020	2019
Current Assets	(a)	$1,433	$984	$705
Current Liabilities	(b)	1,255	917	369
Current Ratio	(a/b)	1.14:1	1.07:1	1.91:1

This ratio indicates how many current asset dollars are available to pay current liabilities at a point in time. The expression "1.14:1" is read, "1.14 to 1." In this case it means that at December 31, 2021, $1.14 of current assets exist to pay each $1 of current liabilities. This ratio is difficult to interpret in isolation. There are two types of additional information that could help. First, what is the trend within BDCC over the last three years? The ratio declined between 2019 and 2020 (from 1.91 to 1.07), then recovered slightly between the end of 2020 and 2021 (from 1.07 to 1.14). The overall decline may be a cause for concern, as it indicates that in 2021 BDCC had fewer current assets to satisfy current liabilities as they became due.

A second interpretation aid would be to compare BDCC's current ratio to a similar company or that of BDCC's industry as a whole. Information is available from various trade publications and business analysts' websites that assemble financial ratio information for a wide range of industries.

Some analysts consider that a corporation should maintain a 2:1 current ratio, depending on the industry in which the firm operates. The reasoning is that, if there were $2 of current assets to pay each $1 of current liabilities, the company should still be able to pay its current liabilities as they become due, even in the event of a business downturn. However, it is recognized that no one current ratio is applicable to all entities; other factors — such as the composition of current assets — must also be considered to arrive at an acceptable ratio. This is illustrated below.

Composition of Specific Items in Current Assets

In the following example, both Corporation A and Corporation B have a 2:1 current ratio. Are the companies equally able to repay their short-term creditors?

	Corp. A	Corp. B
Current Assets		
Cash	$ 1,000	$ 10,000
Accounts Receivable	2,000	20,000
Inventories	37,000	10,000
Total Current Assets	$ 40,000	$ 40,000
Current Liabilities	$ 20,000	$ 20,000
Current Ratio	2:1	2:1

The companies have the same dollar amounts of current assets and current liabilities. However, they have different short-term debt paying abilities because Corporation B has more liquid current assets than does Corporation A. Corporation B has less inventory ($10,000 vs. $37,000) and more in cash and accounts receivable. If Corporation A needed more cash to pay short-term creditors quickly, it would have to sell inventory, likely at a lower-than-normal gross profit. So, Corporation B is in a better position to repay short-term creditors.

Since the current ratio doesn't consider the components of current assets, it is only a rough indicator of a company's ability to pay its debts as they become due. This weakness of the current ratio is partly remedied by the acid-test ratio discussed below.

An exploration is available on the Lyryx site. Log into your Lyryx course to run Current Ratio.

Acid-Test Ratio

A more rigid test of liquidity is provided by the **acid-test ratio**; also called the **quick ratio**. To calculate this ratio, current assets are separated into *quick* current assets and *non-quick* current assets.

Quick Current Assets

Cash
Short-term investments } These current assets are considered to be readily convertible into cash.
Accounts Receivable

Non-quick Current Assets

Inventories } Cash cannot be obtained either at all
Prepaid Expenses } or easily from these current assets.

Inventory and prepaid expenses cannot be converted into cash in a short period of time, if at all. Therefore, they are excluded in the calculation of this ratio. The acid-test ratio is calculated as:

$$\frac{\text{Quick current assets}}{\text{Current liabilities}}$$

The BDCC information required to calculate this ratio is:

		(000s)		
		2021	2020	2019
Cash		$ 20	$ 30	$ 50
Short-term investments		36	31	37
Accounts receivable		544	420	257
Quick current assets	(a)	$ 600	$ 481	$ 344
Current liabilities	(b)	$ 1,255	$ 917	$ 369
Acid-test ratio	(a/b)	0.48:1	0.52:1	0.93:1

This ratio indicates how many quick asset dollars exist to pay each dollar of current liabilities. What is an adequate acid-test ratio? It is generally considered that a 1:1 acid test ratio is adequate to ensure that a firm will be able to pay its current obligations. However, this is a fairly arbitrary guideline and is not appropriate in all situations. A lower ratio than 1:1 can often be found in successful companies. However, BDCC's acid-test ratio trend is worrisome.

There were $0.48 of quick assets available to pay each $1 of current liabilities in 2021. This amount appears inadequate. In 2020, the acid-test ratio of $0.52 also seems to be too low. The 2019 ratio of $0.93 is less than 1:1 but may be reasonable. Of particular concern to financial analysts would be BDCC's declining trend of the acid-test ratio over the three years.

Additional analysis can also be performed to determine the source of liquidity issues. These are discussed next.

An exploration is available on the Lyryx site. Log into your Lyryx course to run Acid-test Ratio.

Accounts Receivable Collection Period

Liquidity is affected by management decisions related to trade accounts receivable. Slow collection of receivables can result in a shortage of cash to pay current obligations. The effectiveness of management decisions relating to receivables can be analyzed by calculating the *accounts receivable collection period*.

The calculation of the **accounts receivable collection period** establishes the average number of days needed to collect an amount due to the company. It indicates the efficiency of collection procedures when the collection period is compared with the firm's sales terms (in BDCC's case, the sales terms are *net 30* meaning that amounts are due within 30 days of the invoice date).

The accounts receivable collection period is calculated as:

$$\frac{\text{Average net accounts receivable}[2]}{\text{Net credit sales (or revenues)}} \times 365$$

The BDCC financial information required to make the calculation is shown below (the 2019 calculation cannot be made because 2018 Accounts Receivable amount is not available). Assume all of BDCC's sales are on credit.

		(000s)	
		2021	2020
Net credit sales	(a)	$3,200	$2,800
Average accounts receivable [(Opening balance + closing balance)/2]	(b)	$ 482[3]	$ 338.5[4]
Average collection period [(b/a) × 365 days]		54.98 days	44.13 days

When Big Dog's 30-day sales terms are compared to the 54.98-day collection period, it can be seen that an average 24.98 days of sales (54.98 days – 30 days) have gone uncollected beyond the regular credit period in 2021. The collection period in 2021 is increasing compared to 2020. Therefore, some over-extension of credit and possibly ineffective collection procedures are indicated by this

---

[2] Average balance sheet amounts are used when income statement amounts are compared to balance sheet amounts in a ratio. This is because the income statement item is realized over a fiscal year, while balance sheet amounts are recorded at points in time at the end of each fiscal year. Averaging opening and ending balance sheet amounts is an attempt to match numerators and denominators to an approximate midpoint in the fiscal year.
[3] ($420 + 544)/2 = $482
[4] ($257 + 420)/2 = $338.5

ratio. Quicker collection would improve BDCC's cash position. It may be that older or uncollectible amounts are buried in the total amount of receivables; this would have to be investigated.

Whether the increase in collection period is good or bad depends on several factors. For instance, more liberal credit terms may generate more sales (and therefore profits). The root causes of the change in the ratio need to be investigated. However, the calculation does provide an indication of the change in effectiveness of credit and collection procedures between 2020 and 2021.

An exploration is available on the Lyryx site. Log into your Lyryx course to run Accounts Receivable Collection Period.

Number of Days of Sales in Inventory

The effectiveness of management decisions relating to inventory can be analyzed by calculating the number of days of sales that can be serviced by existing inventory levels.

The **number of days of sales in inventory** is calculated by dividing average inventory by the cost of goods sold and multiplying the result by 365 days.

$$\frac{\text{Average merchandise inventory}}{\text{Cost of goods sold}} \times 365$$

The BDCC financial data for 2020 and 2021 required to calculate this ratio are shown below.

		(000s) 2021	2020
Cost of goods sold	(a)	$2,500	$2,150
Average inventory [(Opening balance + closing balance)/2]	(b)	$ 668[5]	$ 432[6]
Cost of goods sold		365	365
Number of days sales in inventory [(b/a) × 365 days]		97.53 days	73.34 days

The calculation indicates that BDCC is investing more in inventory in 2021 than in 2020 because there are 97.53 days of sales in inventory in 2021 versus 73.34 days in 2020. BDCC has approximately 3 months of sales with its existing inventory (98 days represents about 3 months). The increase from 2020 to 2021 may warrant investigation into its causes.

A declining number of days of sales in inventory is usually a sign of good inventory management because it indicates that the average amount of assets tied up in inventory is lessening. With lower inventory levels, inventory-related expenses such as rent and insurance are lower because less

---
[5]($503 + 833)/2 = $668
[6]($361 + 503)/2 = $432

storage space is often required. However, lower inventory levels can have negative consequences since items that customers want to purchase may not be in inventory resulting in lost sales.

Increasing days of sales in inventory is usually a sign of poor inventory management because an excessive investment in inventory ties up cash that could be used for other purposes. Increasing levels may indicate that inventory is becoming obsolete (consider clothing) or deteriorating (consider perishable groceries). Obsolete and/or deteriorating inventories may be unsalable. However, the possible positive aspect of more days of sales in inventory is that there can be shorter delivery time to customers if more items are in stock.

Whether Big Dog's increasing days of sales in inventory is positive or negative depends on management's objectives. Is management increasing inventory to provide for increased sales in the next year, or is inventory being poorly managed? Remember that ratio analyses identify areas that require investigation. The resulting investigation will guide any required action.

An exploration is available on the Lyryx site. Log into your Lyryx course to run Number of Days of Sales in Inventory Ratio.

The Revenue Portion of the Operating Cycle

As discussed in Chapter 4, the sale of inventory and resulting collection of receivables are part of a business's operating cycle as shown in Figure 12.1.

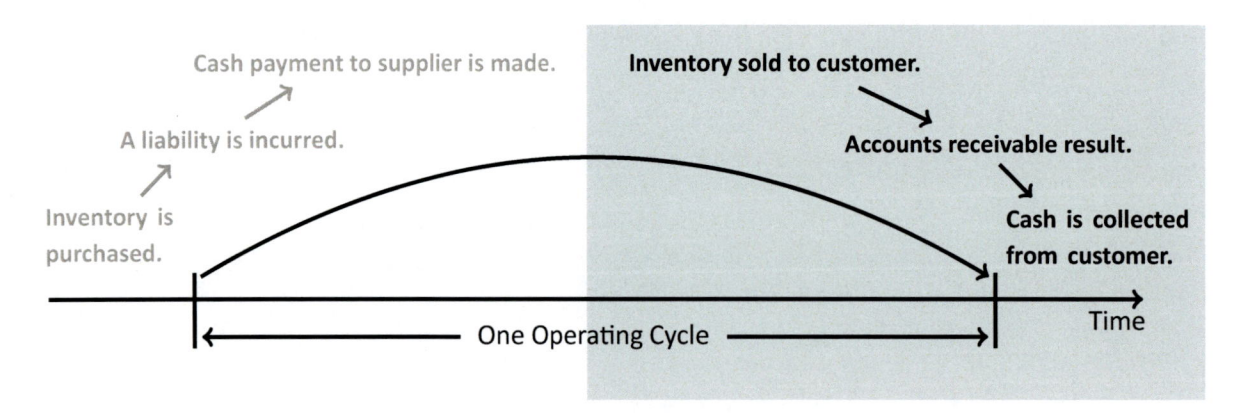

Figure 12.1: Sales and Collection Portion of the Operating Cycle

A business's **revenue operating cycle** is a subset of the operating cycle and includes the purchase of inventory, the sale of inventory and creation of an account receivable, and the generation of cash when the receivable is collected. The length of time it takes BDCC to complete one revenue operating cycle is an important measure of liquidity and can be calculated by adding the number of days of sales in inventory plus the number of days it takes to collect receivables. The BDCC financial data required for this calculation follows.

	2021	2020
Average number of days of sales in inventory	97.53 days	73.34 days
Average number of days to collect receivables	54.98 days	44.13 days
Number of days to complete the revenue cycle	152.51 days	117.47 days

In 2021, 152.51 days were required to complete the revenue cycle, compared to 117.47 days in 2020. So, if accounts payable terms require payment within 60 days, BDCC may not be able to pay them because the number of days to complete the revenue cycle for both 2020 (117.47 days) and 2021 (152.51 days) are significantly greater than 60 days.

Analysis of BDCC's Liquidity

Reflecting on the results of all the liquidity ratios, it appears that Big Dog Carworks Corp. is growing less liquid. Current assets, especially quick assets, are declining relative to current liabilities. The revenue operating cycle is increasing.

12.3 Profitability Ratios: Analyzing Operating Activities

Profitability ratios compare various expenses to revenues, and measure how well the assets of a corporation have been used to generate revenue.

Gross Profit Ratio

The **gross profit ratio**, as introduced briefly in Chapter 6, indicates the percentage of sales revenue that is left to pay operating expenses, creditor interest, and income taxes after deducting cost of goods sold. The ratio is calculated as:

$$\frac{\text{Gross profit}}{\text{Net sales}} \quad \text{OR} \quad \frac{\text{Gross profit}}{\text{Net sales}} \times 100$$

BDCC's gross profit ratios for the three years are:

		2021	2020	2019
Gross profit	(a)	$ 700	$ 650	$ 540
Net sales	(b)	$ 3,200	$ 2,800	$ 2,340
Gross profit ratio	(a/b)	0.2188:1 or 21.88%	0.2321:1 or 23.21%	0.2308:1 or or 23.08%

(000s)

In other words, for each dollar of sales BDCC has $0.22 of gross profit left to cover operating, interest, and income tax expenses ($0.23 in each of 2020 and 2019). The ratio has not changed significantly from year to year. However, even a small decline in this percentage can affect net income significantly because the gross profit is such a large component of the income statement. Changes in the gross profit ratio should be investigated, as it will impact future financial performance.

An exploration is available on the Lyryx site. Log into your Lyryx course to run Gross profit ratio.

Operating Profit Ratio

The **operating profit ratio** is one measure of relative change in these other expenses. This ratio indicates the percentage of sales revenue left to cover interest and income taxes expenses after deducting cost of goods sold and operating expenses. In other words:

$$\frac{\text{Income from operations}}{\text{Net sales}} \quad OR \quad \frac{\text{Income from operations}}{\text{Net sales}} \times 100$$

BDCC's operating profit ratio for the 2019, 2020, and 2021 fiscal years is calculated as follows:

		2021	2020	2019
Income from operations	(a)	$ 300	$ 274	$ 204
Net sales	(b)	$ 3,200	$ 2,800	$ 2,340
Operating profit ratio	(a/b)	0.0938:1 or 9.38%	0.0979:1 or 9.79%	0.0872:1 or or 8.72%

(000s)

For each dollar of sales revenue in 2021, the company had $0.09 left to cover interest and income tax expenses after deducting cost of goods sold and operating expenses. A review of the company's operating expenses (selling, general, and administrative expenses; employee benefits, and depreciation) show that they have all increased. As a result, and despite increasing sales revenue and gross profit, operating income has remained relatively flat. Although it seems reasonable that an increase in operating expenses would follow an increase in sales, the reasons for the operating expense increases should be investigated.

An exploration is available on the Lyryx site. Log into your Lyryx course to run Operating Profit Ratio.

Net Profit Ratio

The **net profit ratio** is the percentage of sales revenue retained by the company after payment of operating expenses, interest expenses, and income taxes. It is an index of performance that can be used to compare the company to others in the same industry. This ratio is calculated by the following formula:

$$\frac{\text{Net income}}{\text{Net sales (or revenues)}} \quad OR \quad \frac{\text{Net income}}{\text{Net sales (or revenues)}} \times 100$$

BDCC's net profit ratios for the three years are calculated as follows:

		2021	2020	2019
		(000s)		
Net income	(a)	$ 116	$ 117	$ 112
Net sales	(b)	$ 3,200	$ 2,800	$ 2,340
Net profit ratio	(a/b)	0.0363:1 or 3.63%	0.418:1 or 4.18%	0.0479:1 or or 4.79%

For each $1 of sales in 2021, BDCC earned $0.04 of net income. The net profit ratio has been relatively stable but needs to be compared with industry or competitors' averages for a better perspective.

Recall that revenues are generated from a business's asset holdings. The financial strength and success of a corporation depends on the efficient use of these assets. An analysis of asset investment decisions can be made by calculating several ratios, and is discussed next.

An exploration is available on the Lyryx site. Log into your Lyryx course to run Net Profit Ratio.

Sales to Total Assets Ratio

Are BDCC's sales adequate in relation to its assets? The calculation of the sales to total assets ratio helps to answer this question by establishing the number of sales dollars earned for each dollar invested in assets. The ratio is calculated as:

$$\frac{\text{Net sales}}{\text{Average total assets}} \quad OR \quad \frac{\text{Net sales}}{\text{Average total assets}} \times 100$$

BDCC's ratios are calculated as follows:

		2021	2020
		(000s)	
Net sales	(a)	$ 3,200	$ 2,800
Average total assets	(b)	$ 2,299[7]	$ 1,764.50[8]
Sales to total assets ratio	(a/b)	1.3919:1 or 139.19%	1.5869:1 or 158.69%

---

[7] ($2,112 + 2,486)/2 = $2,299
[8] ($1,417 + 2,112)/2 = $1,764.50

384 ■ Financial Statement Analysis

The ratio has decreased from 2020 to 2021. Each $1 of investment in assets in 2020 generated sales of $1.59. In 2021, each $1 of investment in assets generated only $1.39 in sales. Over the same period, BDCC's investment in assets increased. The ratios indicate that the additional assets are not producing revenue as effectively as in the past. It may be too soon to tell whether the increase in assets in 2020 will eventually create greater sales but an investigation is required.

As noted earlier, comparison with industry averages would be useful. A low ratio in relation to other companies in the same industry may indicate an over-investment in or inefficient use of assets by BDCC. On the other hand, a higher ratio in comparison to other companies would be a positive indicator.

An exploration is available on the Lyryx site. Log into your Lyryx course to run Sales to Total Assets Ratio.

Return on Total Assets Ratio (ROA)

The return on total assets ratio or ROA is designed to measure the efficiency with which all of a company's assets are used to produce income from operations. The ratio is calculated as:

$$\frac{\text{Income from operations}}{\text{Average total assets}} \quad OR \quad \frac{\text{Income from operations}}{\text{Average total assets}} \times 100$$

Note that expenses needed to finance the company operations are excluded from the calculation, specifically interest and income taxes. This is because all the assets of the company are considered in the ratio's denominator, whether financed by investors or creditors. Average Total Assets are used in the calculation because the amount of assets used likely varies during the year. The use of averages tends to smooth out such fluctuations.

BDCC's returns on total assets for 2020 and 2021 are calculated as follows:

		2021 (000s)	2020
Income from operations	(a)	$ 300	$ 274
Average total assets	(b)	$ 2,299[9]	$ 1,764.50[10]
Return on total assets ratio	(a/b)	0.1305:1 or 13.05%	0.1553:1 or 15.53%

The ratios indicate that Big Dog earned $0.13 of income from operations for every $1 of average total assets in 2021, a decrease from $0.16 per $1 in 2020. This downward trend indicates that assets are being used less efficiently. However, it may be that the increased investment in assets has not yet begun to pay off. On the other hand, although sales are increasing, it is possible that

---
[9] ($2,112 + 2,486)/2 = $2,299
[10] ($1,417 + 2,112)/2 = $1,764.50

future sales volume will not be sufficient to justify the increase in assets. More information about the company's plans and projections would be useful. Recall that ratio analysis promotes the asking of directed questions for the purpose of more informed decision making.

An exploration is available on the Lyryx site. Log into your Lyryx course to run Return on Total Assets Ratio.

Return on Equity Ratio (ROE)

The return on equity ratio measures the return to shareholders — how much net income was earned for the owners of a business. It is calculated as:

$$\frac{\text{Net income}}{\text{Average equity}} \quad \text{OR} \quad \frac{\text{Net income}}{\text{Average equity}} \times 100$$

The 2020 and 2021 returns on equity ratios for BDCC are calculated as follows (note that the 2019 ratio is excluded because average equity cannot be calculated since 2018 ending balances are not provided):

		(000s)	
		2021	2020
Net income	(a)	$ 116	$ 117
Average equity	(b)	$ 1,213[11]	$ 1,121.50[12]
Return on equity ratio	(a/b)	0.0956:1 or 9.56%	0.1043:1 or 10.43%

In both years, shareholders earned, on average, $0.10 for every $1 invested in BDCC, or 10%. Industry averages could help with this analysis. For instance, if the industry as a whole earned only a 5% return on equity in 2021, it could be concluded that BDCC performed better than the industry average in terms of return on equity.

An exploration is available on the Lyryx site. Log into your Lyryx course to run Return on Equity Ratio.

12.4 Leverage Ratios: Analyzing Financial Structure

The accounting equation expresses a relationship between assets owned by an entity and the claims against those assets. Although shareholders own a corporation, they alone do not finance

---

[11]($1,195 + 1,231)/2 = $1,213
[12]($1,048 + 1,195)/2 = $1,121.50

the corporation; creditors also finance some of its activities. Together, creditor and shareholder capital are said to form the financial structureFinancial structure of a corporation. At December 31, 2021, the balance sheet of BDCC shows the following financial structure:

$$\text{ASSETS} = \text{LIABILITIES} + \text{EQUITY}$$
$$\$2{,}486 = \$1{,}255 + \$1{,}231$$

Debt Ratio

The proportion of total assets financed by debt is called the debt ratio, and is calculated by dividing total assets by total liabilities.

$$\frac{\text{Total liabilities}}{\text{Total assets}} \quad \text{OR} \quad \frac{\text{Total liabilities}}{\text{Total assets}} \times 100$$

In BDCC's case, these amounts are:

		(000s) 2021	2020
Total liabilities	(a)	$ 1,255	$ 917
Total assets	(b)	$ 2,486	$ 2,112
Debt ratio	(a/b)	0.5048:1 or 50.48%	0.4342:1 or 43.42%

In other words, 50.48% of BDCC's assets are financed by debt. Therefore, because assets are financed by debt (aka liabilities) and equity, we intuitively know that 49.52% of BDCC's assets must be financed by equity which is the topic of the next section.

An exploration is available on the Lyryx site. Log into your Lyryx course to run Debt Ratio.

Equity Ratio

The proportion of total assets financed by equity is called the equity ratio, and is calculated by dividing total equity by total assets. In BDCC's case, these amounts are:

		(000s) 2021	2020
Total equity	(a)	$ 1,231	$ 1,195
Total assets	(b)	$ 2,486	$ 2,112
Equity ratio	(a/b)	0.4952:1 or 49.52%	0.5658:1 or 56.58%

In 2021, 49.52% of the assets were financed by equity while in 2020 56.58% of the assets were financed by equity. Generally, this is considered an unfavourable trend because as equity financing decreases, we know that debt financing must be increasing as evidenced by the debt ratio above. The greater the debt financing, the greater the risk because principal and interest payments are part of debt financing.

Notice that the sum of the debt and equity ratios will always equal 100% because of the accounting equation relationship: A = L + E where A = 100% and, in the case of BDCC, L = 43.42% in 2020 and E = 56.58% in 2020.

An exploration is available on the Lyryx site. Log into your Lyryx course to run Equity Ratio.

Debt to Equity Ratio

The proportion of creditor to shareholders' claims is called the debt to equity ratio, and is calculated by dividing total liabilities by equity. In BDCC's case, these amounts are:

		2021	(000s) 2020	2019
Total liabilities	(a)	$ 1,255	$ 917	$ 369
Equity	(b)	$ 1,231	$ 1,195	$ 1,048
Debt to equity ratio	(a/b)	1.02:1	0.77:1	0.35:1

In other words, BDCC has $1.02 of liabilities for each dollar of equity at the end of its current fiscal year, 2021. The proportion of debt financing has been increasing since 2019. In 2019 there was only $0.35 of debt for each $1 of equity. In 2021, creditors are financing a greater proportion of BDCC than are shareholders. This may be a cause for concern.

On the one hand, management's reliance on creditor financing is good. Issuing additional shares might require existing shareholders to give up some of their control of BDCC. Creditor financing may also be more financially attractive to existing shareholders if it enables BDCC to earn more with the borrowed funds than the interest paid on the debt.

On the other hand, management's increasing reliance on creditor financing increases risk because interest and principal have to be paid on this debt. Before deciding to extend credit, creditors often look at the total debt load of a company, and therefore the company's ability to meet interest and principal payments in the future. Total earnings of BDCC could be reduced if high interest payments have to be made, especially if interest rates rise. Creditors are interested in a secure investment and may evaluate shareholder commitment by measuring relative amounts of capital invested. From the creditors' perspective, the more capital invested by owners of the company, the greater the relative risk assumed by shareholders thus decreasing risk to creditors.

Although there is no single most appropriate debt to equity ratio, there are techniques for estimating the optimum balance. These are beyond the scope of introductory financial accounting. For now, it is sufficient to note that for BDCC the debt to equity ratio has increased considerably over the three-year period which is generally unfavourable because of the risk associated with debt financing.

An exploration is available on the Lyryx site. Log into your Lyryx course to run Debt to Equity Ratio.

Times Interest Earned Ratio

Creditors are interested in evaluating a company's financial performance, in order to project whether the firm will be able to pay interest on borrowed funds and repay the debt when it comes due. Creditors are therefore interested in measures such as the times interest earned ratio. This ratio indicates the amount by which income from operations could decline before a default on interest may result. The ratio is calculated by the following formula:

$$\frac{\text{Income from operations}}{\text{Interest expense}}$$

Note that income from operations is used, so that income before deduction of creditor payments in the form of income taxes and interest is incorporated into the calculation. BDCC's 2020 and 2021 ratios are calculated as follows:

		2021	2020	2019
		(000s)		
Income from operations	(a)	$ 300	$ 274	$ 204
Interest expense	(b)	$ 89	$ 61	-0-
Times interest earned ratio	(a/b)	3.37:1	4.49:1	n/a

The larger the ratio, the better creditors are protected. BDCC's interest coverage has decreased from 2020 to 2021 (3.37 times vs. 4.49 times), but income would still need to decrease significantly for the company to be unable to pay its obligations to creditors. The analysis does indicate, though, that over the past two years interest charges have increased compared to income from operations. Creditors need to assess company plans and projections, particularly those affecting income from operations, to determine whether their loans to the company are at risk. As discussed above, it may be that significant investments in assets have not yet generated related increases in sales and income from operations.

An exploration is available on the Lyryx site. Log into your Lyryx course to run Times Interest Earned Ratio.

12.5 Market Ratios: Analysis of Financial Returns to Investors

Investors frequently consider whether to invest or divest in shares of a corporation. There are various ratios that help them make this decision. These are called market ratios, because the stock market plays an important role in allocating financial resources to corporations that offer their shares to the public.

Earnings-per-Share (EPS)

Measures of efficiency can focus on shareholder returns on a per-share basis. That is, the amount of net income earned in a year can be divided by the number of common shares outstanding to establish how much return has been earned for each outstanding share. This earnings-per-share (EPS) value is calculated as:

$$\frac{\text{Net income}}{\text{Number of common shares outstanding}}$$

EPS is quoted in financial markets and is disclosed on the income statement of publicly-traded companies. If there are preferred shareholders, they have first rights to distribution of dividends. Therefore, when calculating EPS, preferred shareholders' claims on net income are deducted from net income to calculate the amount available for common shareholders:

$$\frac{\text{Net income} - \text{preferred share dividends}}{\text{Number of common shares outstanding}}$$

BDCC has no preferred shares and thus no preferred share dividends. Recall that 100,000 common shares are outstanding at the end of 2019, 2020, and 2021. For BDCC, EPS calculations for the three years are:

		2021	2020	2019
		(000s)		
Net income	(a)	$ 116	$ 117	$ 112
Number of common shares outstanding	(b)	100	100	100
Earnings per share	(a/b)	$ 1.16	$ 1.17	$ 1.12

Big Dog's EPS has remained relatively constant over the three-year period because both net income and number of outstanding shares have remained fairly stable. Increasing sales levels and the resulting positive effects on net income, combined with unchanged common shares issued, has generally accounted for the slight increase from 2019 to 2020.

An exploration is available on the Lyryx site. Log into your Lyryx course to run Earnings Per Share.

Price-earnings (P/E) Ratio

A price at which a common share trades on a stock market is perhaps the most important measure of a company's financial performance. The market price of one share reflects the opinions of investors about a company's future value compared to alternative investments.

The earnings performance of common shares is often expressed as a price-earnings (P/E) ratio. Price-earnings (P/E) ratio It is calculated as:

$$\frac{\text{Market price per share}}{\text{Earnings per share}}$$

This ratio is used as an indicator of the market's expectation of a company's future performance. Assume Company A has a current market value of $15 per share and an EPS of $1 per share. It will have a P/E ratio of 15. If Company B has a market value of $4 per share and an EPS of $0.50 per share, it will have a P/E ratio of 8. This means that the stock market expects Company A to earn relatively more in the future than Company B. For every $1 of net income generated by Company A, investors are willing to invest $15. In comparison, for every $1 of net income generated by Company B, investors are willing to pay only $8. Investors perceive shares of Company A as more valuable because the company is expected to earn greater returns in the future than is Company B.

Assume that BDCC's average market price per common share was $4 in 2019, $5 in 2020, and $6 in 2021. Its P/E ratio would be calculated as:

		2021	2020	2019
Market price per common share	(a)	$ 6.00	$ 5.00	$ 4.00
Earnings per share (see above)	(b)	$ 1.16	$ 1.17	$ 1.12
Price-earnings ratio	(a/b)	5.17	4.27	3.57

(000s)

BDCC's P/E ratio has increased each year. Although industry and competitor's P/E ratio comparisons would be important to compare, BDCC's increasingly positive ratio also indicates that investors are "bullish" on BDCC. That is, the stock market indicates that it expects BDCC to be increasingly profitable in the coming years. Despite a relatively constant EPS ratio from 2019 to 2021, investors are willing to pay more and more for the company's common shares. This must be because future financial prospects are anticipated to be better than in the past three years.

An exploration is available on the Lyryx site. Log into your Lyryx course to run Price-Earnings Ratio.

Dividend Yield

Some investors' primary objective is to maximize dividend revenue from share investments, rather than realize an increasing market price of the shares. This type of investor is interested in information about the earnings available for distribution to shareholders and the actual amount of cash paid out as dividends rather than the market price of the shares.

The dividend yield ratio is a means to determine this. It is calculated as:

$$\frac{\text{Dividends per share}}{\text{Market price per share}}$$

This ratio indicates how large a return in the form of dividends can be expected from an investment in a company's shares. The relevant information for BDCC over the last three years is shown in the financial statements, as follows:

		2021	2020	2019
Dividends declared	(a)	$ 80	$ 70	$ 60
Outstanding common shares	(b)	100	100	100
Dividends per share	(a/b)	$ 0.80	$ 0.70	$ 0.60

(000s – except per share values)

The dividend yield ratio is therefore:

		2021	2020	2019
Dividends per share	(a)	$ 0.80	$ 0.70	$ 0.60
Market price per share (given)	(b)	$ 6.00	$ 5.00	$ 4.00
Dividend yield ratio	(a/b)	0.13:1	0.14:1	0.15:1

The company's dividend yield ratio decreased from 2019 to 2021. In 2019, investors received $0.15 for every $1 invested in shares. By 2021, this had decreased to $0.13 for every $1 invested. Though the decline is slight, the trend may concern investors who seek steady cash returns. Also notice that total dividends declared increased from 2019 to 2021 even though net income did not substantially increase, and despite the company's poor liquidity position noted in an earlier analysis. Investors might ask why such high levels of dividends are being paid given this situation.

An exploration is available on the Lyryx site. Log into your Lyryx course to run Dividend Yield.

12.6 Overall Analysis of Big Dog's Financial Statements

Results of ratio analysis are always more useful if accompanied by other information such as overall industry performance, the general economy, financial ratios of prior years, and qualitative factors such as analysts' opinions and management's plans.

However, there are some interpretations that can be made about BDCC from the foregoing ratio analyses even without other information. Although BDCC is experiencing growth in sales, net income has not substantially increased over the three-year period 2019 to 2021. The gross profit ratio is relatively constant. Their increasing operating expenses appear to be an issue. The sales to total assets and return on assets ratios have decreased due to a recent investment in property, plant and equipment assets and growth in current assets. Income from operations has not increased with the growth in the asset base. However, it may be premature to make conclusions regarding the timing of outlays for property, plant, and equipment.

The most immediate problem facing BDCC is the shortage of working capital and its poor liquidity. BDCC expanded its property, plant, and equipment in 2020 and experienced increases in revenue that did not correspond to increases in accounts receivable and inventories. The company should therefore review its credit policies and monitor its investment in inventory to ensure that these expand in proportion to sales.

The plant expansion produced an increase in current liabilities (mainly borrowings). The company's ability to meet its debt obligations appears to be deteriorating. The ability of income from operations to cover interest expense has declined. The company's liquidity position is deteriorating, even though it continues to produce net income each year. BDCC should investigate alternatives to short-term borrowings, such as converting some of this to long-term debt and/or issuing additional share capital to retire some of its short-term debt obligations.

Despite these challenges, the stock market indicates that it expects BDCC to be increasingly profitable in the future. Perhaps it views the negative indicators noted above as only temporary or easily rectified by management.

The next section provides further insights into BDCC's operations through trend analysis of the company's financial statements.

12.7 Horizontal and Vertical Trend Analysis

> LO2 – Describe horizontal and vertical trend analysis, and explain how they are used to analyze financial statements.

Trend analysis is the evaluation of financial performance based on a restatement of financial statement dollar amounts to percentages. Horizontal analysis and vertical analysis are two types of trend analyses.

Horizontal analysis involves the calculation of percentage changes from one or more years over the base year dollar amount. The base year is typically the oldest year and is always 100%. The following two examples

12.7. Horizontal and Vertical Trend Analysis

of horizontal analysis use an abbreviated income statement and balance sheet information where 2019 represents the base year. ***For demonstration purposes, the percentages have been rounded to the nearest whole number.***

	2021		2020		2019	
Sales[1]	$100	200%	$70	140%	$50	100%
Gross profit	$ 48	160%	$45	150%	$30	100%
Net income	$ 14	140%	$12	120%	$10	100%

1. Sales in 2020 were 140% of 2019 sales calculated as ($70/$50)x100. Sales in 2021 were 200% of 2019 sales calculated as ($100/$50)x100.

	2021		2020		2019	
Current assets[2]	$ 18	90%	$ 22	110%	$ 20	100%
Long-term investments	$ -0-	N/A	$ 48	60%	$ 80	100%
Total assets	$252	105%	$228	95%	$240	100%

2. Current assets in 2020 were 110% of 2019 current assets calculated as ($22/$20)x100. Current assets in 2021 were 90% of 2019 current assets calculated as ($18/$20)x100.

An alternate method of performing horizontal analysis calculations is to simply calculate the percentage change between two years as shown in the following example.

	2021	% Change	2020
Sales[3]	$100	43%	$70
Gross profit	$ 48	7%	$45
Net income	$ 14	17%	$12

3. Sales in 2021 increased 43% over 2020 calculated as ($100−$70)=$30; ($30/$70)x100=43%.

An exploration is available on the Lyryx site. Log into your Lyryx course to run Horizontal Analysis.

Vertical analysis requires numbers in a financial statement to be restated as percentages of a base dollar amount. For income statement analysis, the base amount used is sales. For balance sheet analysis, total assets, or total liabilities and equity, are used as the base amounts. When financial statements are converted to percentages, they are called common-size financial statements. The following two examples of vertical analysis use information from an abbreviated income statement and balance sheet.

	2021		2020		2019[1]	
Sales	$100	100%	$70	100%	$50	100%
Gross profit	$ 48	48%	$45	64%	$30	60%
Net income	$ 14	14%	$12	17%	$10	20%

1. 2019 Gross profit was 60% of Sales calculated as ($30/$50)x100; 2019 Net income was 20% of Sales calculated as ($10/$50)x100.

	2021		2020		2019[2]	
Current assets	$ 18	7%	$ 22	10%	$ 20	8%
Long-term investments	$ -0-	N/A	$ 48	21%	$ 80	33%
Total assets	$252	100%	$228	100%	$240	100%

2. 2019 Current assets were 8% of Total assets calculated as ($20/$240)x100. 2019 Long-term investments were 33% of Total assets calculated as ($80/$240)x100.

An exploration is available on the Lyryx site. Log into your Lyryx course to run Vertical Analysis.

Notice that the same information was used for both the horizontal and vertical analyses examples but that the results are different because of how the dollar amounts are being compared.

Horizontal and vertical analyses of the balance sheets of Big Dog Carworks Corp. are as follows:

12.7. Horizontal and Vertical Trend Analysis

Horizontal Analysis: Balance Sheet

	2021	2020	Difference	Per Cent
			Change	
Current assets	$1,433 (a)	$984 (b)	+$449 (a-b)	+45.6 [(a-b)/b]
PPE assets	1,053	1,128	-75	-6.6
Total	$2,486	$2,112 (c)	+$374	+17.7
Current liabilities	$1,255	$917	+$338	+36.9
Equity	1,231	1,195	+36	+3.0
Total	$2,486	$2,112	+$374	+17.7

Vertical Analysis (Common-size): Balance

	% 2021	% 2020
Current assets	57.6	46.6 (b/c)
PPE assets	42.4	53.4
Total	100.0	100.0
Current liabilities	50.5	43.4
Equity	49.5	56.6
Total	100.0	100.0

> Notice the two columns introduced here. Analysis of the changes indicates a large increase in current assets (45.6%) together with a large increase in current liabilities (36.9%). There was a small decline in PPE assets (6.6%) and a small increase in equity (3%). The percentage change must always be interpreted together with the absolute dollar amount of change to avoid incorrect conclusions; percentage can sometimes be misleading.

> In the common-size balance sheet, the composition of the assets has changed with an overall shift to current assets in 2019 (57.6% vs. 46.6%). Also, an increase in the percentage of current liabilities has occurred, resulting in an overall shift from equity financing to debt financing from 2020 to 2021.

The same analysis of BDCC's income statement is as follows:

Horizontal Analysis: Income Statements

	2021	2020	Amount	Per Cent
			Change	
Sales	$3,200 (a)	$2,800 (b)	+$400 (a-b)	+14 [(a-b)/b]
Cost of Goods Sold	2,500	2,150	+$350	+16
Gross Profit	700	650 (c)	+$ 50	+8
Expenses	584	533	+$ 51	+10
Net Income	$ 116	$ 117	-$ 1	-1

Vertical Analysis (Common-size): Income Statements

	% 2021	% 2020
Sales	100	100 (b/c)
Cost of Goods Sold	78	77
Gross Profit	22	23
Expenses	18	19
Net Income	4	4

> Although sales and gross profit increased in dollar amounts, net income decreased slightly from 2020 to 2021 (1%). This net decrease resulted because cost of goods sold increased at a faster rate than sales (16% vs. 14%).

> Notice the relative change in the components. For example, cost of goods sold increased in 2021 relative to sales (78% vs. 77%), while expenses in 2021 relative to sales decreased (18% vs. 19%). The overall changes were almost offsetting, as net income remained fairly stable.

The percentages calculated become more informative when compared to earlier years. Further analysis is usually undertaken in order to establish answers to the following questions:

| What caused this change? Is this change favourable or unfavourable? | How do the percentages of this company compare with other companies in the same industry? In other industries? |

These and similar questions call attention to areas that require further study. One item of note becomes more apparent as a result of the trend analysis above. Initially, it was stated that operating expenses were increasing between 2019 and 2021. Based on trend analysis, however, these expenses are actually declining as a percentage of sales. As a result, their fluctuations may not be as significant as first inferred. Conversely, the increases each year in cost of goods sold may be worrisome. Initial gross profit ratio calculations seemed to indicate little variation, and thus little effect on income from operations. The increase in cost of goods sold (78% vs. 77% of sales) may warrant further investigation.

The ratios covered in this chapter are summarized in Figure 12.2.

Analysis of liquidity:	Calculation of ratio:	Indicates:
1. Working Capital	Current assets − Current liabilities	The excess of current assets available after covering current liabilities (expressed as a dollar amount).
2. Current ratio	$\dfrac{\text{Current assets}}{\text{Current liabilities}}$	The amount of current assets available to pay current liabilities.
3. Acid-test ratio	$\dfrac{\text{Quick current assets}}{\text{Current liabilities}}$	Whether the company is able to meet the immediate demands of creditors. (This is a more severe measure of liquidity.)
4. Accounts receivable collection period	$\dfrac{\text{Average net accounts receivable}}{\text{Net credit sales (or revenues)}} \times 365$	The average time needed to collect receivables.
5. Number of days of sales in inventory	$\dfrac{\text{Average inventory}}{\text{Cost of goods sold}} \times 365$	How many days of sales can be made with existing inventory
6. Revenue operating cycle	Average number of days to collect receivables + Average number of days of sales inventory	Length of time between the purchase of inventory and the subsequent collection of cash.

Analysis of profitability:	Calculation of ratio:	Indicates:
1. Gross profit ratio	$\dfrac{\text{Gross profit}}{\text{Net sales}}$	The percentage of sales revenue that is left to pay operating expenses, interest, and income taxes after deducting cost of goods sold.
2. Operating profit ratio	$\dfrac{\text{Income from operations}}{\text{Net sales}}$	The percentage of sales revenue that is left to pay interest and income taxes expenses after deducting cost of goods sold and operating expenses.
3. Net profit ratio	$\dfrac{\text{Net income}}{\text{Net sales (or revenues)}} \times 100$	The percentage of sales left after payment of all expenses.
4. Sales to total assets ratio	$\dfrac{\text{Net sales}}{\text{Average total assets}}$	The adequacy of sales in relation to the investment in assets.
5. Return on total assets	$\dfrac{\text{Income from operations}}{\text{Average total assets}}$	How efficiently a company uses its assets as resources to earn net income.
6. Return on equity	$\dfrac{\text{Net income}}{\text{Average equity}}$	The adequacy of net income as a return on equity.
Leverage ratios:	**Calculation of ratio:**	**Indicates:**
1. Debt ratio	$\dfrac{\text{Total liabilities}}{\text{Total assets}}$	The proportion of total assets financed by debt.
2. Equity ratio	$\dfrac{\text{Total equity}}{\text{Total assets}}$	The proportion of total assets financed by equity.
3. Debt to equity ratio	$\dfrac{\text{Total liabilities}}{\text{Equity}}$	The proportion of creditor financing to shareholder financing.
4. Times interest earned ratio	$\dfrac{\text{Income from operations}}{\text{Interest expense}}$	The ability of a company to pay interest to long-term creditors.
Market ratios:	**Calculation of ratio:**	**Indicates:**
1. Earnings per share	$\dfrac{\text{Net income} - \text{Preferred share dividends}}{\text{Average number of common shares outstanding}}$	The amount of net income that has been earned on each common share after deducting dividends to preferred shareholders.
2. Price-earnings ratio	$\dfrac{\text{Market price per share}}{\text{Earnings per share}}$	Market expectations of future profitability.
3. Dividend yield ratio	$\dfrac{\text{Dividends per share}}{\text{Market price per share}}$	The short-term cash return that can be expected from an investment in a company's shares.

Figure 12.2: Summary of Financial Statement Analysis Ratios

Schematically, the various analytical tools can be illustrated as shown in Figure 12.3.

Liquidity		Profitability		Financial Structure	Market Measures	Trend Analysis
Short-term cash needs	Current asset performance	Returns on sales	Returns on balance sheet items			
Current ratio	A/R collection period	Gross profit ratio	Sales to total assets ratio	Debt to equity ratio	Earnings per share	Horizontal
Acid-test ratio	Number of days of sales in inventory	Operating income ratio	Return on total assets	Times interest earned ratio	Price-earnings ratio	Vertical
	Revenue operating cycle	Net profit ratio	Return on equity		Dividend yield ratio	

Figure 12.3: Categorization of Financial Statement Analytical Tools

Summary of Chapter 12 Learning Objectives

LO1 – Describe ratio analysis, and explain how the liquidity, profitability, leverage, and market ratios are used to analyze and compare financial statements.

Ratio analysis measures the relative magnitude of two selected numerical values taken from a company's financial statements and compares the result to prior years and other similar companies. Financial ratios are an effective tool for measuring: (a) liquidity (current ratio, acid-test ratio, accounts receivable collection period, and number of days of sales in inventory); (b) profitability (gross profit ratio, operating profit ratio, net profit ratio, sales to total assets ratio, return on total assets, and return on equity); (c) leverage (debt ratio, equity ratio, debt to equity ratio, and times interest earned ratio); and (d) market ratios (earnings per share, price-earnings ratio, and dividend yield ratio). Ratios help identify the areas that require further investigation.

LO2 – Describe horizontal and vertical trend analysis, and explain how they are used to analyze financial statements.

Horizontal analysis involves the calculation of percentage changes from one or more years over the base year dollar amount. The base year is typically the oldest year and is always 100%. Vertical analysis requires that numbers in a financial statement be restated as percentages of a base dollar amount. For income statement analysis, the base amount used is sales. For balance sheet analysis, total assets, or total liabilities and equity, are used as the base amounts. When financial statements are converted to percentages, they are called common-size financial statements.

Discussion Questions

1. Ratios need to be evaluated against some base. What types of information can be used to compare ratios against?

2. Explain what *liquidity* means. When a corporation is illiquid, what are the implications for shareholders? ...for creditors?

3. How is it possible that a corporation producing net income each year can be illiquid?

4. What ratios can be calculated to evaluate liquidity? Explain what each one indicates.

5. a. Define working capital. Distinguish between the current ratio and the acid-test ratio.

    b. "The current ratio is, by itself, inadequate to measure liquidity." Discuss this statement.

6. Two firms have the same amount of working capital. Explain how it is possible that one is able to pay off short-term creditors, while the other firm cannot.

7. Management decisions relating to accounts receivable and inventory can affect liquidity. Explain.

8. What is one means to evaluate the management of accounts receivable? ...inventory?

9. Discuss the advantages and disadvantages of decreasing number of days of sales in inventory.

10. What is the revenue operating cycle? How is its calculation useful in evaluating liquidity?

11. a. Identify and explain six ratios (and any associated calculations) that evaluate a corporation's profitability.

     b. What does each ratio indicate?

12. Why are analysts and investors concerned with the financial structure of a corporation?

13. Is the reliance on creditor financing good or bad? Explain its impact on net income.

14. Discuss the advantages and disadvantages of short-term debt financing compared to long-term debt financing.

15. Identify and explain ratios that evaluate financial returns for investors.

16. Distinguish between horizontal and vertical analyses of financial statements.

Exercises

EXERCISE 12–1 (LO1)

The following are condensed comparative financial statements of Stockwell Inc. for the three years ended December 31, 2015.

Balance Sheet
At December 31

Assets

	2015	2014	2013
Current			
Cash	$ 21	$ 8	$ 17
Accounts Receivable	38	30	20
Merchandise Inventory	60	40	30
Prepaid Expenses	1	2	3
Total Current Assets	120	80	70
Property, plant and equipment assets, at carrying amount	260	150	76
Total Assets	$380	$230	$146

Liabilities

	2015	2014	2013
Current			
Accounts Payable	$100	$ 80	$ 50
Non-current			
Bonds Payable, 4%	50	50	-0-
	150	130	50

Equity

	2015	2014	2013
Common Shares	200	80	80
Retained Earnings	30	20	16
	230	100	96
Total Liabilities and Equity	$380	$230	$146

Income Statement
For the Years Ended December 31

	2015	2014	2013
Sales	$210	$120	$100
Cost of Goods Sold	158	80	55
Gross Profit	52	40	45
Operating Expenses	35	32	33
Income from Operations	17	8	12
Interest Expense	2	2	-0-
Income before Income Taxes	15	6	12
Income Taxes	5	2	4
Net Income	$ 10	$ 4	$ 8

Additional information:

i. The company's accounts receivable at December 31, 2012 totalled $20.

ii. The company's merchandise inventory at December 31, 2012 totalled $20.

iii. The company's property, plant and equipment assets at December 31, 2012 totalled $70.

iv. Credit terms are net 60 days from date of invoice.

v. Number of common shares outstanding: 2013–80, 2014–80, 2015–400.

Required:

a. Calculate liquidity ratios and discuss.

b. What is your evaluation of

  i. The financial structure of the corporation?

  ii. The proportion of shareholder and creditor claims to its assets?

  iii. The structure of its short-term and long-term credit financing?

c. What are some other observations you can make about the financial performance of Stockwell?

EXERCISE 12–2   (LO1)

The following information relates to three companies in the same industry:

Company	Latest market price	Earnings per share	Dividends per share
A	$ 35	$ 11	$ -0-
B	40	5	4
C	90	10	6

Required: Explain and calculate the price-earnings and dividend yield ratios. On the basis of only the foregoing information, which company represents the most attractive investment opportunity to you? Explain.

EXERCISE 12–3   (LO1)

Consider the following information:

Salinas Limited
Balance Sheet
At December 31, 2012

Assets		Liabilities and Equity	
Cash	$ 72	Accounts Payable	$ 60
Accounts Receivable	88	Bank Loan, non-current	150
Merchandise Inventory	100		
Prepaid Expenses	40	Preferred Shares	60
Property, Plant, and Equipment,		Common Shares	250
at carrying amount	320	Retained Earnings	100
Total Assets	$620	Total Liabilities and Equity	$620

Salinas Limited
Income Statement
For the Year Ended December 31, 2012

Sales		$240
Cost of Goods Sold		144
Gross Profit		96
Operating Expenses		
Salaries	$ 44	
Depreciation	6	50
Income from Operations		46
Less: Interest		8
Income before Income Taxes		38
Less: Income Taxes		18
Net Income		$ 20

Assume that 80% of sales are on credit, that the average of all balance sheet items is equal to the year-end figure, that all preferred share dividends have been paid and the total annual preferred dividend entitlement is $6, and that the number of common shares outstanding is 10.

Required: Calculate the following ratios and percentages

    a. Current ratio

    b. Return on total assets

    c. Sales to total assets

    d. Acid-test ratio

    e. Times interest earned

    f. Earnings per common share

    g. Accounts receivable collection period

    h. Return on equity

EXERCISE 12–4   (LO2)

The following data are taken from the records of Cronkite Corp.:

	2012	2011
Sales	$2,520	$1,440
Cost of Goods Sold	1,890	960
Gross Profit	630	480
Other Expenses	510	430
Net Income	$ 120	$ 50

Required: Perform horizontal analysis on the above date and interpret your results.

EXERCISE 12–5   (LO2)

Assume you are an accountant analysing Escalade Corporation. Escalade has expanded its production facilities by 200% since 2010. Its income statements for the last three years are as follows:

Escalade Corporation
Comparative Income Statements
For the Years Ending December 31

	2012	2011	2010
Sales	$250	$150	$120
Cost of Goods Sold	190	100	60
Gross Profit	60	50	60
Other Expenses	35	34	35
Net Income	$ 25	$ 16	$ 25

Required:

a. Prepare a vertical analysis of Escalade Corporation's income statement for the three years.

b. What inferences can be drawn from this analysis?

Problems

PROBLEM 12–1 (LO1)

Belafonte Corporation's books were destroyed in a fire on April 20, 2011. The comptroller of the corporation can only remember a few odd pieces of information:

a. The current ratio was 3.75 to 1.

b. Sales for the year were $73,000.

c. Inventories were $20,000 and were equal to property, plant and equipment at carrying amount, and also equal to bonds payable.

d. The accounts receivable collection period was 40 days.

e. The bonds payable amount was 10 times cash.

f. Total current assets were twice as much as common shares.

Required: Using this information, prepare Belafonte Corporation's balance sheet at April 30, 2011. Assume balances at April 30, 2011 are the same as average balances for the year then ended, and besides retained earnings, there are no accounts other than those mentioned above.

PROBLEM 12–2 (LO1)

The incomplete balance sheet of Hook Limited is given below.

Hook Limited
Balance Sheet
At December 31, 2011

Assets

Current		
Cash	$30,000	
Accounts Receivable	?	
Merchandise Inventory	?	
		$?
Property, plant and equipment assets	?	
Less: Accumulated Depreciation	100,000	?
Total Assets		$?

Liabilities

Current		
Accounts Payable	$50,000	
Accrued Liabilities	?	
		$120,000
Non-current		
8% Bonds Payable		?

Equity

Common Shares		?
Retained Earnings		?
Total Liabilities and Equity		$?

Additional information for 2011 year-end:

a. The amount of working capital is $150,000.

b. The issued value of the shares is $10 per share.

c. Market price per share is $15.

d. Price-earnings ratio is 3.

e. Income before payment of interest and income tax is $80,000.

f. The ratio of shareholder's equity to total assets is 0.60 to 1.

g. Income tax expense equals $30,000.

h. The acid-test ratio is 1.5 to 1.

i. The times interest earned ratio is 8 to1.

Required: Complete Hook Limited's balance sheet.

Chapter 13

Proprietorships and Partnerships

Chapter 1 introduced the three forms of business organizations — corporations, proprietorships, and partnerships. The corporation has been the focus in Chapters 1 through 12. This chapter will expand on some of the basic accounting concepts as they apply to proprietorships and partnerships.

Chapter 13 Learning Objectives

LO1 – Describe the characteristics of a proprietorship, including how its financial statements are different from those of a corporation.

LO2 – Describe the characteristics of a partnership including how its financial statements are different from those of a corporation.

Concept Self-Check

Use the following questions as a self-check while working through Chapter 13.

1. What are some of the characteristics of a proprietorship, that are different from those of a corporation?
2. What is the journal entry to record the investment of cash by the owner into a proprietorship?
3. How are the closing entries for a proprietorship different than those recorded for a corporation?
4. Why is there only one equity account on a sole proprietorship's balance sheet and multiple accounts in the equity section of a corporate balance sheet?
5. What is mutual agency as it relates to a partnership?
6. How is a partnership different than a corporation?

NOTE: The purpose of these questions is to prepare you for the concepts introduced in the chapter. Your goal should be to answer each of these questions as you read through the chapter. If, when you complete the chapter, you are unable to answer one or more the Concept Self-Check questions, go back through the content to find the answer(s). Solutions are not provided to these questions.

13.1 Proprietorships

> LO1 – Describe the characteristics of a proprietorship including, how its financial statements are different from those of a corporation.

As discussed in Chapter 1, a proprietorship is a business owned by one person. It is not a separate legal entity, which means that the business and the owner are considered to be the same entity. As a result, for example, from an income tax perspective, the profits of a proprietorship are taxed as part of the owner's personal income tax return. Unlimited liability is another characteristic of a proprietorship meaning that if the business could not pay its debts, the owner would be responsible even if the business's debts were greater than the owner's personal resources.

Investing in a Proprietorship

When the owners of a corporation, known as shareholders, invest in the corporation, shares are issued. The shares represent how much of the corporation is owned by each shareholder. In a proprietorship, there is only one owner. When that owner invests in their business, the journal entry is:

General Journal				
Date	Account/Explanation	PR	Debit	Credit
	Cash....................................		XXX	
	Owner's Capital.....................			XXX
	To record the owner's investment into their business.			

Distribution of Income in a Proprietorship — Withdrawals

A corporation distributes a portion of income earned to its owners, the shareholders, in the form of dividends. In a proprietorship, the owner distributes a portion of the business's income to her/himself in the form of **withdrawals**. Typically, the owner will withdraw cash but they can withdraw other assets as well. The journal entry to record a cash withdrawal is:

General Journal				
Date	Account/Explanation	PR	Debit	Credit
	Withdrawals............................		XXX	
	Cash....................................			XXX
	To record the owner's withdrawal of cash.			

Closing Entries for a Proprietorship

The closing entries for a corporation involved four steps:

Entry 1: Close the revenue accounts to the Income Summary account

This would be identical for a proprietorship.

Entry 2: Close the expense accounts to the Income Summary account

This would also be identical for a proprietorship.

Entry 3: Close the income summary to retained earnings

Instead of closing the balance in the income summary to retained earnings, a proprietorship would close the income summary to the Owner's Capital account.

Entry 4: Close dividends to retained earnings

The equivalent to dividends for a proprietorship is withdrawals. There is no Retained Earnings account in a proprietorship. A corporation separates investments made by the owners (shareholders) into a Share Capital account while dividends and accumulated net incomes/losses are recorded in retained earnings. In a proprietorship, all owner investments, withdrawals, and net incomes/losses are maintained in the Owner's Capital account. Therefore, the fourth closing entry for a proprietorship closes withdrawals to this Owner's Capital account.

Figure 13.1 compares the closing entries for a proprietorship and a corporation.

Proprietorships and Partnerships

Proprietorship			Corporation		
Entry 1: Close the revenue accounts to the Income Summary account.					
Revenues	XXX		Revenues	XXX	
Income Summary		XXX	Income Summary		XXX
Entry 2: Close the expense accounts to the Income Summary account.					
Income Summary	XXX		Income Summary	XXX	
Expenses		XXX	Expenses		XXX
Entry 3: Close the Income Summary account					
...to the Owner's Capital account.			...to the Retained Earnings account.		
Income Summary	XXX		Income Summary	XXX	
Owner's Capital		XXX	Retained Earnings		XXX
When there is a net income.			*When there is a net income.*		
OR			**OR**		
Owner's Capital	XXX		Retained Earnings	XXX	
Income Summary		XXX	Income Summary		XXX
When there is a net loss.			*When there is a net loss.*		
Entry 4: Close					
...withdrawals to the Owner's Capital account.			...dividends to the Retained Earnings account.		
Owner's Capital	XXX		Retained Earnings	XXX	
Withdrawals		XXX	Dividends		XXX

Figure 13.1: Comparing Closing Entries for a Proprietorship and Corporation

An exploration is available on the Lyryx site. Log into your Lyryx course to run Closing Entries.

Financial Statements

The financial statements for a proprietorship are much the same as for a corporation with some minor differences. As shown in Figure 13.2, the income statements only differ in that the proprietorship does not include income tax expense since its profits are taxed as part of the owner's personal income tax return.

Proprietorship			Corporation			
ABC Consulting			ABC Inc.			
Income Statement			Income Statement			
Year ended December 31, 2015			Year ended December 31, 2015			
Revenues		$400	Revenues			$400
Operating expenses		180	Operating expenses			180
Income from operations		$220	Income from operations			$220
Other revenues and expenses			Interest revenue		$20	
Interest revenue	$20		Loss on sale of equipment		(5)	
Loss on sale of equipment	(5)	15				15
Net income		$235	Income before tax			$235
			Income tax expense			50
			Net income			$185

Figure 13.2: Comparing the Income Statement for a Proprietorship and for a Corporation

The statement of changes in equity for each of a proprietorship and corporation includes the same elements: beginning equity, additional investments by the owner(s), net income/loss, distribution of income to the owner(s), and the ending balance in equity. However, the statements are structured differently because in a proprietorship, all the equity items are combined in one account, the Owner's Capital account. In a corporation, equity is divided between share capital and retained earnings. These differences are illustrated in Figure 13.3.

Proprietorship			Corporation			
ABC Consulting			ABC Inc.			
Statement of Changes in Equity			Statement of Changes in Equity			
Year ended December 31, 2015			Year ended December 31, 2015			
				Share Capital	Retained Earnings	Total Equity
Owner's capital, January 1, 2015		$12,000	Balance, January 1, 2015	$9,000	$3,000	$12,000
Add: Owner investment	$1,000		Issuance of share capital	1,000		1,000
Net income	235	1,235	Net income/loss		185	185
Total		$13,235	Dividends		(150)	(150)
Less: Withdrawals		150	Balance, December 31, 2015	$10,000	$3,035	$13,035
Owner's capital, December 31, 2015		$13,085				

Figure 13.3: Comparing the Statement of Changes in Equity for a Proprietorship and for a Corporation

Although both statements are based on identical dollar amounts, notice that the total equity at December 31, 2015 for the proprietorship is $13,085 which is $50 more than the $13,035 shown for the corporation. The $50 difference is the income tax expense deducted on the corporation's income tax.

The balance sheet for each of a proprietorship and corporation includes the same elements: assets, liabilities, and equity. However, the equity section of the statement differs because in a proprietorship, all the equity items are combined in one account, the owner's capital account. In a corporation, equity is divided between share capital and retained earnings. These differences are illustrated in Figure 13.4.

Proprietorship			**Corporation**		
ABC Consulting			ABC Inc.		
Balance Sheet			Balance Sheet		
December 31, 2015			December 31, 2015		
Assets			Assets		
Cash		$ 4,000	Cash		$ 3,950
Other assets		86,000	Other assets		86,000
Total assets		$90,000	Total assets		$89,950
Liabilities		$76,915	Liabilities		$76,915
Equity			Equity		
Owner's capital		13,085	Share capital	$10,000	
Total liabilities and equity		$90,000	Retained earnings	3,035	
			Total equity		13,035
			Total liabilities and equity		$89,950

Figure 13.4: Comparing the Balance Sheet for a Proprietorship and for a Corporation

The $50 difference between the proprietorship's and corporation's balances in each of cash and total equity is because the corporation paid $50 income tax which the proprietorship is not subject to. The equity sections of the two balance sheets are different only in terms of the types of accounts used.

An exploration is available on the Lyryx site. Log into your Lyryx course to run Financial Statements.

13.2 Partnerships

LO2 – Describe the characteristics of a partnership, including how its financial statements are different from those of a corporation.

As discussed in Chapter 1, a partnership is a business owned by more than one person. Partners should have a partnership contract that details their agreement on things such as each partner's rights and duties, the sharing of incomes/losses and withdrawals, as well as dispute and termination procedures. A partnership is not a separate legal entity, which means that the business and the partners are considered to be the same entity. As a result, for example, from an income tax perspective, each partner's share of the profits is taxed as part of that partner's personal income tax return. Unlimited liability is another characteristic of a partnership, meaning that if the business could not pay its debts, the partners would be responsible even if the business's debts were greater than their personal resources.

The exception to this would be the formation of a **limited liability partnership (LLP)** that that is permitted for professionals such as lawyers and accountants. In an LLP, the **general partner(s)** is/are responsible for the management of the partnership and assume(s) unlimited liability, while the **limited partners** have limited liability but also limited roles in the partnership as specified in the partnership agreement. Partnerships also have a limited life and are subject to *mutual agency*. **Mutual agency** means that a partner can commit the partnership to any contract because each partner is an authorized agent of the partnership. For example, one partner could sign a contract to purchase merchandise that falls within the scope of the business's operations.

Investing in a Partnership

Recall that when the owners of a corporation, known as shareholders, invest in the corporation, shares are issued. Recall as well that in a proprietorship there is only one owner whose investments into the business are credited to their capital account. A partnership is similar to a proprietorship in that each partner's investment into the business is credited to an owner's capital account. The difference is that in a partnership there will be more than one owner's capital account. For example, assume Doug Wharton, Lisa Bartwiz, and Tahanni Butti started a partnership called WBB Consulting and invested cash of $20,000, $15,000, and $40,000, respectively. The journal entry to record the investment is:

	General Journal			
Date	Account/Explanation	PR	Debit	Credit
	Cash.....................................		75,000	
	Wharton, Capital			20,000
	Bartwiz, Capital.....................			15,000
	Butti, Capital			40,000
	To record each partner's investment into the business.			

Distribution of Income in a Partnership — Withdrawals

Recall that a corporation distributes a portion of income earned to its owners, the shareholders, in the form of dividends. In a proprietorship and partnership, the owner/partners distribute a portion of the income to themselves in the form of withdrawals. Assume Wharton, Bartwiz, and Butti each withdraw $5,000. The journal entry is:

\multicolumn{5}{c	}{General Journal}
Date	Account/Explanation	PR	Debit	Credit
	Wharton, Withdrawals		5,000	
	Bartwiz, Withdrawals.		5,000	
	Butti, Withdrawals		5,000	
	Cash.			15,000
	To record the partners' withdrawal of cash.			

Closing Entries for a Partnership

The closing entries for a partnership are much the same as those for a proprietorship except that for a partnership there is more than one withdrawals account and more than one capital account. The only complexity with the closing entries for a partnership is with closing the Income Summary account to the capital accounts. The complexity stems from the partnership agreement which details how incomes/losses are to be allocated. Let us review several scenarios.

Example 1: Assume WBB Consulting earned $60,000 during the year and the partnership agreement stipulates that incomes/losses are to be allocated equally. The journal entry to close the income summary to the partners' capital accounts would be:

\multicolumn{5}{c	}{General Journal}
Date	Account/Explanation	PR	Debit	Credit
	Income Summary		60,000	
	Wharton, Capital			20,000
	Bartwiz, Capital.			20,000
	Butti, Capital			20,000
	To close the income summary based on equal allocation.			

An exploration is available on the Lyryx site. Log into your Lyryx course to run Allocating Income - No Partnership Agreement.

Example 2: Assume WBB Consulting had a net loss of $70,000 during the year and the partnership agreement stipulates that incomes/losses are to be allocated on a fractional basis of 2:1:4, respectively. The journal entry to close the income summary to the partners' capital accounts would be:

General Journal				
Date	Account/Explanation	PR	Debit	Credit
	Wharton, Capital....................		20,000	
	Bartwiz, Capital.....................		10,000	
	Butti, Capital		40,000	
	Income Summary.................			70,000
	To close the income summary based on 2:1:4 fractional allocation; calculations: 2/(2+1+4) x 70,000 = 20,000; 1/(2+1+4) x 70,000 = 10,000; 4/(2+1+4) x 70,000 = 40,000.			

An exploration is available on the Lyryx site. Log into your Lyryx course to run Allocating Income/Loss – Fractional Basis.

Example 3: Assume WBB Consulting had a net income of $100,000 during the year and the partnership agreement stipulates that incomes/losses are to be allocated on the ratio of capital investments. The journal entry to close the income summary to the partners' capital accounts would be:

General Journal				
Date	Account/Explanation	PR	Debit	Credit
	Income Summary......................		100,000	
	Wharton, Capital			26,667
	Bartwiz, Capital...................			20,000
	Butti, Capital			53,333
	To close the income summary with the allocation based on a ratio of capital investments; calculations: (20,000/75,000) x 100,000 = 26,667 (rounded to the nearest whole dollar); (15,000/75,000) x 100,000 = 20,000; (40,000/75,000 x 100,000 = 53,333 (rounded to the nearest whole dollar).			

An exploration is available on the Lyryx site. Log into your Lyryx course to run Allocating Income – Ratio of Investments.

Example 4: Assume WBB Consulting had a net income of $60,000 during the year and the partnership agreement stipulates that incomes/losses are to be allocated based on salaries of $70,000 to Wharton; $20,000 to Bartwiz; zero to Butti; and the remainder equally. The journal entry to close the income summary to the partners' capital accounts would be:

416 ■ Proprietorships and Partnerships

Date	General Journal Account/Explanation	PR	Debit	Credit
	Income Summary		60,000	
	Butti, Capital		10,000	
	Wharton, Capital			60,000
	Bartwiz, Capital			10,000
	To close the income summary with the allocation based on salaries and the remainder allocated equally; calculations:			

	Wharton	Bartwiz	Butti	Total
Net income				60,000
Salaries:	70,000	20,000	0	-90,000
Remainder to be allocated:				-30,000
-30,000 x 1/3	-10,000	-10,000	-10,000	30,000
Balance of net income to be allocated				0
Total to be allocated to each partner	60,000	10,000	-10,000	60,000

*The sum of the totals **must** reconcile (be equal to) the net income/loss being allocated.*

Notice in Example 4 that Butti is receiving a negative allocation which results in a debit to her Capital account.

An exploration is available on the Lyryx site. Log into your Lyryx course to run *Allocating Income – Remainder to be Allocated*.

Example 5: Assume WBB Consulting had a net income of $90,000 during the year and the partnership agreement stipulates that incomes/losses are to be allocated based on a combination of: (a) 20% interest of each partner's beginning-of-year capital balance; (b) salaries of $70,000 to Wharton, $20,000 to Bartwiz, $15,000 to Butti; and (c) the remainder equally. The journal entry to close the income summary to the partners' capital accounts would be:

Date	General Journal Account/Explanation	PR	Debit	Credit
	Income Summary		90,000	
	Wharton, Capital			64,000
	Bartwiz, Capital			13,000
	Butti, Capital			13,000
	To close the income summary with the allocation based on a combination of interest and salaries with the remainder allocated equally; calculations:			

	Wharton	Bartwiz	Butti	Total
Net income				90,000
Interest:				
20%x20,000; 20%x15,000; 20%x40,000	4,000	3,000	8,000	-15,000
Salaries:	70,000	20,000	15,000	-105,000
Remainder to be allocated:				-30,000
-30,000x1/3	-10,000	-10,000	-10,000	30,000
Balance of net income to be allocated				0
Total to be allocated to each partner	64,000	13,000	13,000	90,000

The sum of the totals **must** reconcile (be equal to) the net income/loss being allocated.

The total income allocated to each partner is carried into the net income line of the Statement of Changes in Equity (as shown next).

An exploration is available on the Lyryx site. Log into your Lyryx course to run Allocating Incomes/Losses – Interest, Salaries, Remainder.

Financial Statements

The income statement for a partnership is identical to that for a proprietorship. The statement of changes in equity for a partnership is similar to a proprietorship's except that there is a Capital account and Withdrawals account for each of the partners.

Assume that on January 1, 2015, the first year of operations for WBB Consulting, the partners, Wharton, Bartwiz, and Butti, invested $20,000, $15,000, and $40,000, respectively. During 2015 they each withdrew $5,000. The statement of changes in equity would appear as illustrated in Figure 13.5 given a net income for the year of $90,000 allocated as shown in Example 5 previously.

WBB Consulting
Statement of Changes in Equity
Year Ended December 31, 2015

	Wharton	Bartwiz	Butti	Totals
Capital, January 1, 2015	$ 0	$ 0	$ 0	$ 0
Add: Investments by partners	20,000	15,000	40,000	75,000
Net income	64,000	13,000	13,000	90,000
Subtotals	$84,000	$28,000	$53,000	$165,000
Less: Withdrawals by partners	5,000	5,000	5,000	15,000
Capital, December 31, 2015	$79,000	$23,000	$48,000	$150,000

Figure 13.5: Statement of Changes in Equity for a Partnership

An exploration is available on the Lyryx site. Log into your Lyryx course to run *Allocating Income – Remainder to be Allocated*.

In the equity section on the balance sheet there will be more than one owner's capital account as shown in Figure 13.6.

WBB Consulting
Balance Sheet
December 31, 2015

Assets		
Cash		$ 35,000
Other assets		143,000
Total assets		$ 178,000
Liabilities		$ 28,000
Equity		
Wharton, capital	$79,000	
Bartwiz, capital	23,000	
Butti, capital	48,000	150,000
Total liabilities and equity		$ 178,000

Figure 13.6: Balance Sheet for a Partnership

Summary of Chapter 13 Learning Objectives

LO1 – Describe the characteristics of a proprietorship, including how its financial statements are different from those of a corporation.

A proprietorship is a business owned by one person. It is not a separate legal entity, which means that the business and the owner are considered to be the same entity. The profits of a proprietorship are taxed as part of the owner's personal income tax return. Unlimited liability is another characteristic of a proprietorship meaning that if the business could not pay its debts, the owner would be responsible even if the business's debts were greater than the owner's personal resources. Owner investments, owner withdrawals, and net incomes/losses are closed to one permanent account: the Owner's Capital account.

LO2 – Describe the characteristics of a partnership, including how its financial statements are different from those of a corporation.

A partnership is a business owned by more than one person. Partners should have a partnership contract that details their agreement on things such as each partner's rights and duties, the sharing of incomes/losses and withdrawals, as well as dispute and termination procedures. A partnership is not a separate legal entity, which means that the business and the partners are considered to be the same entity. Each partner's share of the profits is taxed as part of that partner's personal income tax return. Unlimited liability is another characteristic of a partnership meaning that if the business could not pay its debts, the partners would be responsible even if the business's debts were greater than the partners' personal resources. The exception to this would be the formation of a limited liability partnership (LLP) that is permitted for professionals such as lawyers and accountants. In an LLP, the general partner(s) is/are responsible for the management of the partnership and assume(s) unlimited liability while the limited partners have limited liability but also limited roles in the partnership as specified in the partnership agreement. Partnerships also have a limited life and are subject to *mutual agency*. Mutual agency means that a partner can commit the partnership to any contract because each partner is an authorized agent of the partnership. The closing entries for a partnership are the same as those for a proprietorship except there is more than one capital account and more than one withdrawals account. The closing of the income summary to each partner's capital account is based on the allocation details in the partnership agreement.

Discussion Questions

1. Define a partnership and briefly explain five characteristics.
2. What are the advantages and disadvantages of partnerships?

3. How does accounting for a proprietorship, partnership, and corporation differ?

4. How can partnership profits and losses be divided among partners?

5. Why are salary and interest bases used as a means to allocate profits and losses in a partnership?

6. How are partners' capital balances disclosed in the balance sheet?

Exercises

EXERCISE 13–1   (LO2)

You are given the following data for the partnership of B. White and C. Green.

B. White and C. Green Partnership
Trial Balance
December 31, 2015

Cash	$41,000	
Accounts Receivable	68,400	
Merchandise Inventory	27,000	
Accounts Payable		$45,800
B. White, Capital		30,000
B. White, Withdrawals	7,000	
C. Green, Capital		20,000
C. Green, Withdrawals	5,000	
Sales		322,000
Cost of Goods Sold	160,500	
Rent Expense	36,000	
Advertising Expense	27,200	
Delivery Expense	9,600	
Office Expense	12,800	
Utilities Expense	23,300	
Totals	$417,800	$417,800

Each partner contributed $10,000 cash during 2015. The partners share profits and losses equally.

Required:

a. Prepare an income statement for the year.

b. Prepare a statement of changes in equity for the year in the following format:

Statement of Changes in Equity
For the Year Ended December 31, 2015

	White	Green	Total
Opening Balance	$	$	$
Add: Investments during 2015			
Net Income			
	$	$	$
Deduct: Withdrawals			
Ending Balance	$	$	$

c. Prepare a balance sheet at December 31, 2015.

d. Prepare closing entries at year end.

EXERCISE 13–2   (LO1,2)

Refer to Exercise 13–1.

Required: Prepare the equivalent statement of changes in equity at December 31, 2015 assuming that the partnership is instead:

a. A proprietorship owned by B. White called White's (Combine C. Green balances and transactions with those of B. White.)

b. A corporation named BW and CG Ltd. with 100 common shares issued for $1 per share to each of B. White and C. Green. Assume opening retained earnings equal $29,800 and that 20,000 common shares were issued during 2015 for $20,000. Assume the net income of $52,600 is net of income tax.

EXERCISE 13–3   (LO2)

Refer to Exercise 13–1.

Required: Prepare the journal entry to allocate net income to each of the partners assuming the following unrelated scenarios:

a. Net income is allocated in a fixed ratio of 5:3 (White: Green).

b. Net income is allocated by first paying each partner 10% interest on opening capital balances, then allocating salaries of $30,000 for White and $10,000 for Green, then splitting the remaining unallocated net income in a fixed ratio of 3:2 (White:Green).

EXERCISE 13–4 (LO2)

Walsh and Abraham began a partnership by investing $320,000 and $400,000, respectively. They agreed to share net incomes/losses by allowing a 10% interest allocation their investments, an annual salary allocation of $75,000 to Walsh and $150,000 to Abraham, and the balance 1:3.

Required: Prepare the journal entry to allocate net income to each of the partners assuming the following unrelated scenarios:

a. Net income for the first year was $210,000.

b. A net loss for the first year was realized in the amount of $95,000.

Problems

PROBLEM 13–1 (LO2)

On January 1, 2015, Bog, Cog, and Fog had capital balances of $60,000, $100,000, and $20,000 respectively in their partnership. In 2015 the partnership reported net income of $40,000. None of the partners withdrew any assets in 2013. The partnership agreed to share profits and losses as follows:

a. A *monthly* salary allowance of $2,000, $2,500, and $4,000 to Bog, Cog and Fog respectively.

b. An annual interest allowance of 10 per cent to each partner based on her capital balance at the beginning of the year.

c. Any remaining balance to be shared in a 5:3:2 ratio (Bog:Cog:Fog).

Required:

1. Prepare a schedule to allocate the 2015 net income to partners.

2. Assume all the income statement accounts for 2015 have been closed to the income summary account. Prepare the entry to record the division of the 2015 net income.

Made in the USA
Columbia, SC
12 May 2017